Shooter's Bible

GUIDE TO
BOWHUNTING

Shooter's Bible
GUIDE TO
BOWHUNTING

DR. TODD A. KUHN

SKYHORSE PUBLISHING

Skyhorse Publishing books may be purchased in bulk at special discounts for sales promotion, corporate gifts, fund-raising, or educational purposes. Special editions can also be created to specifications. For details, contact the Special Sales Department, Skyhorse Publishing, 307 West 36th Street, 11th Floor, New York, NY 10018 or info@skyhorsepublishing.com.

Skyhorse® and Skyhorse Publishing® are registered trademarks of Skyhorse Publishing, Inc.®, a Delaware corporation.

www.skyhorsepublishing.com

10 9 8 7 6 5 4 3 2 1

Library of Congress Cataloging-in-Publication Data is available on file.

ISBN: 978-1-62087-812-5

Printed in China

CONTENTS

SECTION 1
COMPOUND BOWS

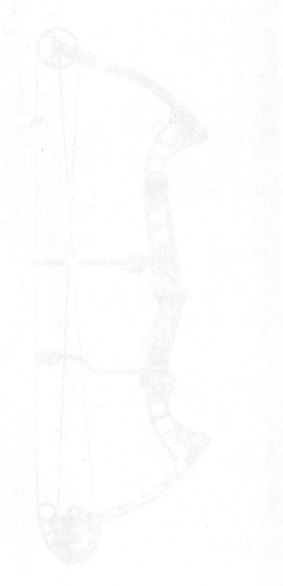

I. Pursuit of the Perfect Arrow

My first "bow," hand-fashioned from a heavy willow branch, was as crooked as a dog's leg. It was strung with cotton cord spooled on a wooden spindle that had been bought from a dusty mercantile in upstate New York. The cord was destined for my grandmothers clothes line.

My grandfather, an outdoorsman, squirreled away the remnant twine on a hand-hewed header in a tool shed he'd built in the early 1920s. Its roof pitched and yawed, having grown temperamental, afflicted from decades of heavy snows and legume growth that enshrined the ancient structure. Teetering on its floor joists, its once firm stance had succumbed to the roots of a neighboring balsam fir.

To a four-year-old, that shed held a unique fascination for a vivid imagination and a spirit for adventure. Rusty tin-lidded jars of milky glass held untold treasures: snelled hooks, brass buttons, curtain rings, and a pocketknife that was bequeathed to me when I turned old enough to handle it with respect and care.

On the front step of this shed, my grandfather spun dramatic tales of his adolescence and fascination with the bow. Once he finished, I'd run off with that stick and twine in hand, searching for rabid grizzlies and other foe worthy of attention from my finely-crafted weapon.

My first real bow was a Fred Bear. I remember it vividly. I stood tall in the backyard of our house in central Florida, my lemonwood Ranger a thing of beauty in the eyes of a youthful beholder. It had its share of nicks and scratches—all badges of courage etched by mighty warriors from distant lands who too stood tall behind this bow. Mighty men of stern resolve who'd fought hand-to-hand against overwhelming odds. They'd been

▲ Author on an early morning South Dakota turkey hunt.

bloodied in battles, but had emerged victorious. The spoils of victory were theirs.

My knobby knees rattled as I strained to bend those limbs and stretch the frayed string. I longed to be a warrior, too. Years later, my mom told me the bow's patina wasn't earned in battle but from bouncing from one garage sale to the next. Nonetheless, for one scrawny kid, the seed was sown and the dream was born.

Fast Forward

Those who haven't been exposed to archery often ask me why I shoot. For me, (and hundreds of thousands of other archery fanatics), the answer is relatively simple: I love it. For us, the bow and arrow are somehow addictive, casting a spell of intrigue and romance over those who shoulder it.

I consider myself an atypical archer, shooting around sixty arrows a day on weekdays, close to double that on weekends. For anyone who drops by my house,

it's immediately obvious that I'm an addict. For starters, there's a hundred-yard range in my backyard. Well-worn bag targets hang on pressure treated 4x4s, arranged incrementally and staggered at twenty, forty, sixty, eighty, a hundred yards. The ragged target faces are testament of the hundreds, if not thousands, of arrows they've been pounded with over time.

Now that I live north of the Mason-Dixon line, there are occasions when the weather turns persnickety. When it does, I move indoors to my twenty-yard range in my basement. While my wife isn't overly thrilled with the idea of arrows zinging around in the basement, I've yet to hit anything down there of real or sentimental value.

Archery has since morphed into a lifetime pursuit of perfection—perfection in the sense of the human machine (that of muscle, tendon, and bone) mastering the mechanical machine (the bow's components).

As I mentioned, I have a hundred-yard range. A bag target hanging 100-yards away is a daunting sight. For

▲ Cause for Intrigue: 100-yard backyard range.

most visitors, it holds such intrigue. Those uninitiated to the archery game immediately assume they've stumbled on a neighborhood gun range. Once I explain the function of my range, visitors are stupefied. The first question out of everyone's mouth is "How far is it to that target down there," there being the farthest target. And so begins my sermon on the virtues of archery.

You see, archery is an odd sport—one of solitude. Not unlike that of the long distance runner. It's a sport of seclusion and relative recluse for those who choose to participate. There are no referees, no umpires, or line judges. There's no clock to run out other than when daylight recedes into night on a day's hunt. There's no overtime—no mulligan, handicaps, or cheering crowds. For team members, the uniform is a favorite brand of camouflage.

Archery is a sport requiring discipline of the hand, head, and heart. You see, to excel you must train the hand through much repetition and discipline the head through mental calisthenics. And to *really* excel, you must possess a heart whose desire is to achieve.

In engineering terms, a compound bow is a simple machine. It's so simple, you'll be hard pressed to name

▲ A bowhunter's team uniform is his favorite camo brand.

more than five or so components that actually move. In contrast, an automobile has more than 20,000 moving parts. But how could this mechanical contrivance, one of such rudimentary intent—that of casting arrows downrange—possess such a degree of intrigue for countless generations of archery enthusiasts?

When the compound was first introduced, it was much maligned by traditionalists. It was, after all, like shooting a gun, right? Well, not so much. The modern compound, with its array of accessories, is at best only as accurate as the human machine throttling it.

While the act of drawing the bow isn't too difficult, it is extremely challenging to do it with a complete concert of an amalgam of muscles. When working in perfect concert, the mind and body achieves flawless form and the perfect shot. While most believe that is defined as a "pie-plate sized group at twenty yards," that is far from "perfection attained."

Achieving the perfect arrow with a compound is rare. No matter how good you get (or think you are), you can still improve. No archer can consistently hit the mark. In fact, it is for that reason we keep coming back to the sport. It's what draws newbies and challenges the most ardent of archers to continue improving. It is, in its purest form, a lifetime pursuit of the perfect arrow.

▲ Archery is a sport of solitude, not one given to crowds.

Making a Case for Compounds and Bowhunting

Bowhunting has experienced unparalleled growth as a sport. A sport of meager beginnings, the first "compound" was kludged together by Holless Wilbur Allen in the mid-1960s. Allen's contraption was a longbow with the limb tips cut off. He then lashed crude pulleys to the limbs and configured a makeshift string and cable system. Crude at best, the first "compound" cobbled together would be the predecessor of all that is "compound" today.

Today's modern compound is an astounding feat of mechanical engineering and materials science. From its meager beginnings in a tinkerer's crowded Missouri garage, the compound has morphed into a stealthy, powerful machine capable of clustering arrows into tight target groups at exaggerated distances.

Weird Science

With the whirlwind of advances that we witness each year, it seems these machines are only physically limited by the imagination of those who use them. Advances in materials science continue, offering compound designers more options. Solid fiberglass limbs have been replaced by limbs reinforced and lightened with space-age carbon fibers. Carbon nanotube technology will be available in compound limbs within the next year or so, offering even more stout and resilient materials from which to design and build archery components.

New copolymers blend resins with long-strand carbon fibers, and other proprietary fillers are incorporated into designs with improved performance. This slurry is molded into parts and assemblies that rival machined aircraft quality aluminum for structural integrity and are physically lighter.

Scientific advancements in coatings have contributed to the rapid advancements in compounds. Progress in fluoropolymers, aluminum surfacing science, and elastomeric coatings have led to reduced friction on bow component surfaces, as well as resistance to wear. All of these have led to more mechanically efficient bows.

Cam systems are modeled using complex computer aided design (CAD) programs that plot their efficiencies and match them perfectly to the compound's limbs, riser, string, and cable systems. These programs can actually simulate drawing and firing the compound; enabling design engineers to predict where structural inefficiencies may manifest prior to cutting the first prototyping part. These efficiencies make a more rugged bow with higher mechanical efficiencies, tighter tolerances, and top-end performance while lowering the overall mass weight.

Technology Rules

As compounds have evolved, so has the sport of bowhunting. Modern compounds are capable of harvesting animals at dizzying distances. Consequently, the evolution of accessories and hunting tactics has accelerated to keep pace with the quantum leaps in bow performance.

Early bowhunters carried compounds into the field that were capable "of astounding performance" (as one was advertised) comparable to lobbing arrows at 180 feet-per-second with a whopping 30-some foot pounds of kinetic energy. These modern-day compound predecessors limited the bowhunter to shoot distances of 20 yards or less. In stark comparison, today's compounds are capable of shooting arrows more than 360 feet-per-second and carry over 100 foot pounds of kinetic energy. Today, a bowhunter's effec-

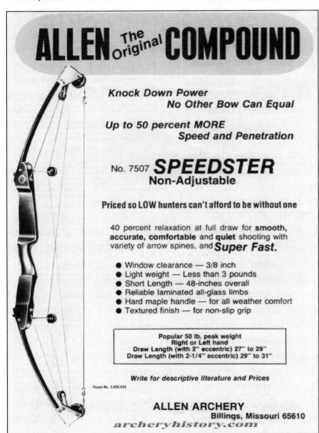

▲ The original Wilbur Allen compound bow advertisement.

tive range is limited only by his or her physical ability, not by his or her equipment.

Beyond the bow itself, modern archery equipment has evolved, keeping pace with the advances in compound technologies. As we will see in later chapters, sights, arrows, arrow rests, stabilizers, quivers, and other ancillary equipment have made the bow more efficient while increasing the enjoyment of shooting.

Even with a bow's impressive performance, it's still a primitive weapon. So why bowhunt? Well, the answer is quite rudimentary. For me, bowhunting presents challenges unparalleled by other forms of hunting, and the up-close-and-personal style of bowhunting adds to the challenge. Having to slip within a short physical distance from the animal for a shot also adds to the excitement. Narrowing this distance also requires the hunter to be more skilled, both in woodsmanship and in the skill required to make an ethical kill shot.

▲ Bowhunter glassing field from the confines of a ground blind fashioned from native prunings.

▲ A bowhunter glasses from his elevated perch.

Neither of these are easy nor are they learned anywhere other than in the woods or afield.

Contrast this with hunting using high-powered rifles. Please understand first and foremost that I hold no prejudice or malice toward rifle hunters. I have hunted with a rifle and loved every minute of it. However, I prefer bowhunting. That being said, rifle hunting removes some (not all) of the woodsmanship factors—those skills requiring the hunter to negotiate close to his or her target animal.

Spot-and-Stalk, Treestands, and Ground Blinds.

The need to get close presents significant challenges, depending on your method of hunting—spot-and-stalking, tree standing, or ground blinding. Getting close using a tree stand or ground blind requires hours of scouting and surveillance. Each observation is used to paint a tactical picture of what a particular deer is doing.

Once this is decided, the bowhunter can formulate a hunting strategy. But it doesn't end once you're committed to a specific tree or ground blind position—the game has typically just begun. Rarely does a new tree stand or ground blind position pay off with an animal. As you hunt and observe the movement of the animals,

▲ Spot-and-stalking requires an archer be able to execute shots from a number of positions.

the strategy changes and so the hunter must evolve and adapt.

The same rigors apply to spot-and-stalking. However, for me, spot-and-stalking is the most challenging (and rewarding) bowhunting technique. It demands incredible bowmanship, that of being capable of executing the most difficult of nontraditional shots. Nontraditional as in kneeling, seated, crouched, angled, leaning, and so on.

Adding to the difficulty is the need to be physically capable of closing the distance between the animal and yourself. This may include literally hours of crawling, slipping, jogging, and anything in between. All require the bowhunter to be in top physical shape.

The challenge is not all physical, however. You must also consider the mental chess match you enter into with the animal and the environment. Every move made to negotiate closer to the animal is predicated on past experiences, those that educate the bowhunter on what can be done tactically and those that cannot be done tactically but are still successful. In most cases, sadly, the animal and the environment win the chess match. Whether the animal sees you or the wind changes, tipping the animal of your approach—you lose. That's what makes it challenging.

An Economy of Scale

One of the last reasons folks are flocking to bowhunting (both compounds and crossbows) is there simply isn't enough contiguous ground on which to rifle hunt. Larger tracts of farmlands have been split, segmented, and subdivided throughout the past few decades. The family farms of yesteryear simply don't

appear with the frequency they once did. Challenging economic times have led to family farms being sold off in small plots.

So a depressed economy has led to an economy of space for hunters. These plots, sometimes as small as a few acres and once a large aggregate of property, were hunted with high-powered rifles. Now, they no longer offer a safe opportunity to gun hunt. However, in contrast, these small tracts offer ample bowhunting space. In fact, my largest deer to date was taken on a postage stamp-sized tract of land in a neighborhood that was adjacent to a farm. These small tracts often times offer protected sanctuary for mammoth whitetails.

An Abridged History of Archery

Early historical facts surrounding the bow and its development are sketchy at best. As a weapon, it dates back a few millenniums As such, much of what is surmised about early archers has been discovered through archeological digs. To date, the oldest archery relics were unearthed in Africa. Arrowheads discovered in the area date back to approximately 25000 BC.

More than 5,000 miles south of Africa, scientists discovered a burial tomb in Italy containing a skeleton with a fragmented flint arrowhead lodged in the pelvis. Through carbon dating, scientists estimate that the flint dates back to 11000 BC. Ancient Egyptian drawings dating from 7500 to 5000 BC depict humans using early bows for hunting food and for warfare.

Scientists estimate that around 2800 BC, the first composite bow (built from two separate materials glued together) was made of wood, tipped with animal horn, and lashed together with animal sinew and some

▲ Large expansive tracts of land are shrinking at an accelerated pace.

type of ancient glue. The bowstring was made of sheep intestines, which launched very light arrows.

In battles, early Egyptian armies utilized archers on chariots to outflank the enemy on the battlefield. The chariots and skilled archers proved too much for opposing foot soldiers and their handheld weaponry. Literature found in ancient China dated between 1500 and 1027 BC included the first description of crossbows built and used in China.

Somewhere around 250 BC, the Parthian civilization (now modern Iran and Afghanistan) mounted expert archers on horseback. These archers developed an odd but highly effective battle technique. The archers would pretend to flee the battlefied, and the enemy would give chase. Once their opponents were in bow range, they would turn around on their horses and launch arrows back at the advancing army. Historians venture that this is where the term "parting shot" came from.

Qin Shihuang, the first emperor of China, was buried with six-thousand life-sized terracotta figures, some of which modeled carrying primitive crossbows. In Rome, a fellow named Sebastian was the commander of the Praetorian Guards for the Roman Emperor. He was shot to death with arrows when his deep Christian faith was discovered in 228 AD. Oddly enough, after being shot repeatedly and assumed dead, he was found alive and nursed back to health by family friends.

Once he was again healthy, Sebastian announced his Christian faith on the steps of the Emperor's palace. The guards were ordered to beat him to death with their clubs. After he was pummeled to death, his body was recovered by friends (probably the same ones that found him the first time) and was secretly buried in the catacombs under Rome. Sebastian became known as the Patron Saint of Archers.

Infamous Mongol warrior Genghis Khan was documented as utilizing composite bows of seventy pounds of draw weight and thumb ring releases to unleash the bowstring in 1208 AD. These bows were far superior to those used by other armies. These same Mongol soldiers would wrap silk cloth under their clothing as an arrow shield. When struck by an enemy's arrow, the silk fabric wrapped around the enemy's arrowhead, impeding penetration.

In 1307 AD, the legendary William Tell refused to bow (in a display of indentured servitude) to the imperial power and was thus ordered to shoot an apple off his son's head. Legend has it that Tell had another arrow hidden just in case he injured or killed his son. If he had, he was going to kill the government official who had ordered him to shoot at his son. Naturally, as the story goes, he successfully shot the apple off his sons head, sparing the official's life, too.

In 1346 AD, the French army included crossbow-equipped soldiers. Their crossbows were powerful because they were drawn via hand crank. During the Battle of Crécy, Edward III of England led his army into battle against the French. The French were defeated handily when rain moistened their bowstrings the night before the battle, causing them to stretch. The waterlogged strings misfired and broke during the battle. The French, knowing the rain would compromise their strings, had placed them under their helmets during the rainstorm. The dry strings proved deadly.

Both crossbows and compound bows were considered the most effective battle weapons throughout what is modern day now modern day Europe and Asia until the early 1500s when the musket was invented. The year 1588 AD marked the last time bows were used in warfare when 10,000 soldiers from the English fleet, armed with muskets, defeated the Spanish Armada which was armed with bows. In the latter half of the 1600s, contests of archery skill became vogue in England.

In 1545, *Toxophilus*, a book about longbow archery by Roger Ascham, was published in London. Dedicated to King Henry VIII, it was the first book on archery written in English. According to legend, Ascham was a keen archer and scholar, lecturing at St John's College, Cambridge. The premise of the book was his defense of archery as a sport fitting of the educated.

The beginning of modern archery arguably dates back to 1879 when inventor Ephraim Morton of Plymouth, Massachusetts, was granted a United States patent for his wood handled bow equipped with steel rod limbs.

Archery gained international exposure as a sport when it was included in the Olympic Games in 1904, 1908, and 1920. It was discontinued for a while, and then reinstated during the 1972 Olympics. Meanwhile, in 1934, the first bowhunting season opened in Wisconsin, and in 1937, the first modern sights were used in target archery competitions.

In 1939, James Easton began tinkering with manufacturing arrows out of aluminum instead of the traditional wood. By 1941, Larry Hughes won the American National Championship using Easton's alu-

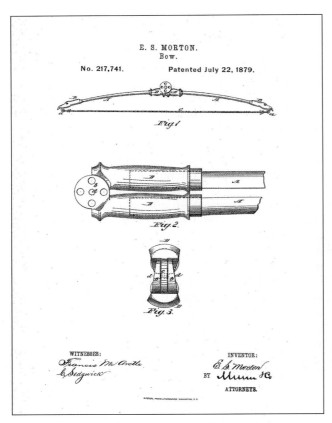

▲ The patent Ephraim Morton of Plymouth received for a bow equipped with steel rod limbs marked the beginning of modern archery.

▲ James Easton, inventor of the aluminum arrow.

minum arrows. Easton, of course, went on to found Easton Technical Products, which continues to be a leader in the archery industry. Easton produced its first trademarked aluminum arrows, the 24 SRT-X, in 1946.

In 1942, Earl Hoyt, Jr. founded Hoyt Archery, Co. In the decades to follow, Hoyt's company would go on to become one of the largest and most successful archery companies in the world. In 1951, Max Hamilton introduced the first plastic fletching, the Plastifletch, which marked the start of today's arrow vane industry.

Meanwhile, Fred Bear of Bear Archery introduced the first recurve bow in 1953. Previous bows were longbows, that is, bows with straight limbs. Bear's recurve had oddly shaped limbs that were purported to improve accuracy and increase speed.

By 1956, Earl Hoyt developed the first pistol grip bow handle, and Easton introduced his new XX75 aluminum arrow shaft in 1958. In 1966, Easton continued innovating arrows, extruding their X7 aluminum shaft.

However, the largest advancement in modern archery is attributed to a Missourian.

Holless Wilbur Allen was born on July 12, 1909. Allen was a tinkerer and avid archer. Legend has it that Allen had grown tired of the drawbacks of traditional

► Earl Hoyt, founder of the company that bears his name.

▲ Archery icon Fred Bear in his shop.

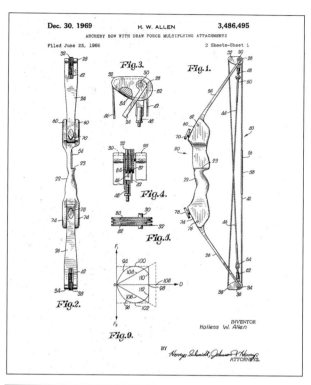

bows and longed for something faster and a bit easier to shoot.

So one day in his garage, Allen decided to cut the limb tips off his recurve and added two pulleys to decrease the amount of effort it took to draw the bow. With that, he had unknowingly launched the modern archery industry. His new prototype performed considerably better than his recurve, though it was very, very crude.

On June 23, 1966, Allen applied for a patent titled "Archery Bow with Draw-Force Multiplying Attachments." In December of 1969, the US Patent and Trademark Office issued Allen his patent (patent number 3,486,495). Allen joined forces with Tom Jennings, a revered traditional bowyer, to begin manufacturing of the first compound bows. Tragically, Allen was killed in a two-car collision on June 28, 1979.

In 1970, the compound bow and release aid made their national debut at the United States National Archery Competition. In 1971, Andy Simo, founder of New Archery Products (NAP), invented the first flipper-style rest, increasing archery accuracy ten-fold over shooting off a padded bow shelf. Simo's NAP would grow into one of the largest archery accessory companies, offering a wide variety of over-the-top engineered shooting components. That same year, archery legend Pete Shepley founded Precision Shooting Equipment (PSE) in Illinois. Shepley, an engineer by education, worked for Magnavox as a product engineer. Shepley's love for shooting led him to tin-

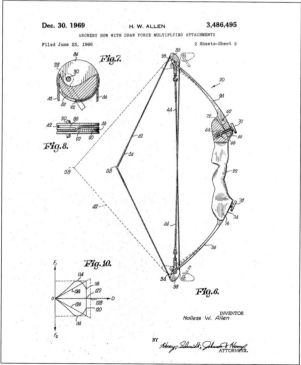

▲ Holless Allen's original compound patent **USPTO Patent 3,486,495 Archery Bow with Draw Force Multiplying Attachments**

ker with different designs. The company he founded continues to lead the archery industry in innovative engineering today.

In 1974, archery legend Freddie Troncoso invented the first dual prong arrow rest, elevating archery accuracy even further over Simo's flipper-style rest. The year 1982 marked the first time compounds with actual lobe-shaped cams were introduced (previous compounds featured round wheels). The following year, Easton introduced the first carbon arrow shaft. From here on out, the timeline of improvements begin to blur as innovations are developed seemingly overnight and more archers and hunters become archery inventors and manufacturers. We will review these improvements and the history of these accessories and bows in detail in subsequent chapters.

▲ Precision Shooting Equipment's founder Pete Shepley, today and circa 1969.

The Arch of Innovation

Archery companies are pressured to one-up their products each year. Throughout the late 1960s and early 1970s, improvements in compound design were happening on an almost daily basis. The compound design was in its adolescence, and improvements came quickly and easily. These quantum leaps in technological advances continued through the eighties and nineties. The new millennium saw technological

▲ Andy Simo, founder of New Archery Products.

advances slow as the fundamental design of the compound had matured.

As is the case with any industry, the bowhunting industry evolved in cycles and eventually matured. The improvements that followed became incrementally smaller. For instance, solar power was harnessed and collected in the late 1760s. Swiss scientist Horace de Saussure was credited with building the world's first solar collector in 1767. Yet some 245 years later, our government still pitches "new" solar power green initiatives as though this idea is something new.

As a student of the game of archery, I watch each year for new and innovative improvements, yet they have appeared less frequently in the past twenty years. Admittedly, small tweaks in design are made by manufacturers and then advertised as earth-shattering new designs. In reality, these are simple twists on current designs polished with marketing hype.

For example, about ten years ago, one bow company espoused at length about their new and innovative cam system. Ads screamed of this breakthrough technology; cutting-edge science, engineering, and manufacturing melded together to form the ultimate power propulsion system for compounds. Well, truth be told, the design had been patented some twenty years earlier and never really marketed with zeal. So much for the latest and greatest innovation!

When asked where I see the industry going in the next decade, I hesitate to provide a definitive answer. This is because, barring any new discoveries in materials science, the industry and their compounds have squeezed almost every pound of power out of the compound machine.

In Chapter Two, I discuss what it will take, in purely theoretical terms, to break the mystical 400-feet-per-second barrier with a compound. I think that once you read this, you'll understand the limitations that bow designers are faced with and what it will take to break the next great barrier of compound design.

Despite its limitations, the archery game continues to intrigue many. I'm hoping you'll find something to your liking in this book—something that will enlighten or stir your interest in bowhunting.

Up Close and Personal

Humidity drapes on you like a warm, wet bed sheet. You struggle against gravity and impending sunrise, inching your climber ever higher. Your lungs offer their objection, burning as you quietly gasp to draw your next breath of this air you wear.

Once you've reached hunting height, you settle into the pre-dawn darkness—one so dark you need a flashlight to find your pocket. Your heart pounds uncontrollably and your temples throb with each rustle of leaves and snap of a twig. The anticipation of what the first fingers of sunlight will reveal on the forest floor some thirty feet below is deafening.

The acrid smell of repellent fills your nose and stings your eyes as it shoulders itself against the airborne horde that clouds around your head and hands. The early light stretches through nature's mossy hardwood window shades, and you stare cross-eyed as a salty bead of sweat trickles down the bridge of your nose.

Resolute to remain motionless, you battle the urge to brush it aside. Finally, it drips onto the standing platform with a gentle, yet discernible "tink." Welcome to the archery opener and early season bowhunting!

This precious time is what the fraternal brotherhood of bowhunters yearns for. To the uninitiated, this ritual is remotely odd and seemingly painful. To those of the order, those with unwavering resolve, it's what defines our being. Adrenaline is our drug of choice. We are, proudly and passionately, after all, bowhunters. I invite you to join the ranks. Here's why.

Learn to be a Better Hunter

I'm not going to beat around the bush or sugarcoat this for any number of reasons; bowhunters are the best hunters in the woods. Don't get mad at me; it is what it is. Consider the following.

Close your eyes and picture the first days of the war in Iraq. Remote images of sorties dropping smart bombs filled our living rooms and dens. We cheered as bombs dropped several miles away found their way to the intended targets.

Gun hunting, to me, is much the same. There you sit in a shooting house, covering a 100-acre agricultural field with a high-powered rifle. In stark contrast, a bowhunter has an effective range on a good day in the south of about forty yards. With this diminutive affective range, a bowhunter must get into a deer's comfort zone, into their living room if you will, to deliver a lethal arrow.

Scent Control

Being a good bowhunter means being a master woodsman. As such, many individual facets must be considered and contemplated. Scent control is exponentially more important to a bowhunter than someone hunting with a gun. Make a mistake here with

▲ Author and his Texas Axis deer.

the wind and it's over. Much has been written on the subject, so we won't be laver the point.

Stand Management and Etiquette

Stand management is another consideration that's critical. Several factors require forethought including shooting lanes, animal travel direction, sunrise and sunset, predominant wind direction, hunting height, stand orientation, and more.

Stand etiquette is also of paramount importance. There are two distinct entities here: 1) management of yourself and 2) equipment management. Managing "yourself" refers to the ability to cloak yourself from an animal's eyes and ears. This is not an easy skill to learn. Curbing or minimizing movement takes practice.

Equipment management takes time to perfect as well. This affects your ability to setup your hunting platform (stand) in the most ergonomically and efficient manner. You must know how to place your

▲ Author with his Wyoming antelope.

essentials about the stand to make you as comfortable negotiating them as you are driving your automobile.

Early Season Patternability

A distinct advantage early season bowhunters have is that deer are very predictable now. While many hunters center their season's hopes, dreams, and much-coveted vacation time around the rut, rutting bucks wander willy-nilly in search of breed-able does. This search may take them miles from their core area. Conversely, during early season, whitetails fall into a predictable pattern, one that puts grounding one in your favor.

Early season deer are driven by the need to feed and rehydrate themselves. When the temperature rises, a deer's metabolism goes into overdrive. As whitetail binge on readily available nutrition, their need for water increases. This need for water makes them susceptible. Locate their water and food source and you'll find success.

Go Where No One Has Gone Before

As urban sprawl continues to cast its shadow across the landscape, whitetails are being pinched out of their natural habitat. No matter if you agree with urban expanse, more whitetails are forced to live within the confines of this urbanscape.

Hardwoods, swamps, and other intimate places of refuge are diminishing. Whitetails are squeezed like frosting through a batter bag into backyards, small woodlots, and neighborhoods. The family farm and its corn fields and CRP succumb to suburbia, concrete, condos, and corporate America.

▲ Author with an Illinois buck shot with a muzzleloader, although he prefers archery equipment.

▲ Author with a rare white deer—not an albino, but a completely white whitetail deer.

Significantly more opportunities to hunt pristine areas where no other hunters have been before now exist. Moreover, we're able to hunt very small tracks of lands where guns are considered off-limits. Along these same lines, the owners of these small tracts are much more likely to allow bowhunting than that of high-powered rifle hunting. In many cases, the animals are unpressured and relatively tolerant of humans and their presence.

It's Just Fun!

Admittedly, shooting a gun has its distinct appeal. The smell of gunpowder and seeing a quarter-size group at 100 yards is satisfying. However, the thrill of attaining a shaft-to-shaft arrow group at thirty yards eclipses high-powered, magnification-assisted groupings.

Archery and bowhunting can be addictive. It's a sport that can be done year-round in most cases and is one the entire family can enjoy together. There's an archery setup for any age, gender and skill level. It's also relatively inexpensive to get into. Complete combination (i.e., bow, sight, arrow rest, arrows, and quiver) kits retail for as little as $199.

II. Speaking "Bow"

Merriam Webster's definition of compound is "to put together (parts) so as to form a whole: combine." In its simplest form, a compound bow is a combination of various components that, when assembled into a complete mechanical machine, produces a vehicle capable of sending arrows downrange at speeds that exceed those of a traditional bow.

Anyone who has spent time around the archery game has probably learned to speak the "language of compounds." For the archery insider, the jargon and odd nomenclature of those in the know comes easily.

Typically weighing around four odd pounds, compound bows are capable of shooting arrows at amazing speeds. But to fully understand these incredible machines, it is important to understand the vernacular of the sport. Such oddities as "brace height," "idler," "eccentrics," "tiller," "cam lean," "hysteresis," "draw force curve" and so on can leave the head swimming in short order.

Here's an introduction to the compound and what you'll need to know to fit in.

The Fundamentals

Compounds all share common components—those parts that make a compound tick.

Limbs

For a bow to propel an arrow, it must generate and store energy. Pulling the bow string generates this energy and the bow limbs store the energy. When this energy is unleashed and applied to the arrow, it is propelled downrange.

Limbs come in a number of styles. Most commonly, they are *solid limbs*. Solid limbs are simply one-piece units with a slot cut in the limb tip for receiving and mounting the cam axle and cam. *Split limbs* became very popular in the late 1990s. In theory, split limbs have several advantages over solid limbs.

First, split limbs are lighter as the center section of the limb has been removed. Some manufacturers have gone as far as to claim split limbs have less aerodynamic drag, arguing that air flows between the limbs as they are thrust forward during the shot. They further postulate this makes the limbs "faster reacting" and thus the bow faster. For me, this is a stretch.

Split limbs have a disadvantage as each is manufactured independently of others. As such, each limb exhibits its own flexure (the way they bend) characteristics. The problem lies in attempting to match a pair of limbs on the top and bottom of the bow. Independently flexing limbs can cause cam lean (*see Cam Lean*).

Riser

The functional purpose of a bow's riser is to anchor the two limbs and offer a place for the archer to grip

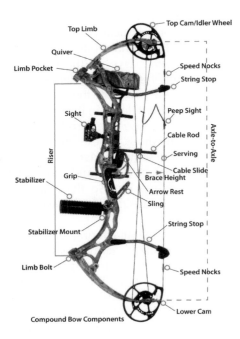

Top Limb
Quiver
Limb Pocket
Top Cam/Idler Wheel
Speed Nocks
String Stop
Sight
Peep Sight
Cable Rod
Serving
Riser
Cable Slide
Grip
Brace Height
Stabilizer
Arrow Rest
Sling
Axle-to-Axle
Stabilizer Mount
String Stop
Limb Bolt
Speed Nocks
Lower Cam
Compound Bow Components

▲ Compound components.

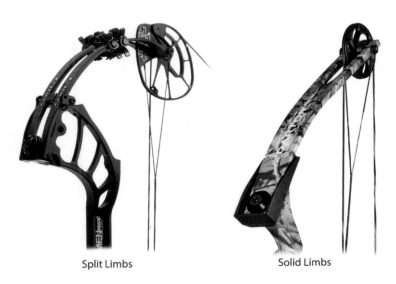

Split Limbs   Solid Limbs

▲ Split limbs versus solid limbs. Makers of split limbs claim advantages over solid limbs while solid limb manufacturers tout their limbs advantages.

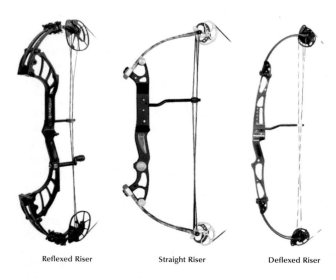

Reflexed Riser   Straight Riser   Deflexed Riser

▲ Riser configurations vary from one model and manufacturer to the next.

the bow. Risers come in a myriad of styles and shapes. However, there are three general geometries. They are: 1) deflexed, 2) reflexed, and 3) straight.

When discussing riser geometry, one must consider the relationship of the shooter's bow hand to the string.

Each riser geometry offers both advantages and disadvantages. A *reflexed riser* positions the handle back toward the shooter. By moving the bow's handle back further, the bow's *brace height* (the measure in inches from a resting string to the bow's grip at the farthest point) is decreased. As brace height is decreased, the bow's *power stroke* is increased as the string must travel further before releasing the arrow.

By increasing the distance the string has to travel, it also increases the distance the bow can accelerate the arrow (hence its power stroke). Thus, a shorter brace height generates more arrow speed. However, there are trade-offs for this added speed. By shortening the bow's brace height, the length of the lever arm between the string at rest (referred to as *equilibrium*) and the handle is decreased. By decreasing this lever, it multiplies, or compounds, any shooter-induced errors.

If the shooter torques the bow to the left during the shot, the effect of that error is multiplied downrange. Additionally, a shorter brace height and longer power stroke increases the time the arrow is physically on the string. By increasing the shot's time, the shooter has

more time to make slight errors in shooting technique. This, in turn, leads to errant arrow flight and delivery to the target.

A *deflexed riser* is the polar opposite of a reflexed riser. Instead of the riser bending inward, the riser geometry flexes outward, away from the shooter. This increases the bow's brace height, shortening the power stroke and slowing the bow's top speed. However, while speed suffers, accuracy is increased as the riser's length of the lever arm between the string at rest (remember equilibrium) and the handle is increased. By increasing this lever length, shooter errors are minimized. Additionally, with a shortened power stroke, the effect of shooter errors is diminished as the arrow is on the string a shorter amount of time. Traditionally, deflexed risers are typically found on target-style bows.

Bows with *straight risers* are a compromise between reflexed and deflexed risers. Straight risers have a neutral geometry, that is, they are neither reflexed nor deflexed. Straight risers are a compromise for archers who want speed and accuracy but are unwilling to settle for the compromises of the reflexed and deflexed riser designs.

Riser Manufacturing Processes

High-end compounds typically have risers manufactured using a CNC (computer numerical control) machine. The CNC utilizes a complex computer program to automatically or robotically cut the intricate riser profile. Either solid aluminum billets are used or extruded aluminum blanks serve as the base material. Risers milled in this fashion are referred to as a *machined riser*. Machined risers are the most precise risers and demand the highest dollar in the bow market.

Cast magnesium alloy risers are produced using conventional casting methods. These include sand castings, permanent and semi permanent mold and shell castings, investment castings, and die-castings. Production is fast and less precise than machined risers. As such, cast risers are found on lower-priced compounds in general.

Forged risers utilize a manufacturing process that shapes metal with localized compressive forces. Depending on the manufacturer, forging can be performed "cold," "warm," or "hot." The type of forging used is dependent on temperature. Forging produces a part that is stronger than an equivalent cast or machined part. Due to the complexity of equipment required to produce forged risers, few manufacturers opt to manufacture them.

Cam System

The basic cam system on a compound bow is made up of a string, one or two *eccentrics* (cams), and one or two harnesses or cables. According to Robert Norton and his *Design of Machinery,* "In mechanical engineering, an eccentric is a circular disk solidly fixed to a rotating axle with its center offset from that of the axle" (hence the word "eccentric," off center). Refer to Chapter Three for a detailed discussion of *cams.*

Bowstring and Cables

The bowstring on a compound launches the arrow. Most modern bowstrings are made of advanced, man-made materials that do not stretch. In the past, compound bowstrings had a problem of stretching after being installed. When the bowstring stretches, it changes the timing and tune of the bow. As the string

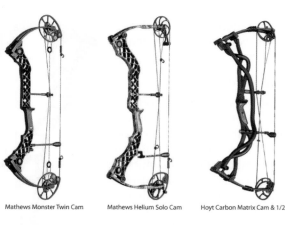

Mathews Monster Twin Cam   Mathews Helium Solo Cam   Hoyt Carbon Matrix Cam & 1/2

▲ **Various cam configurations exist. Each cam system offers distinct advantages. No one stand-alone cam system is perfect or offers the best of all worlds.**

stretches non-uniformly, the cams rotate in an unsymmetrical manner, and one rotates out of sync with the other.

Most compound bow manufacturers now use prestretched strings that do not stretch. Common bowstring materials include Dacron B50 (stretch equals 2.6 percent), Spectra (a composite ultra-high molecular weight polyethylene), Dyneema (high modulus polyethylene), Fast Flight S4 (high modulus polyethylene; stretch equals 1 percent), polyester, Kevlar (para-

aramid synthetic fiber; stretch equals 0.8 percent), and Vectran (a spun fiber of liquid crystal polymer).

Bowstring Serving

The point where the arrow nocks (mounts) to the bowstring would wear very quickly, leading to failure, if not "served" with an additional wrap of *serving* material. Serving materials are typically made of nylon.

Cables

Compound bows utilize pulleys, wheels, or cams to load the limbs with energy. These are physically lashed together cables. Refer to Chapter Three for a detailed discussion of cables.

Grip

When we discussed the compound riser, we mentioned the grip. A bow's grip is just that, a place where the archer physically holds the bow. Bow grips come in an array of shapes, styles, and construction materials. They range from very large to very demur. Grip style and shape is a matter of shooter preference.

Hoyt Narrow Full Grip   Mathews Full Grip   PSE Side Plates

▲ **Various grips range from the diminutive to the bulbous, each designed for individual tastes and preferences.**

Arrow Shelf

Modern compounds have a horizontal shelf manufactured into the riser that contains the arrow and allows for the mounting of an *arrow rest.* Early compounds did not have an arrow shelf, and archers were often injured when a broadhead-equipped arrow would drop off early arrow rests and onto the archer's hand.

Axle-to-axle Measurement

The axle-to-axle measurement of a bow is from the top cam axle (or *idler wheel*) to the bottom cam axle. Axle-to-axle measurements provide the archery consumer with a general idea of the overall physical size of the compound. Keep in mind that this measure does not take into account the eccentrics (i.e., cams and/or idler wheel).

Berger Hole

In an effort to standardize certain compound features so the mounting of archery accessories can be standardized (i.e., sights, stabilizers, and arrow rests), manufacturers drill and tap a Berger hole just above the arrow shelf. The hole is named after Victor Berger, who invented the "Berger Button," an early plunger-style arrow rest. Most bow technicians center the arrow horizontally on this hole.

Bow Sling

This bow accessory mounts on the front of the bow's riser to the *stabilizer mounting hole*. Because the compound bow lurches forward following the shot, slings serve to keep the bow contained or lashed to the shooter's hand.

Brace Height

The *brace height* is the measurement, in inches, from the crotch (or throat) of the grip to the bowstring when the compound is at rest or equilibrium. In general, the brace height of a bow is indicative of how "forgiving" the bow will shoot.

In most cases, a brace height of less than seven inches indicates the manufacturer is attempting to achieve fast arrow speeds. Brace heights over seven inches are indicative of more a forgiving bow (one more tolerant of shooter error). The distance between the string at rest and the throat of the grip determines the lever arm distance of a bow. Refer to the "riser" section of this chapter for a detailed discussion of the effect brace height has on accuracy.

Cable Guard

Compound bows utilize pulleys, wheels, or cams to load the limbs with energy. These are physically lashed together with cables. The cable guard is a perpendicular rod that holds the cables off-center of the riser's mid-line so they do not interfere with the bow's string. Cable guards come in various sizes and configurations. Some are as simple as a rod with a slide. Others are machined parts with dual bearing equipped rollers that the cables track in.

Cable Slide

When a cable guard rod is utilized to manage the cables, many manufacturers use a plastic slide (or some type of thermoplastic) in which the cables are mounted. This allows the cables to slide along the cable guard rod via the slide almost friction-free.

Cam Lean

The buss cables are connected directly to the cable guard or rod. The cable guard keeps the buss cables from interfering with the arrow leaving the bow by pulling the cables off to the side. When pulling the buss cables to the side, the cams are affected on draw as they are pulled to the side. The result is what is referred to as *cam*

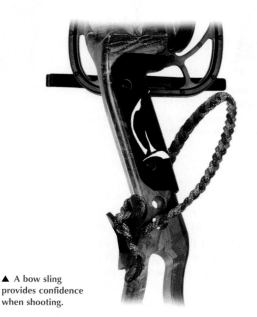

▲ A bow sling provides confidence when shooting.

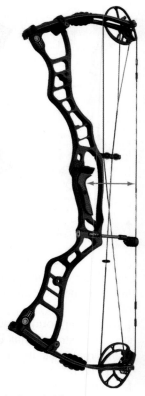

▲ Brace height measure determines how forgiving of shooter-induced error a bow will be.

lean. Longer axle-to-axle bows have less cam lean as the angle is not as acute, whereas shorter axle-to-axle bows have more cam lean as the angle is more acute.

Cam lean is a relatively simple phenomenon. Cams are mounted on cam axles. As the bow is drawn, the cams are rotated and forces are placed on the cams, axles, and limb tips. As these forces are not equal, the cam is forced to lean to one side or another on the axle.

No bow is void of cam lean. Some will argue that cam lean is bad; others relish it. While both arguments have merit, there is not, in my opinion, a definitive argument for one side or the other. I personally know a few top-level professional 3-D archers who introduce severe cam lean into their rigs to get perfect arrow flight.

If you talk to a few other top-level 3-D professionals, they'll tell you cam lean is the work of the devil. I'll leave it up to you to decide for yourself as experience will be your best teacher. The one thing I can say without hesitation is this: Solid limb bows have less cam lean than split limb bows. This is due to the torsional strength and rigidity of the limbs at the tips. Split limb bows have less torsional rigidity and thus flex more and result in more cam lean.

D-Loop

When using a mechanical release attached directly to the bowstring, repetitive shots can cause wear and abrasion to the bowstring. In many cases, this can lead to breakage. Most archers attach a short length of looped cord to their bowstring. This looped cord, or D-Loop, allows attachment of the mechanical release to the loop, eliminating bowstring wear and subsequent breakage.

Draw Weight

The *draw weight* is the amount of force required to draw a compound bow. This is measured in pounds.

Feet-Per-Second (FPS)

This is the numerical measure of how fast a projectile is moving. In archery, it typically refers to arrow speed. Feet-per-second can be converted to miles-per-hour by multiplying fps x 0.682 = mph.

Grains

This is a unit of mass measurement nominally based on the mass of a single seed of wheat . This method of measuring dates back to the Bronze Age.

IBO Speed

The International Bowhunting Organization, or IBO, established a standard for measuring a compound bows speed in feet-per-second (FPS).

IBO Speed is equal to 350-total-grain-weight arrow (shaft, fletchings, nock, and point) shot from a bow with 30-inch draw length and the draw weight set at 70 pounds

Idler Wheel

On solo-cam bows, or bows with one cam, the top wheel is referred to as the idler wheel.

Let-Off

An advantage of the compound bow is its ability to load the bow limbs with energy and then reduce the weight at the conclusion of the draw to a manageable weight. This reduction in draw weight at full draw is referred to as *let-off*. Let-off is articulated in a percentage. If a bow has an 80 percent let-off, at a draw weight of seventy pounds, the shooter will be holding the equivalent of fourteen pounds at full draw.

Mechanical Release

This is a device capable of securing the bowstring during draw, which gives the archer a mechanical advantage over drawing the bow using his fingers. Multiple designs exist, however. Generally speaking, mechanical releases contain a set of jaws to grip the bowstring or D-Loop, a trigger, and some sort of wrist strap or grip.

Nock

A nock is the plastic (some may be manufactured of aluminum) appendage on the rear of an arrow that the bowstring slides into.

Nocking Point

The point or position on a bowstring that the archer positions his or her arrow prior to drawing and releasing it is known as the *nocking point*.

Peep Sight

Compound bows are typically aimed using a *sight* (refer to sight on the next page). Sights are mounted to the bow and are positioned at arm's length when the bow is drawn. Peep sights are installed into the bowstring. This hollow, donut-shaped device allows the shooter to look through the hole at full draw and

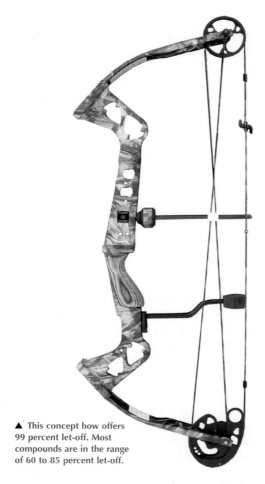

▲ This concept bow offers 99 percent let-off. Most compounds are in the range of 60 to 85 percent let-off.

▶ Arrow nock serves as the physical connection between the string and the arrow shaft.

align his sight pins on the target. The peep sight operates much like a rear sight on a rifle.

Quiver

Dating back to ancient times, the quiver is a receptacle for arrows. Usually mounting on the bow's riser, the quiver holds one to nine arrows. Quivers come in an array of sizes and shapes. Most are detachable from the compound bow. Quivers hold broadhead-equipped arrows safely, shielding the razor edges from the shooter.

Sight

The archery *sight* is a relatively crude aiming device that is mounted on the bow's riser. Three types of sights are available: 1) pins, 2) crosshairs, and 3) laser dot.

▲ Peep sights allows for precision aiming.

▲ A mechanical release allows for precise release of the bowstring.

◀ A hooded peep sight shades the sun on bright days.

▲ Quivers provide safe and easy arrow access.

▲ Modern sights are marvels of engineering. A quality sight makes accurate arrows easy.

Silencers

These are typically rubber appendages that either glue-on, stick-on, or mechanically attach to the compound bow in any number of positions along the bows framework. These appendages do little to quiet a bow's shot noise or minimize vibration as they only add mass to the compound bow.

Stabilizer

The stabilizer is an accessory that mounts to the compound's riser. A plethora of designs are currently available. Originally designed to counter-balance a bow's mass for target shooters, modern stabilizers are now marketed as "vibration and noise eliminating devices." While their value as a counterweight is undeniable, their ability to reduce vibration or noise is highly suspect.

Tiller

The tiller measurement is the measurement from the point where the limb meets the riser and the string in a perpendicular line. Each bow will have two tiller measurements and generally should be the same.

Weird Science: Building the 400+ FPS Compound

Like some strange spring ritual, archers annually migrate to local pro shops to pour over the newest of industry offerings. Undoubtedly when fondling the recent arrivals, the first words the faithful will utter are "how fast is it?" Like candy apple red muscle cars, no bow can be "too fast." If it'll peel the paint off the house with blistering speed, folks will flock in droves to it.

The modern compound had its meager beginnings in the one-car garage of Missouri's Holless Allen in the early 1960s. It's hard to imagine that the anemic and frail recurve that Allen lashed with pulleys would morph into today's compound powerplants.

In the fifty-some odd years since, evolutions in co-polymers, metallurgy, and man-made fibers have been mindboggling. Synergistically, these scientific and engineering advancements have pushed the speed envelope right up against a brick wall.

Even with these technological achievements, compounds still haven't reached the holy grail of speed: the magical 400 feet-per-second benchmark.

What the Desaguliers?

France's John Theophilus Desaguliers first described the phenomenon of friction in the 1600s. Friction, in an engineering sense, is the force that opposes the relative motion or tendency of such motion of two surfaces in contact. Okay, simple enough—stuff rubbing against stuff keeps it from moving freely.

Friction, as it relates to bows, is the primary reason why compounds haven't attained 400 feet-per-second. You see, it's this friction that limits the efficiency of the simple machine we call a bow. Friction in machines produces unwanted side effects—those of heat, noise, and vibration. Admittedly, other factors contribute to energy losses, but we'll not focus on these.

Theoretically, if we could eliminate friction, or significantly reduce it, we could improve a bow's efficiency and exceed the 400-feet-per-second barrier. So it's this friction, or hysteresis, that we'll minimize in our new theoretical 400-plus feet per second mega ground pounder bow.

Bio-Kinetic Limbs

Bow limbs are under two distinct physical forces when they are flexed. The face (i.e., the portion of the limb facing the shooter) is under *compression* (i.e., withstanding axially directed pushing forces), and the back (i.e., the portion of the limb facing the target) is under *tension* (a force that stretches or elongates a material).

Human bones have complex internal and external structures, making them lightweight, yet exceptionally strong. One of the types of tissue that makes up bone is the mineralized osseous tissue, also called bone tissue. Osseous tissue gives bone its rigidity and honeycomb-like three-dimensional internal structure.

To minimize friction and weight, our bio-kinetic limbs are molded using a carbon-to-carbon molecularly bonded matrix. Our artificial matrix mimics bone tissue's honeycomb-like structure with a synthetic mineral component. Our new limbs are stiff in compression while offering little friction in the tension mode. *Net Speed Gain: +13 fps*

Tri-Cam System

The centerpiece of eccentrics will be a double pulley system mounted on our near-parallel bio-kinetic limbs. Our new cam system will provide a 5:1 ratio of movement between the bio-kinetic limbs and the arrow.

To accomplish this, our cams (pulleys) will not rotate as complete disks, but as narrow rings sliding on a highly polished hollow cylinder only slightly dimensionally smaller than the cams. A single-cam will be centrally placed near the handle to reduce mass on the bio-kinetic limb tips. Raised micro-grooves will be machined into the cam groove surfaces. These grooves minimize string and cable friction by reducing surface area. *Net Speed Gain: +8 fps*

Off-Season Tune-Up and Storage

Winter's chill sets in, and the season has closed. Now's a great time to drop off your rig for an annual check-up. Off-season service is both fast and inexpensive. It's also an opportunity to avoid the crowds that jam shops prior to the next opener.

Your local tech will put your bow in a press and remove the string. Once removed, they'll check for wear, as well as check the axles, cam bearings, or bushings.

Keep in mind that an inevitable wet weather outing can negatively affect the performance of these, so an annual checkup is prudent. Depending on your particular make and model, it's a good idea to have them lubricate axles, bushings, or cam bearings as deemed appropriate.

Prior to mothballing your bow, apply a generous amount of bowstring wax to the string and cables. Additionally, store your bow in a climate controlled space where it won't be exposed to extreme temperature swings.

When storing your bow, consider a quality hard case to keep it nestled in safety. It's also a good idea to remove broadheads from arrows. Store these prickly critters somewhere other than with your bow. For some reason, their honed edges have a propensity for finding strings and cables.

The International Bowhunting Organization (IBO) developed a standard formula for measuring arrow speeds. Arrow speed is tested using an arrow with a mass weight of 350-grains, a thirty-inch draw length, and seventy-pound draw weight. By using this formula, bow manufacturers rate the speed of their bows in a uniform manner. This apples-to-apples rating system allows consumers to compare relative bow speeds.

The Archery Manufacturers and Merchants Organization (AMO) now known as the Archery Trade Association (ATA) developed a standard for measuring arrow speed. A bow must have a maximum draw weight of sixty pounds. The arrow must weigh 540-grains with a draw length set at thirty inches.

Cable Guard and Pulley Bio-Cylinders

Traditional pulleys have significant mass that has to start rotating, which uses up energy and adds to the weight at the end of the limb that has to accelerate as the arrow is released. In our bow, the conventional pulley or cam is reduced to a thin ring that rotates on a hollow axle shaft, about an inch in diameter, anchored to the limb.

The outside of the ring is grooved to guide the string or cable, and it rotates on the axle on a film of synthetic lubricating fluid similar to the synovial fluid in your joints, reducing both inertia and friction. *Net Gain: +2 fps*

Nano-Tech String/Cable System

Our string and cable system will take advantage of cylindrical carbon nanotubes woven into "rope." Using nanotubes will exponentially decrease the string, cable diameters, and surface area.

Reducing the surface area decreases surface friction and increases the string's velocity. An anti-wear coating is bonded onto the surface of the cylindrical carbon weave nanotube strings and cables, which offers substantial protection. *Net Gain: +8 fps*

Uni-Lite Aeros

Arrow shafts will be considerably smaller in diameter and lighter than their traditional carbon counterparts (thus minimizing aerodynamic drag). Our shafts and their components (i.e., field points, vanes, and nocks) will be molded of one-piece thin-walled, radially woven composite. Field points and broadheads are molded into the shaft and of the same composite, eliminating the weight of the ferrule.

Uni-composite components reduce arrow shaft weights and increase arrow speeds while minimizing the criticality of arrow spine. Vanes are replaced with integrally molded ultra low-profile airfoil equipped fins that high-speed spin-stabilize our low mass Uni-Lite Aeros. A pulverized magnetic dust is added to the radial complex to enhance arrow rest performance. *Net Gain: +18 fps*

Magna-Force Arrow Rest

A powerful magnetic field will levitate our Uni-Lite Aeros without any rest-to-shaft contact. Floating in this field, the arrow will leave the bow in a friction-free state. Pulverized magnetic dust in the arrow shaft provides the repulsion force. *Net Gain: +8 fps*

Zero-Resist Release

Much like our arrow rest, the centerpiece of our mechanical release will be a powerful magnet that holds our Nano-Tech string during the draw cycle. As the trigger is engaged, the magnetic field releases the string effortlessly, increasing string velocity and ultimately arrow speed. *Net Speed Gain: +2 fps*

Post-Hunt Checklist

You labored from dawn-to-dusk on your stand, struggling to remain motionless while aloft in your white-tail haunt. Or conversely, you scratched and clawed your way up, negotiating nauseating miles of altitude challenging terrain, in pursuit of your trophy.

At day's end, the dirt under your nails, melded with the sweat and blood soaked soil that's been ground into the cracks of your palms, usher credit to your resolve to "just get it done."

Busted, broken, and exhausted, you return to camp. Your thoughts now focus on anything other than hunting. Before grabbing that steamy cup of Joe, perform these tasks to ensure your next hunt doesn't result in a costly equipment meltdown.

1. "Pluck" the bowstring to check for any loose components. The vibration induced from the bowstring will ferret out any nuts, bolts, or screws in need of tightening.
2. Check the knock loop for any obvious signs of fraying or wear. Rest assured that worn knock loops only break when attempting to draw on that animal of a lifetime.
3. Check your bowstring, peep sight serving, and string serving for any wear. Sticks, limbs, and rocks can make quick work of these. Reserve and re-wax as deemed appropriate.
4. Visually check limbs for any signs of fatigue. These may include chips, splinters, or cracks. Oddly enough, limbs are susceptible to failure as they are under tremendous stress. Once you've completed your visual inspection, gently run your fingers over the limbs to tactically check for defects.
5. Check arrow nocks to ensure that they are aligned correctly. A misaligned nock, one quickly knocked and released during the heat of battle, results in horrific flight. This is not an option when attempting to harvest prized game.
6. Broadheads have a strange capacity to loosen up. Check these to make sure they are both tight and sharp. Bees wax (string wax) applied to the threads can help ensure they remain tight no matter how tough the going gets.
7. Fiber-optics revolutionized the archery sight game. However, these extrusions are also fragile and prone to breakage. Visually check these for damage. In addition, if you have a battery-operated sight light, fire it up to ensure the battery is up to snuff.
8. Arrows can get damaged during transit in vehicles, on four-wheelers hauling them up a hillside, or at the end of a pull-up rope. Flex each shaft to check for damage. If defects are found, cull these from your quiver. Additionally, check vanes for damage.
9. Cams are the powerplants central to your arrow launcher. Give them a visual for any foreign debris that might have inadvertently become lodged there.
10. By all means, if possible, shoot a few arrows to make sure that your bow is still sighted in.
11. Draw your bow and check peep alignment. Peeps have an ugly tendency to creep and move. Drawing on an animal is not the time to discover yours has gone south.
12. Limb pockets are wonders of modern engineering; most archers have no idea how integral these are to bow performance. Typically, manufacturers heavily lubricate these. As such, they are prone to attracting dust and dirt. Check for these and clean as necessary.
13. Exercise your release several times to ensure it's working properly. Hook it to the string and gently put some tension on it. *(Note: Don't pull your string back any further than half an inch.)*

Where to Buy? That is the Question.

So you're in the market for a new bow. You've essentially got three options. It's either big retailer, discount catalog, or the local mom-and-pop shop.

Both meglo-mart retailers and discount catalog houses offer great pricing. Granted, both deal in enormous volume. However, while they shine on price, they lose this luster in a lack of archery knowledge.

Consider this: Local archery pro shops have hardcore archery nuts that can whip your new setup into shape without blinking. The downside is this—you're going to pay a bit more for your dream rig (typically about $50–75 on a complete rig).

An extra $75 may sound like a lot, but consider this: When ordering your dream setup, you are left to make all the decisions. That includes bow, arrow rest, sight, release, arrows, silencers, loop, quiver, field points, broadheads, sling, etc.

So do you consider yourself enough of an archery expert to gather all these components together? One capable of planting carbon shafts in the bull's eye at fifty and beyond?

III. How Compounds Are Made

I was fortunate enough to be invited to visit the BowTech manufacturing plant in Eugene, Oregon. While I was there, I was allowed to see how they produce their bows. Here is a pictorial tour of their manufacturing facility and a look into how compounds are made.

▲ The CNC machining facility is equipped with state-of-the-art Mori Seiki NH6300 DCG machines, each capable of turning out precision quality components while maintaining exacting tolerances. The result is tight fitting, accurate bows.

▲ BowTech is located in Eugene, Oregon. The factory, boasting some 80,000 square feet, houses arguably some of the most technologically advanced manufacturing equipment and processes in the bow industry.

▲ Raw aluminum riser blanks, or plugs, start as either an extrusion or a solid one-piece casting. Here, castings await their turn in the CNC machining center.

▲ At the Eugene, Oregon location, BowTech operates their BowTech Factory Pro Shop. It's worth a visit for those traveling through the area.

◀ The BowTech manufacturing manager holds a solid aluminum casting.

◀ Some risers are machined from extruded aluminum. A FLOW brand water jet cutting machine prepares to cut riser blanks from a solid aluminum extrusion.

◀ The water jet begins cutting the extrusion. Once cut, they are sent to the CNC machining center.

▶ The water jet operator programs the machine for an exacting cut.

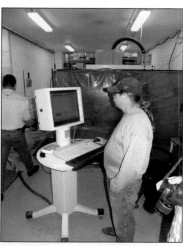

▶ After spending time in the CNC machine, the carousel comes out of the CNC machine with machined risers. The CNC operator removes each riser one at a time. The manufacturing manager holds in his right hand, a raw, cast blank.

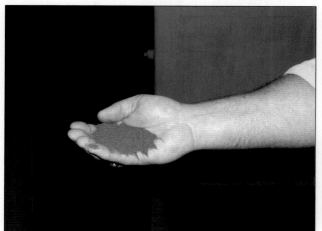

▲ Garnet is used as an abrasive in the water jet. Grains of garnet pass through the water jet and are concentrated into a 60,000 psi stream of water that cuts solid aluminum like butter.

▲ Risers are then placed in tumblers with abrasives to remove all the sharp edges left by the CNC machining operation.

▲ Tumbled risers are then stacked and await the next step in their journey from raw material to new BowTech compound bows.

▲ A CNC machine cuts limb pockets from the stock material.

◄ Thousands and thousands of pounds of recyclable aluminum chips are produced during the manufacturing process. These will be sent to the recycler and processed back into aluminum billet and raw stock. Keeping the process "green" is one of BowTech's paramount objectives.

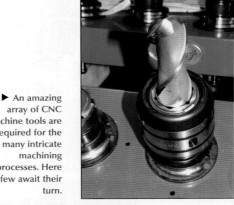

► An amazing array of CNC machine tools are required for the many intricate machining processes. Here a few await their turn.

► Limb pockets are critical to any bow setup. BowTech machines theirs from solid blocks of aluminum. The raw stock is in the manufacturing manager's left hand. He holds a finished limb pocket in his right hand.

◄ Limbs are custom cut and laminated in-house. Here, the manufacturing manager holds a raw limb billet in his right hand and one that has been cut via CNC machine in his left hand. Limbs are high on the criticality list. As such, they must be built to exacting tolerances.

◀ Limbs are hand laminated one-by-one. Here, limbs await the pressure and "cooking out" process. Limbs are placed under 16,000 psi and "cooked" for an extended period of time to ensure proper bonding of the internal laminates.

◀ Following their dip in the dipping tank, components are then sent through an exhaustive wash process that removes all impurities and readies them for the coating process. Hand-applied coatings protect their finishes against the toughest of elements.

▲ BowTech film dips all their components in-house at their Water Dog facility.

▲ Dipped components are clear-coated with a secret formula referred to as "in velvet." This finish keeps the bow looking new for years and feels great to the touch.

▲ Here, risers that have been dipped await the next step in the build-up process. Risers go into the dipping tank where various camo patterns are applied. The result is bows that are "decorated" to match every consumer's personal camouflage pattern preference. Risers "rise" from the dipping tank, magically transformed into works of camo art.

▶ It's now time to assemble the components. Here, cams are assembled and readied for installation on a new Destroyer 340 custom built for me. Every part is torqued to specific tolerances, inspected, and then re-inspected. Cam components await the build-up.

◀ A technician installed the cams on the limbs using a jig built specifically for my Destroyer 340.

◀ A setup technician checks the bow for cam lean. If found, they adjust the harness and retest. This exhaustive attention to detail ensures customers receive a properly tuned bow right from the box.

▲ With the limbs assembled and installed, another technician shows me the tricks of the trade for installing a fresh bowstring. All bowstrings are built in the BowTech plant from the best materials available. The results are strings that won't stretch and are very rugged.

◀ After the bow has been tuned, arrow clearance is checked to ensure all components are working synergistically. If not, it's back to a build-up technician for corrections and adjustments. Draw length and draw weight are checked prior to shooting the new Destroyer 340.

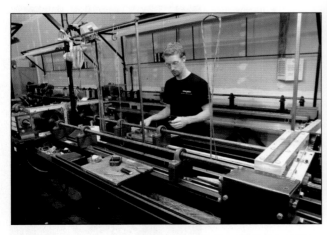

▲ A bowstring technician builds a bowstring for the new Destroyer. The string build-up shop is one of the busiest areas in the factory.

▲ Hot off the assembly line, I shoot my new Destroyer through the chronograph to make sure its performance is up to snuff. It chronos at 346 feet-per-second at 31 inches of draw length and 61.6 pounds of draw weight. Impressive numbers for sure!

◄ After the shot, and a final once-over, my new Destroyer receives its "birth certificate."

▼ After the BowTech factory tour, what would you expect? I'm turned loose on the Oregon turkeys. Sadly, the turkeys would rule the day.

IV. How a Compound Works

To the uninitiated modern compound bows can be intimidating. They come in a dizzying array of shapes, sizes, cam options, draw weights, draw lengths, and axle-to-axle lengths. They have odd looking appendages and strings that seem to head in every direction.

Adding to the confusion is the jargon, the insider nomenclature of those who know bows. Oddities like brace height, idler, eccentrics, tiller, cam lean, hysteresis, draw force curve and others can leave any amateur or outside confused. So how is your average joe to make heads or tails of all this? Heading back to college for a course in mechanical engineering is out.

But I've got good news. While these compounds may look like something that might have a Ph.D. physicist puzzled, it is a relatively simple mechanical machine, one not too unlike a simple block and tackle.

In this chapter, I am going to explain, in the most simplest of terms, what every compound shooter should know (and needs to know) about a compound bow. Although we went over some of these parts

▲ Compound confusion can afflict anyone.

briefly in Chapter Two, this section will add a bit more detail to the basics I've previously provided. If you're new to the sport of archery, I'll guide you through all the jargon and technical hoopla and help to make you sound like a well-seasoned pro next time you step into your local archery pro shop. You'll be spitting out words and phrases like spiral cams, nock travel, and hysteresis with the best of them.

The modern compound bow is an amazing machine. Typically weighing around four pounds, these mechanical machines are capable of delivering arrows at amazing speeds. Anyone who spends time around the archery game will quickly gain an appreciation for these.

The Basics: How a Compound Works

A compound bow is a simple mechanical machine capable of harnessing an amazing amount of energy and then releasing it on command. Imagine you have a simple bungee cord in your hand. As it lays there at rest, it has no energy. However, grab it with both hands and stretch it, and you now have a mechanical machine—one capable of storing energy and releasing it according to your will. A compound bow is nothing more than a bit more complicated mechanical machine.

On a compound bow, the limbs act as our "springs." The cams, or *eccentrics* (a cam that rotates around an off-centered pivot point) are mounted at the tips of our compound limbs. To store energy in the limbs, we must flex them just as we must stretch our bungee cord to store energy in it. To flex the limbs, we add a string. The bowstring is what allows us to rotate the cams.

So now we have a complete mechanical system. We have our limbs, cams, and string. To load our limbs with kinetic energy, we must draw the bowstring, which in turn rotates the cams, which in turn bends the limbs. Once bent, we now have stored kinetic energy.

We may now use the stored kinetic energy to send our arrow downrange. To do so, we must release the string. Once the string is released, the stored energy in the limbs is transferred to the arrow as the limbs move upward (the reverse of how they moved when we bend them to store energy in them). As the limbs move upward, the string is pulled tight (moving it forward), allowing the arrow to propel forward and down to the target.

Once this cycle of sending the arrow downrange is complete, the bow returns to rest. It now does not have any stored energy in the limbs, so it is in a state referred to as *equilibrium*. What we have done is perform what

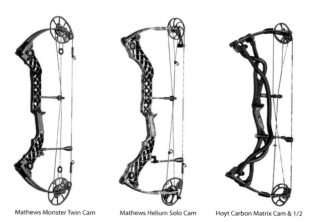

Mathews Monster Twin Cam   Mathews Helium Solo Cam   Hoyt Carbon Matrix Cam & 1/2

▲ Different cam profiles are as plentiful as bowhunters themselves.

▲ Bungee cords that have been stretched hold kinetic energy. Upon release, the energy is turned loose and performs work, sending the arrow downrange to the intended target.

is called a *shot cycle*. The shot cycle is the loading of energy into the limbs and releasing of said energy to send the arrow downrange. It's just that simple.

Types of Cams

Any number of cam systems is available on modern compounds, ranging from the simple to the exotic. Since the early advent of the compound, eccentric

systems have evolved as technology has progressed. Original compounds were built using two round wheels. In the early 1990s, round wheels gave way to more sophisticated cam designs. Eventually, the twin-cam bow was the norm.

As time passed, more cam variations were introduced. Today, four basic styles of cams are available: the two cam (or twin-cam), single cam (sometime referred to as a solo-cam), hybrid, and a combination of the two cam with a modification called the binary cam. Each cam system has its advantages and its share of disadvantages.

Two Cam or Twin-Cams

A two-cam system is just that: two mirrored cams on opposite ends of the bow's limbs. Typically those archers who desire blazing arrow speeds opt for two cams. The distinct advantages of two cams are their ability to load a large amount of kinetic energy into the bow. As such, two-cam bows are typically faster than other cam combinations.

The disadvantage to two-cam systems is that they must be perfectly synchronized at all times. This synchronization is referred to as a bow's *timing*. For a two-cam to perform at its mechanical best, the two cams must work in perfect concert. The bow is out of time when one cam rotates sooner or later than its twin. An out-of-time bow will not launch arrows consistently.

The most common cause of a two-cam bow getting out of time is the string or buss cable system stretches over time, leading to the bow losing its timing. However, while manufacturers of other types of cam systems argue two-cam designs are archaic, new advances in materials sciences (particularly those for synthetic string materials) make today's two-cam bows very stable, and they stay in time under normal use.

In all my years of shooting and testing compounds, I have never found a modern two-cam bow to be difficult to keep in time. In fact, I prefer two cams over single-cam systems. It is simply my personal preference for shooting a really fast setup.

Single Cam

A single-cam system is exactly that—one cam and an *idler wheel*. The single cam is designed to load both limbs when drawn while the idler wheel rotates. Single-cam bows are typically easier to draw than two-cams because you are rotating one cam instead of two. The single cam's claim to fame is that there aren't two cams to synchronize, meaning timing is less critical.

Single-cam manufacturers will also tell consumers that their single-cam bow is quieter than other cam systems. In all my years of testing bows, I have not found this to be true. I have also found that they aren't particularly easy to tune because they can be persnickety and have difficulty achieving *level nock travel*.

Hybrid Cams

The word "hybrid" congers up visions of new and cutting-edge technology. Well, in the case of archery's *hybrid cam,* the technology was developed by Rex Darlington, owner and founder of Darton Archery.

The hybrid cam system was reintroduced and has gained enormous popularity over the past decade after Hoyt archery introduced their version: the Cam & ½. These hybrid cam systems feature two asymmetrical elliptically shaped cams. The top cam on the bow serves as a control while the bottom cam serves as the power cam. Both the top and bottom cams are linked using a split harness, a control cable, and a main bow string.

The distinct advantage of the hybrid system is the level knock travel and the synching of the two cams without the problems of timing associated with two-cam systems.

Binary Cams

A further improvement in cam systems was recently introduced by BowTech Archery. Their binary cam system is basically a two-cam system with both cams slaved together by a cam-to-cam control cable. By slaving the two cams together, the problems associated with timing two-cam bows are eliminated since the cams must rotate as they are lashed together.

▲ Matt McPherson is credited with the advent of the single-cam compound.

▲ Rex Darlington owns in excess of twenty US patents for compound bow technology.

Supporters of the binary system venture that by lashing the cams together, inconsistencies in limb flexure and cable and control cables are automatically compensated for by the two cams working in unison.

While many archery gurus logged into internet chat rooms debate the pros and cons of the various cam systems, I personally think the hybrid and binary cam systems are the wave of the future. These, in my opinion, provide a smooth drawing bow with ample speed and are virtually immune to tuning issues associated with past two-cam designs.

Cam Profiles

Now that we have discussed the various cams and their systems, it is a good place to explain what it is that makes one cam differ from another. I'm often asked the following question by inexperienced archers and newbies to the sport: what bow would I recommend they shoot? While it is flattering to be trusted by these folks to recommend a specific bow for them, it isn't something I nor anyone else can do.

Bows are a matter of individual taste and preference, much like pairs of shoes. Manufacturers have been tasked with providing a wide selection of bows and cam combinations in an attempt to "fit" each and every individual archer.

For a bow to fit properly, it must accommodate any number of *anthropometric* measures. Anthropometry is Greek and loosely translates to "measurement of man." These measures are unique to every human being and are what determine our overall build and physical being.

When archery manufacturers design a bow, they must accommodate all of us, literally tens of thousands of shooters in one bow line. A daunting task, huh? As such, a wide array of cam configurations is available to choose from. A bow's particular shooting demeanor is determined from a conglomerate of these configurations.

So when looking for a bow, you must consider the type of bow *you* like. I personally like a really fast shooting bow. This means the cam profile you'll be shooting is harsh and aggressive, as these are required to put enough energy into the limbs to propel arrows at top speeds. Other archers may opt for a smooth drawing bow that's easy to hold. In this case, you'd choose a mild cam that draws easily, storing a moderate amount of energy in the limbs and shooting a bit slower than aggressive cams.

The Draw Cycle

You've probably heard much ado about the *draw cycle* when folks talk about the way a compound bow shoots. As with most things related to the compound bow, the draw cycle is very simple. The draw cycle is the portion of the shot when the bow is drawn from equilibrium (when the bow string is stationary) until the bow is at full draw.

The draw cycle is the portion of the shot cycle that loads the limbs with kinetic energy. When folks talk of how a bow "feels," they are referring to its draw. There are as many eccentric combinations (cams) as there are bows. The combination of cams you have on your bow determines how the bow will draw and its draw cycle.

Typically, compound bows will have any number of cam or eccentrics combinations. Manufacturers use these various combinations to make a compound bow shoot in a certain way. For instance, there are speed bows that are designed for blistering arrow speeds. For a bow to be incredibly fast, you must load the amount of energy it takes to propel the arrow super fast into the bow.

As you can imagine, the faster the bow, and subsequently the arrow, the more energy must be put into the bow. There is nothing magical about a compound. No bow exists that can be effortlessly drawn and still be blisteringly fast. The amount of energy introduced to the system *is* the amount of energy you can get out. We will discuss bow efficiencies later.

Draw Force Curves

After discussing cam profiles, it is prudent that we discuss draw force curves. At its most basic, the *draw force curve* is a graphical representation of the way draw weight changes in pounds from an "at rest" position to the "full drawn" position. The curve is plotted on a graph as draw weight over the duration of the draw length.

As we have discussed, it is the profile of the cam that determines how a bow draws. Manufacturers have graphically put these cam profiles on paper. These graphical representations of the draw cycle are called draw force curves. Now don't panic when you look at these. At first glance, they can be a bit overwhelming. However, they're no more than a line drawing of what you feel when you draw a bow. Simple, huh?

Typically there are three types of cams: 1) round wheel, 2) mild, and 3) aggressive\harsh. While these are generalities, they do describe most cams. The round wheel cam offers shooters a gentle pulling, smooth drawing bow that holds nicely but shoots rather slow arrow speeds. A mild cam offers archers a more aggressive cam and better top-end arrow speeds. Harsh, aggressive cams typically are difficult to draw, ramping up to maximum draw weight quickly and storing the most energy in the bow. Due to their aggressive nature, they shoot the fastest and send arrows downrange at top speeds.

Bow Let-Off

One of the biggest advantages of the compound bow is that it stores plenty of energy to propel arrows quickly to their target. What makes a compound bow a pleasure to shoot is its ability to store maximum energy in the limbs and then ramp down at the end of the draw cycle. It is this ramping down that is referred to as *let-off*.

Let-Off occurs after the bow's cam system has transferred your muscle energy into the limbs and is ready to shoot. During the last portion of the draw cycle, the cam(s) taper(s) off, allowing you to hold the bow more comfortably at full draw.

Manufacturers have assigned numeric values to these let-offs so you, the consumer, can gauge how easy the bow is to hold at full draw. These cam let-offs are expressed in percentages. For instance, if a bow has a 65 percent let-off, and you are drawing 70 pounds, you'll be holding around 24.5 pounds at full draw.

Calculated: 70 (draw weight) x 0.35 = 24.5 pounds

Let-Offs range from 30 percent (on very old compounds) to 99 percent on some specialty bows. Most modern compounds have let-offs that are in the 65 to 85 percent range.

Effective Let-Off Versus Actual Let-Off

As with most things "compound," you need additional information when looking at let-off. While the concept of let-off is a simple one, the manner in which manufacturers advertise let-off can be a bit misleading. Enter "effective" let-off and "actual" let-off. These two entities report two separate types of let-off. Huh? Hang in there.

When drawing a bow there is a certain amount of friction in the system. This degradation or loss of effec-

tive draw weight due to these frictional forces is called *hysteresis*. When letting down a bow there is less friction in the system (less friction than when drawing the bow). So to calculate let-off, you need: 1) maximum draw weight and 2) the holding weight at full draw. So if there is less friction when letting the bow down, the percentage of "let-off" will be higher on the way down. This is called *effective let-off*.

Conversely, *actual let-off* is the percentage in pounds that you will be holding at full draw. Reporting "effective let-off" is a good way for manufacturers to fudge the numbers, making it appears like the bow has more let-off while generating more arrow speed with a lower "actual let-off." When reading through the specs, see if you can tell which is being reported.

How Let-Off Affects Shooting Accuracy

Much has been written on shooting form. In fact, it has been covered ad nauseum in bowhunting publications. However, little has made it to print about the effect of let-off on your shooting form. In my opinion, there is a point of diminishing return as let-offs increase. The idea behind high let-offs is to allow the shooter to relax as much as they can at full draw. However, a shooter can relax too much, and form then deteriorate.

Biomechanical engineering is the study the human machine and the application of mechanical engineering to biological systems. Biomechanics tell us that muscles are designed to work in pairs. Skeletal muscles attach to the skeleton and rely on one muscle to move the bone in one direction and another to move it back the other way.

When a bow is drawn to full draw, muscles are at work to steady the bow arm, contract the drawing arm, fix (make stationary) the shoulders, grip the handle, rotate the head into the shooting position, etc. Everything is working under tension. When the arrow is released, the recoil forces are transmitted to the bow hand, but the muscles that hold it are already under tension and can hold it steady.

When compound let-offs become too great, the muscles relax, particularly the muscles that keep the bow arm extended. When you release the arrow, the bow accelerates the arrow, and the recoil forces are suddenly transmitted to the bow hand; it takes a fraction of a second for the muscles to again contract so as to hold it steady. Keeping a moderate force on the bow arm keeps the muscle fibers firing and active and

The Pope & Young Club is a record keeping organization for bowhunting. To qualify for a record, you must comply with their rules and regulations. They define let-off for bowhunting equipment in the following manner:

1. Definition of let-off: that characteristic of a bow that results in a reduction of the force necessary to increase the draw length after the highest level of draw force has been reached. This is a characteristic generally associated with, but not restricted to, compound bows.
2. The maximum let-off on a compound bow shall be measured at a point in the draw cycle after the peak draw weight has been attained. It shall be measured near the end of the draw cycle where the minimum holding force is reached. This point in the draw cycle on a compound bow is known as "the bottom of the valley."
3. Determination of the percent of let-off: The values of the peak draw force and the let-off force shall be used to calculate the percent of let-off. The peak force is the maximum force obtained during the draw cycle. The let-off force is the lowest force reached following the peak force during a single uninterrupted draw cycle. In all cases, both the highest and lowest force shall be read from a scale during a single and continual pull condition, without relaxation. This technique eliminates the introduction of hysteresis, which can distort the reading. % Let-Off = 100 X [(Peak Draw Force) – (Minimum Holding Force)] / (Peak Draw Force)
4. Effective January 1, 2004, animals taken with bows that have a nominal percent of let-off greater than 65 percent shall be listed with an asterisk (*) in the Records. It is recognized that variations in draw length and/or draw weight can affect the percent of let-off on compound bows. For these reasons, minor variations in let-off are acceptable.

allows them to react much more quickly, minimizing movement when the arrow is released.

The Role of Draw Length in the Shooting Equation

Earlier we discussed anthropometric measures, those measures of humans that are unique to every human being and determine our overall build and physical being. When discussing *draw length*, these measures become very important.

Modern compound bows are built to specific draw lengths. According to the Archery Manufacturers and Merchants Organization (AMO) Standards Field Publication, FP-3/2000 draw length is measured according to the following information:

Draw length is a specified distance, or the distance at the archer's full draw, from the nocking point on the string to the pivot point of the bow grip (or the theoretical vertical projection of a tangency line to the pivot point parallel to the string) plus 1 ¾". Draw length from pivot point shall be designed at DLPP and shall be called true draw length. Example: 26 ¼" DLPP plus 1 ¾" is the equivalent of 28" draw.

As I mentioned, bows are built to draw to a specific length. When engineers design a bow, they design the cams to operate at peak efficiency at a very specific draw length. This is how they get the most efficiency out of the cams (eccentrics) and ultimately the compound bow.

The advantage to having a long draw length is that the bow has a longer power stroke and is therefore able to generate more arrow speed. As a general rule, for every additional inch of draw length, the bow will generate an additional 10 feet-per-second (fps) of arrow speed. So if a bow shoots 250 feet-per-second at a 26-inch draw length, that same bow will shoot 290 feet-per-second at a 30-inch draw length (4 additional inches of draw length x 10 fps = +40 fps).

Conversely, if a bow has an advertized International Bowhunting Organization (IBO) speed rating of 330 fps (IBO speed rating is calculated by shooting a bow at 30 inches of draw length at 70 pounds of draw weight with a 350-grain arrow) and your draw length is 26 inches, you should expect your bow to shoot in the ballpark of 290 fps (330 fps minus 4 inches less of draw length x 10 fps per inch (40 fps) of draw length = 290 fps).

Shooting a Bow That's the Wrong Length

From time to time, folks shoot bows that are not sized correctly for them. Some shoot bows with draw lengths that are too long or too short. Both situations lead to shooting form errors and errant arrows.

Too Short a Draw Length. In all reality, few archers shoot bows that are too short. However, for those who do, you'll run into some basic shooting form errors. A bow that is too short typically results in the shooter's inability to settle into his natural anchor point(s).

For most archers, they anchor at full draw on some portion of their face with their mechanical release. Most archers anchor their strings to their nose tips, corners of their mouths, or behind their ears. When drawing a bow that's too short, the string never makes it far enough backward to settle the string on any of these anatomical reference points. As such, the shooter must lean their head forward awkwardly as they try to look through their peep and attain their anchor point(s).

You also bend or collapse your bow arm to allow the bow to move back toward the torso. Once this is done, the grip tightens, torquing the bow and canting it to the left or right depending on your handedness. By the time you release the arrow, the body is contorted in all kinds of odd manners, leading to some of the ugliest shots on the range or in the woods.

Too Long a Draw Length. More often than not, if draw length is the culprit of a shooting ill, it's because an archer is shooting a bow that is too long. For some unknown reason, some archers insist on shooting a bow that is too long for their physical build, and they pay the price in accuracy. Several years ago, I went on a hunt with a fellow who was not too terribly tall. He insisted that he had a thirty-one-inch draw length.

For this gentlemen to have a thirty-one-inch draw length, his knuckles would have had to literally drag on the ground. Naturally, they didn't (I checked). We were getting ready for the afternoon hunt and he insisted on shooting my bow. I'm six foot five and have a thirty-one-inch draw length. Needless to say, after much struggling, groaning, and horribly funny facial expressions, he was finally able to draw the bow.

When he anchored, the string wrapped around the back of his head. Before he could shoot, I leaned over and mentioned that I thought the string would remove his ear when he released the arrow. He just winced and let her fly. Luckily for him, his ear remained intact.

There is a moral to this story: Don't shoot a bow that's too long in an effort to gain any extra arrow speed. Rest assured, you're sacrificing an enormous amount of

Quick and Easy Way to Measure Your Draw Length

Shooting a bow that's the correct draw length is critical to shooting comfortably and accurately. Shooting a compound that's too short or too long will negatively affect your accuracy; a bow that doesn't fit you will cause multiple shooting issues. So fitting a bow to your body is of utmost importance.

To measure your draw length, determine the length of your wingspan in inches. To do so, stand facing a wall with your arms outstretched and your palms facing the wall. Have someone mark the tips of your outstretched fingers on the wall. Make sure you don't strain to reach further out—just remain relaxed.

Now, measure the distance between your marks and divide that number by 2.5. The number you come up with is your draw length in inches.

▲ While leaning against a flat wall, measure fingertip to fingertip and divide by 2.5.

accuracy for the little amount of arrow speed you're gaining. There is a really old archery saying, "a fast miss is still a miss." Though a bit silly, it's true.

Technically, if you're shooting a bow that's too long, you'll encounter plenty of problems. For starters, your peep sight will be too close to your eye to effectively frame your pins. Not to mention your anchor points will be in some odd anatomical position (anchoring behind your head is not recommended).

Although you'd naturally anchor on your nose when shooting the correct length bow, that anchor point might change to your ear if your bow is too long for you. When you have unnatural anchor points, your form suffers. When form suffers, you miss.

Other shooting maladies include stiffening your bow arm and rotating your elbow inward, locking your arm out at full draw. Locking your arm leads to pushing your shoulder girdle forward in an effort to lengthen your upper body. As you attempt to lengthen your body, you pull the head backwards to keep it away from the string and gain focus through the peep.

All of these contortions lead to some of the ugliest arrow groups you'll ever see. And to think you're going through all these gyrations to be able to get a few more feet-per-second out of your bow. When the string slaps your forearm and raises a giant welt every time you shoot an arrow, you'll be reminded of your errant thinking and poor choice in draw lengths.

The Role of Draw Weight (Force) in the Bow Equation

Draw weight has served as a badge of courage for many throughout the years. I cannot count the times I've heard archers brag about the amount of draw weight they pull as though there is a merit badge for successfully drawing a ridiculous amount of pound-age.

For some, it's like there is a magical number in pounds that separates the men from the boys and the women from the girls. I once had an archery acquaintance who would shop a new bow every year with the goal of finding the bow with the highest draw weight that shot the fastest arrow speeds.

Every year, he'd call me asking for my annual report of the newest and hottest bows available. Like clockwork I'd report my findings, and off he'd go in search of the new, "hot" bow. And so it went for many years. It was years before I actually was able to witness him shooting one of his radical bows. Let me tell you, it was comical.

▲ Shooting a bow that's too long.

▲ Shooting a bow that's too short.

There he stood, attempting to draw that ninety-pound bow. He pointed it straight skyward, like a Greek statue of a mythical hero. His head cranked acutely to the side. He put his chin down and squinted his eyes tightly, like someone had punched him in the gut. His body squirmed and gyrated. While I'm relatively sure it's impossible, I swear to this day, I

String Loops?

Does adding a string loop change your draw length? This is an often debated topic. The simple answer is no. Here's why.

A bow's draw length is measured from the string at full draw. Now adding a ½-inch loop or more to the string does not change this draw length measure as it is still a measure from the string. If adding a string loop to a bow increased its draw length, it would increase the bow's top speed as the power stroke would also increase. Right? But it doesn't.

However, adding a string loop *does* increase the perception that the draw length is longer as your anchor point(s) move(s) backward, just as they would if drawing a longer bow. So when buying a new bow, it is important to take into consideration your use of a string loop.

▲ String loops can make an average shooter a good shooter.

actually heard his rotator cuffs creak and moan as he awkwardly attempted to muscle that devil bow.

Once at full draw, he stood shaking like he was suffering from hyperthermia. Gritting his teeth, he leveled his arrow at the twenty-yard target. At that point, I reached up and placed my fingers in my ears like a gun was about to go off. With one god-awful trigger punch and huge lurch, he launched that ultrafast, barn

▲ Drawing a bow that's too heavy negatively affects every aspect of the shot. Most importantly, an accurate arrow is never achieved.

burning, blistering arrow. It screamed over the target, off on its way into the next zip code, leaving behind nothing but a vapor trail.

In that brief moment, I'm confident my face reflected the sheer terror, confusion, and concern for what I had just witnessed. Archery is, after all, a beautifully orchestrated, fluid melding of man with machine—not a poorly scripted rendition of someone riding their first bucking Brahma bull at the county fair.

That was fifteen years ago, and I still chuckle and shake my head each time I recount that experience. I must admit that was one of the fastest arrows I have ever seen go whistling off into the great blue yonder.

It was now my turn to shoot (and give him time to towel off the sweat and ice down his shoulders). I gently and effortlessly drew my 62-pound bow back, nestled my 20-yard pin on the center circle, and drilled it with little fanfare. As I turned, he extended his arms, offering me his ridiculous setup. I passed, saying, "Oh, no thank you. I'm sure I couldn't move that string more than a quarter-inch at that draw weight." Sadly enough, I swear I saw a look of satisfaction on his face. *Really?*

When discussing draw weight, it is important to note that today's compounds are feats of mechanical engineering and materials science. While seemingly simple machines, they convert the power of our muscles into stored energy and then send arrows downrange with incredible accuracy and speed.

The role draw weight plays in this equation is quite simple. In general, the higher the draw weight, the more energy is loaded into the bow. The more energy, the faster the bow propels the arrow. What follows are some very general guidelines for draw weight compiled using average shooter body weights. These will vary greatly for individuals that do not fit the "standard" index. In other words, I know several small children that can draw as much as an adult. This happens, of course, after several years of shooting experience.

	Physical Weight	Draw Weight
Very Small Child	55-70 lbs.	10-15 lbs.
Small Child	70-100 lbs.	15-25 lbs.
Larger Child	100-130 lbs.	25-35 lbs.
Small Frame Women	100-130 lbs.	25-35 lbs.
Medium Frame Women	130-160 lbs	30-40 lbs.
Athletic Older Child (Boys)	130-150 lbs.	40-50 lbs.
Small Frame Men	120-150 lbs.	45-55 lbs.
Large Frame Women	160+ lbs.	45-55 lbs.
Medium Frame Men	150-180 lbs.	55-65 lbs.
Large Frame Men	180+ lbs.	65-75 lbs.

Recommended Draw Weight

The Function of the Valley

As we've seen, compound bows store energy when the string is drawn. As one might imagine, at some time during the drawing of the bow, it reaches peak weight. Once a bow has reached peak weight, the shooter has loaded as much energy as the bow is capable of storing. That point in the draw stroke before full draw is reached is called "the valley."

Bows built for speed typically have a very short valley—that is, nearly their entire draw cycle is needed to load as much energy into the bow as possible. Less aggressive bows, however, require less distance of the draw to generate and load the bow with energy, so their valleys are typically longer. In general, bows with short valleys are more difficult to shoot because they fire quicker due to the short valley, while longer valleys are more comfortable to shoot.

Bow Length: How Long is Long Enough?

A bow's length is measured from the pins or axles the cams are mounted on. This is referred to as the "axle-to-axle measurement." An axle-to-axle length reflects the approximate measure of a bow's overall length. It is, however, *not* the real measure of the bows length as it does not account for the cam height.

The length of a bow has more to do with the time period in which it was made than with the bow's performance. Prior to the mid-1990s, most archers thought that longer axle-to-axle bows were easier to shoot and more forgiving than their shorter cousins. In fact, during this period, compounds averaged forty–forty five inches long.

Sometime around the mid-1990s, a company began an advertising campaign (more of an advertising blitz) that purported short axle-to-axle bows were now "in." From that day forward, other companies followed suit, making their bows shorter and shorter while reporting that these new diminutive bows were a shooter's best friend.

Today, the average compound is about 34 inches axle-to-axle. It appears all the great shooting attributes of longer bows have been forgotten. Typically, compounds can be grouped into three size categories: 1) short axle-to-axle bows less than 32" long; 2) mid-range axle-to-axle 32" to 37" long; and 3) long axle-to-axle bows that are over 37" long. Each of these bows has their merits and applications.

Short axle-to-axle bows are generally best suited for bowhunters who hunt from treestands and ground blinds where maneuverability is at a premium. At these shorter lengths, the shooter is less affected by hanging limbs and the physical constraint of the roof of a ground blind. However, minimum axle-to-axle bows make for an acute string angle when drawn. This "string pinch" makes a small, short bow more difficult to shoot well.

Mid-range length bows are the most popular length bows. These compounds are well-suited for treestand hunters as well as those who hunt from ground blinds. Due to their size, they are also a good candidate for hunters who prefer to spot-and-stalk. However, they are perfect for close distance shots when spotting-and-stalking because their accuracy diminishes as the shot distance increases.

Long compounds, that are 38 inches or longer are great for target shooters looking for the easiest, most forgiving of compounds. The long axle-to-axle measure minimizes string pinch and offers excellent accuracy. Most western hunters opt for these longer bows as most shots on western big game are taken from exaggerated distances where pin-point accuracy is required. The extra axle-to-axle distance helps make the bow a more stable platform from which to shoot. Long axle-to-axle bows are also a good choice (if not their only choice) for those who desire to shoot their compounds using their fingers.

How Fast is Fast Enough?

There is plenty of advertising hype over how fast compounds shoot. In fact, I am of the opinion that most archers consider speed first and foremost when shopping a new bow. While speed is important, it is not, however, the single most important consideration.

Probably a decade or so ago, bows were struggling to break the three hundred-feet-per-second mark. At the time, three hundred was the Holy Grail for bow designers. With the recent advent of preloaded parallel limbs, arrow improvements, limb refinement, and CAD cam design, bow manufacturers have been able to exceed the 300-feet-per-second mark, and now several manufacturers offer compounds that eclipse the 360-feet-per-second mark. This is truly amazing.

IBO Versus AMO Speeds

There are two bodies who have issued standards for measuring bow speeds—the IBO and AMO (Archery Manufacturers and Merchants Organization). If a compound is advertised with an *(IBO)* speed rating, it has been tested shooting at thirty inches of draw length and at seventy pounds of draw weight with a 350-grain arrow.

If a bow is advertised with speeds recorded in AMO, the bow in question will have a maximum draw weight of sixty pounds. The arrow will have a grain weight of 540-grains. The draw length will be set at thirty inches.

For both standards, the bow is then shot through a chronograph to obtain a speed reading. Almost all manufacturers report compound bow speeds as an IBO speed. The reason is simple—these speeds are always more impressive than bow speeds reported as AMO because these speeds are always slower due to the diminished draw weight and the increased arrow weight.

One important note on advertised arrow speeds: beware of them. Many manufacturers shoot their bows specifically to get top speeds. To do so, some manufacturers will shoot their compounds with a smaller string (with less strands) and everything stripped off the bow. That includes a peep sight, arrow rest, etc. The bow will be shot at the lowest let-off setting, with a bare shaft (no fletching) and, in many cases, overdrawn

(i.e., drawn past the back wall that increases the power stroke and draw length).

It is also not unusual for the manufacturer to fudge their speed numbers, too. As a matter of fact, in the ten plus years that I have been testing bows for *Outdoor Life*, I have found very few bows that shoot the same speed during my testing as those advertised for the bow. One other word to the wise: beware of bows with the advertisement "speeds up to." If a bow says speeds up to 330 feet-per-second, keep in mind that 290 feet-per-second is well within that range as the "up to" range is 0 feet-per-second to 330 feet-per-second.

The Speed Factor

If there is so much hype over speed, why is more better? The answer is simple: the faster a bow shoots, the flatter the trajectory of the arrow. Without getting too technical, the laws of physics dictate that an arrow traveling slower (fewer feet-per-second) will drop greater than a faster moving arrow.

Imagine taking a ball and throwing underhand to someone a few yards away. You'd notice the ball had a distinct arc to it as it dropped quickly on its way to the other person. Now imagine taking that same ball and throwing overhand with some oomph on it to the same person. Of course, it is not going to have the visual drop or arc since it has enough momentum to overcome the gravity attempting to pull it down.

The same holds true for arrows. Fast compounds shoot arrows fast enough to eliminate (or minimize) the effect of gravity along their flight path. A slower bow, shooting the same distance, will have a pronounced arc to the arrow's flight. The slower arrow, the one with the greater arc, has less of a chance of striking the target as the likelihood of the arrow's path intersecting the target is less than the probability of a faster arrow striking the target where its path intersects the target.

Line of Sight. A major misconception some beginners—and even some advanced archers—have is their arrow follows their line of sight to the intended target. This has caused much heartache for the bowhunter who assumes as much.

Depending on your compound and your setup, your arrow's flight begins as much as six inches below your line of sight. *It is critical that you understand your arrow's trajectory starts below your line of sight.* When released, the arrow rises into your line of sight and then begins to drop as its momentum begins to deteriorate.

I learned this valuable lesson many years ago while hunting from a makeshift ground blind for turkeys. Given two ideal opportunities to harvest a couple of tremendous birds, I ended up shooting the brush I had placed in front of me for cover. The first time I did it, I was stupefied at what I had done. After giving it much thought, sitting there with an arrow stuck in a pine limb, I realized my error. On my next shot, I did it again because I was excited about making the shot (hard learner). Since then, I haven't made the same mistake a third time.

Understanding your line of sight is very important when hunting from ground blinds. The awfully small windows you're expected to shoot through can be a real challenge when trying to slip an arrow through them.

A Compound's Effective Range

Every archer has an "effective range," at which they're confident shooting. For some, it's thirty yards. For others, it's sixty yards. Compound bows have an effective range, too. In this case, the range is the distance at which the bow is capable of delivering a lethal arrow.

A bow's effective range is determined by a couple of things: 1) arrow speed and 2) the kinetic energy the arrow carries. The laws of physics dictate that as an arrow travels downrange, its trajectory decays as gravity and aerodynamic drag affect its flight.

Every compound delivers arrows at a defined speed at certain target distances. This, in essence, is the bow's effective range. So if we can determine how our bow performs at different distances, we can make an educated decision on which sight pin to use at varying shot distances. You'll calculate your bow's effective range using the sight pins. When we're done, you'll know the range of distances at which each pin is capable of delivering a lethal shot.

Let's assume we're hunting whitetail deer. The kill zone on a whitetail is about an eight-inch circular area (give or take some) when standing broadside. An arrow placed anywhere in that zone will result in a kill shot. Placed outside that zone, the shot will be nonlethal.

We'll start by shooting at the eight-inch kill zone at twenty yards with your twenty-yard pin. You may want to actually mark the eight-inch area on your target. The arrow should hit in the middle of the 8-inch zone as your pin is sighted in for twenty yards. Now move for-ward one yard. Shoot again. Move one yard closer to the target with each shot. At a certain distance, you'll notice your arrows are above the kill zone. At this distance, you have exceeded your twenty-yard pin's ability to deliver a lethal arrow. Write down that distance.

Now repeat this starting at twenty yards and moving back one yard with each successive shot. At some point, your arrows will drop out of the kill zone. Write this distance down. Now, you have a range of yards in which your twenty-yard pin is capable of delivering a lethal shot. Repeat this process for each pin. When you finish, you'll know your bow's effective range.

Shooting Acute Angles

Grounding a trophy animal with bow and arrow often carries bowhunters beyond the flatlands and into steep terrain. Acute uphill or downhill shots are often unchartered territory for bowhunters. Make the wrong decision here and your trip will be logged as a disaster.

Get Anchored

Successful conversion of tough inclined or declined shots requires picture-perfect shooting form. Your anchor point(s) when drawing on flat ground changes when drawing on uneven terrain. Multiple anchor points such as a string kisser button, peep sight, bow string to nose, and nestling the release hand on the neck, jaw, or face helps keep your shot geometry tight.

Shot Geometry

For most bowhunters, there's a natural tendency to either lean backward or forward when shooting up or downhill. Your bow arm geometry should remain unchanged from shots on level ground. Consciously check your torso at full draw. If you're leaning in any direction, your anchor points have changed drastically. Bend at the waist to keep your upper body and bow arm the same as when executing level shots.

Footwork

Steeply angled shots can have you searching for a solid footing. To achieve the best footing, work the sides of your boots or heels into the terrain until you're comfortable. On occasion, you'll find the need to bend your back leg on extreme uphill shots. If necessary, kneel. Keep in mind that your upper body must remain static as it does on flatland shots.

Get Level

If your bow is canted in one direction or another, you're going to miss your target. Prior to releasing an arrow, glance at your sight level. If it is canted, level the bow. If your sight doesn't have a level, line your bow's riser up with the trees on the hillside. Trees generally grow straight up. On occasion, leaning into the hillside will help keep your shooting form level.

Practice

No one can learn to shoot reading about it. Find terrain that simulates where you'll be hunting and practice there. More than one bowhunter's trip has been ruined by not preparing for angled shots. *Practice!*

How Far?

Judging distances to an uphill or downhill target is the toughest assignment in bowhunting. These shots involve that nasty word mathematics. Most of us aren't statisticians, so do yourself a favor—invest in a high-quality rangefinder equipped with an inclinometer. These rangefinders eliminate all guesswork by automatically calculating shot angle and providing the exact distance to the target.

Flattening a Bow's Trajectory

There is no debating the fact that a faster-shooting bow produces flatter arrow trajectories, making judging target distances easier. A flat flying arrow is the goal of every archer. While we have discussed the trade-offs for achieving speed previously, I will explain simple ways to get a flatter shooting arrow from your current rig.

Several factors affect arrow speed, including 1) fletching (vane) size and configuration; 2) arrow weight; 3) geographical elevation; 4) draw weight; 5) draw length; and 6) brace height. Of these, the easiest to manipulate are arrow weight, fletching size and configuration, and draw weight. Your elevation is dependent on where you hunt and is unchangeable (unless you change your hunting location). Your draw length is a fixed distance that remains unchanged unless you're still growing. Your brace height is determined by the bow you shoot. Short of buying a new bow, you are stuck with what you have.

Reducing Arrow Weight

Let's look at arrows first. If you opt to reduce the weight of your arrows, they will fly faster. The rule of thumb is for every five grains of arrow weight you can eliminate, you will gain an additional 1 feet-per-second. So reducing an arrow's weight by fifty grains will give you an estimated ten additional feet-per-second. Now, keep in mind that as with everything, there will be trade-offs for reducing arrow weight.

If you reduce your arrows' weight too much, they can become unsafe to shoot. For a bow to operate efficiently and safely, it must have a sufficient mass (which is the arrow) to move. That means a bow must have an arrow loaded to provide enough resistance in the system to dissipate most of the kinetic energy stored in the compound. If there isn't enough mass, the bow will explode. This is why when a bow is *dry-fired* (i.e., shot without an arrow loaded), the bow typically explodes. There isn't enough resistance in the system for the bow to convert its energy into propelling the arrow. So it converts the extra energy into breaking the limbs, strings, and cables.

Additionally, when you decrease arrow weight, you decrease its mass. As arrow mass decreases, so does the amount of kinetic energy it can carry to the target. So you may be shooting an incredibly fast arrow, however, once it arrives at the target, it might not have enough mass to enter the target. Remember, there are trade-offs for everything you change on a compound bow.

When changing arrow weights, it is recommended that you have at minimum of 5-grains of arrow weight per pound of draw weight. That means if you're drawing 70 pounds, you must have at least a 350-grain arrow (5 x 70 = 350). A few companies do make arrows that are extremely light and built specifically for shooters who want to shoot underweighted arrows. While these arrows do offer incredible speeds, they do eventually damage the bow, as the bow is not designed to shoot underweight arrows.

Arrow Vanes

There are more old wives' tales about arrow fletching than any other archery component. Many of these tales have spawned misconceptions about fletching that inevitably keep archers from attaining the best performance from their equipment.

Modifying your fletching setup can increase arrow speeds. Today several manufacturers produce small, low-profile vanes. These vanes are approximately 1-inch long. For eons, archers have believed that large, high-profiled vanes steer their arrows and stabilize them in flight. Nothing could be further from the truth. In its basic form, an archery arrow is a projectile. A projectile is defined as an object (the arrow) thrown obliquely (shot) near the earth's surface that moves along a curved path (trajectory). The science and analysis of the motion associated with a projectile is referred to as *projectile motion*. The projectiles path is directly influenced by gravity.

While in the perfect world of theoretical physics, a projectile is not acted upon by any force other than gravity. In our real-world application with an arrow, aerodynamic drag also acts upon our arrow projectile. Aerodynamic drag is the fluid drag force (air) that acts on any moving solid body (our arrow) in the direction of the fluid free stream flow (the air in front of the arrow).

So to increase arrow speeds, we have to reduce the amount of aerodynamic drag causing friction on our arrow and slowing it. As we have discussed, by making the size of your vane smaller, you decrease the amount of surface area of your vane. When surface area is reduced, so is aerodynamic drag. So that makes the arrow fly faster. The same is true with the fletching configuration. Many archers believe, a *helically fletched* or *offset fletched* arrow "spin-stabilizes" the arrow.

While these configurations do make the arrow rotate slightly, they do not, however, do so in an efficient manner. The rotation induced by these arrangements is the result of aerodynamic drag. In other words, the rotation is the result of friction on the vanes. Instead of stabilizing flight, they are actually slowing the arrow with exaggerated drag.

This is the same misconception that many archers have about fletching their arrows with feathers. They firmly believe large feathers "steer" their arrow shafts and broadheads. The fact is, applying extra large feathers to an arrow shaft dramatically increases the drag on the aft end (rear of the arrow) of the arrow shaft. In the case of broadheads, the arrow is dramatically slowed by friction reducing the effect of the broadhead. You are actually detuning or slowing the bow down to an arrow speed that is not affected by arrow planing. In the case of broadhead flight, a well-tuned bow will shoot broadheads perfectly; there is no reason to slow the arrows down by adding feathers to get good flight.

Draw Weight

The simplest way to flatten arrow trajectory is to increase your bow's draw weight. For every one pound you add to the draw weight, you increase your arrow speeds by approximately two feet-per-second. So an increase in draw weight of ten pounds will increase arrow speed by about twenty feet-per-second. But remember that there is a trade-off for everything you do in an effort to increase arrow speeds. Increasing draw weight makes the bow much harder to draw and hold at full draw. As you increase draw weight, you

Dry Firing a Bow?

We have all been told to not dry fire a bow; That is, release the string without an arrow nocked. I have personally witnessed three bows dry fired in my career. Two were compounds and one was a crossbow. In all three instances, the result was the same—catastrophic. So what is it that happens when a bow is misfired? Simple physics are at work when the bow is fired sans the arrow.

All bows, whether compound or crossbow, are mechanically designed to function with an arrow loaded. The limbs, cams, strings, and cables work in concert to load energy into the bow and store it there until it is released when the bow is triggered.

Should you attempt to fire a bow without an arrow, the bow has to displace all the stored energy somewhere other than into the arrow. In physics, this is called performing "work." Or in other words, the bow focuses its stored energy into the arrow shaft. Now, not all the energy is transferred into the bow. This is because mechanical machines are not totally efficient. They lose some of their energy to things like noise, vibration, and friction (heat).

If the arrow is not present, the bow now has to transfer this energy somewhere else. With so much stored energy, the bow absorbs the energy and then attempts to dissipate it. The only way the bow can do this is to perform "work" on the bow assembly. That is, the limbs, cams, riser, strings, cables, and so on. The result is a bow that explodes.

also increase the number of pounds you're holding at full draw. This is very important; if a bow is difficult to hold at full draw, it is also difficult to aim as you struggle to keep the pins still and on target.

One last note: It is not the speed of the bow that determines how accurately you shoot, but the ability of the archers, the one who stands behind the bow, to execute the perfect shot. Increasing arrow speeds does nothing to increase your shooting ability. Practice and confidence in your equipment improves your shooting ability.

Shooting a Drop Away Arrow Rest

Another way to flatten an arrow's trajectory is to reduce the friction between the arrow shaft and the arrow rest. Today bristle-style full-capture rests are very popular with bowhunters. And for good reason—they work really well. However, these style rests are not the best when trying to eliminate friction and increase arrow speeds.

Drop away rests, those that are triggered to drop away from the arrow during release, greatly reduce arrow-to-arrow rest friction. During testing, I have personally found this style of rests add about three to four feet-per-second over bristle-style arrow rests. However, as with everything else, you'll sacrifice the security that comes when your arrow is captured in the by the bristles in the arrow rest.

▲ This QAD drop-away style arrow rest minimizes arrow-to-rest friction.

Kinetic Energy: How Much is Enough?

There is plenty of talk in archery circles about kinetic energy. In the *Textbook of Engineering Physics,* Jain offers this insight:"The kinetic energy of an object is the energy which it possesses due to its motion."

Francis Sears, in his *Introduction to the Theory of Relativity,* further postulates, "the speed, and thus the kinetic energy of a single object is frame-dependent (relative): it can take any non-negative value, by choosing a suitable inertial frame of reference. For example, a bullet passing an observer has kinetic energy in the reference frame of this observer. The same bullet is stationary from the point of view of an observer moving with the same velocity as the bullet, and so has zero kinetic energy."

While this seems interesting enough, it isn't much more than engineering-speak for geeks. So what is this "kinetic energy"? For the bowhunter, kinetic energy is important as it is directly correlated to the amount of oomph your arrow is carrying. Think of kinetic energy the same way you think of horsepower in an automobile.

Imagine you have a choice of two cars: on one hand, you've got the four-cylinder economy car with a little itty-bitty motor—a motor with just enough power to merge onto the freeway given a long enough head start. It has squirrels winding a rubber band for power. On the other hand, you have the fire-breathing performance car that muscles along the highway, capable of blinding acceleration and top speeds that'll peel the paint off the hood. It drinks testosterone for fuel. Now, imagine that economy car, the one that can't get out of its own way, as your arrow. If it were to shoot something, it would lack the energy to do much damage; it just doesn't have the horsepower—much like a compound bow that shoots arrows slowly.

Now imagine that shiny, candy apple red sports car is your arrow. Send it off downrange, and it will blast through anything in its way. It's all about the horsepower. A high-powered arrow (one that has ample kinetic energy) like our sports car, is capable of incredible penetration because it is oozing horsepower. Keep in mind that it is our compound bow that loads the "horsepower" into our arrow.

Measuring Kinetic Energy

So we have our two cars, the high-powered machine and the grocery getter. Like horsepower, kinetic energy can be readily measured or assigned a quantitative measure. In archery, the kinetic energy carried by the arrow is expressed as *foot pounds*. The foot pound is the amount of force and is symbolized as ft/lb$_f$ or ft/lbf, or in the case of archery, "ft-lbs." In the most basic of terms, foot pounds is a unit of measurement used to show how much work or energy exists. For those in the know, ft-lbs. are the equivalent of the joule in the International System of Units (SI).

In the shooting sports, firearms and handguns use the foot pound as the unit of measure for muzzle energy in ballistics. The archery industry has adopted the foot pound as a descriptor of arrow energy or kinetic energy.

Calculating Kinetic Energy

As you can see, kinetic energy is simply a measure of how much energy an arrow contains during the shot. When calculating kinetic energy, only two numbers are needed: the first is the arrow mass in grain weight and the second is the arrow's speed measured in feet-per-second (fps).

From our exhaustive discussion of the compound bow, we know these two commodities are easily measured. Arrow weight is easily measured with a digital grain scale and arrow velocity is measured using a chronograph. Once you have these two numbers, simply enter them into the following formula:

$$\text{Kinetic Energy} = (\text{mass} \times \text{velocity}^2) \text{ divided by } 450{,}240$$

For those of you who aren't math whizzes, you can go online, type in the search box "calculate arrow KE," and you'll get numerous sites that merely require you enter these two numbers and the program will spit out the KE number for you. Here is the math worked through using a 450-grain arrow (mass= *m*) and a velocity of 300 fps (*v*).

KE = (mv^2) / 450,240
KE = [(450 arrow mass)(arrow velocity 300^2)] / 450,240
KE = [450 x 90,000] / 450,240
KE = 40,500,000 / 450,240 = 89.96 ft-lbs.

How Much Kinetic Energy?

So we have discovered how to measure kinetic energy for our rig. But how much of this stuff do we need to go out and kill (or "harvest," using the politically

correct term) something? As you can imagine, different animals have varying anatomies. The physical size of different animals presents us with decisions to make concerning just how much "bow" (i.e., to produce enough KE) we need.

Thankfully, the folks at Easton Technical products have provided hunters with this general guide to the *minimum* amount of kinetic energy required for various sized game. Here's what they recommend:

Small Game (rabbits, squirrels, etc.) 25 ft-lbs. KE
Medium Sized Game (whitetail deer, antelope, coyotes, etc.) >40 ft-lbs. KE
Large Game (elk, black bear, wild boar, etc.) 42–65 ft-lbs. KE
Extra Large, Thickly Skinned Animals (grizzly bear, African animals, etc.) >65 ft-lbs.

To put these numbers into perspective, here is what a compound bow would have to shoot to attain these kinetic energy numbers, assuming you are shooting an arrow weighing a total of 350-grains.

25 ft-lbs. KE = ~175 fps
>40 ft-lbs. KE = ~227 fps
42 – 65 ft-lbs. KE = ~227 fps – 290 fps
>65 ft-lbs. KE = ~290 fps

The Role of Compound Efficiencies

As we have seen, compounds are physically loaded with energy simply by pulling the string back. This rotates the cams, moving the cables and flexing the limbs. Once at full draw, the bow is now loaded with energy and is ready to shoot.

But as most know, the amount of energy put in the machine doesn't equal the amount of energy you get out of the machine. Some of that energy is lost to friction in a process called hysteresis. Friction is introduced into the system from the limbs, which have internal friction. This means that as the fibers of the limbs are flexed, they create resistance to the bending. This is cause for friction. Bearings, cam string tracks, axles, strings, cables, and arrow rests all contribute friction that slows the compound machine, limiting its efficiency.

Energy is also lost to vibration and the resulting generation of noise. *Compressive forces* acting on the arrow also rob some of the stored kinetic energy in the system. This compression of the arrow shaft and subsequent flexing of the shaft acts as a shock absorber, absorbing precious energy during the shot. Calculating a bow's mechanical efficiency is done as follows:

Kinetic energy (KE) / stored energy (draw weight) x 100 = bow efficiency expressed as a percentage (%)

Here is the math worked through for a bow shooting 59 ft-lbs. of kinetic energy at a draw weight of 70 pounds.

50 (KE) / 70 (draw weight) = 0.843 x 100 = 84.29% mechanical efficiency

Interestingly, the amount of noise and vibration generated by a bow is a general indication of the bow's mechanical efficiency. Both of these are generated by the excess energy left in the bow following the shot. This noise and vibration is how the compound dissipates the excess energy in the system that was not transferred directly to the arrow upon release.

Higher efficiency bows have a distinct advantage as they have less wear and tear because they are not exposed to excessive shock and vibration following the shot. Additionally, an efficient compound is a joy to shoot as it has very little *hand shock* and is quiet. A stealth shooting bow is an advantage for hunters who worry of spooking their quarry with an excessively loud bow.

The Mass Weight Factor in Compounds

Modern compound manufacturers are in a constant quest to design a bow that is whisper quiet, blazing fast, helium light, has no vibration, draws nicely, has an attractive retail price, requires no tuning, and looks good. As we have seen, designing all these into a compound bow is nearly impossible as there are trade-offs for each of these.

If a bow is feather-light, it probably will have considerable hand shock because light bows are easily set into vibratory motion when shot. If a bow is blazing fast, then you must input enough energy for that bow to shoot blistering arrows. If you struggle to pull that bow to input enough energy to shoot fast, then the bow doesn't draw well, and so on. You get the point.

So when shopping for a bow, you must understand there is no "perfect" bow no matter what the manufacturers tell us. If their ads were true, every bow ever made would be church mouse quiet, top-fuel dragster fast, lighter than hot air, ridiculously easy to draw, and able to leap tall buildings in a single bound—and chew gum at the same time.

When it comes to *mass weight*—that is, the physical weight of a compound—there are two distinct schools of thought. It is important to note that each individual shooter has their own list of requirements for their equipment. They also have varying shooting styles that dictate the best style of bow for them.

In one corner, there are folks who feel lighter is better. In some cases, this is true. A light bow excels when used for a Western spot-and-stalk style of hunting. (That is, when the bowhunter is using their equipment to sneak up on game.) Imagine crawling through hip-high plains grass dragging an 8-pound bow. It should wear you out after a few minutes. In this case, a light mass weight bow is perfect.

For those who do most of their hunting from treestands, the Northeastern archers for instance, super light bows are not necessary. In fact, a slightly heavier bow may be the right prescription as treestand hunters typically hang their bow on a bow hook so they aren't holding it for extended periods of time. A heavier bow is easier to hold steady on an animal since it takes more force to move it. This is great when aiming at an animal when you have the shakes. In this case, a heavier bow makes the shot steadier. Most target shooters opt for a heavier bow for this reason. The heavier bow holds steady and thus is more accurate in this situation. But like all the other attributes of a compound, like draw weight and length, it is best to shoot plenty of bows to determine what fits *your* shooting style.

The Role of Brace Height in the Bow Equation

The term *brace height* is thrown around quite often in archery circles. Brace height is simply the distance, measured in inches, from the bow string at rest to the furthest point of the grip (sometimes referred to as the "pivot point" of the grip). Brace height is a measurement that gives you an idea of how the bow was designed. That is, was it designed as a speed-burner or was its design intended to make it a forgiving sweet shooter?

Let's look at that word "forgiveness" for a moment. When people say a bow is forgiving, what exactly does that mean? Brace heights vary by several inches. Typically compounds have brace heights from 5½ to around 9 inches (give or take a few eighths). Imagine for a moment what a short brace height bow looks like.

You will see that the string is closer to the handle than a longer brace height bow.

The brace height measure determines how long the bow's power stroke will be. For bows with short brace heights, those less than seven inches, the power stroke is longer because the arrow must travel a longer distance to return the string to the neutral position. This extra distance keeps the arrow on the string longer, increasing its speed.

Conversely, on a bow with a long brace height, those with measures of more than seven inches, the arrow gets to the neutral string position faster. By doing so, the power stroke of the bow has been shortened considerably. With a more abbreviated power stroke, the bow cannot generate as much speed.

So we have two very different designs, but how does brace height affect accuracy or ease of shooting? Increasing the distance the string has to travel on the short brace height bow, it also increases the distance the bow can accelerate the arrow. However, by shortening the bow's brace height, the length of the lever arm between the string at rest and the handle is decreased. By decreasing this lever, it multiplies or compounds any shooter errors.

If the shooter torques the bow to the left during the shot, the effect of that error is multiplied downrange. Additionally, a shorter brace height and power stroke increases the time the arrow is on the string. By increasing the time of the shot, the shooter has more time to make slight errors in shooting technique. This then leads to errant arrow delivery.

Bows with a long brace height in contrast with short power strokes have longer lever arms between the strings at rest and the handles. By increasing this lever length, shooter errors are minimized. Additionally, with a decreased power stroke, the effect of shooter errors is diminished as the arrow is on the string a shorter amount of time.

The Great Limb Migration of the 90s

Anyone who has paid close attention to the archery industry, and compound bow design in particular, over the past two decades has noticed a drastic change in limb design. While the change has been dramatic, it has taken years for it to occur. What I am referring to is what I call the "migration" of compound bow limbs from a relative vertical orientation to the horizontal plane and beyond.

Since their introduction in the 1960s, compound bows have sported limbs that have been vertically arranged. Early compounds, and even those of a few years ago, shot accurately. However, after launching the arrow, these compounds had a tendency to vibrate excessively. Oddly enough, until just the last few years, no one cared, or noticed for that matter, that their bow vibrated.

Enter the marketing gurus. At some point, a marketing genius decided it was time to make unwanted vibration an issue with consumers. Most in the industry credit this to an accessory manufacturer that thought it had a cure for unwanted vibration. So the "vibration phenomenon" was born. Literally overnight, "unwanted vibration" became the archery industry's favorite buzz words.

Products sprung up everywhere, from bulbous hunks of glue-on rubber vibration "dampers," to little oddities inserted into the bow riser that magically eliminated vibration. Taking it one step further, these accessory manufacturers and bow companies expounded on the prowess of their "vibration-free" products and these products' ability to shoot more accurately, smoothly, quickly, quietly, and so on. And the consumers ate it up—hook, line, and sinker.

Today bows are advertised as being "noise-free," "shock-free," "ultra-quiet," "vibration-free," etc. While this marketing hype has done wonders for these companies' bottom lines, consumers are left with bows that are, although somewhat improved, not as described in these over-the-top ads.

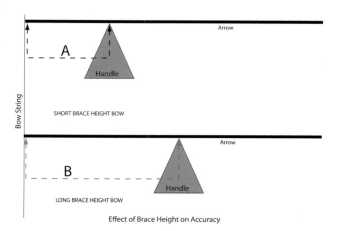

▲ The role of brace height in the accuracy equation.

but there are *always* trade-offs when we modify something on a compound to get a desired result.

You see, vertical limbs, when loaded and then released, yank the bow string forward, causing the bow to jump violently. On the other hand, parallel limbs, when loaded and then released, snap upward, pulling the string from both ends upward and downward. The net result is a bow that remains stationary and does not leap forward. *Viola!* Hand shock gone.

However, when moving to parallel limbs, manufacturers discovered the limbs had to be much shorter than their longer vertical limbs. Axle-to-axle measurements on older vertical bows were typically longer and the riser was short and supported long limbs. Hence, the length of bows was long. Once parallel limbs were introduced, the long limbs presented a problem. The response was to shorten the limbs. Compound designers quickly learned short limbs led to short axle-to-axle bows, which was a distinct problem, as consumers had always been told short bows were difficult to shoot and long bows more accurate.

So manufacturers lengthened the risers. Great! However, when they lengthened the riser, it added more mass weight to the bow. You can see the vicious cycle beginning. The first few parallel limb bows were very short axle-to-axle, and one manufacturer advertised these diminutive bows were now the rage. Well, it caught on, and now 95 percent of all compounds are short axle-to-axle (32–37"). So it appears that longer axle-to-axle bows are a thing of the past and long compounds are nearly impossible to build with parallel limbs unless they weigh six or seven pounds.

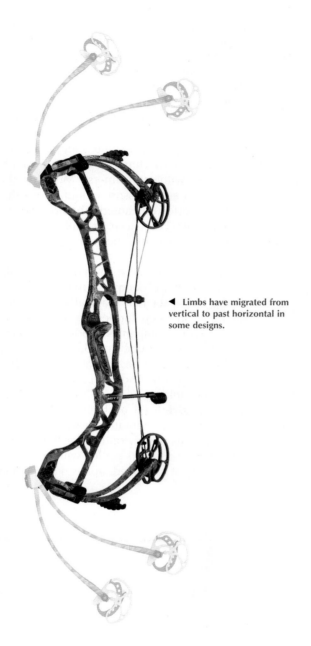

◀ Limbs have migrated from vertical to past horizontal in some designs.

Enter the Limb

In an effort to reduce noise and vibration, bow designers discovered arranging limbs in a "parallel" configuration significantly reduced hand shock and vibration. In turn, noise was minimized. This is great,

Emergency Travel Repair Kit

Many hunts of a lifetime have been ruined by small equipment malfunctions. Snap a peep sight tube, fray a nock loop, or break a sight pin and your trip is over.

Carrying an emergency repair kit can save the day (and trip). Your kit should include the basics: replacement peep sight tubing (if you use one), multi-tool, Allen wrench assortment, nocks, spare sight pins, knock loop material, lubricant, spare release, and bowstring wax.

Brace Me

Mechanically speaking, nothing affects a bow's efficiency (top speed) and accuracy more than brace height. While it sounds like some complicated, mystical engineering term, brace height is simply the measured distance (in inches) between the string and the bows grip.

Brace height directly affects two things: 1) how fast a bow pushes an arrow through the chronograph and 2) how "forgiving," or shootable, a bow is.

While forgiveness is an odd, abstract term, it is nothing more than a measure of how much of a fulcrum effect is introduced to your shot. Let's have a look at both.

Every bow has a power stroke. The power stroke is the distance that the arrow remains on the string. Long power strokes (on short brace height bows) produce greater speeds. Shorter power strokes (on long brace height bows) produce slower arrow speeds.

Forgiveness on a long brace height bow is a factor of its short power stroke. The arrow remains on the string for an abbreviated amount of time, so fewer shooter errors are introduced.

Short brace height bows have longer power strokes and faster speeds. A safe rule of thumb is this: brace heights of less than seven inches tend to be less forgiving than those that exceed seven inches.

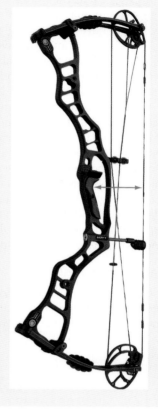

Measuring brace height. ▶

V. Arrow Rests and Sights

*J*ust as the compound has undergone monumental advancements in technologies, so have archery sights and arrow rests. Both are from primitive roots originally based around traditional bows. However, the real evolution of these accessories can be traced to the invention of the compound bow in the 1960s.

Traditional archers were immune to fitting their bows with anything that wasn't considered primitive. That train of thought is still pervasive among traditionalists. It is easily understood as primitive archery is just that: primitive. However, the new wave of modern archers that poured into the sport with the advent of the compound bellowed for anything and everything technological. As such, manufacturers quickly ramped up their design departments in an effort to keep pace with the demand for the newest and most advanced bows and accessories.

Early Arrow Rests

Quantum leaps in designs and function have been seen in the arrow rest market. As compounds' top speeds increased, a need was created for a better arrow rest. Early arrow rests were simple shelves on which arrows rested during the shot sequence. These were very noisy and did little or nothing to take advantage of the compound's newfound speed. Early rests did not capture the arrow or control it during the shot sequence. The simple act of drawing a bow led to the arrow falling off the rest. A better design was needed.

In 1931 C.J. Cameron applied for a US Patent for his shoot-through bow. The idea was simple: an opening sufficiently large enough for the arrow and feathers to pass and a centrally supported arrow support (arrow rest). Mr. Cameron's patent, US Patent 1,847,593, also discussed the use of an adjustable mounted sight. Both were accessories for a longbow.

John O. Lowell of Kirkwood, Missouri, applied for a patent on June 19, 1937 for his crude arrow rest, which was centered in the bow's riser. His idea was a supporting structure (arrow rest) with low-friction to guide the arrow through the riser and off to the target. He was awarded US Patent 2,186,386 on January 9, 1940.

Early arrow rests were simple flipper-style rests—small appendages that supported the arrow with no moving parts.

Modern Arrow Rest Design

Arrow rests have evolved since the early days of archery, changing to keep pace with the development and advancements of the compound. As bows have gotten faster, arrow-rest manufacturers have had to evolve their products. This evolution has kept pace with faster arrows and the need to allow the launch of an arrow without contacting the arrow rest and allowing the arrow to track true.

A shooter has any number of arrow rests to choose from. They range from the simple to the very complex. Their prices also range from relatively inexpensive to very pricey.

Arrow Rests Styles

Arrow rests have varying degrees of complexity, depending on their intended use and application. As anyone who has been in the archery game long enough knows, if an archer can dream it, he or she will build it and market it as the newest and the greatest. There are five categories of arrow rests: 1) shoot-through rests, 2) drop-away rests, 3) containment rests, 4) plunger rests, and 5) target rests.

Shoot-Through Rests

Shoot-through rests are very basic in design. In most cases, they are simply two prongs, bent to accept the

▶ C.J. Cameron's patent, arguably the first patented arrow rest. Circa 1932.

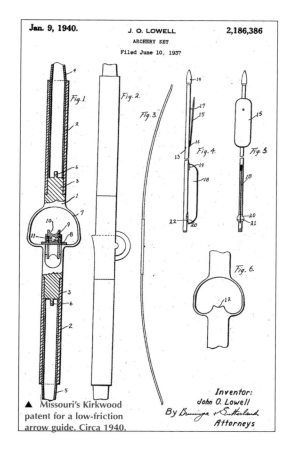

Jan. 9, 1940.   J. O. LOWELL   2,186,386
ARCHERY SET
Filed June 10, 1937

Inventor:
John O. Lowell
By Bruninga & Sutherland
Attorneys

▲ Missouri's Kirkwood patent for a low-friction arrow guide. Circa 1940.

United States Patent [19]   [11]   4,344,409
Barner   [45]   Aug. 17, 1982

[54]   ARROW REST APPARATUS
[76]   Inventor: Roland K. Barner, 119 Sunset Blvd., Bozeman, Mont. 59715
[21]   Appl. No.: 172,386
[22]   Filed: Jul. 25, 1980
[51]   Int. Cl.³ F41B 5/00
[52]   U.S. Cl. .... 124/24 R; 124/41 A
[58]   Field of Search .... 124/41 A, 124/24 R, 88, 124/22

[56]   References Cited
U.S. PATENT DOCUMENTS
2,975,780   3/1961   Fisher .... 124/24 R
3,504,659   4/1970   Babington .... 124/41 A X

Primary Examiner—Richard C. Pinkham
Assistant Examiner—William R. Browne
Attorney, Agent, or Firm—Arthur L. Urban

[57]   ABSTRACT
An arrow rest apparatus capable of being mounted on an archery bow adjacent the point of contact of an arrow with the bow. The arrow rest apparatus includes support structure, a shaft member rotatably carried by the support structure, the shaft member being oriented so that the axis thereof is substantially perpendicular to the axis of the arrow, first biasing mechanism associated with the shaft member urging rotation of the shaft member in one direction, arrow supporting structure affixed to the end of the shaft member closest to the arrow, and a latch mechanism associated with the shaft member. The latch mechanism includes a portion affixed to the shaft member, an arm portion pivotally mounted on the support structure, the arm portion being engageable with the shaft affixed latch portion. The arm portion includes a weighted section remote from the shaft affixed latch portion, second biasing mechanism urging the arm portion away from the shaft affixed latch portion, and structure for mounting the apparatus on an archery bow.

14 Claims, 8 Drawing Figures

▲ This is the Roland Barner patent for the first drop-away arrow rest. Mr. Barner applied for a US Patent in July of 1980 and receiving it on August 17, 1982 for his "Arrow Rest Apparatus" (US Patent 4,344,409).

arrow and keep it above the bow's riser during the shooting sequence. Typically spring-loaded, these rests are capable of moving under the arrow, either up or down, to accommodate an arrow's downward pressure on launch. Once the arrow has passed through the rest, the spring returns the rest to its original support position. All of this occurs, of course, in the blink of an eye. Interestingly, these rests are called "shoot-through" because the cock feather or vane is placed down when placed on the string. During the shot, the cock vane slips through the gap in-between the prongs without any contact or interference. Hence the "shoot-through" name.

Shoot-through rests are reasonably priced and simple in construction and operation. Shoot-through rests are relatively easy to tune, and great arrow flight is easily achieved. However, this type of rest is not suited for bowhunting as arrows fall off the rest if the bow is tilted, canted, or jiggled. (They are very sensitive to being shaken when the arrow is drawn by nervous archers drawing a bow on an animal.)

Another drawback of shoot-through rests is that archers are limited by the type of vane configuration they can actually shoot through these rests. Straight vanes are about the only configuration that will clear the tightly spaced prong gap.

Drop-Away Rests

Drop-away arrow rests have seen their popularity grow exponentially in recent years. The first commercially manufactured and marketed drop-away arrow rest, the Barner, was the brain child of Roland Barner.

The Barner worked theoretically by a slide that was triggered and allowed the spring-wire arrow support

▲ Shoot-through designs, like this NAP QuickTune 800, provide a good arrow foundation and low-friction. However, they are tough to hunt with as the arrow tends to fall off the rest when it is not captured.

to drop out of the way. Years later, high-speed photography revealed that Mr. Barner's arrow rest dropped out of the way long after the arrow had already left the bow.

Prior to Mr. Barner's invention, J. C. Fisher invented an "Archer's Bow" in 1958, which included an arrow rest capable of falling out of the arrow's path after the arrow had been released. His bow was, of course, a longbow, not a compound. In 1968, Charles E. Babington of Ohio applied for a patent for his "Pivoted Bowstring Responsive Arrow Support Device." His new arrow rest would raise and lower as the bow was drawn and released via a cord that was lashed to the bowstring. His patent was granted in April of 1970 (US Patent 3,504,659). The Babington design was arguably the first true drop-away style arrow design, as it was actuated via the bowstring.

Since these early designs, many drop-away arrow rests have been developed, manufactured, and sold. To date, it is still argued that none of them have solved *all* of the ills associated with launching the perfect arrow. However, modern drop-aways have come a long way from the original Barner arrow rest.

The fundamental function of a drop-away arrow rest is just as the name implies: during the release of the arrow, the arrow rest physically drops away right out of the arrow's flight path. Many designs are currently available. There are those that drop forward, split apart, scissor, shutter, snap, flip, and slide away. And I am sure that I am forgetting a couple other mechanical means that allow them to physically drop away.

By moving out of the arrow's path, nothing on the rest can negatively affect the arrow's flight. The theory is, if the arrow leaves the string straight, it will fly straight. If it is skewed as it leaves the bow, then it will be skewed in flight as well.

The advantages of drop-away style arrow rests are significant. The most obvious being there is little or no contact between the arrow and the arrow rest. When this occurs, the arrow flies true and it also picks up some speed because of the lack of friction between the arrow and rest. Another advantage is that since they are removed from the arrow's path, any style of arrow fletching configuration will pass through without interference. This is a huge advantage to those who shoot large, helically arranged vanes or feathers.

However, they do have some disadvantages. Most of these rests are expensive, costing as much as $200. With the cost comes the need to have a competent archery pro shop install them, as it can be difficult to install properly. While the average archer can install them, it is better to have an archery technician install them because they must be timed to the bow. The rests are typically synched to the buss cables using a trigger cord. The cord acts as a trigger for the rest, triggering it to move when the buss cables begin to move during the shot.

Another disadvantage that some drop-away rests don't react fast enough when the arrow leaves the bow. This leads to unwanted contact with the arrow. It may also lead to a disruption in the path of the arrow; as they drop away, they can actually bounce back up. Once again, just like an arrow rest that doesn't drop fast enough, the bouncing back motion and arrow contact causes errant arrow flight as the arrow is knocked off its path.

Containment Arrow Rests

The introduction of the containment arrow rest has been a blessing to the bowhunting community. Containment rests are exactly that: they contain the arrow throughout the entire shot sequence. There are plenty of different designs. Some of the first containment arrow rests utilized metal fingers to keep the arrow in place. However, these fingers did not flex sufficiently during the shot and resulted in errant arrow flight. The introduction of springs into the metal arms helped; however, the metal-to-arrow contact made horrific noise when shot.

These containment rests also introduced a large amount of friction to the arrow, which meant arrow speeds dropped. Teflon launchers (fingers) were created in an effort to quiet the arrow rest and speed arrows up with less arrow friction. Mediocre results were achieved. Then, in the mid-1990s, Isaac Branthwaite

◀ This is an octane drop-away style arrow rest. The external "cage" theoretically keeps the arrow contained during the hunt.

United States Patent [19]

Branthwaite et al.

[11] Patent Number: 5,896,849

[45] Date of Patent: Apr. 27, 1999

[54] **ARROW REST**

[76] Inventors: **Wilfred Isaac Branthwaite**, 2617 Sweetbriar Rd., Durham, N.C. 27704; **Stephen Charles Graf**, 940 Sanford Rd., Pittsboro, N.C. 27312

[21] Appl. No.: **09/050,171**

[22] Filed: **Mar. 30, 1998**

[51] Int. Cl.⁶ **F41B 5/22**

[52] U.S. Cl. **124/44.5**

[58] Field of Search 124/24.1, 44.5

[56] **References Cited**

U.S. PATENT DOCUMENTS

4,282,850	8/1981	Warnicke	124/24.1
4,351,311	9/1982	Phares	124/44.5
4,372,282	2/1983	Sanders	124/24.1
4,858,589	8/1989	Chang	124/24.1
4,917,072	4/1990	Chang	124/44.5
5,042,450	8/1991	Jacobson	124/44.5
5,253,633	10/1993	Sisko	124/44.5
5,456,242	10/1995	Ruhoff	124/44.5
5,460,153	10/1995	Huntt	124/44.5

Primary Examiner—John A. Ricci

Attorney, Agent, or Firm—Mills Law Firm PLLC; Clifford F. Rey

[57] **ABSTRACT**

An improved arrow rest for use in combination with an archery bow is disclosed. The present arrow rest provides complete radial support to an arrow disposed in a ready-to-draw position even if the bow is tilted or rotated radially relative to an axis of the arrow. Such radial support is provided by an inverted coil brush comprising a disc-shaped structure having a plurality of radially disposed, inwardly projecting bristles of a predetermined length attached therein forming a central opening in the arrow rest wherein the arrow shaft is radially supported. The bristles are arranged within the coil brush so as to impart no significant hindrance to the passage of an arrow therethrough. Thus, no angular orientation of the arrow vanes to the arrow nock is required which permits the use of the arrow rest with any configuration of arrow fletching or number of vanes. In addition, the present arrow rest can be used with any diameter of arrow shaft while maintaining both vertical and horizontal position without adjusting the rest position. Further, the present arrow rest improves the stability of an arrow in flight by dampening arrow vibration in all directions as it is released from the bowstring.

9 Claims, 6 Drawing Sheets

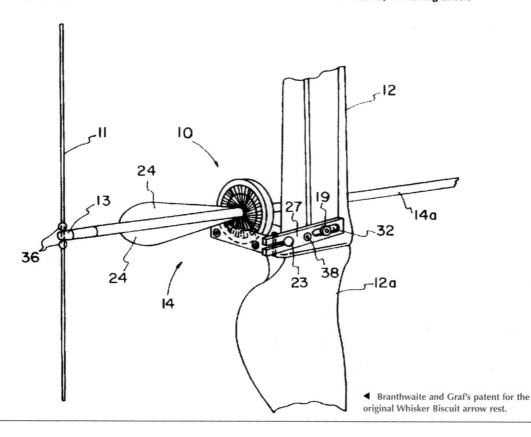

◀ Branthwaite and Graf's patent for the original Whisker Biscuit arrow rest.

and Stephen Graf, two engineers in North Carolina, tried using bristles as a support structure for the arrow.

Their idea was to contain the arrow with 360 degrees of nylon brushes, or bristles. They theorized that the arrow vanes would slip through the brushes and the arrow would fly true. The two applied for a US Patent in 1998 and were subsequently granted US Patent 5,896,849 for their "Arrow Rest." Their invention would be introduced at the annual archery trade show as the Whisker Biscuit.

The Whisker Biscuit's introduction at the annual archery trade show received little fanfare. The archery community, one paranoid of any arrow-to-arrow-rest contact, had a hard time envisioning how this arrow rest, which contacted the arrow shaft around the entire circumference, would be accepted by the bowhunting community.

Over the next couple years, the Whisker Biscuit slowly gained followers and converts as the rest proved to be fantastic for holding the arrow in place during the hunt and producing very accurate shots with little arrow speed loss (around 1 to 3 fps). Today, their arrow rest is installed on close to 60 percent of all hunting bows.

Oddly configured containment rests have followed the Whisker Biscuit. Designs built to improve the Branthwaite-Graf biscuit design have included plastic funnel-shaped "biscuits," "half-biscuits," and any other number of poorly designed knock-offs.

However, one notable improvement over the Branthwaite-Graf was made in 2004. Kevin Yoder of North Carolina applied for a US Patent for his arrow rest, which mimicked the Whisker Biscuit but supported the arrow using three distinct bristle cartridges oriented equal distance around the arrow shaft.

This eliminated the 360-degree contact of the Whisker Biscuit, allowed the arrow to slip through the arrow rest with no vane contact, and created minimum arrow shaft contact. This allowed the rest to give great top speeds with no vane damage. The new design virtually eliminates the two distinct disadvantages of the Whisker Biscuit product. In February 2006, Yoder was awarded US Patent 6,994,080.

Plunger Arrow Rests

Plunger style arrow rests are manufactured specifically for finger shooters. These are folks who prefer to shoot their bow using their fingers to draw and release the string instead of a mechanical release aid.

When shooting a bow using one's fingers, pressures are put on the string that differ from those applied by a mechanical release aid. These pressures are from the side, pushing the arrow off the rest in a sideways manner. Plunger rests account for these pressures and allow the shooter to adjust the rest for perfect arrow flight when shooting fingers.

Plunger-style rests have been around for many, many years; they date back to the golden age of stick bows, or traditional bows. Original plunger-style rests have their foundations in the watch-making trade. R.H. Konikoff applied for a patent in 1944, for a "Spring Bar." was described as:

> **Consisting of two trunnion members, one of which is a solid rod and the other of which is a sleeve provided with a solid end part formed with a stud for reception in the aperture in a watch-case lug, the rod being within the sleeve for the greater part of its length to regulate the overall length of the spring bar . . .**

Mr. Konikoff's patent application described what would later become the plunger arrow rest. His spring bar was a hollow body with a spring inside and a floating bar (much like a modern watchband pin)—the same components shared by the plunger-style arrow rest. Mr. Konikoff's design was mentioned in subsequent patent applications for plunger rests (US Patent 2,392,092).

An early plunger rest was designed by G.B. Guyton in 1962. Mr. Guyton's plunger rest was an adaptation of Konikoff's watch spring bar. However, it featured a one-sided plunger with threads on the outside that made it mountable into the bow's riser. Guyton was

▼ The original Whisker Biscuit arrow rest has undergone several design changes. Here is a modern Whisker Biscuit. Its simplicity and functionality make it one of the premier arrow rests for serious bowhunters.

(12) **United States Patent**
Yoder

(10) **Patent No.:** **US 6,994,080 B1**
(45) **Date of Patent:** Feb. 7, 2006

(54) **ARROW REST**

(76) Inventor: **Kevin L. Yoder**, 309 Michelle La., Mt. Holly, NC (US) 28120

(*) Notice: Subject to any disclaimer, the term of this patent is extended or adjusted under 35 U.S.C. 154(b) by 3 days.

(21) Appl. No.: **10/914,514**

(22) Filed: **Aug. 9, 2004**

(51) Int. Cl.
F41B 5/22 (2006.01)

(52) U.S. Cl. **124/44.5**

(58) Field of Classification Search 124/24.1, 124/44.5
See application file for complete search history.

(56) **References Cited**

U.S. PATENT DOCUMENTS

4,351,311	A	*	9/1982	Phares 124/44.5
4,759,337	A	*	7/1988	Suski 124/24.1
4,858,589	A		8/1989	Chang
5,025,773	A		6/1991	Hintze et al.
5,031,601	A		7/1991	Gunter
5,042,450	A		8/1991	Jacobson
5,161,515	A		11/1992	Hammonds
5,245,980	A		9/1993	Colvin
5,253,633	A		10/1993	Sisko
5,261,383	A		11/1993	Halamay
5,419,303	A		5/1995	Stewart
5,447,284	A		9/1995	Heinz
5,456,242	A		10/1995	Ruholl
5,460,152	A		10/1995	Specht
5,460,153	A		10/1995	Huntt
5,462,041	A		10/1995	Solecki
5,490,491	A		2/1996	Troncoso
5,526,800	A	*	6/1996	Christian 124/44.5
5,896,849	A		4/1999	Branthwaite et al.
RE38,096	E		4/2003	Branthwaite et al.
6,557,541	B2		5/2003	Pinto, Jr.
6,561,175	B1		5/2003	Tidmore
6,725,851	B1		4/2004	Graf

* cited by examiner

Primary Examiner—John A. Ricci
(74) *Attorney, Agent, or Firm*—Adams Evans P.A.

(57) **ABSTRACT**

An arrow rest for guiding and supporting an arrow on an archery bow. The arrow rest includes a base, a plurality of spaced apart arrow supports, and a mounting bracket. Each of the arrow supports include a support shoe and a plurality of bristles. The support shoe is attached to the base. The bristles extend inwardly from the support shoe for supporting an arrow. The mounting bracket attaches the base to the archery bow.

17 Claims, 5 Drawing Sheets

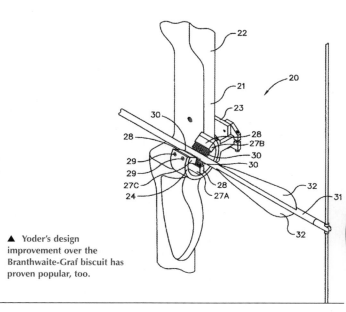

▲ Yoder's design improvement over the Branthwaite-Graf biscuit has proven popular, too.

▼ An octanel arrow rest that incorporates the Yoder intellectual property.

▲ A modern plunger-style arrow rest.

awarded a patent for his design in 1966 (US Patent 3,232,286).

Target Arrow Rests

While bowhunting is the major subject of this book, we would be remiss if we did not mention target arrow rests. Many bowhunters enjoy competing in 3-D tournaments and other forms of competitive archery. Specialty arrow rests have been designed to enable target archers to shoot with more accuracy.

The most popular of target arrow rests is the "lizard tongue" style rest. While that may sound odd, it makes sense when looking at the rest designs. Lizard tongues are rudimentary rests, sometimes referred to as "feeler gauge" rests, because their ultrathin arrow blade resembles a feeler gauge.

▶ A Trophy Taker lizard-tongue/ target arrow rest.

Archery Sights

The archery sight has played a major role in perfecting the accuracy of the compound bow. Traditional bows—longbows and recurves—are shot in an instinctive manner. That is, they are shot without the aid of a sight. Traditional archers rely on their natural skills and hand-to-eye coordination to deliver arrows to their target.

With the invention of the compound bow came a clamor for all that was new and technologically advanced. If it would help a compound archer hit their target more consistently, they wanted it. So archery sights quickly became available as manufacturers attempted to design and build these sighting systems to help compound shooters stay on target.

Archery sights have a long tradition. Many designs have their roots in the nineteenth century. The original pendulum-style archery sight, developed by Charles R. Keller (US Patent 4,120,096), was designed along the same lines as James E. Abbott's "Improvement in Combined Level, Square, Compass, and Plumb-Staff" in 1865 (US Patent 51,675), Albert Dieffenbach's "Rear Sight for Small Arms" in 1895 (US Patent 533,003), and J. A. Kennedy's "Gun Sight" (US Patent 937,244) circa 1909.

Keller's "Tree Stand Pendulum Sight" was the first commercially popular archery sight designed specifically for calculating the shot angles presented with elevated bow shots to the ground below. Its design was the result of morphing years of prior designs.

The modern archery sight has evolved throughout time. This evolution has witnessed changes in materials, from brass pins to surgical stainless hollow tubes that encase fiber-optic cables for ease of sight in low-light conditions. Heavy ferrous metal mounts and cages have given way to lightweight thermoset plastics and, as of late, carbon fiber and even carbon nanotube technology. Every year, the complexity and refinement of sights improves, as does their performance, as manufacturers strive to build a better mousetrap.

All sights, with the exception of a few specialty sights (e.g., gun-style archery sights, no peep sights, etc.) that are beyond the realm of this book, operate on a simple principle. They are mounted to universal mounting holes with location and specifications dictated by the AMO Standards. The AMO Standard for mounting sights states:

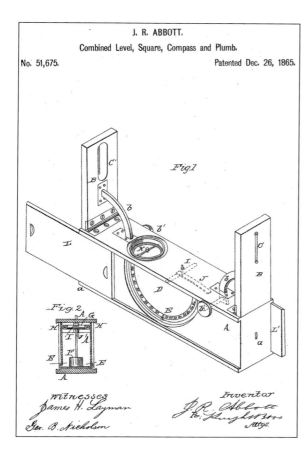

J. R. ABBOTT.
Combined Level, Square, Compass and Plumb.

No. 51,675.

Patented Dec. 26, 1865.

Fig 1

Fig. 2

Witnesses
James H. Layman
Geo. B. Nicholson

Inventor
J. R. Abbott
Per Knight & sons
Attys.

◄▲ Abbott's patent for a combination level, square, compass, and plumb staff. Circa 1865.

Two holes located on the outside of the bow window are to be 10–24 threaded holes spaced 0.312 + - 0.010 center to center. Minimum thread depth shall be 0.250. Mounting holes in sights or other side mounting accessories should conform to these dimensions. A line through the axis of the holes shall be parallel to the bowstring. EXPLANATION: 10–24 threaded holes are used to provide a secure fastening for bow quivers, fishing reels, etc.

Once mounted to the bow's riser, the sight provides a forward pin for reference when aiming at a target. A *peep*, or a string-mounted circular objective manufactured of aluminum or plastic, is served into the bow string and acts like the rear sight on a rifle barrel. It allows the user to draw the bow and look through the peep that is close to their dominant eye. Through the peep, the front sight pin is centered. The system worked just like shooting a rifle, but using a compound bow instead. Adjustments in elevation (up and down) and wind (left and right) are made by moving the individual sight pins; moving the entire assembly of pins left or right, up and down, or both; or moving the entire sight in what is referred to as a *gang adjustment*.

There currently exists four major types of archery sights: 1) fixed-pin; 2) moveable pins; 3) pendulum; and 4) target. Of course, each has their strengths, just as each has their weaknesses.

Fixed-Pin

Fixed-pin sights are just that: three to five individual pins are contained in some type of housing. Each pin is capable of independent adjustment. Individual pins are designed to be set to a designated distance. For instance, on a three-pin sight, the top pin might be adjusted and set as the twenty-yard pin. This is the pin you shoot when aiming at a target estimated to be at a distance of twenty yards from the shooter.

The next pin down might be adjusted as the forty-yard pin and the third pin adjusted as the sixty-yard pin. Note these distances change as the requirements of each hunter changes. Some folks may sight in their

United States Patent [19]

Keller

[11] **4,120,096**

[45] **Oct. 17, 1978**

[54] **BOW SIGHT**

[76] Inventor: **Charles R. Keller,** 411 Old Evans Rd., Martinez, Ga. 30907

[21] Appl. No.: **805,743**

[22] Filed: **Jun. 13, 1977**

[51] Int. Cl.² **F41G 1/02**
[52] U.S. Cl. **33/265;** 33/260; 33/283; 33/292
[58] Field of Search 33/265, 260, 273, 283, 33/282, 290, 259

[56]   **References Cited**

U.S. PATENT DOCUMENTS

51,675	12/1865	Abbott	....	33/273
533,003	1/1895	Dieffenbach	....	33/260
937,244	10/1909	Kennedy	....	33/260
2,925,656	2/1960	Genovese	....	33/265
3,013,336	12/1961	Pennington	....	33/265
3,212,190	10/1965	Larson	....	33/265

FOREIGN PATENT DOCUMENTS

527,783 12/1956 Belgium 33/283

Primary Examiner—William D. Martin, Jr.
Attorney, Agent, or Firm—Bailey, Dority & Flint

[57]   **ABSTRACT**

A sight for use on a bow for aiding an archer in sighting on a target from both elevated and level shooting positions. The sight includes an elongated sighting element which has a plurality of sighting beads thereon. The elongated sighting element is pivotably mounted on a horizontally extending shaft and is balanced so that the top bead on the elongated sighting element pivots about said horizontal shaft as the bow is tilted for automatically determining the proper elevation of the bow when shooting from an elevated position. The elongated sighting element may be locked in various arcuate positions when shooting on the ground.

4 Claims, 5 Drawing Figures

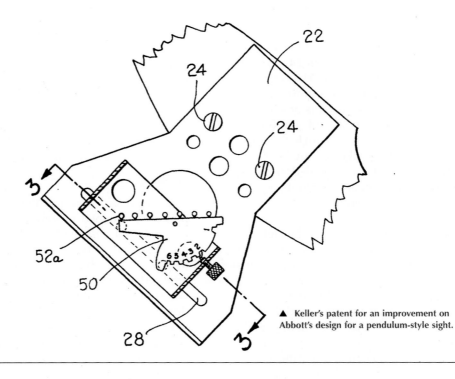

▲ Keller's patent for an improvement on Abbott's design for a pendulum-style sight.

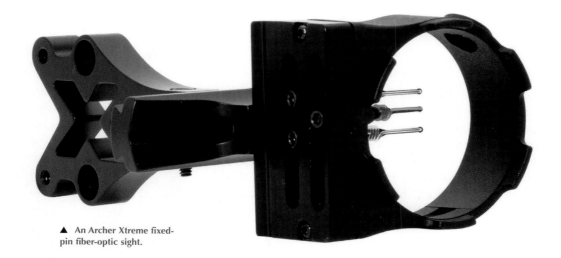

▲ An Archer Xtreme fixed-pin fiber-optic sight.

pins for 15, 30, and 45 yards, or maybe even 10, 20, and 30 yards. It is dependent on your particular hunting situation and your style of shooting. And, of course, the distance to which you feel comfortable shooting.

Fixed-pin sights have some distinct advantages. First, most are simple in design, and there is no learning curve to using them. Additionally, you can get a quality three-to-five pin sight for a reasonable price. On the other hand, you can also spend several hundred dollars for a fixed-pin sight. Typically, the bowhunter will feel that the simpler the sight, the better his experience. Once you introduce levels of complexity into the sight's design, you also introduce more ways for the sight to fail.

In most cases, a good-quality fixed-pin sight for the bowhunter should cost between $40–80. I always recommend buying the sight that has the brightest pins. This means fixed-pin sights are almost all equipped with fiber-optics. These pins have short lengths of fiber-optic cable threaded through or around the pin. As shooting light begins to wane, the fiber-optic cable (more like thread, but technically called "cable") gathers ambient light and focuses it at the end of the cable, appearing as a glowing dot. This dot helps bowhunters get a few extra minutes of shooting light at the day's end or early in the morning. In many cases, this may make a difference in whether they execute a successful shot on an animal in low-light conditions.

One of the disadvantages of fixed-pin sights occurs when an animal or target presents itself at an odd shot distance. For instance, if the hunter has their sight pins set at twenty, thirty, and forty yards and a target is at thirty six yards, which pin should they use to make the shot? Some archery experts have suggested a method of "gap shooting" for these instances.

Gap shooting is done by placing the forty-yard pin below the target and the thirty-yard pin above the target. The bull's eye of the target is then centered in between the two pins (called the gap). While this system may work for some shots, it is not a reliable method of ethically shooting. I recommend determining what your bow's effective range is.

Today, fiber-optic sight pins are the industry standard. Previous designs used tritium painted pins—a low-level radioactive paint that emits a constant glow. These pins proved mostly ineffective because the paint chips easily and the ends of the pins were physically too large, in most cases, covering the intended target when leveled on the target.

Moveable Sight Pin

A *moveable sight* is a variation of the fixed-pin sight. It uses one fixed pin, mounted on a lever arm capable of moving up and down. The user, once they have determined the distance to a target (hopefully via a laser rangefinder), moves the sight pin either up or down to a preset distance marked on the sight. The sight housing is marked with varying distances.

If a target presents itself at thirty seven yards, the user simply slides the sight to the position marked for thirty seven yards. Now the sight is set for that exact distance. In some circles, these moveable sights are called "ranger" sights because of their ability to shoot to all different ranges.

There are plenty of advantages to this type of sight. This most obvious is that, as the shooter, you're always dialed in to the exact shot distance. This eliminates much of the guesswork involved in executing a shot.

Game Changer: The Fiber-Optic Revolution

In December 1993, Paul LoRocco applied for a US Patent titled "Sight Pin and Holder for Archery Bow." In the early days of fixed-pin archery sights, the overwhelming problem was being able to see the sight pins in periods of low-light, typically early morning and late afternoon. During these times, if an animal presented itself to the bowhunter, the hunter was unable to make a shot because he or she was unable to see their pins.

Mr. LoRocco, the founder of Tru-Glo, was granted a patent by the US Patent and Trademark Office on August 22, 1995 (US Patent 5,442,861). Mr. LoRocco's invention utilized small lengths of fiber-optic cable—designed to gather and transmit light—to replace the traditional brass sight pin with the small section of annealed fiber-optic cable. Now when animals presented themselves during low-light situations, the bowhunter was able to place their pins on the target and successfully complete their hunt.

▲ Paul LoRocco, the father of fiber-optics.

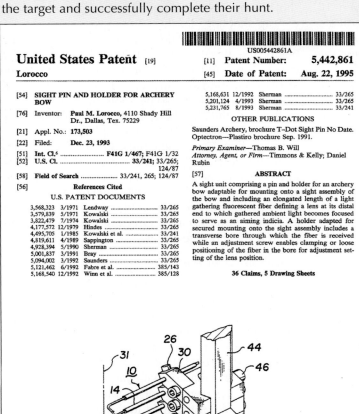

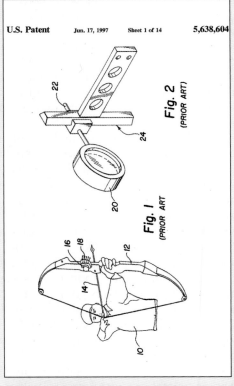

▲ The LoRocco patent for incorporating fiber-optic material into an archery sight revolutionized the sight industry and changed the way we hunt today.

These sights are also very ruggedly built. They can withstand all the abuse even the roughest of users can send its way.

Of course, there are a few disadvantages too. First and foremost, you must be able to judge distances. Now this is much easier if you simply use a laser rangefinder. However, when a target presents itself, some archers don't like having to reach for their rangefinders. While ranging an animal really only takes a split second, some hunters argue that the additional time it takes to adjust the sight and the added movement can spook game. And I don't disagree. However, with a bit of practice it can be accomplished with little fanfare.

Moveable pin sights are also a bit on the heavy side, adding unwanted weight in some cases to already heavy compounds. I personally think a moveable pin sight is an absolute necessity if hunting out west where shot distances can range from point blank to long-distance affairs. These ranging sights offer uncompromising accuracy for those who learn or grow accustomed to their setup and use.

Pendulum Sight

Anyone who has spent much time in an elevated tree stand knows elevated shots can be very tricky. Acutely angled shots (upward or downward) present special shot considerations for the archer. As mentioned in the opening of this section, Georgia's Charles Keller knew these shots were very difficult and developed and patented his Keller Tree Stand Sight in the 1970s. The idea behind his product, and all other pendulum sights, is rather simple: Mount a pin on a pivoting arm. When the bow is angled or canted, the pendulum arm pivots and adjusts the pins placement for accurate angled shots downward from treestands.

During the 1970s, bows were much slower and arrows were affected much more by the forces of gravity. Today's compounds have greatly improved arrow speeds.

In recent years, as compound bow speeds have increased exponentially, the need for these pendulum sights has decreased. However, folks still do make them, and people still use them. In many southern states, where shot distances are short and people climb high, they're still popular.

Fiber-Optic Pins

Fiber-optic pins have been a god-send for the archery industry. They offer excellent low-light transmission of light, allowing sight pins to "glow" with sufficient intensity to allow low-light shots on target. However,

▲ An A.X. Driver sight moves to accommodate differing target distances with one pin.

▶ This TruGlo pendulum sight adjusts itself from an elevated shooting position to compensate for varying target distances and hunting heights. These sights are great for tree stand hunters who limit their shooting distances to less than thirty yards.

hunters always have the same question about Fiber-optic pins: Which size is best?

Fiber-optic pins come in a variety of sizes. These range from 0.010" to 0.040" in diameter. Naturally, the larger fiber-optic cable, the more light can be transmitted down its length and out the end, which appears as the glow associated with Fiber-optic pins. Each of these pin sizes has distinct advantages.

A 0.040" fiber-optic pin gathers the most light and is, therefore, the brightest. While they are the brightest, they also take up the most physical area. This can be an issue in some circumstances. These pins are large on the ends with a large profile. In most cases, when hunting or shooting at targets at long distances, smaller Fiber-optic pins allow the target to remain in the sight window uncovered.

The 0.029" fiber-optic pin are by and far the most popular sized pins. These offer a compromise between large 0.040" pins and tiny 0.010" pins. This sizes features great light transmission and brightness while remaining sufficiently small enough not to cover the target.

Finally, 0.010" pins have become popular in recent years as they offer excellent sight window clarity that rarely physically covers the target. They do have several drawbacks, however. The diminutive pins are easily bent or snapped off due to their size. If you damage these fragile pins while on an expensive hunt at a distant locale, your entire trip can be ruined. They also don't transmit much light because they are so small in diameter. This can be a distinct disadvantage in low-light situations.

Bubble Levels

The effectiveness of bubble levels have been debated for years. Some archers say they are useless, while others argue the level keeps their shots on track. Personally, I use a bubble level only on rare occasions.

For most archers, having a bubble level lets them quickly check to see if their bow is canted to the left or to the right. A canted bow will result in errant shots. However, most experienced archers can level their bow with their eyes literally closed and without any conscious thought. The place where I have found a level to be of significant help is when hunting uneven terrain, such as in hilly country when spot and stalking.

When attempting a shot from unlevel ground, the bubble can help you get your bow level on uneven terrain. If you cant your bow on uneven terrain shots, your shot will suffer greatly. I also find a bubble is of great help for elevated shots from treestands. If a shot presents itself up very close to your stand, you will be bending from the waist to make the shot. The bubble helps keep your bow level at this odd angle when your mind isn't used to leveling your bow at such strange shot angles.

VI. Arrows

elivering a carbon shaft with a surgically-sharp payload with precision is bowhunting nirvana. A perfectly placed arrow grounds animals quickly and humanely and abbreviates blood trails.

For some reason, arrow flight is shrouded in a cloud of mysticism. For many, achieving the perfect projectile is seemingly beyond their grasp. Well, getting arrows to fly true and group tightly isn't black magic, nor is it reserved for archery's innermost circle.

Here's the inside scoop on arrows and their workings.

History of the Modern Arrow

The archery arrow is one of the most primitive weapons known to man. Its evolution has occurred over thousands of years, with the most dramatic changes in the last fifty years. Early arrows were built of wood, as it was a readily available commodity. Metals had yet to be discovered, so early bow men would whittle down limbs into arrow shafts.

In 1921, James Douglas Easton was hunting with a shotgun in California. He had placed his loaded shotgun against a car. The shotgun was bumped, and it fell, discharging when it hit the ground. The shot hit the young Easton in both legs at point-blank range.

Easton, fifteen years old at the time of the accident, spent the next year in the hospital recovering from his near fatal wounds. During that time, a friend of Easton's brought him the book *Hunting With the Bow & Arrow* written by Dr. Saxton T. Pope. (The Pope & Young Club was named in the author's and Arthur Young's honor.)

During his year of recovery, Easton studied the book for days on end. Once he was released from the hospital, he began handcrafting traditional bows and wooden arrows. Easton's arrows quickly earned a reputation for being some of the finest available.

In 1939, Easton began experimenting with different materials he felt could replace wooden arrow shafts. After much experimentation, Easton decided on alu-

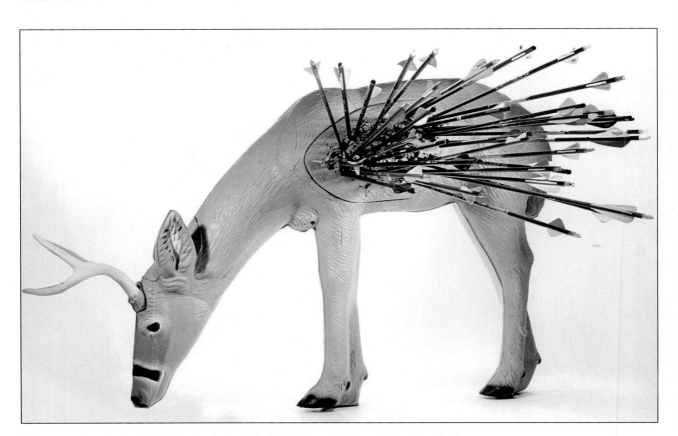

▲ Arrows are the only physical link from the shooter to the intended target. Photo credit Lucas Zarebinski.

▲ Doug Easton shooting an archery tournament with traditional equipment.

▲ Easton's early shop.

▲ Easton's early woodworking equipment, which was utilized to make wooden shaft arrows.

▲ Wood being delivered to Easton's shop for arrow building.

▲ An early Easton cedar arrow.

minum. He gave one of his first sets of metal arrows to Larry Hughes, a champion archer of the day. In 1941, Hughes won the National Championship with Easton's arrows. However, World War II was now in full swing, and aluminum was in short supply for anything other than the war effort. Easton had no choice but to put his arrow business on hold until the end of the war.

By 1946, aluminum was available again, and Easton resumed his testing of the aluminum for his arrow shafts, eventually discovering a process to make them harder. The new hardened shafts were very lightweight, straight, and durable.

By the end of 1946, Easton was selling his newly trademarked aluminum arrow shaft, the 24SRT-X. For

years following, the Easton aluminum shaft was the gold standard in archery arrows.

Enter the compound bow. In 1969, Holless Wilbur Allen invented the compound bow. With the advent of improvements in the compound design, stronger and more powerful bows were designed. These compounds quickly evolved into mechanical machines that could easily outpace wooden longbows and recurves. The new energy available in these bows created a need for a new arrow—one stronger and capable of rugged use without damage. Aluminum arrow shafts were straight, but they were prone to damage when struck by another arrow during practice sessions. Everyone knows a bent arrow is not safe to shoot.

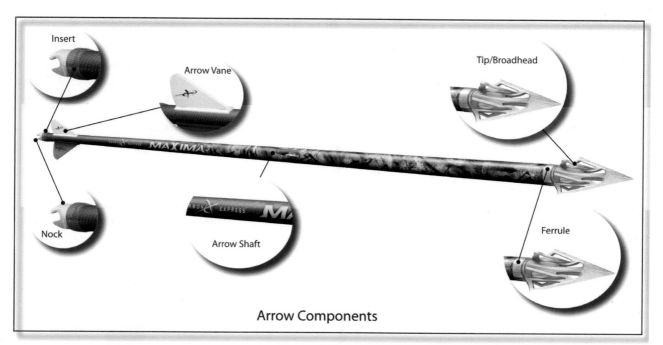

▲ Easton's first aluminum shaft arrow—the 24SRT-X.

So the Easton Company experimented with carbon arrow shafts. In 1983, Easton introduced the first commercially available carbon arrow shaft. Since its introduction, carbon arrows have improved tenfold. Modern arrow shafts incorporate carbon nanotube technology for stronger, stiffer, and lighter shafts.

Anatomy of an Arrow

An arrow shaft is very simple: it has no moving parts and very few components. For the most part, arrows have five components. They are: 1) the arrow shaft, whether aluminum or carbon; 2) the nock; 3) the fletching or vanes; 4) the ferrule or insert; and 5) the point, whether a field, broadhead, or target point (or an adaptation of the target point such as a bludgeon tip, judo point, etc.).

Arrow Shaft

Arrow shafts are made of two materials: 1) aluminum and 2) carbon. Both arrow shaft materials have distinct advantages. Aluminum arrows are available in more sizes than carbon arrow shafts. Aluminum shafts weigh consistently the same, from one shaft to another. This is due to the fact that they are extruded. Extruding is a process by which aluminum is pressed through a die (in this case, a cylindrical die) to form the tubing that ultimately becomes the arrow shaft. Aluminum extrusions are consistent, and the wall thickness very rarely deviates. Aluminum shafts are cheaper to build and hence cost less to buy over carbon arrow shafts.

In contrast, carbon shafts are handmade, one at a time, on stainless steel mandrels. These mandrels are long rods unto which a carbon "tape" is laid. Carbon fibers are peeled off the decal-like substrate and wrapped or laid onto the stainless mandrel. Successive layers are wrapped on top of each other, forming the arrow shaft. These are then coated with proprietary coatings (most like a gel-coat in fiberglass boat making) and baked or cured in an industrial oven. Once cured, the mandrel is removed, and the exterior of the shaft is sanded or sometimes painted. This hand wrapping of the carbon shaft introduces imperfections and leads to variations in arrow spine and shaft mass weight from one shaft to the next.

Arrow Components

▲ Anatomy of a modern arrow.

▲ Easton arrows awaiting quality assurance checks in preparation for sorting and packaging.

▲ Easton arrows ready to be shipped to packaging department.

On the down side, aluminum shafts are prone to bending and damage when struck by other arrows in a target. Carbon shafts have better penetration over aluminum shafts, as their shaft diameters are smaller than their carbon counterparts. Smaller diameter shafts have less surface area and thus less friction when passing through a target.

Nock

To attach the arrow shaft to the bow string, there must be an attachment point. Small plastic, or sometime aluminum inserts called *nocks*, are inserted into the aft end of the arrow shaft. These nocks have a small slot that receives the bow string, allowing the arrow to remain in place until the archer releases the string.

In recent years, illuminated nocks have received much press and have become very popular. These nocks have small LED lights that are powered by very small batteries. When the arrow is released, the nock lights up. This allows the archer to track the flight of the arrow to the target and beyond. Lighted nocks are great for hunting because it helps the hunter visualize where his arrow strikes the animal and where it goes once it passes through. Lighted nocks are also great for helping keep track of arrows that miss the target when practicing, as today's arrows are very expensive.

Inserts

Whether aluminum or carbon arrow shaft, every arrow needs an *insert* into which a field/target point, broadhead, or other tip can be installed on the arrow shaft. Inserts are made of various materials, ranging

▶ Quality Archery Design's Tune-A-Nocks

▲ Lighted nocks have exploded in popularity in recent years. Here is an Easton Tracer lighted nock.

from aluminum to thermoplastics. Some inserts fit inside the arrow shaft, while others fit on the outside of the arrow shaft.

Fletching

The amalgam of vanes on the rear of the arrow is called the fletching. Fletching arrangements can vary from two, three, or four vanes. They can be arranged in any manner of ways, including straight, offset, heli-

cal, or any other manner limited only by an archer's imagination.

The functions of the fletching are simple. They are there to provide aerodynamic drag to the aft end of the arrow. This aerodynamic drag keeps the aft end of the arrow from cavitating, or becoming loose when in flight. When fletching is arranged in a manner other than straight, it produces sufficient aerodynamic drag to allow the arrow shafts to rotate or spin-stabilize themselves. These arrangements include helicals and off-sets. A common misnomer is that these fletching arrangements cause the arrow to spin-stabilize due to aerodynamic lift. This is simply not the case. It is a function of aerodynamic drag that causes the rotation of the arrow shaft. In an off-set or helical arrangement,

▲ This is a brass arrow insert into which a field point or broadhead is screwed.

▶ The very popular Blazer vanes.

the air flow is turbulent, not laminar as is the case for airfoil-shaped airplane wings.

Feathers are also commonly utilized as fletching. Again, there is a misconception that these large feathers "steer" the arrow from the rear. This too is simply not true. Again, the large surface area of a feather offers a larger surface area to the air column through which the arrow moves. The result is more turbulent

Feather Fletching

Feathers have been the cure-all fletching material for years. Some of the most hardcore of archers still insist natural feathers fly best and provide the best broadhead flight. Feathers do have advantages over rubber, silicon or vinyl vanes.

Feathers are considerably lighter than their synthetic counterparts. Three four-inch feathers weigh somewhere in the neighborhood of 7- to 10-grains. A matching set of four-inch vinyl vanes weigh in at around 24-grains. So feathers will give you faster arrow speeds. They also provide more surface area, which induces more aerodynamic drag, stabilizing the arrow a bit better than synthetic vanes.

However, feathers do have several drawbacks. First, they are brittle and easily damaged under tough use conditions. However, with proper attention, you'll be hard pressed to damage them.

Feathers are also prone to becoming water logged. While this is a problem, with a little care it isn't an issue. Several years ago, I was hunting in Maine. It had been raining all day, and my feathers had become drenched. A deer approached, and without giving it any thought, I drew back and let my arrow fly. Much to my chagrin, it didn't make it halfway to the deer below. The soaked feathers acted as a wet rag, and my arrow fell hopelessly to the forest floor. Lesson learned. Since that day, when using feathers, I spray them down with boot waterproofing spray. It works wonders; the rain and moisture roll off harmlessly.

The last drawback is price. Feathers are much more expensive to make than stamped vinyl vanes, which are produced by the thousands in a matter of a few minutes. For those with the adventurous spirit, give feathers a try.

airflow, the arrow and brings it into a stable flight configuration.

Fletching Configurations

There are a number of fletching configurations to choose from. Each provides benefits and each has drawbacks. It is the archer who has to decide which configuration is best suited for their setup. There are essentially five ways to fletch an arrow: 1) left helical; 2) left offset; 3) straight; 4) right offset; and 5) right helical.

Left Helical. I am always intrigued at how few people understand what a "helical" is. The term is thrown around in bow circles regularly. Merriam Webster defines a helical as, "turning around an axis like the thread of a screw." So a helically arranged vane is one which wraps around the arrow shaft (looks much like a boat propeller or the thread on a wood screw). So a "left helical" is a vane which is configured to give an arrow a left-handed rotation.

Right Helical. Same as left helical, only with a right configuration.

Advantages to Helicals. Good rotational spin-stabilization of the arrow shaft.

Disadvantages to Helicals. Excessive aerodynamic drag; very difficult to get arrow through arrow rests without fletching clearance issues; arrow is very noisy when in flight.

Left Offset. Offset fletching configuration is often confusing to archers, too. A left offset simply requires laying the vane on the arrow shaft shifted to the left. The vane's foot remains straight, but the entire vanes is cocked to the left. To the naked eye, it appears that the vane has been put on crookedly. Left offsets induce left-handed rotation.

Right Offset. The same as a left offset, only offset to the right.

Advantages to Offsets. Provides the least amount of aerodynamic drag, yet still retains some rotational spin-stabilization; considerably faster arrow speeds than left helical fletching configuration; very little arrow rest clearance issues.

Disadvantages to Offsets. Some loss of arrow speed; may cause arrow clearance issues on a select few arrow rests.

Straight. You may be able to guess the orientation of this fletch. When fletched straight, the vane's foot runs parallel to the arrow shaft or straight down the arrow shaft. Straight fletching induce no rotation and provide the least amount of aerodynamic drag. This style of

If I am going to get in trouble with the readers of this book, it will be now. Literally hundreds or thousands of articles have been written on how to "tune broadheads" for perfect flight. Others have been written on how to choose the best arrow vane configuration to make your broadheads fly true. An entire industry—the mechanical broadhead industry—is founded on the fact that folks can't get their fixed-bladed broadheads to fly true. Millions of dollars worth of these heads have been sold to archers promising "field-point" accuracy and flight. Well, here goes.

Broadhead flight is predicated on a bow's tune. There, I said it. It has little to nothing to do with your fletching. Any archer worth their salt with a well-tuned bow can get any broadhead to fly like a dart out of a tuned bow.

A well-tuned bow propels the arrow out of it perfectly. That is, it is pushing the arrow in a direct line forward, without side or up and down pressure. All the energy is being focused directly into the nock and the arrow.

fletching of course provides the fastest arrow speeds of all fletching configurations as it has the least amount of aerodynamic drag.

Advantages. Fastest arrow speeds due to minimal aerodynamic drag; no arrow rest clearance issues.

Disadvantages: Some archers will argue straight fletches are less accurate than offset or helical. This has not yet been proven by any reputable source.

Arrow Selection Guide

Arrow Length

Correct arrow length is of paramount importance. While this may sound strange, some folks overlook this. For true flight, arrows must be sized to your rig.

With the arrow nocked on your string, and a helper near, gently draw your bow (while pointing it in a safe direction). Have your helper mark your arrow one-inch in front of where the arrow contacts the arrow rest with an indelible marker. You now have determined your arrow length.

A word to the wise: resist the temptation to mark your arrows as short as you can get them. This practice leads to plenty of problems—none of which you want.

Arrow Spine

Arrow spine, quite simply, is how rigid an arrow shaft is. Absolutely nothing more. For an arrow to fly true, it must have the right amount of "flex" or spine. Too stiff an arrow means that there is not enough flex. Not stiff enough means that there is too much flex.

Determining proper spine is easy as arrow manufacturers have figured it out for us. To find the right arrow

spine for your bow, you'll need two numbers: 1) your bow's draw weight in pounds and 2) your arrow length. After choosing the brand arrow you want to shoot, visit the arrow manufacturer's website, input these numbers, and you'll know which arrow is right for you.

Arrow Weight

Arrows are either heavy or light. Light arrows fly faster (more feet-per-second [fps]) with a flatter trajectory than heavy arrows. Because they're light, having less mass than a heavier arrow, they deliver less kinetic energy to the target.

Heavy arrows fly slower (fewer fps) and drop faster; however, they deliver more punch to the target. You should strive for a happy medium. Not too light, not too heavy—just right.

There's two methods for determining the right arrow weight. As with all this arrow stuff, neither one is complicated. I enthusiastically recommend using the IBO formula. The IBO formula calls for five grains per pound of draw weight. So if you're shooting sixty-five pounds of draw weight, you'd want a 325-grain arrow (65 x 5=325). Easy, huh?

Arrow Shafts

Anyone who has spent quality time tucked behind a stretched bowstring has pursued "it"—that something, whether a profound advancement in cam technology, or something all together nondescript, that enables us to push our personal accuracy envelope to heights above and beyond. Whether it's the latest cure-all target panic eliminating release, or a simple truth

▼ Arrows come with various different spines and weights.

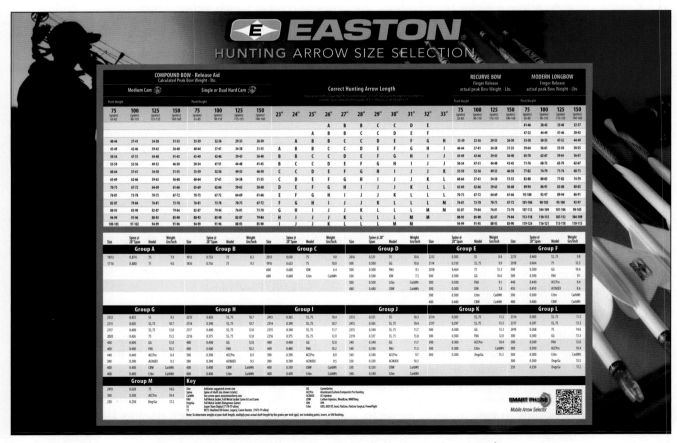

▲ Easton and Beman arrow spine charts. Selecting the right arrow is as simple as looking it up on these charts. ▶

COMPOUND BOW – Release Aid
Calculated Peak Bow Weight - lbs.

Medium Cam	Single or Dual Hard Cam	23"	24"	25"	26"	27"	28"	29"	30"	31"	32"	33"	RECURVE BOW Weight - lbs. Finger Release
27-31	22-26									A	B	C	22-26
32-36	27-31								A	B	C	D	27-31
37-41	32-36							A	B	C	D	D	32-36
42-46	37-41						A	B	C	D	D	E	37-41
47-51	42-46					A	B	C	D	D	E	F	42-46
52-56	47-51				A	B	C	D	D	E	F	G	47-51
57-61	52-56			A	B	C	D	D	E	F	G	H	52-56
62-66	57-61		A	B	C	D	D	E	F	G	H	H	57-61
67-72	62-66	A	B	C	D	D	E	F	G	H	H		62-66
73-78	67-72	B	C	D	E	F	G	H	H				67-72
79-84	73-78	C	D	D	E	F	G	H	H				73-78
85-90	79-84	D	D	E	F	G	H	H					79-84
91-96	85-90	D	E	F	G	H	H						85-90

If your arrow shaft is longer than that shown on the chart, round up to the next inch increment. For example, if your arrow length measures 28 3/4", then your correct length is 29".

Size	Spine	Model	Weight Grs/Inch	Size	Spine	Model	Weight Grs/Inch	Size	Spine	Model	Weight Grs/Inch	Size	Spine	Model	Weight Grs/Inch	Size	Spine	Model	Weight Grs/Inch
Group A				**Group B**				**Group C**				**Group D**				**Group E**			
500	0.500	BC	8.1	500	0.500	BC	8.1	500	0.500	BC	8.1	400	0.400	BC	9.0	400	0.400	BC	9.0
500	0.500	Classic	9.7	500	0.500	Classic	9.7	500	0.500	Classic	9.7	400	0.400	Classic	10.4	400	0.400	Classic	10.4
500	0.500	ICSH/B	7.3	500	0.500	ICSH/B	7.3	500	0.500	ICSH/B	7.3	400	0.400	ICSH/B	8.4	400	0.400	ICSH/B	8.4
500	0.500	ICS/HPRO	7.5	500	0.500	ICS/HPRO	7.5	500	0.500	ICS/HPRO	7.5	400	0.400	ICS/HPRO	8.1	400	0.400	ICS/HPRO	8.1
500	0.500	SPEED	6.8	500	0.500	SPEED	6.8	500	0.500	SPEED	6.8	400	0.400	SPEED	7.4	400	0.400	SPEED	7.4
Group F				**Group G**				**Group H**											
340	0.340	BC	9.5	340	0.340	BC	9.5	300	0.300	BC	10.7								
340	0.340	Classic	11.2	340	0.340	Classic	11.2	300	0.300	ICSH/B	9.5								
340	0.340	ICSH/B	9.3	340	0.340	ICSH/B	9.3	300	0.300	ICS/HPRO	9.6								
340	0.340	ICS/HPRO	8.8	340	0.340	ICS/HPRO	8.8	300	0.300	SPEED	8.9								
340	0.340	SPEED	8.1	340	0.340	SPEED	8.1												

Size indicates suggested shaft sizes.	**BC**	MFX Bone Collector
Spine Spine of arrow size shown (static).	**Classic**	MFX Classic MFX
Model Designates arrow model.	**ICSH/B**	ICS Hunter, ICS Bowhunter
Weight Listed in grains per inch.	**ICS/HPRO**	ICS HunterPro
	SPEED	ICS Speed

Visit www.beman.com for complete shaft size selection and component information.

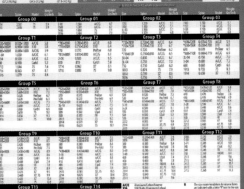

extracted from the tired ramblings of a mystic archery savant, the substance of *it* matters little.

Hardcore archers rarely consider the source. If a product's hype sounds good and seems to hold merit—hey, sign us up. Sadly enough and selfishly so, a bowhunter's only concern is that *it* translates into crowded arrow groups on range and the delivery of lethal shots when seated aloft on bench, holding court over our favorite early-season green field or late-season transitional trail.

I'm here to tell you, reaching the next level of accuracy and then stepping beyond, requires nothing more than close examination of what's under your nose when settled in at full draw. Oddly enough, for most bowhunters, achieving that "next level" of accuracy has been there for years, you just haven't been able to sniff it out—until now.

Arrow shafts are *not* created equal. There are vast differences between carbon shafts and manufacturers. Any number of factors dictates how well arrows perform while on stand or roaming the archery range. When ready to pony up for your next dozen arrows, consider these.

Arrow performance is measured in three ways: 1) weight; 2) spine; and 3) straightness.

Weight. High-end carbon shafts placed on a grain scale are typically within a grain or two of each other. Interestingly, the use of "grains" as a measure has ancient roots. The grain was derived from the weight of a single grain seed from an ear of barley wheat. So if we consider the weight of a single seed of barley, the accuracy and minuteness of grain weight becomes much more implicit. . . . Shafts of lesser quality have greater variations in grain weight, causing an inability to achieve consistent arrow groups.

Spine. This is a five-dollar word for arrow stiffness. Spine is the most critical criteria when it comes to accuracy. Not just spine, but more specifically, *spine around shaft* (or SAS), which is the spine deflection around the 360-degree circumference of the shaft.

Spine is a difficult concept for some bowhunters to understand. You can't see it, touch it, or taste it—it's intangible. In stark contrast, arrow straightness and the consistency of arrow weights are straightforward and measurable. Spine is more difficult to measure by the average archer or pro shop.

Spine is calculated by suspending an arrow shaft cut to 29 inches from both ends. Then a weight weighing 1.94 pounds (880 grams) is suspended from the center of the arrow shaft. The amount an arrow deflects, or doesn't, is its spine or stiffness. Measuring SAS requires sophisticated testing equipment to test spine around an arrow's circumference. Arrows that do not have a consistent SAS won't group because they flex inconsistently when shot from a bow.

Straightness. As a rule of thumb, the straighter an arrow, the more expensive it is. A human hair is about 0.004 inches in diameter. A carbon shaft of 0.006-inch straightness is plenty straight; in fact, you need relatively sophisticated measuring equipment to reveal an arrow's straightness. But since some bowhunters desire the best-of-the-best, arrows are offered in straightness's up to 0.0001 inches, with some manufacturers advertising even straighter shafts.

Setting Shafts Apart

What determines an arrow's quality? The answer is two-fold and relatively simple and yet somehow also complex. In short, construction material composition and manufacturing tolerances dictate what is, or isn't, a quality shaft.

Construction Material Composition. There are three grades of carbon fiber used when manufacturing arrow shafts. These are 1) recreational or standard modulus; 2) intermediate modulus; and 3) high modulus carbon. Obviously, standard modulus is the least expensive and most readily available carbon fiber, and high modulus carbon is the most costly. High modulus carbon fiber costs range from 5 to 100 times that of standard fiber.

Different grades of carbon offer varying degrees of filament counts, translating into inconsistencies between shafts. Tensile strength and modulus, flexural strength, flexural modulus, compression strength, and compressive modulus all impact the quality of materials. Just as quality varies among fibers, resins are another important piece of the carbon shaft puzzle.

Literally thousands of combinations of fiber and epoxy resins are available for manufacturing. Resin grades range in cost from as little as $10 per pound to those exceeding thousands of dollars per pound. Carbon fiber/resin combinations produce a multitude of products, ranging from arrow shafts to the intricate components carried aboard communication satellites orbiting Earth in microgravity.

Manufacturing Tolerances. Typically, in manufacturing, the tighter the tolerance held, the more expensive the component. In the arrow industry, there simply isn't a shortcut to quality. The birth of a quality shaft takes considerable time, and as all of us know all too well, time is money.

Harris and McKinney on the Record

I talked with two of the industries arrow experts, Easton's Jason Harris and Carbon Tech's Rick McKinney. I posed my toughest question to both. Can the average archer tell the difference between a low-end hunting shaft and a high-end shaft?

Harris, who works in Easton's Marketing Department offered this: "I believe the average bowhunter can tell a difference. However, how much of a difference depends on their shooting form, consistency, and how well their bow is tuned."

He continued, "Say you can reduce your group size by 10 percent using a high-end carbon arrow. A ten-percent difference in groups at extended hunting ranges, such as thirty and forty yards, can easily mean the difference between a hit or miss on deer-sized game."

Harris added, "I'm a stickler when it comes to equipment. I use equipment that is better than me, that way *I'm* the limiting factor. I can practice and get better, however, if I'm shooting equipment that compromises consistency, then it's limiting my progress."

McKinney, a three-time US Olympic Archery Team member and two-time silver medalist said, "The aver-age bowhunter can tell the difference, but unfortunately they've been led to believe that arrow group inconsistencies are their fault. Arrows are the most critical portion of an archer's arsenal."

McKinney continues, "Using a quality arrow that is consistent and accurate that can be tuned easily will have you enjoying tighter, more consistent groups. Unfortunately, there are a lot of people with shafts that have inconsistent spines who cannot figure out what the problem is with their groups."

Shaft Selection Miscues

Most would agree by now that the right arrow is critical to accuracy. Here are the most frequent miscues archers make when selecting shafts.

Information Shortage. Simply not being in "the know" about the differences in carbon shafts can lead to arrow selection slip-ups. Informed archers, those armed with the knowledge to make the right shaft selection decisions, can be found crowding the range target bull's eye with shafts and hanging expansive ivory on den walls.

Catalog Shopping. Buying shafts from a mail-order catalog can be perilous. Do yourself a favor: read past the product descriptions and marketing hype. Scrutinize the critical shaft performance descrip-

Broadheads Anyone?

For those who struggle yearly with unruly flying broadheads, here's some advice that should tighten your groups and increase your confidence when pointing the business end of your arrow towards that trophy buck:

While ultralight carbon shafts offer incredible speed, they're significantly more difficult to tune, especially with fixed-blade broadheads. Bowhunters often become disgruntled and turn to mechanical heads for better flight with the same shaft. That's a mistake.

If you're scratching your head over errant broadhead flight, try switching to a heavier shaft. Heavier shafts (those with more spine) are less affected by a fixed-bladed broadheads tendency to wind-plane. Additionally, shoot your rig through paper to get a read on its tune. If you're getting less than a perfect bullet hole, odds are your broadheads won't hold tight groups with your field points.

Another factor to remember is this: If your arrow is flying as little as five degrees off-center when it impacts the target, you'll lose a considerable amount kinetic energy (i.e., penetration).

If your nock isn't directly behind your broadhead's point-of-impact, energy is dissipated elsewhere—away from the broadhead and the animal. This significantly reduces your penetration power as the arrow's kinetic energy isn't delivered squarely to the impact point.

There's nothing separating you from that trophy below other than space and time. Your arrow is the only mediator capable of crossing this time-space continuum to deliver a lethally placed broadhead.

If you've overlooked your shaft selection in the past, it's time for serious reflection. Quality shafts usher you into the archery express lane and the fast track to ultimate tack driving, deer-whacking accuracy.

Converting FPS to MPH

It's always fun to stand around in an archery shop and listen to all the resident archery gurus share their expertise on all aspects of the archery game. It's also entertaining to hear all the exaggerated hunting stories about the giant that narrowly missed being the next addition to someone's interior décor.

Next time you find yourself growing bored with all the same old stories, ask anyone if they know how to convert feet-per-second into miles-per-hour. Once the dust has settled, flex your mental muscle and share the formula. Arrow speed in feet-per-second can be converted to miles-per-hour by multiplying by 0.682—and that's it! 300 fps equals 204.6 mph. How simple is that?

tors—straightness, grains per inch and weight tolerances—before you decide to hand over your credit card number.

Buying arrows based solely on advertisements, celebrity endorsements, or flowerily product description will leave you with that lingering bitter diet cola aftertaste as you swallow hard when missing that "once in a life-timer."

Price Shopping. If you find yourself shopping shafts by price, it's time for you to pack it in. Spend a couple more weeks saving a bit more green, then make your shaft selection based on quality. The few bucks you save won't make up for the frustration you face when trying to acquire consistent groups.

Defer to the Professionals. If the arrow game has you confused, defer to a professional. Drop by your local pro shop and ask the folks there for the best arrow for your specific hunting needs. They'll walk you through your choices and make sure you score the right shaft.

VII. Mechanical Release Aids, Quivers, and Stabilizers

When deciding on a mechanical release, quiver, or stabilizer, it all comes down to personal preference. Each of these product categories are rich with choices—so many that you'll probably be overwhelmed when trying to decide on just one. The reasons for selecting each individual model are as numerous as the product options themselves, which doesn't make the decision any easier.

Mechanical Releases

The style of release you shoot is incredibly important. I have been in pro shops on numerous occasions when someone is buying his first bow and he's asked what style of release he'd like. At this point in the purchase, he has, in most cases, spent almost his entire allotted bow budget. So when it comes time to choose a release, it isn't uncommon for him to opt for "the least expensive one you've got."

While this may save him a few bucks in the short term, he will be disappointed with his *bow* purchase in the long run. The reason is simple: it somehow doesn't perform as advertised. In most cases, the mechanical release is the culprit.

There are huge differences between a $30 release and a $100 release. Now, don't get me wrong, there are some less expensive releases that work fine, however, that is the exception not the rule. In most cases,

when it comes to mechanical releases, you get what you pay for.

Nock Loop Releases

Nock loops have become very popular in the last few decades. These simple loops improve accuracy, as they keep the archer from torquing the string when directly connected to it with a release. They also keep the peep nicely aligned and eliminate any string serving wear.

Mechanical releases designed for nock loops have a post or exposed hook that the nock loop slides into. When the release is triggered, the post or hook releases the nock loop and the arrow is turned loose.

These releases are great for steady-handed archers, as they induce very limited friction on the nock loop. They are very easy to attach to the nock loop and are very reliable. On the down side, they can be difficult to use for archers who tend to torque their release hand on draw. If the release hand is torqued during draw, the nock loop will pop off the post or exposed hook and turn the arrow loose. This is very unsettling, to say the least.

I learned the hard way just how badly I torque my release when attempting to use one of these releases for the first time several years ago. After dry firing my bow about a quarter of the way into my draw, I decided I would stick to my caliper-style release and leave this style of release for the "professional shooters."

Caliper Releases

This style of release is, hands down, the most popular release in bowhunting—and for good reason.

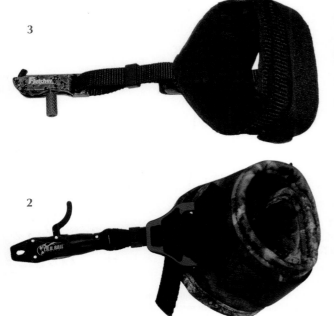

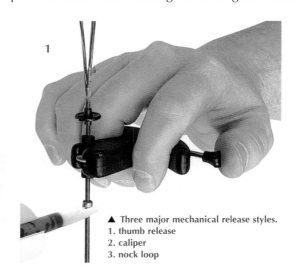

▲ Three major mechanical release styles.
1. thumb release
2. caliper
3. nock loop

Caliper releases work just like the brake calipers on your car or bicycle. Caliper releases have a set of jaws that squeeze the bowstring or nock loop. The design is decades old and operates flawlessly. In fact, the original caliper release was designed and patented by Charles Mead Beard of Elroy, Wisconsin. Mr. Beard's release was called the "Clutch for Bow-Strings" and filed with the patent office way back in 1880. He received his patent that same year, US Patent 228,302.

Caliper releases provide great user feedback. Typical designs require the user to push the trigger forward to engage the jaws. By doing so, the release "snaps," letting them know the release is indeed engaged. Most come equipped with wrist straps that adjust with either a buckle or Velcro closures.

Thumb Releases

This style of release clips onto the string or nock loop and can remain there without the archer needing to touch it. These releases are triggered, as the name implies, with the thumb instead of the index finger. The paramount advantage to this style release is the fact you can set it on the string and forget it. The release will remain connected until you remove it. This ability to keep your hands free while hunting is very advantageous.

However, thumb style releases do have their drawbacks. Because there is no wrist strap (like on caliper releases), you have to draw the weight of the bow using only your fingers. This can be an issue when the day turns cold, and you have limited use of your fingers when they're freezing cold. I have tried this style of release to hunt, and I am always a bit uncomfortable with my release

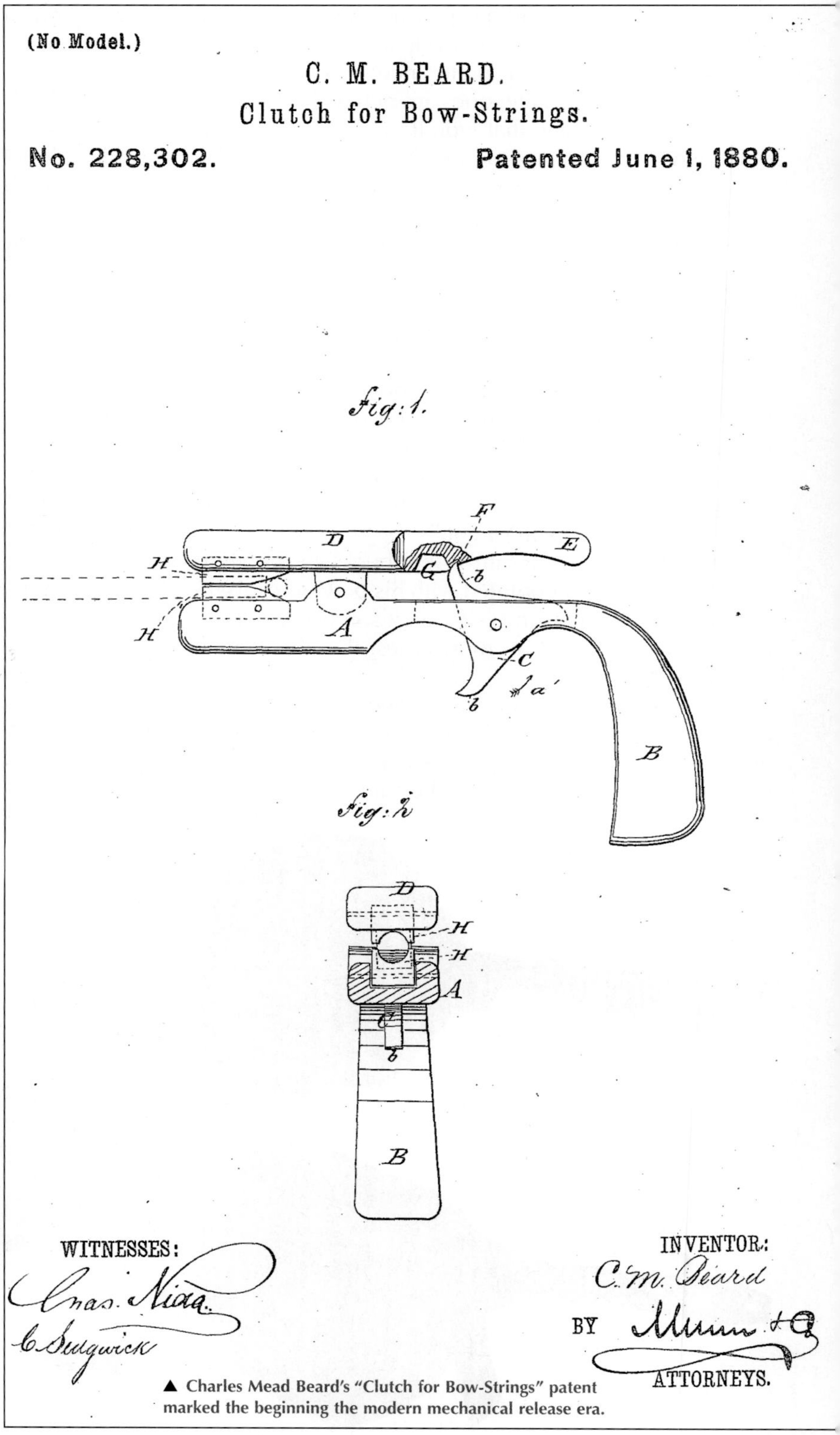

(No Model.)

C. M. BEARD.
Clutch for Bow-Strings.

No. 228,302.   Patented June 1, 1880.

Fig: 1.

Fig: 2.

WITNESSES:
Chas. Nixa.
C. Sedgwick

INVENTOR:
C. M. Beard
BY Munn & Co.
ATTORNEYS.

▲ Charles Mead Beard's "Clutch for Bow-Strings" patent marked the beginning the modern mechanical release era.

UNITED STATES PATENT OFFICE.

CHARLES M. BEARD, OF ELROY, WISCONSIN.

CLUTCH FOR BOW-STRINGS.

SPECIFICATION forming part of Letters Patent No. 228,302, dated June 1, 1880.

Application filed March 6, 1880. (No model.)

To all whom it may concern:

Be it known that I, CHARLES M. BEARD, of Elroy, in the county of Juneau and State of Wisconsin, have invented a new and Improved Arrow-Holder, of which the following is a specification.

The object of my invention is to provide a new and improved arrow-holder which holds the arrow while the bow is being drawn and releases it by means of a trigger, thus permitting the bow-string to force the said arrow forward.

The invention consists of a portable clutch for seizing a bow-string, which is adapted to be held in the hand, and is provided with an unlatching device or trigger, by means of which the bow-string, when strained to the desired point, may be instantaneously released without any relaxation of the muscles of the archer's arm.

In the accompanying drawings, Figure 1 is a side elevation of my improved arrow-holder. Fig. 2 is a partial cross-sectional and front elevation of the same.

Similar letters of reference indicate corresponding parts.

The lever A, provided with a curved handle, B, is provided with a longitudinal slot, in which the trigger-wheel C, provided with two or more rounded arms, $b\ b$, is pivoted.

A straight lever, D, is pivoted on the upper side of the lever A, and has the under side of its rear end, E, slightly recessed on a curved line. At the end of this curved under side a small notch, F, is cut into the same, and next to this notch a recess, G, is provided on the under side of the said lever.

The front ends of the levers A and D are provided with cushions H, preferably made of rubber or some other similar material, and provided with a longitudinal groove in the adjoining sides, so as to obtain a better gripe on the end of the arrow.

The operation is as follows: The arrow, which is preferably a little thicker at the rear end, is placed between the cushions H H, the string of the bow having been previously placed into the groove on the end of the arrow. By rotating the trigger-wheel C in the direction of the arrow a' the rounded end of one of the arms b glides along the curved recessed under side of the rear end, E, of the lever D, thereby raising said rear end and pressing the front downward, and thus holding the arrow firmly. The end of the arm b then passes into the notch F and locks the lever D in the above-described position. The bow-string is then drawn by pulling on the handle B, and as soon as aim has been taken the trigger is slightly touched, so as to cause the end of the arm b to pass out of the notch F into the recess G, thereby releasing the lever D, and consequently, also, the arrow and the bow-string, which is drawn forward with great force by the bow and forces the arrow forward with great speed.

With the herein-described apparatus the arrow can be firmly held while drawing the bow, the string can be drawn with great ease, and very accurate aim can be taken.

Having thus described my invention, I claim as new and desire to secure by Letters Patent—

1. The combination of the bent piece A B, the straight lever D, having notch F and recess G, and the trigger b, as and for the purpose specified.

2. As a new article of manufacture, a hand-clutch for straining a bow-string, provided with an unlocking device, by the operation of which the bow-string may be instantaneously set free, substantially as set forth.

3. In a hand-clutch for drawing a bow-string, the combination of a hook or angular projection to hold the string while being drawn and a trigger to discharge the string when it is drawn, as specified.

CHARLES MINOR BEARD.

Witnesses:
N. B. WILKINSON,
E. S. ROGERS.

just hanging on the string. In my mind, it's just waiting to fall to the ground below.

Back Tension Releases

These releases are the choice of competitive target and tournament archers. A small contingency of bowhunters out there use back tension releases. The design is simple: they are loaded under tension and, as you apply tension to the release, it is triggered. The catch here is that they are designed to release the arrow unexpectedly. This is to help archers relax when shooting targets. In my opinion, back tension releases are the least desirable design for hunting because you really should know exactly when you are going to release the arrow. Otherwise, you'll miss plenty of animals.

Beating Target Panic

Punching a mechanical release is the worst affliction you can have as an archer. It causes more misses than any other shot malady. Those who are plagued with target panic are some of the most desperate folks I've ever met. They are willing to do most anything to relieve this painful disease.

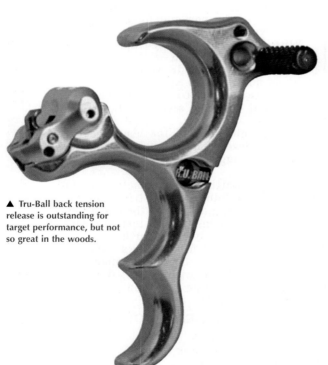

▲ Tru-Ball back tension release is outstanding for target performance, but not so great in the woods.

Tuning Your Trigger

Mechanical releases do two things: 1) they open and 2) they close. Not too complicated, is it? However, maladjusted releases are the culprit of inconsistent groups. There are two ways for a release to be adjusted incorrectly. First, the trigger can be set with too light. Archers have been led to believe that a light trigger cures target panic. False! An overly light trigger leads to punching.

Second, a release can be set too heavy. A tight trigger causes you to fight the pull, resulting in a panicked punch.

When asked, I always recommend a stiffer trigger. A *moderately* tight trigger allows you to gently squeeze through the trigger, avoiding the dreaded punch.

To prove to you just how badly you punch your trigger, the next time you're practicing with a buddy, trade releases. On your first shot, whether set light or heavy, you'll punch it—badly. Don't be embarrassed, most bowhunters punch their trigger. Now don't try and shrug it off as "an unfamiliar release." You punched it because, well, that's how you shoot.

Try this: Increase the trigger tension on your release. Now shoot it. Undoubtedly, you'll flinch, lurch, and probably squint your eyes at the point where it usually releases the arrow.

Practice with the tighter trigger until you can gently pull through it. When you can, reduce the tension slightly. Soon enough, you'll have quit punching the trigger.

While there's no magical elixir or medication that will immediately relieve this condition, rest assured—there's hope for those infected.

Remedies for target panic range from the sublime to the extravagant. As one who is constantly struggling to control my trigger punching, I have tried all with varying degrees of success. If it seems as if you're afflicted, you'll always be afflicted to one degree or another.

Trigger Fingers. For me, one of the simplest of remedies is to simply change the finger you trigger the release with. Of course, 99.99 percent of all shooters use their index finger to pull their mechanical release trigger. Try this instead: When easing your finger up to the trigger, switch to your middle finger.

Now, now, hear me out! Switching to your middle finger will be very uncomfortable, as it is not naturally in line with the release's trigger. In fact, it can be a struggle for some to get the middle finger on the trigger. However, therein lies the beauty. Once you reach the trigger with your middle finger, you will notice it's not a "natural" for pulling the trigger. You will actually have to *slow down* and give what you are doing some thought. *Voila*! You have just slowed your shot sequence and dumbed down your trigger finger. Try this for a few practice sessions and then switch back to your trigger finger. In most cases, you'll be miraculously cured.

Blind Bailing. Believe or not, shooting your bow with your eyes closed can help cure what ails you. Of course, you'll want to be really close to your target when doing so. Otherwise you'll run the risk of lobbing arrows onto your neighbors roof or into their vinyl siding.

Blind bailing is a term coined for standing a few feet from the target. You then draw with your eyes closed and level the bow on the target. Then you slowly squeeze the trigger and release the arrow into the target. By doing this, you eliminate looking at your sight pins and rushing the shot the minute they are on the target.

Back Tension. Back tension releases, while designed for target archers, can be just what the doctor ordered for target panic. Designed to go off when not expected, these releases can save the day. If you don't already have one, I recommend trying to borrow one for a week or two. Back tension releases are not cheap; sometimes they cost several hundred dollars.

Once you have secured one, practice just as you would with your normal hunting release. A word to the wise: make sure you have your bow pointed in the right direction, as these releases will initially have you flinging arrows in every direction.

Once you've gotten the hang of the triggering, you'll be on your way to controlling your target panic. If you can, I also recommend you have someone who knows how to use a back tension release present when you're testing it. They can help walk you through their operation and help you find all the arrows you'll have spread about the archery range.

Wrist Straps. When it comes to releases, I am a firm believer in a wrist strap-equipped model. Wrist straps allow for easier drawing of the bow; they recruit more muscles of the arm and back. They also increase accuracy over handheld releases, such as concho or grip releases, as they provide a repeatable installation.

I highly recommend wrist straps with buckle closures over Velcro closures for a couple reasons. First, the buckle closure can be replicated time and time again by putting the strap on and using the same hole each time. By doing so, your draw length (the track along which you draw the string) remains the same, as do your anchor points.

Secondly, buckle wrist straps are considerably quieter than Velcro wrist straps. For years, I used a Velcro wrist strap and loved it. However, when I was hunting one evening, I drew back on a deer and the Velcro made that horrible sound we all recognize when it is pulling apart. Needless to say, the deer wasn't too fond of that sound either and peeled off.

▲ Switching to your middle finger can minimize or eliminate trigger panic because your mind will focus on the trigger trip instead of rushing the shot.

▼ Tru-Ball buckle-style straps helps you put the mechanical release on the same way every time. The buckle and its holes ensures the length is always the same.

Velcro wrist straps are also noisy going on and coming off, in addition to readjusting when hunting. All of these ills are eliminated with a buckle wrist strap. I can actually put my release on while in complete darkness, as I need only to count the holes in the strap with my fingers and cinch the buckle to the appropriate hole for me. It's that simple.

Wrist Strap Length. I am of the opinion the majority of bowhunters have never consciously given any real thought to the length of their release wrist strap. And why should they? It's not like it's a complicated thing, right? Well, maybe not. However, the length of your wrist strap is *very* important to your shooting form and accuracy.

Most hunters put their wrist straps on so the tip of their trigger finger comfortably touches the trigger—much like a rifle. Here lies the rub: allowing the tip of your finger to touch and trip the trigger sets you up for

punching the trigger. Why? Fingertips are innervated with tons of nerve endings; they must be ultrasensitive to allow us as humans to manipulate objects and afford us fine motor skills with our hands (fine motor skills like punching our bow's trigger).

If you're one of the thousands of archers who set the length of their wrist strap to accommodate the trigger trip with the fingertip, stop. Instead, adjust your wrist strap so that its length only allows the second finger crease from the tip to reach the trigger. In other words, your fingertip will be past the trigger when the wrist strap is correctly adjusted. By effectively shortening your wrist strap, you're keeping your finger tip away from the trigger and using the lower portion of your finger.

This means that you're "dumbing down" your trigger finger, allowing a less sensitive, and mechanically disadvantaged portion of the trigger finger to trip the

▼ Tru-Ball Velcro style wrist strap. The velcro is noisy and it is difficult to get the same length adjustment every time. Small changes in mechanical release length can result in errant shots.

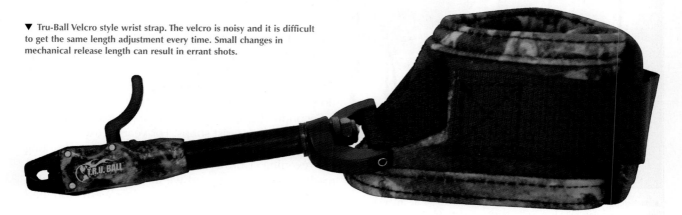

trigger. By using the lower portion of the finger, you're far less likely to punch the trigger.

Grip. A bow is a physical extension of the shooter—an innate connection of machine and man, manifested via mechanical release, anchor point(s), and grip. The tactile connection between the palm and bow's riser affects shooting consistency more than any other. In the big scheme of things, two distinct grips exist.

The *death grip* introduces excessive torque to the bow and results in ugly groups. When we talk about torque, we are referring to the residual forces built up in the wrist and hand, which cause the bow to start rotating (twisting) away from the target the instant you release the string. What the bow does after the arrow is launched is an indication of what it was doing while the arrow was at rest at full draw.

Then there's the *relaxed grip*. When applied correctly, shots are torque-free and arrows track true with high-powered rifle accuracy.

The most popular yet worst grip (for bowhunting) is the *open grip*. This grip has plagued every archer in search of the Holy Grail of handholds. The open grip places the bow handle in the crouch of the hand, fingers extended forward. The thinking here is that if nothing touches the grip, there's no torque, right? Wrong. As arrows leave the string, the laws of physics propel the bow forward. Keep this in mind: The only control of the bow is the minimal side pressure asserted by the thumb.

As the bow lunges forward, contact with the hand is lost. The instinctive reaction is to grab. It's hard to put into words just how much shooter error this panic grab introduces.

▼ Tripping the trigger with the fingertip leads to punching. By moving the trigger back in your finger, you reduce the tendency to punch it.

If you insist on an open grip, try this: Gently place the index and middle finger on the front of the riser while keeping your ring and pinky fingers extended. When the arrow is released, you'll grip the bow without introducing unwanted torque.

Trigger Tension. Incorrectly set trigger tension is quite common. In fact, I would guess that over half of all hunting release triggers are set too loose. Now, what I have just said goes against what the majority of the archery gurus out there would say.

There are numerous reasons to set a trigger light. They include getting off a shot with little effort and interference with the bow—pulling too tight on a trigger tends to make the bow torque in one direction or another. However, as mentioned previously, a loose trigger leads quickly to target panic and punching.

I personally like a trigger set a bit tighter, as it does two things. First, it keeps the shooter from punching. When the trigger is set tighter, it makes the shooter pull through the shot. If the shooter must pull through the trigger, the release is smooth and with less punching.

Secondly, a tighter trigger is more hunter-friendly than a soft trigger. In most cases, but not all, bowhunters hunt with some type of gloves. While some hunters keep their trigger hand ungloved, they are often surprised when their fingers don't work well enough to trigger the release when a shot presents itself because their digits have become too cold.

A firmer trigger allows the bowhunter to shoot with gloves on, as the firmer trigger provides more feedback through the gloves than a soft trigger. In fact, trying to trip a light trigger wearing gloves almost always ends up in a very errant shot as the gloved hand cannot sense when it is about to trigger the release.

Not to beat a dead horse, but I recommend practicing shots during the summer with the clothing you'll be wearing during the season (as does every single article you've ever read on bowhunting practice). Although this is standard advice, I know of almost no one who has ever practiced in the summer months wearing insulated gloves. Skipping this step has the potential to lead to costly mistakes come wintertime.

Quivers

For me, quivers are almost as exciting as dirty laundry. After all, these things are designed and built to hold your arrows. While some manufacturers claim their product eliminates vibration, helps to balance the bow, and so on, it's important to keep quivers in perspective.

▲ The very popular open grip has caused more errant shots than almost any other shot aberration. Upon release, or worse yet, before release, the shooter grabs the bow anticipating it lunging forward. This is easily corrected by gently holding the bow and allowing the fingers to rest front and center on the riser.

While I make light of quivers, they do serve a useful and meaningful purpose in the hunting game. Choose the wrong one, one that doesn't fit your hunting or shooting style, and you'll be hamstrung in the field.

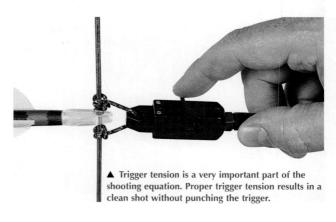

▲ Trigger tension is a very important part of the shooting equation. Proper trigger tension results in a clean shot without punching the trigger.

There are several considerations to take into account when thinking about a new quiver—things like the type of hunting you'll be doing. Are you spot-and-stalking or hunting from a tree stand or ground blind? How many arrows are you comfortable carrying? Do you shoot with your quiver on the bow in the off-season? Do you like a heavy bow or a light bow?

Two-Piece Quivers

A *two-piece quiver* is just that: two separate pieces or units that bolt onto your bow. There is a top unit, typically the hood, and a bottom unit, typically the base grippers. Two-piece quivers mount on the bow permanently (you can remove them, but you'll need tools) so they are not designed to remove once installed.

Two-piece quivers were made for archers who like to hunt with their quiver on the bow. A two-piece quiver is lighter than a one-piece quiver because the middle section of the quiver (the stem) has been eliminated. Two-piece quivers are also the most rigid quiver, providing rugged support for arrows. They are also the quietest of quiver designs as they mount securely to the bow's riser using hardware, as opposed to one-piece quivers that snap into place on the bow.

The downside to two-piece quivers is that they're permanent. That is, if the need arises to remove the quiver—you can't. I personally like removing my quiver when I shoot. It lightens the bow considerably and makes the bow balance better (the bow was designed to shoot without a quiver installed, after all). A permanent quiver also makes shots in heavy winds difficult; it increases the bow's aerodynamic profile, which then increases the surface area, which can be blown around by even gentle breezes.

Another disadvantage is that removing an arrow from the quiver when practicing changes the balance of the bow with each successive shot. While the difference is small, it *does* exist. And rest assured, this small difference does make the bow shoot differently with each successive shot.

One-Piece Detachable Quivers

As I mentioned, I personally favor this type of quiver. A one-piece detachable quiver fits my style of shooting and hunting. One-piece quivers are designed to be put on and then taken off. Their one-piece design includes a hood for the broadheads (or any type of arrow point),

▶ Trophy Ridge two-piece quiver saves on weight, however, it is not detachable from the bow.

a stem that connects the hood to the bottom arrow grippers, and the grippers themselves.

The advantages to one-piece quivers are numerous. First and foremost, you're able to remove the quiver while shooting. This is a huge advantage while in a tree stand or in a ground blind where elbow room is limited. Once the quiver has been removed, the bow's profile is reduced and is capable of making shots in tighter quarters than quiver-equipped bows. Another advantage that has been already briefly mentioned is that the bow is much more maneuverable and more agile without a quiver attached. Without the quiver, the bow is less susceptible to being affected by the wind during the shot.

Hip and Back Quivers

Quivers are also available in hip and back models. These quivers mount on the hip or are carried across the back. These two quiver types are not too popular, as they are generally in the way. They are also noisy; the arrows rattle around inside of the quiver. However, there are some archers who still demand this style of arrow holder.

To my knowledge, the Martin Super Quiver holds the most arrows at a whopping total of ten. Now, I under-

▲ Detachable one-piece G5 quiver. This is distinctly advantageous for those who like to hunt with as light a bow as possible.

stand wanting to be ready for all situations, but unless you're caught in the middle of an alien invasion (or you are the worst shot on the planet), you don't need that many arrows.

The majority of bowhunters opt for either three- or five-arrow quivers. I personally use a three-arrow quiver and have never run out of arrows on my many trips afield. However, I do not subscribe to the notion of shooting at squirrels, raccoons, and various other distractions while I'm hunting. If I'm hunting whitetails, I'm hunting whitetails—not any of the other furry critters around me. But to each his own. If you're comfortable with seven arrows, then by all means take seven. And if it takes ten to make you feel warm and fuzzy, by all means load 'em up.

Stabilizers

Another accessory that gets plenty of play in archery debates is the stabilizer. Modern stabilizers are designed to snuff out noise and vibration while stabilizing the bow. That's a tall order for sure. For years now, we've been bombarded with advertising hype about all sorts of stick-on, glue-on, and wrap-on rubber thingies, whatchamacallits, and thingamajigs that claim to magically "reduce noise and vibration by up to 65 percent." Incredible feats of engineering, indeed!

Having spent the last twenty years testing product claims, such as the one from the previous paragraph, I can tell you these miracle products do not work as advertised. It is also very important to note that when a company claims a product "reduces vibration and noise by *up to* 65 percent," 1 percent or 2 percent is included in that "up to" scale of noise elimination. It's called creative embellishing in the advertising world. In most southern states, it's referred to simply as lying.

If there really was a magical hunk of rubber one could peel-and-stick on a machine (a bow is a simple machine), and 65 percent of its noise and vibration

How Many Arrows?

There is an ongoing debate among archers as to how many arrows you really need. I know of one popular hunting television personality who looks to be packing a cord of wood when he goes bowhunting because he carries so many arrows. After seeing him shoot, I've realized that he needs each and every one of those arrows.

▲ Kwikee Kwiver Three-Arrow is compact and minimalistic. It holds just enough arrows for the hunt.

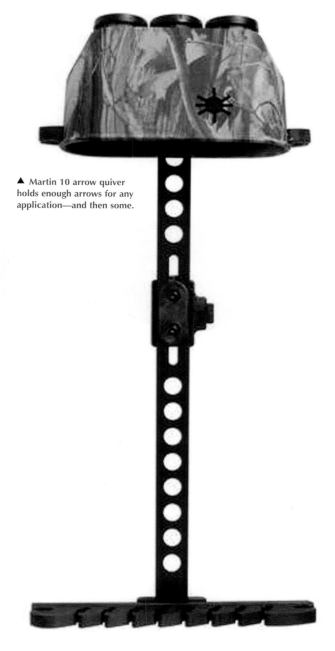

▲ Martin 10 arrow quiver holds enough arrows for any application—and then some.

could be eliminated, then jet engines would purr and top-fuel dragsters would hum instead of roar.

As with anything in the archery game, it's important to approach advertising claims with hesitation and a measure of common sense. Otherwise, you'll be paying out the nose for products that promise modern-day miracles, only to be disappointed by reality.

One last favorite: Car dealers advertise "all credit applications will be accepted." Great. They may all be *accepted*, but they all won't be *approved*. Get my point?

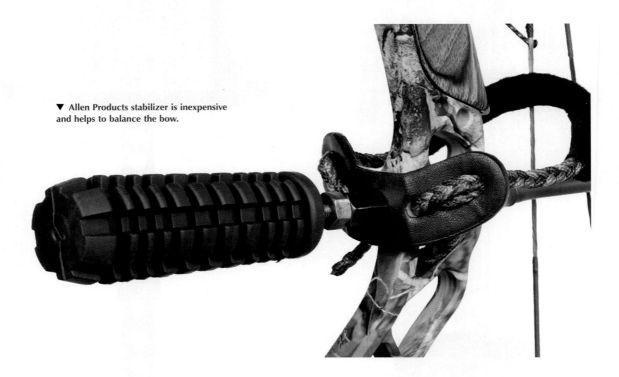

▼ Allen Products stabilizer is inexpensive and helps to balance the bow.

Stabilizers do serve a useful purpose, though. When chosen correctly, they can be beneficial for stabilizing a bow. They are capable of providing a counterweight to offset the weight of other accessories, such as the sight, that may give the bow an unwieldy balance.

Now, back to the vibration reduction part of stabilizers: admittedly, they do reduce some vibration in a bow. In all my testing using accelerometers, measuring vibration in both the x- and y-axis (front-to-back and up-and-down), I've found the best a stabilizer can do is reduce vibration by a little less than 1 percent. What I have found is the heavier the stabilizer, the more vibration it reduces. However, the amount of reduction is almost directly proportional to the increase in mass you're adding to the bow.

So if you're looking for a stabilizer to make some large reduction in vibration, you'll be disappointed. However, if you're trying to improve your hunting bow's balance, a stabilizer will work wonders.

VIII. Broadheads: The Business End of the Arrow

Broadheads have been around since what seems like the dawn of time. Early broadheads were called arrowheads. In the Stone Age, people used sharpened bone, knapped stones, flakes, and chips of rock as weapons and tools. Such items remained in use throughout human civilization, with new materials used as time passed. As archaeological artifacts, such objects are classed as projectile points without specifying whether they were projected by a bow or by some other means, such as throwing.

Arrowheads can be found worldwide as early civilizations developed weapons simultaneously. Arrowheads were handmade using naturally occurring materials like rocks (i.e., flint, obsidian, and cherts). Early arrowheads fashioned of bone and metal have also been recovered.

A team of scientists from the University of Witwatersrand published a report in August 2010 on stone-projectile points dating back 64,000 years that were excavated from layers of ancient sediment in Sibudu Cave, South Africa. Examinations led by a team

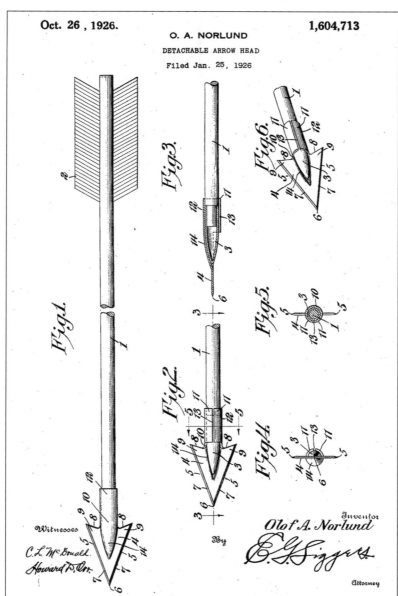

◀ O. A. Norlund's patent was the first issued for a modern broadhead.

Patented Oct. 26, 1926.

1,604,713

UNITED STATES PATENT OFFICE.

OLOF A. NORLUND, OF WILLIAMSPORT, PENNSYLVANIA, ASSIGNOR TO PHILLIP ROUNSEVILLE, TRADING AS THE ARCHERS COMPANY, OF PINEHURST, NORTH CAROLINA.

DETACHABLE ARROW HEAD.

Application filed January 25, 1926. Serial No. 83,674.

This invention relates to arrow heads, and has for its object to provide a metallic head, formed, preferably, of hardened sheet steel, and so shaped and proportioned as to be readily applied to the nose ends of ordinary arrows used by archers for target shooting and amusement, to convert said arrows into weapons for killing game animals, etc.

Another object is to provide a detachable arrow head for the above purpose which has the necessary penetrating point, cutting edges along the flaring sides thereof and the usual retaining hooks or barbs, and which may be readily formed of a single piece of sheet metal, suitably cut and pressed into a form having means for frictionally engaging the said nose end in a manner to rigidly hold the same in position during use of the same, and which may be as readily removed when it is desired to use the arrow again either for target practice or as a weapon with another head applied.

A full and complete understanding of the invention may be obtained from a consideration of the following detailed description, taken in connection with the accompanying drawing forming a part of this specification, it being understood that while the drawing shows a practical form of the invention, the latter is not confined to strict conformity with the showing thereof, but may be changed or modified, so long as such changes or modifications mark no material departure from the salient features of the invention, as specifically pointed out in the appended claims.

In the drawing, in which similar reference characters designate corresponding parts throughout the several figures:—

Figure 1 is a side elevation of an ordinary archer's arrow having the improved arrow head applied thereto.

Figure 2 is a reverse side view of the nose end of the arrow and the head.

Figure 3 is a longitudinal section on the line 3—3 of Figure 2.

Figure 4 is a front end view of the device.

Figure 5 is a transverse section on the line 5—5 of Figure 2.

Figure 6 is a perspective view of the head applied to the arrow.

Archers, in ordinary target shooting, generally use an arrow such as shown in the drawing and which comprises a staff 1 formed of suitable strong and tough wood of light weight and having at the trailing end, opposite feathers or other thin webs or fins 2 to guide and steady the arrow in its flight. At the front end the staff is usually provided with a thin metal ferrule or nose 3, which may be provided with a rounded or tapered end or striking point, the said ferrule being set into the staff and frictionally held thereon, so that the outer surface of the same is flush with the surface of the staff.

The improved, detachable arrow head comprises a body member 4 formed of thin, flat, hardened steel and is of triangular shape, having its opposite tapering side edges 5 converging towards the front, at an acute angle to each other, to provide the sharp penetrating point 6. The side edges 5 are bevelled on each side to provide cutting edges 7 for facilitating the entrance of the arrow into the object, and the rear edge of the triangular arrow head, at either side of the staff 1, is inclined forwardly as indicated at 8, to provide opposite side hooks or barbs 9 which serve, in the usual manner, to prevent the arrow head from being easily removed from the wound.

Projecting from the rear edge of the body portion 4 is an extension 10 which is normally provided with side wings 11, and the said extension is bent or formed into concave form longitudinally thereof, and the said wings are accordingly bent to complete the circle and provide a tubular sleeve or extension 12, joined integrally with the body member, the said sleeve having the longitudinal slit 13, co-extensive therewith, and formed by the abutting outer edges of said wings, to provide an expansible sleeve to be forced on over the nose end of the arrow, and to exert a constant pressure inwardly to frictionally retain the head in position thereon.

The concavity of the extension 10 is extended on into the body member 4 and tapered to a point somewhat in advance of the center of the head, to form a half-round seat 14 for the tapered nose or ferrule 3 of the arrow, and it will be noted that, when the latter is fully seated therein, the outer end of the sleeve or tubular extension 12 overlaps the open end of the ferrule or nose and clamps also on the wooden staff 1, so that the frictional engagement of the nose from the University of Johannesburg found traces of blood and bone residue and glue made from a plant-based resin, which was used to fasten the points to wooden shafts.

Modern broadheads, as they have come to be known, get their name from their "broad" appearance. If we fast forward to the 1920s, archery was becoming a popular sport in the United States. However, while it increased in popularity, there were few archery manufacturers in the twenties. During this time, archers would fashion the majority of their equipment by hand, including their broadheads. As one can imagine, the level of complexity in design and manufacture was directly commensurate with the archer's ability to design and build these components.

During this archery era, homemade broadheads were all flat, two-bladed heads fashioned from flat stock. In most instances, the materials used were anything archers could get their hands on, as raw materials were scarce. Broadheads routinely weighed anywhere from seventy-five to a whopping three hundred grains. Most were two-piece designs, with a soldered, brazed, or welded ferrule fastened to the flat blade. Empty bullet casings were popular means of attaching the blades to makeshift ferrules.

▲ Krieger's Special Triple Blade Metal Arrowhead is credited with being the first broadhead with three blades. Interestingly, it was molded of aluminum into a one-piece design. The manufacturing process was considered very advanced for the time period. Credit: Don Williams.

Interestingly, even though manufactured broadheads did not yet exist at this time, the first commercially built broadhead was a tie-on model sold via mail order by the Peck & Snyder Corporation of New York. The year was 1878. In 1923, a very large barbed broadhead built by the California By-Products Company was made available to the public.

In 1925, the O. A. Norlund Company of Williamsport, Pennsylvania, offered their Yeoman No. 1. It retailed for a mere ten cents and was the first broadhead to receive a patent from the US Patent and Trademark Office. It was filed on January 25, 1926 and issued on October 26, 1926 (US Patent 1,604,713).

In the 1930s, several landmark improvements to broadhead design were made. J.H. Mahler of New York created the Mahler Interchangeable broadhead. Mahler's design was the first to incorporate a threaded ferrule that could be unthreaded and swapped out for another head.

In 1938, the Krieger Manufacturing Company of St. Clair Shores, Michigan, introduced the first American three-bladed broadhead via their Krieger Special Triple Blade Metal Arrowhead. The Krieger head was molded aluminum, a real technological advancement way back in the 1930s.

The most popular of the first mass produced broadheads was the skeleton ferrule design of Pearson Archery. These flat-bladed broadheads featured a ferrule that had cut outs. These cut outs did not have any functional purpose; however, the design was easily mass produced at a greatly reduced cost to the consumers. The design was an overnight success and Pearson sold literally tens of thousands of the broadheads in various blade configurations.

Meanwhile, Cliff Zwickey of Minnesota was experimenting with a new broadhead design that would bear his name. Zwickey longed for a quality-made head that featured good steel and would hold an edge unlike the modern broadheads of that era. In 1939, Zwickey introduced his new "Black Diamond." Mr. Zwickey's broadheads enjoyed tremendous popularity. Not one to rest on his laurels, in 1942 Zwickey punched two small areas in his blade and folded the tabs perpendicular to the main blade surface. The result was the first broadhead with four blades introduced in the United States. Zwickey named his new creation the Eskimo. Zwickey's Eskimos are still manufactured today and are the longest running broadhead mass produced in the United States.

By the 1940s, wind-planing had become a real issue with flat-bladed broadheads as bow speeds increased. Mr. Earl Hanson of California began tinkering with the idea of eliminating some of the surface area of a broadhead to limit the wind-planing effect. In 1944, Hanson introduced his "Hanson No-Plane Arrowhead" to the general hunting public.

▲ The Mechanical Killer and the Hinged Fang mechanical style heads were some of the first introduced to the bowhunting community. However, the invention of the compound bow, with sufficient kinetic energy to open these heads efficiently, was almost two decades off. Credit: Don Williams.

During the 1950s, W.W. Rice of Leeds, New York, introduced a very important broadhead. Mr. Rice's "Bo 'n Arrer Rocket" broadhead featured a ferrule design with slots milled into it. The slots would accept four razor blades. These razor blades were then held in place by screwing a conical-shaped tip onto the front of the broadhead ferrule. Thus, the first interchangeable bladed broadhead was introduced. As a practice point, the "Bo 'n Arrer Rocket" could even be shot without the blades in it.

Meanwhile, Fred Bear of Bear Archery was developing a new head that featured replaceable blades much like the Rice head. However, the new Bear broadhead was capable of being shot only using two or four blades. In 1956, Bear introduced his new Razorhead.

The 1960s came and went with little in the way of major improvements. However, in 1972, Dick Maleski of Connecticut introduced his Wasp broadhead to the archery community. Maleski was a machinist by training and was thus able to experiment with different shapes, configurations, and designs. The basis of his design was a machined aluminum ferrule with a hardened steel tip and three highly modified Shick Injector razor blades. The blades were held in place with steel spring locking collars.

The new Wasp broadheads created a dramatic stir in the archery industry and the design proved to be an overnight success. Maleski literally worked day and night to manufacture enough Wasps to keep up with demand for his new and greatly improved broadhead design. In fact, he ran 24-hour shifts and still couldn't produce enough heads.

Since the early 1970s, broadhead designs have made limited progress. Most of the improvements have come in the form of improved materials. Ferrules that were once machined are now metal injection molded (MIM) for better structural integrity. Blade steel has gotten much better and now holds an edge no matter how rugged its use. Advanced manufacturing techniques have led to consistency between heads, with each weighing nearly the same.

Looking ahead to the future of broadheads and their design, it is hard to imagine any real significant advancements will be made. But then again, such was the thought of the Peck & Snyder Corporation of New York in 1878 when they introduced their tie-on broadhead.

Antique Broadheads

BROADHEADS FROM THE LARRY WHIFFEN COLLECTION.

▶ *Bear Razorhead;* built by Bear Archery of Grayling, Michigan, in 1956. Some referred to it as the "Bubble Head." It's one of the most successful broadheads of all time.

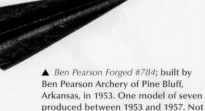

▲ *Ben Pearson 6x6 Skeleton Barbed;* built by Ben Pearson Archery of Pine Bluff, Arkansas, in 1942. Very inexpensive head used for big game and bow fishing. This is just one of twenty-three models Pearson Archery made using the skeleton design from 1937 to 1965.

▲ *Ben Pearson Forged #784;* built by Ben Pearson Archery of Pine Bluff, Arkansas, in 1953. One model of seven produced between 1953 and 1957. Not a real successfull head.

▲ *Ben Pearson Deadhead;* built by Ben Pearson Archery of Pine Bluff, Arkansas, in 1964. Ben Pearson Sr. used the prototypes of this head to harvest a world-record polar bear and grizzly in the same year.

▶ *Bigras Big Game Missile* with cutting ring. Built by Norm Bigras of Alpna, Michigan, in 1956. Built until 1969. Achieved very limited commercial success.

▲ *Blood Trail;* built by John Hauch of Stephenville, Michigan, in 1956. The design was limited to the bow it was shot from. It required a very powerful bow to drive the head in deep enough to harvest an animal due to the oddly shaped tip with the coring section.

◀ *Bow 'n Arrer Shop Rocket;* built in Leeds, New York, in 1955. One of the first "take apart" broadheads with replaceable blades. The Screw-in design made it possible to change to field point or blunt for hunting.

▲ *Browning Serpentine;* invented by Lou Brozina of Grand Junction, Colorado. Built by Browning Firearms of Ogden, Utah, in 1971. Although a very novel design, archers had a particularly difficult time getting the head sharp as the blades were curved. The Serpentine led to many states enacting the "all cutting blades must be in the same plane as the arrow shaft" regulation as this head would not penetrate.

▶ *Case Kiska*; invented and built by Roy Case of Racine, Wisconsin, in 1928. Roy Case made and sold broadheads from 1926 until 1953. Numerous models in both finished heads and in kit form were sold worldwide. Mr. Case was known as "The Dean of Broadhead Collectors." The Case Kiska was adopted as the logo of the American Broadhead Collectors Club (ABCC).

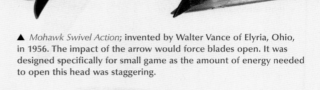

▲ *Mohawk Swivel Action*; invented by Walter Vance of Elyria, Ohio, in 1956. The impact of the arrow would force blades open. It was designed specifically for small game as the amount of energy needed to open this head was staggering.

▲ *Three Vent Geronimo*; invented and designed by Perry Mecham of Salt Lake City, Utah, in 1959. It was a very unique broadhead in the day due to the auxiliary blades that deployed on impact. Five models were made between 1957 and 1959. Ultimately, the head saw limited use as it was very difficult to drive the head through the animal with bows of the day.

▲ *Spitfire*; invented and designed by Fred Mosher of Grand Rapids, Michigan, in 1940. There were ten different models built in the 1940s and were named after the after World War II fighter plane.

▲ *Hawkeye Nylon 2*; built by the Hawkeye Feather, Corp. of Salem, Oregon, in 1959. It was designed as a small game head. Molded of nylon, it had threads inside the ferrule so it could be screwed onto wooden shafts.

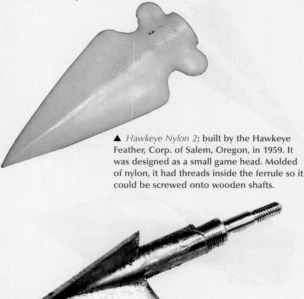

◀ *SR100*; built in Minneapolis, Minnesota, in 1960. It has a very large three blade built in two models. Very rare broadhead with one selling at an auction for $2,125.

▲ *Krieger*; invented by Ralph S. Krieger of Saint Clair Shores, Michigan, in 1938. A cast head way ahead of its time. Ultimately, exorbitant manufacturing costs would cause its demise. A very sought after broadhead by collectors.

▲ *Stemmler Big Game*; designed by L.E. Stemmler of Queens Village, Long Island, New York, in 1937. Stemmler produced over a dozen different heads. All are very rare and very collectible.

▲ *Terrible Terry;* invented by Ken Moore, co-owner of King Moore Archery in Los Angeles, California, in 1945. There are six total cutting edges on this unique head.

▲ *Barbed Zwickey;* designed and built by Cliff Zwickey of St. Paul, Minnesota in 1939. One of the most sought-after heads by collectors. The laminated head was very strong in the day, and the heads are still built by Cliff Zwickey's son today. The Zwickey is the longest continuously produced broadhead. For years the barbed heads were outlawed in many states and fell out of favor with manufactures. In 2010, Jack Zwickey reintroduced the Barbed Zwickey after most states lifted the ban. It is again a popular head. Zwickey's motto is "the sun never sets on a Zwickey head"

The Advent of Mechanical Broadheads

In 1948, Beryl H. Steinbach had grown tired of ill-flying broadheads. He designed a new style of head that was capable of expanding on impact. His broadhead had small wings that would deploy the blades when pushed backward. Mr. Steinbacher applied for a patent that same year. On September 18, 1951 he was issued US Patent 2,568,417 for his "Arrowhead Assembly." The Steinbacher patent is considered by broadhead collectors to be the original mechanical broadhead.

Subsequently, in the 1950s, several other mechanical heads were introduced. Early mechanical designs were riddled with operational problems. Some failed to open due to their radical design. Large wings required enormous amounts of kinetic energy to open and the stick bows of the time were incapable of producing enough speed to open these monstrosities.

Also during the 1950s, several mechanical heads were introduced by manufacturers. These heads seems to be ahead of their time, as they would require the power of a compound bow to operate correctly—an invention that was almost two decades away. The mechanicals from the fifties included the Star Point, which was designed, manufactured, and distributed by the Red Bow Manufacturing Company of Vermont in 1953. The Mechanical Killer was introduced in 1955, the Mohawk Swivel Action in 1956, the Geronimo in 1957, and the Hinged Fang in 1960. Because of the day's inefficient bows, mechanicals died a slow death as they proved ineffective when shot from recurves and longbows.

Blueprint of a Bow Kill

A strategically placed arrow dispatches animals quickly. But how is it exactly that a well-placed arrow proves lethal to an animal? I am often intrigued by hunters when they recount the tracking of an animal that proved unsuccessful. Most often the story goes, "I found plenty of blood, like it was pouring out of them, but no deer."

But how much blood does it take for a shot to be lethal? A thimble? A cup? More? And what does it take for an animal to expire when hit in the lungs? What physiologically happens to an animal after being shot? Oddly enough, these are questions that have remained unanswered for decades. Well, here's both the logistics and the how-to behind the shot.

Biology Meets Ballistics 101

Living tissue is composed of about 60 percent non-compressible water. For hunters using high-powered rifles, they rely on extreme muzzle velocities to put game on the ground. Modern rifles can generate muzzle velocities from 2,000 to more than 4,000 feet-per-second, placing the projectile in the supersonic range (objects traveling in dry air of a temperature of 68 °F (20 °C) at a speed exceeding around 343 m/s, 1,125 ft/s, 768 mph, or 1,235 km/h). These velocities create the violent impact and resulting shockwave that radiates throughout the surrounding tissue of an animal.

A bullet creates a bludgeon point when it comes in contact with incompressible tissues. As the incompressible tissue slows the bullet by friction and hydraulics, a hydraulic shockwave is created. This sends out a shockwave that radiates throughout surrounding tissues, organs, and nerves, inflicting irreparable damage. This immense pressure wave of destruction is called *hydrostatic shock*.

The Broadhead Equation

Low-velocity broadheads, however, travel at top speeds of maybe 400 feet-per-second (i.e., out of a select few crossbows). This speed is classified as *subsonic*. Subsonic speeds are those that fall below 343.2 meters per second (1,126 ft/s) in dry air at 68 °F (20 °C). Arrows and their broadheads are lethal for a dramatically different reason than high-velocity bullets; an arrow's lethality lies in its ability to cleanly sever arteries and veins and rupture vital organs.

To understand just how a broadhead harvests an animal, think of an animal's circulatory system as an elaborate, pressurized plumbing system—one that runs throughout the animal's body. A broadhead's job is then to compromise the system and spring a leak somewhere in the plumbing.

When a broadhead compromises the system, the circulatory leak leads to an abrupt loss of blood. When blood is loss rapidly, blood pressure drops quickly, halting transport of oxygen-rich blood to vital organs (like the brain). A fatal condition called hemorrhagic shock is induced.

Experts generally agree that animals must lose one-third (33 percent) of their total blood by volume to die from hemorrhagic shock. Whitetail deer have approximately 1 ounce of blood-per-pound of body weight. So a 200-pound whitetail deer carries 1.56 gallons (5.91 liters) of blood. Mathematically speaking, a loss of 0.52 gallons (1.97 liters) would lead to its demise.

Now consider for a moment that you are given a half gallon of blood to disperse along a trail. You would soon find that there would be an incredible amount on the ground. Give that some thought next time you're trailing an arrowed animal.

By the Numbers

Physiologically speaking, as blood loss reaches 10 percent (0.243 gallons for a 200-pound whitetail deer), the heart rate dramatically increases. This is an autonomic response by the body to attempt to maintain the system's equilibrium. The increased heart rate is attempting to elevate the blood pressure back to normal.

At the 20-percent mark (0.312 gallons for a 200-pound whitetail deer), the heart loses its prime and is now unable to keep pace with the ever-increasing loss of blood from the circulatory system. At this point, the animal's blood pressure begins to drop.

At the 30-percent mark (0.468 gallons for a 200-pound whitetail deer), the animal begins showing the dramatic signs of hemorrhagic shock: low blood pressure, loss of consciousness, and loss of *perfusion*. Perfusion is the process of delivery of blood and oxygen to a capillary bed in the biological tissue.

Faulty Jets

An automobile's carburetor mixes fuel with air. The human lungs function in much the same manner. As oxygen is inhaled into the lungs, it is infused into the blood. This life sustaining cocktail is passed throughout the body via the circulatory system.

The lungs are housed in the pleural cavity where the pressure is slightly lower (during inspiration) than that of outside air. The expansion of the chest wall keeps slightly negative pressure in the pleural cavity which, in turn, maintains the expansion of the lungs. This negative pressure holds the outer walls of the lung tissue against the chest wall, while the elasticity of the lung tissue keeps air passages open.

When an arrow compromises this space—that of the lungs—air rushes into the pleural cavity from inside the lungs and through the chest wall, breaking the vacuum and collapsing the lungs. With the lungs collapsed, oxygen cannot be mixed with the blood—this condition is medically referred to as *pneumothorax* (the prevention of the transfer of oxygen into the blood). The subsequent oxygen starvation of the brain leads to hypoxemia. *Hypoxemia* is generally defined as decreased partial pressure of oxygen in blood, sometimes specifically as less than 60 mmHg (8.0 kPa), or causing hemoglobin oxygen saturation of less than 90 percent.

Hypoxemia results in a loss of consciousness, while the oxygen-starved heart begins beating abnormally. The process is called *dysrhythimias*. Oddly enough, a whitetail hit in the lungs may succumb to suffocation (hypoxemia) before it has a chance to bleed to death. The result of a lung shot is the motor (muscular system) running out of fuel (oxygen).

The Ethical Shot

Quartering-Away

Shots to the chest cavity—those that damages the liver, diaphragm, lungs, and heart—are highly effective. In this quartering-away shot, the arrow passes through the animal diagonally, entering through the thin abdominal wall and passing forward into the chest cavity. The lethal disruption of any number of vital organs, as well as both the blood and oxygen delivery systems, occurs.

Remember: always use the opposite front leg as your aiming point.

Broadside

This shot offers the highest probability of a pass-through. Geometrically speaking, a broadside shot is the shortest distance through an animal.

Remember: Your aiming point should be right behind the front leg, one-third up from the bottom of the chest cavity. To avoid hitting the heavy bones of the shoulder, wait until the animal presents itself with its leg forward.

Abdominal Cavity

The large abdominal cavity houses the stomach, kidneys, liver, and small and large intestines. While

Why Mechanicals Require More Kinetic Energy

We've all heard that mechanical-style broadheads (those with blades that are fixed in the closed position during launch and flight that deploy when they strike the target) consume considerable energy when opening, but I can't recall seeing an explanation of this phenomenon anywhere.

As any broadhead-tipped arrow enters a target (in this case, an animal) its momentum begins to decay as a function of friction. This friction comes from both the broadhead blades, as well as the arrow shaft. As we have seen, animal flesh and tissue is comprised mostly of incompressible water. As a fixed-bladed broadhead (i.e., a broadhead with blades mounted and exposed at all times) enters an animal, it begins as the rearward swept blades pass through flesh. Since the blades are already "deployed," no additional energy is used. Fixed blades also have a significant mechanical advantage over mechanical-style designs.

A *mechanical advantage* is defined as a measure of the force amplification achieved by using a tool (i.e., a broadhead). Our fixed-bladed broadhead offers a mechanical advantage as it concentrates the energy into a sharp point and the rearward sweeping blades.

In contrast, as a mechanical broadhead hits an animal, the blades begin to be forced open. At this moment, the friction system (rubber band, slip-cam, spring, o-ring) that holds the blades shut must be overcome. Overcoming this friction system consumes energy. After the target has been struck, the arrow shaft has continues to move forward, leaving the blades stationary as they pivot open.

Once they are deployed, they again begin to move forward, jotting the arrow as it is forced to drag them through the target. This instantaneous shock, or application of drag, slows the arrows forward progress considerably, robbing yet more energy from the arrow. It is much like a dragster deploying a parachute at the end of a drag race. Additionally, dragging the deployable blades, which in most cases are placed at acute angles to gain large cutting diameters, robs yet more energy from the arrow.

Arrow Shafts. I cover arrow shafts comprehensively in Chapter Six. For argument's sake, when searching for the perfect hunting arrow, remember that arrows are, like all other compound components, governed by the laws of physics. As such, when looking for the perfect hunting arrow, general rules apply. First, the larger the diameter of the shaft, the more fluid drag it has when entering and passing through a target.

For the best penetration, you should choose the smallest diameter shaft you're comfortable shooting. I also recommend that you choose an arrow with the smoothest finish. The finish contributes directly to the amount of surface friction an arrow has. The smoother the finish, the less surface friction it generates, and the easier it slips through a target. In all cases, the diameter of the arrow shaft must not exceed that of the broadhead's ferrule diameter. If you are shooting an arrow/broadhead combination that demonstrates this, you are decreasing your penetration by some 30 percent.

an expansive target, avoid it at all costs. Shots here are mostly lethal, yet recovery rates are dramatically low. Usually there's little bleeding, but the stomach or intestines are cut, and their contents seep out into the animal's abdomen. Massive infection, called *peritonitis*, results. Death can take up to twelve hours.

Facing-To or Facing-Away

Neither of these shot angles present a high-percentage of success and should not be taken. In either case, heavy bones and muscle lead to minimal shot penetration.

Quartering-To

For much the same reasons not taking facing-to or facing-away shots, quartering-to shots should be avoided. Heavy bones and muscle of the shoulder shield the chest cavity.

Spine

While spine shots make for some spectacular video, they almost never work. The upper third of the body contains the bones of the spine and the heavy muscles of the back. It's unlikely an arrow will penetrate through this mass to the vital organs.

The Perfect Hunting Arrow and Shaft

Much has been written and much has been debated over the perfect broadhead design and the "best" hunting shaft. While there are plenty of both to choose from, few possess all the right stuff for optimum performance. As with many facets of the archery game, there are numerous old wives' tales and misinformation surrounding the perfect hunting shaft. We will dispel several of those here.

As you have seen previously, a hunting shaft's lethality is dependent on its placement. A poorly placed arrow, no matter how fast it was shot, will not kill the animal if it doesn't compromise one or more of the animal's life support systems (i.e., circulatory system, respiration system, etc.). Here are some tips on getting the most out of your hunting rig.

Maximize the Machine

As we have seen, compounds are amazing machines. They're capable of sending arrows to their intended target with incredible speed. To maximize the efficiency of the compound, select an arrow heavy enough to make use of all the bow's mechanical advantage. As the weight of an arrow increases, so does the mechanical efficiency of the compound. To do so, you'll need to shoot varying weight arrows through a chronograph and compare arrow speeds to arrow weight. At some point, the bow will begin to lose mechanical efficiency as it attempts to push an arrow that's too heavy.

Achieve Perfect Arrow Flight

A bow that is not shooting arrows with perfect flight is not functioning at peak efficiency. An arrow that is porpoising, fishtailing, minnowing, etc. is dissipating precious kinetic energy to do so. A perfectly tuned bow that shoots perfect arrows is using all of the available kinetic energy in the correct manner.

If your arrows aren't flying perfectly, or if you suspect they aren't, shoot your bow through paper to check its tune. If you don't know how to do this, visit a local pro shop and have them do so for you. They can easily correct any problems and maximize your arrow's flight.

Spine, Spine, Spine

To shoot the perfect arrow, you must select the perfect arrow spine. Selecting the proper arrow spine for your compound is a relatively simple task. Arrows shot with the wrong spine significantly decrease your bow's mechanical efficiency.

Which Broadhead is Best?

Broadheads are available in three styles: cut-on-contact, fixed-blade, and mechanicals.

For those who shoot low poundage (forty to fifty pounds), I recommend cut-on-contacts. Cut-on-contacts penetrate best because the tip is a sharpened razorblade. Cut-on-contact broadheads begin their cuts the moment they engage the animal. The tips cut as they enter and lead into the animals via lacerations. This is in contrast to chisel points, which lead with a blunter point.

For those shooting heavier poundage (sixty and above), fixed-blades are an excellent choice. Fixed-blades are durable and fly true if you take the time to set them up correctly. Typically, fixed-blade style heads have the aforementioned chisel points. While they require a bit more kinetic energy to penetrate than cut-on-contact heads, chisel points are more durable and less prone to bending.

Mechanicals, while getting plenty of ad time as of late, require additional kinetic energy when deploying their blades. Mechanicals are at a disadvantage when presented with a quartering shot—typically deflected shots and disappointment are the norm. Mechanicals do shine as they require little or no tuning to get them to fly field-point true.

Perfect Broadhead Flight

Weigh-In

Arrow-to-arrow consistency is absolutely necessary for tight, repeatable groups. With a digital grain scale, weigh your arrows. Shoot only those that are the exact same weight (within a few grains). Be sure all your broadheads weigh the same, too.

Wobblers

Believe it or not, not all carbon arrows are straight. With an arrow spinner and a field point, spin-test each arrow making sure it's straight. Cull those that are not.

Shooters

Once your arrows weigh the same and are straight—shoot them with field points. Take note of the ones who fly consistently. Set those aside from the group that don't.

Sharp Shooting

Once you've culled down your arrows, install your broadheads and start the process over. It's best to do this over several shooting sessions. Don't rush. After a couple sessions, you'll have a handful of perfect flying arrows.

Attitude Adjustment

On occasion, rotating the knock a quarter turn can transform an underachieving arrow into a standout. Rotate it until it flies better. If it won't, delegate it to the off-season practice range.

Keep 'Em Separated

Mark your best flying arrows. Put one dot on the cock vane of your best flying broadhead arrow, two dots on the next best flying arrow, and so on. Never shoot an ill-performing arrow at an animal.

The American Broadhead Collectors Club (ABCC)

The American Broadhead Collectors Club (ABCC) was established in 1974 by a small group of archery enthusiasts. Today, members are located in all parts of the world. The goal of the Club is to record and preserve the history of broadheads and fish points.

The ABCC has assembled a master list of all the commercially made broadheads from 1927 to today. The broadhead master lists are divided into categories: tie-ons, glue-ons, and screw-in broadheads. To date, the master list contains some 4,500 broadheads and fish points.

A large number of broadheads listed are from New Zealand and Australia. Fish points were added to the master list several years ago, with more 400 known commercially made fish points.

Once a year, the ABCC holds an annual meeting and its members can attend and bring their collections to put on display and trade for others.

The ABCC prints a quarterly newsletter with articles on old and current broadheads. Several books on broadheads and fish points meant for identification purposes have been printed under the ABCC's supervision.

▲ ABCC members display their collection at an ABCC meeting.

IX. Accessories That Make the Hunt

Anyone who has spent time in a tree stand, in a ground blind, or spot-and-stalking knows the right accessories can make or break a hunt. Whether it's a great backpack or a quality rangefinder, the right accessories can mean the difference between success and failure.

Treestands

Taking to a lofty perch for the day can be very exciting. Being prepared for the long sit can make the hours spent motionless almost bearable. There are plenty of styles and models to choose from. The trick is to select the one that's right for you, your hunting style, your physical ability, and your limitations. Here's how to pick the one that's right for you.

Climbers

Nearly four decades ago, James Baker and Fred Walters teamed up to create the first climbing tree stand. The "Baker" planted innovative seeds of thought leading to contemporary climbers. Modern climbers are alloy light and cleverly compact. Hunters are privy to ascenders capable of sending hunters up considerable distances and into remote areas.

I.J. Westad of Minnesota received credit for the original climbing tree stand, which differed from and heavily influenced Baker and Walters's work. In 1911, Westad patented a "Rope Climbing Device" that allowed users to ascend rope easily (US Patent 983,335).

▼ A bowhunter is filmed by a friend while elevated in treestands.

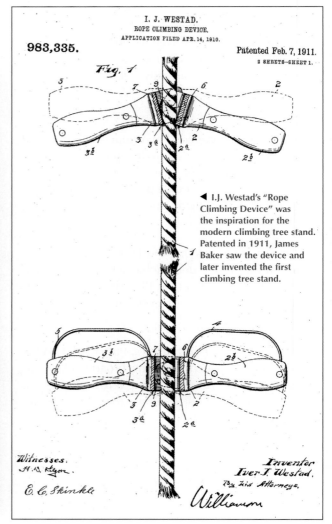

◀ I.J. Westad's "Rope Climbing Device" was the inspiration for the modern climbing tree stand. Patented in 1911, James Baker saw the device and later invented the first climbing tree stand.

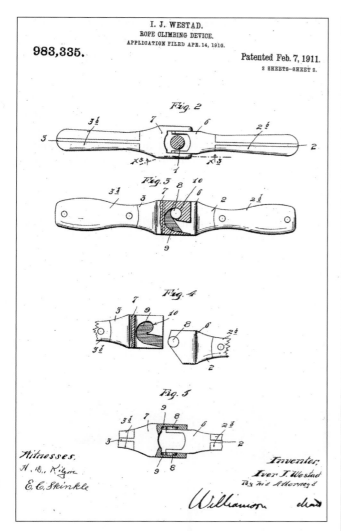

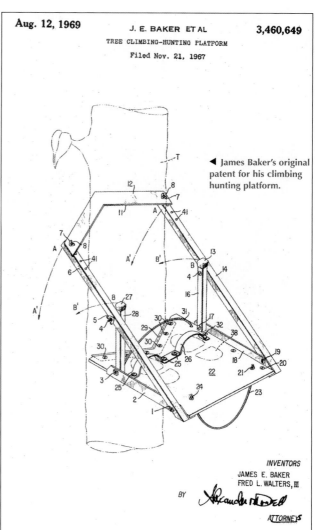

◀ James Baker's original patent for his climbing hunting platform.

Baker would later file for a US patent, and on August 12, 1969, he was awarded a patent for his "Tree Climbing Hunting Platform" (US Patent 3,460,649).

Climber Pros

Climbers are suited for hunters addicted to patterning individual trophy animals. When chasing down record book animals, you've got to be able to adapt. This flexibility includes being mobile and able to quickly relocate as the situation dictates.

Climbers allow you to change stand locations as the season progresses. You can follow game through early season, pre-rut, rut, post-rut, and well into late season. One climber can replace multiple hang-ons and ladders.

Climber Cons

Climbers are noisy when scratching and biting into bark on ascent. Their use is limited to straight trees devoid of limbs. They require the hunter be in good physical condition and are dangerous to use in the dark or when inclement weather compromises climbing conditions.

Hang-Ons

North Carolina's Ben Southard fathered the hang-on. Southard built and sold the first commercially available "Loc-Ons" in the early 1960s. Since their introduction, hang-ons have remained popular.

tree growth and animals. As such, when someone attempts to enter them during the following season, they can collapse, injuring or killing the hunter.

Ladderstands

Ladderstands have been around forever. In fact, it'd be difficult to establish the point of their origin. Ladders are well-suited to those hunting hot spots that don't have trees that accommodate climbers or hang-ons or for hunters who appreciate these granite-solid hunting platforms.

Ladderstand Pros

These are rock-solid hunting platforms for trees in the perfect location but aren't candidates for portable climbers or hang-ons. Ladders are perfect for hunters who choose not to use climbers, scale screw-in steps, or climb sticks on their way up to their favorite perches.

▼ Loc-Ons, or hang-on style stands, are very popular with hunters who do not desire to climb trees with climbing tree stands but want a permanent tree stand to use when they are ready to hunt.

▲ This is a Summit climbing tree stand. Modern climbers are alloy-light and able to climb safely to dizzying hunting heights.

Hang-Ons Pros

Hang-on stands are well-suited for hunters who favor a tree or have their own top-secret spot. Hang-on style stands are attractive to those who shy away from the climber setup fuss.

Hang-ons offer solid hunting platforms that most people leave installed year round. As such, critters on the ground below become acclimated to their presence.

Hang-Ons Cons

Most have postage stamp-sized platforms and horrifically uncomfortable seats. They can also be a pain to install. For the rifle hunter, hang-ons don't offer a gun rest. Many hunters leave these in the trees year-round. Here they rust, are stolen, are vandalized, or are damaged by

▲ **Ladder-style stands let hunters install once and enjoy a strong, steady hunting platform that is easily accessed via rungs. Models now allow hunters to access hunting heights as high as twenty-two feet.**

Ladderstand Cons

This class of tree stand is both heavy and awkward. In most cases, you'll need the help of several hunting buddies and a four-wheeler to tote one to your favorite tree. Typical ladder designs are complicated and a chore to setup and lean in the woods. You're limited in the height you can climb. (Yes, some ladders are built to stretch over twenty-feet, however, these are nearly impossible to erect.)

Rangefinders

Rangefinders date back to the early nineteenth century. These early rangefinders, sometimes referred to as telemeters, were designed for cameras. The first commercially available rangefinder was sold by the Kodak Company around 1915. These rangefinders were installed in cameras to assist the auto focusing function.

Laser rangefinders, those most common in the outdoor industry (and those used in golf, for architecture, builders, and in the military) emit a laser beam that is projected onto a distant object. The laser bounces off the target and returns to the source: the rangefinder. As light travels incredibly fast, the entire process takes literally milliseconds. The rangefinder calculates the amount of time it takes for the beam to bounce back, then converts it into a physical distance.

I personally consider the laser rangefinder the single most important piece of equipment any bowhunter can carry along on his hunt. Misjudging distances is the number one cause of missed animals and, worse, wounded, unrecoverable animals. I strongly believe any ethical hunter owes it to themselves and the game they pursue to make ethical shots. Those include knowing beyond a shadow of a doubt the distance at which you are shooting at an animal.

After spending decades in the field, I can honestly say I have never had an occasion when a rangefinder could not have been used to range an animal. The only instance I have found when one might be a bit less

▼ Bushell's Truth laser rangefinder has come a long way from the original rangefinders found in early Kodak cameras.

than convenient occurred when hunting in the deep south from a tree stand in early season when canopies were dense and shots happened to be up close and personal.

In these instances, when visibility is limited, I always make it a habit to range all the landmarks that surround my tree. I mentally note these distances, then spend time rehearsing possible shots and figuring out the distances to those shots. This system works very well and has never failed me, no matter how quickly an animal has presented itself.

Rangefinders are also a necessity when hunting in unruly terrain that rolls, has steep inclines, or declines. These are, by far, the toughest shots in the archery game. I have personally never met a bowhunter who could consistently make an uphill or downhill shot without the help of a quality rangefinder that has an angel compensation feature (for calculating distances while accounting for the upward or downward shot angle).

Knickknacks

Typically archers are gadget people. We love our little trinket stuff—the stuff we can screw in a tree and hang stuff from and other odds and ends. I think a great part of the fun of archery is assembling and gathering up our "stuff" for the hunt. While in hunting camp, I'll often ask my fellow hunters to show me their "system," or the gear they carry on the hunt. I can honestly say I have never been bored by a hunter when they are reviewing their gear.

I think bowhunters are like those Bond characters in the 007 movies. We've definitely got the knickknacks that would leave Q scratching his head in dismay. Whether it's a fanny pack, backpack, pull-up rope system, hydration pack, camera arm, or whatever else, bowhunters never run out of ways to improve the hunt.

Full-Body Fall Arrest Harnesses

If you're hunting from an elevated position, in my opinion, a full-body fall arrest harness is the single most important accessory you can carry to the woods with you. Each and every year, hunters are seriously injured or killed while hunting. Falls from treestands never have a good ending. As such, you should never hunt elevated unless you are attached to the tree.

Reaching the Summit Safely

It's simple enough—climb up, sit down, hunt, climb down, go home. However, this rudimentary task can be deadly. Here's how to keep yourself safe while climbing next time you're out.

Stay Well Connected

Full-body fall arrest harnesses save lives. However, they cannot save your life if you're not wearing one. Tragically, every year hunters are killed while wearing their harnesses because they forget to connect it.

◀ The Seat-O-Pants full-body fall arrest harness is lightweight, comfortable, and most importantly, will save your life should you experience a fall while hunting aloft.

While climbing, remember to stay connected. For portable climbing stands, this means from the time you leave the ground until you are safely back down. To do so, connect your tether to the tree belt while on the ground, moving it up and down as you climb.

Staying attached while using climbing stands also makes you slow down. Slowing down gives you time to think and plan your next move. Rushing up or down a tree leads to slips and, ultimately, falls.

On a Short Leash

All full-body fall arrest harnesses have tethers and tree belts. While some may be called by other names, they all function the same. Remember: your tether is the only thing between you and the ground below.

While using climbing stands, keep your tether length to a minimum. For ladders and hang-ons, minimize the tethers length once you're seated. There shouldn't be any slack in the tether while you're seated.

Hang On!

Hang-on or loc-on style stands have gained popularity recently as the economy has seen consumers knuckling down on expenditures. While they're an economical option for the small budget, they are also very, very dangerous to hang.

When installing hang-ons, hunters sometimes attempt to do so without the aid of a linesman belt. A linesman belt securely positions you while hanging these stands, freeing both hands to attend to stand installation chores.

Ignore the urge to forgo the linesman belt, opting to cling onto a tree by wrapping your legs around the trunk for support. If you so insist, you're guaranteed extended "down time" when you bounce unceremoniously off the ground immediately following a fall.

Transitioning

Many falls occur while hunters attempt to climb up into, or over and into, hang-on stands. When installing climbing aids (i.e., climbing sticks, stacking steps, screw-in steps, etc.), extend them above the standing platform.

Climbing aids should extend high enough so that when transitioning from your climbing aid to the stand, you have a hand-hold. You should step *down* onto the standing platform. And remember: attach your harness to the tree as high as you can reach before disconnecting your linesman belt.

Under no circumstances should you step *up* to transition from your climbing aid onto your standing platform, nor should you rely on pulling yourself into a stand by holding onto the stand itself. No tree stand is designed to support this side loading. Side loading a tree stand will teach you first-hand how gravity works.

Lifelines

The first lifeline was manufactured about ten years ago, and its commercial success was less than stellar. Today, lifelines remain an unheralded lifesaver. For ladders and hang-on stands, lifelines are installed when the stand is placed. Once placed, lifelines remain installed on a semipermanent basis.

When climbing, the user attaches the lifeline to himself, sliding the attachment up as they ascend (or descend). Should you slip, the lifeline reacts, holding you in place until you can regain your position.

Mistakes to Learn From—Before You Make Them

Unfortunately, some hunters tragically lose their lives or are confined to wheelchairs due to debilitating injuries each year. Most of the time, these injuries and fatalities occur after falling from a tree stand. In a sense, these horrible events don't ever have to happen because *falls are preventable*. Here are the most common mistakes and how to avoid them so you can return home safely from every hunt.

High Wire Act

Leaning out from a tree stand to execute a difficult shot is a prescription for disaster. Treestands are not designed to support the weight of a hunter leaning awkwardly out of the stand. Additionally, using a full-body harness to help support your weight when leaning out for a shot is dangerous. Full-body harnesses aren't designed for use as a positioning device; they simply mean to arrest your fall should you slip.

Fit Club

America's sedentary lifestyle has made us an overweight and out-of-shape population. If you plan on climbing this hunting season, seriously consider your physical ability to do so. Climbing a tree using a portable climber is a grueling activity that taxes the entire body.

Likewise, erecting a ladder stand or hanging a lock-on style tree stand is physically demanding, requiring elevated cardio-fitness and agility. If you insist on hunting from one of these style stands, ask for help installing them. If you're overweight or past your physical prime, consider hunting from the ground.

Hazard Pay

Volumes of sage deer hunting how-to have been penned on being out in the thick of the worst weather. This is reinforced by manufacturers who bombard us with ads depicting hunters fighting the horrid environmental conditions to get it done.

Simply put: hunting from a tree stand during bad weather is asking for trouble. Rain, sleet, lightning, high winds, snow, and other conditions make treestands particularly dangerous as rungs, seats, standing platforms, and tree bark become dangerously slick or unstable.

I heard a wise old hunter once say, "No deer is worth dying for." Those words have resonated with me since I first heard them. When the weather turns adversarial, head back to camp. Ignore the deer pundits urging you to stay and hunt. Anyone who advocates hunting in bad weather is an idiot. And you can tell them I said so.

Home Brew

In an effort to save money, folks fashion homemade stands from remnant 2x4s, rebar, scrap lumber, pallets, and any number of other building materials. From a simple pine plank to stand on to the elaborate "shooting house," these monstrosities rot quickly, rendering them unsafe. Boards lashed to tree trunks or limbs using nails or screws tend to loosen as the wind blows and the tree sways, compromising these connections and the integrity of these stands.

Mr. Goodwrench

Hunters love to tinker. Any new gadget that hits the market becomes the object of our obsession. While countless accessories are available for treestands, few are safe. Bow and gun holders that mount on stands can structurally compromise a stand's integrity by crushing or creasing the metal.

Resist the temptation to mechanically modify your tree stand in any way. This includes removing safety straps or installing a tree stand in a manner inconsistent with the owner's manual. Connector straps, tie-downs, bracing, standoffs, cross straps, and stabilizer bars are designed to solidify a treestands installation. If the manufacturer says to install these, then by all means, install them.

Read Me

Treestands are dangerous; no one will argue that point. As such, manufacturers have taken considerable time to outline the safe usage of their products in the instruction manual and through the application of warning labels.

Prior to attempting to climb a tree or install a tree stand, read the instructions completely and follow it religiously. The information contained there may help save your life.

The Great Equalizer

Statistics show that 82 percent of all tree stand-related accidents are due to the user not wearing their full-body fall arrest harness. It seems so simple: wear your harness and stay safe. For those of you who don't wear a harness, heed this warning: Chances are high that you will eventually fall.

Since 2005, every tree stand is required to come with a full-body fall arrest harness. If you don't have one, do yourself a favor and buy one. While in the woods, stay connected from the moment you leave the ground until you're back on it.

Visit hunterexam.com and click on the tree stand safety link for a short tree stand safety refresher.

Selecting the Right Harness

When you're twenty-five feet up in a tree, the only thing between you and the unforgiving ground below is your harness. Falls from elevated treestands seriously injure and kill hunters every year.

Here's what to look for when shopping for one of these life-saving gear essentials:

Fit Check

Hunters come in all shapes and sizes. In fact, no two are the same. When looking for a new harness, try on several models and brands. Never choose a harness from the package label or the marketing hype.

Every manufacturer has their own design features— research the brands you are interested in and choose according to their product merits. And *please* check the weight capacity of the harness to ensure you don't exceed it.

Cinch It Up

After slipping on a harness, tighten the leg straps, waist belt, and shoulder straps. Once buckled in, move around and lift your legs as if climbing and extend your arms as if drawing a bow or aiming a rifle. If the harness binds, try another until you find one that fits.

Gadgets

At some point, harness manufacturers thought gadgets would sell more harnesses. While some gadgets are nice, most are a distraction or nuisance. While shopping, consider the gadgets and ask yourself if you really need them. Remember that in most instances, they'll be under several layers of thick outerwear, rendering them useless. If you won't use them, don't pay for them.

Bulkiness

Nothing is more frustrating than wearing a cumbersome harness. Typically, the less expensive the harness, the more bulky it is. Large, obtuse buckles and stiff, nonconforming webbing is cheaper than diminutive hardware and supple webbing. If a harness doesn't conform to your curves and the hardware bites you, we both know you won't wear it.

"Underwear"

When trying on harnesses, remember that they're worn under your layering. Trying on a harness in a short sleeve T-shirt won't produce the same feeling as wearing one over heavy undergarments.

When trying on harnesses, wear your base hunting garments. While you'll look a bit odd, you'll leave the retailer confident that your harness fits.

Durability and Quality

Before buying, give the harness a close once-over. Check the tightness of stitching and the quality of junctures (i.e., where the webbing overlays other webbing and is sewn). Inspect the hardware. Is it ruggedly designed and easily operated (even while wearing gloves)? Is it silent? Hardware that clanks together will have you muttering words I won't mention here under your breath. Make sure the harness meets the Tree Stand Manufacturer's Association (TMA) standards. If it doesn't say so, put it down and grab one that does.

Warranty

Typically, the better the harness, the better the warranty. On harnesses that meet the TMA standard, you'll find a date of manufacture on the label. Check to make sure the harness has been manufactured recently, as they have a three- to five-year expiration date.

Stick to mainstream manufacturers to minimize warranty issues. "Valued-priced," "econo-" or "budget" harnesses are usually just that.

Price

Once you've targeted the harness you want, shop around. Many times you'll find closeouts or clearances during the off-season. Check the web, too. Internet sellers have less overhead than brick-and-mortar retailers. Always consider shipping charges, too, as they can occasionally sneak up on you. And remember: never sacrifice quality for price—your life depends on it.

How It Works

The Velocitip System includes a computerized 100-grain field point with three-axis accelerometer to continuously measure arrow aerodynamic drag in flight. Arrow drag and time of flight are stored by the field point for each shot and downloaded to a handheld unit. The handheld unit, a ballistic calculator, immediately determines the difference between performance at the bow and performance at the target by processing the stored flight data along with a user-supplied shot distance and arrow weight.

Aerodynamic Drag

Drag is a measure of how quickly an arrow slows down. The greater the drag, the faster the arrow slows down. Drag can be affected by a variety of factors including bow tune, bow design, arrow and vane selection, and shooting form. Arrow launch is extremely dynamic because of the speed with which the bow's stored energy is transferred to the arrow during the power stroke.

A look at the high speed videos available online quickly gives a sense of the effects this rapid transfer of energy has on an arrow shaft. Cam design, cam timing, nock travel, static spine, and arrow dynamic spine can all affect the efficiency of the energy transfer to the arrow and the amount of shaft oscillation and speed of recovery as it flies downrange.

Time-of-Flight

Arguments at hunting camps and target ranges often revolve around who has the flattest shooting rig. Simply put, the arrow that arrives at the target first is the flattest shooting. Time-of-Flight (TOF) is an immediate measure of the flattest shooting archery setup. The effects of aerodynamic drag on the arrow (the dynamic efficiency of the bow and arrow in combination) means the greatest bow speed does not always result in the flattest shooting arrow. In the 2012 bow test, at least one pair of top compound bows with closely competing bow speeds had the slowest start of the two, but delivered the arrow quickly to the target 20 yards downrange. These differences are more pronounced with increased shooting distance.

Retained Energy

A fast TOF also results in a greater percentage of retained energy delivered to the target. Of course, a fast TOF means less time in the air during which the arrow can be slowed down and energy is lost. However, everything else is equal; low drag also contributes to an increase in retained energy and a more lethal arrow. The KE/20 data introduced in the 2012 bow test provides an easy metric for directly comparing the energy delivered to the target by the bows tested.

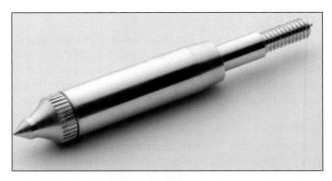

▲ Smart tip: The 100-grain field point houses 3-axis accelerometers that download flight data that is downloaded to the main control unit where software dissects it and then provides users with easy-to-use performance metrics.

The *Outdoor Life* bow test uses identical arrows for all testing to ensure that arrow selection does not introduce any variation in the test results. The Velocitip System also provides a percentage of Retained Energy, or measure of dynamic efficiency, for use in comparing equipment.

The Ultimate Tinker-Toy for Archers

Archery equipment testing traditionally only measures performance at the bow because of the difficulty in accurately measuring downrange performance with available test equipment. With the introduction of the Velocitip Ballistic System in 2011, direct measurement of the downrange performance of archery equipment is now possible. Unlike static measurements taken only at the bow, the full-flight data delivered by the Velocitip System provides information on the dynamic operation of the selected bow and arrow. These dynamic measurements offer insights into bow performance, arrow flight, arrow selection, and archery equipment tuning that can be used to improve archery performance.

▲ Velocitip system provides arrow-flight data sure to assist users in setting up their bows correctly and achieving optimal performance.

When we performed the annual *Outdoor Life* bow test in 2012, two new dynamic performance standards were made possible with the Velocitip System: AD/40 and KE/20. AD/40 predicts arrow drop at forty yards while KE/20 provides a true measurement of kinetic energy at twenty yards. Each of these metrics reflects the speed at which the arrow leaves the bow and the aerodynamic drag experienced by the arrow and its compliments in flight.

Greater aerodynamic drag increases AD/40 while decreasing KE/20. Increased arrow drop magnifies the effect of errors in yardage estimations, for example, when hunting or in 3-D competition. Decreased kinetic energy reduces the effectiveness of shots on poorly placed game.

Electronic Bow Tuning

Accuracy and repeatability in archery are the combined result of the selection and adjustment of your equipment and the consistency of your shooting form. Historically, paper tuning provided the most widely used approach for understanding the stability of an arrow in flight. With electronic bow testing, a new level of precision and granularity are available for archery equipment tuning.

For example, TOF is measured in milliseconds and drag is measured in milli-g's by the Velocitip System. Distinct differences in the flight ballistics for each shot can now be measured and quantified to determine whether the bow and arrow combination are well tuned. For the first time, the effects of changes in dynamic spine—a result of arrow shaft static stiffness and arrow front of center (FOC)—can also be quantified to aid the archer in proper equipment selection.

The ability to deliver quantitative comparative data is enhanced because the data is the result of measurements for the full flight of the arrow. Compare this approach to paper tuning, which only captures a fraction of an arrow's flight.

Physics Background

Dynamic electronic bow testing delivers results without requiring the user to have a PhD in physics.

However, all of the ballistic data is the result of fundamental physical relationships. These relationships are inescapable and worth keeping in mind when you look at test results. For example, if all other factors are equal, a faster moving arrow experiences more drag than a slower moving arrow because the aerodynamic drag force increases as a square of velocity. That's why a crossbow bolt traveling at 400 feet-per-second typically loses speed more quickly than an arrow shot from a compound bow at 300 feet-per-second. Because of the relationship between speed and aerodynamic drag, the arrow's drag will decrease as it flies further downrange. This means comparative testing should be done at a set distance for the equipment under test.

Conclusion

The addition of microelectronics to an arrow provides an easy way for archers to measure and quantify dynamic performance so they can optimize equipment selection and tuning. The innovation is made possible by the availability of today's small, rugged, and precise microelectronic sensors. The high performance microelectronics included in Full Flight Technology's Velocitip Ballistic System result in a tool used today that also provides a glimpse of the future for anyone using stick and string.

X. Degrees of Accuracy

You're comfortable and confident out to forty. It's opening day of the archery season and the local legend walks into your green field, hanging up at forty-seven. An eternity later, he disappears back into the hardwoods.

Before your season had a chance to begin, it's over. You've just passed up the biggest buck in the county. Don't feel too bad; the world hasn't ended. Plenty of bowhunters are forced to pass on shots that are marginal due to their extended distance.

I am dedicating this chapter to relating what I have learned throughout the years on improving your accuracy while extending your ability to shoot to protracted distances—distances that, until now, would seem inconceivable. In most instances, becoming a better archer is a matter of making a form tweak or expanding your mental game. Becoming a better archer does not involve hypnotists, Zen-doctors, or Buddhist priests. In most cases, shooter ills can be quickly diagnosed and remedied allowing you to send arrows downrange at dizzying distances.

The Basics

Shooting a bow well is not that difficult. In fact, I would argue that the longer you shoot a bow, the more likely you are to develop some bad shooting habits. I have taught plenty of folks how to shoot a bow over the years. Having done so, I have made a stark observation: beginners seem to shoot better than seasoned archers. Now, before you get bent of out shape, here's why:

When a newbie first picks up a bow, they haven't developed any bad habits. They have no preconceived notions about the journey on which they are about to embark. When instructed by a competent coach, they quickly become proficient. How many times have you seen this happen? A newbie picks up a bow for the first time, someone explains what they need to do to hit the target, and minutes later, they are stacking arrows in the bull's eye.

Are these new folks "naturals," "phenoms," or future Olympic gold medalists? Of course not. They're people who have no preconceived notion of what to expect.

▼ A bowhunter checks his equipment for accuracy before heading to the woods, ensuring it is tack-driving accurate.

As such, they are deadly right out of the gate. In my opinion, the most difficult aspect of shooting a bow for a beginner is drawing it. For those who can do so with little struggle, they become proficient quickly.

Contrast this to the folks who have been shooting for years or decades. These people, as a group, have more shooting ills than they can count on both hands and feet. These ills crept in throughout the years when they found themselves in a shooting slump. Think about it for a minute: You're practicing one afternoon and you're not doing so great. After some thought, you deduct (or your shooting buddy decides) that your grip is wrong. So off you go on a tangent, changing your grip to one you saw on a hunting show or in a magazine.

Changing your grip now changes everything else in the shot sequence. You now draw the bow differently because the center of gravity has shifted with your new grip. Well, if you now draw differently, you have to adjust your stance. As you can imagine, you've now changed every facet of your shooting style. You lob a

few arrows off course and suddenly doubt whether you can shoot at all. You've gone from a physical shooting issue to a mental one.

I am of the opinion that every archer should develop a style, and then never deviate too far from it. As you'll see here, this style involves the basics, such as stance, head, grip, anchor point, follow through, release, and aiming.

Stance

Shooting a bow is no different than hitting a golf ball, a baseball, a tennis ball, or rolling a bowling ball. Each requires you have a good, stable platform, or stance, from which to start. Now, I'm a bit different than most folks when recommending a stance to new archers. Rather than tell you to use a "shoulder width" stance, I prefer you use whatever stance is natural and comfortable.

I believe this is advantageous for several reasons. First, if you set your feet shoulder-width apart, and it is not a comfortable, natural stance, you're going

▲ A bowhunter with a relaxed style and tight form. Repeatability from one shot to the next is the key to shooting success.

to be uncomfortable. I personally shoot with my feet only several inches apart from each other. Why? Well, the majority of my hunting is done from treestands in the Northeast and the Midwest. I used to practice and shoot with a shoulder-width stance. Come opening day, I found myself very uncomfortable when attempting to shoot from the narrow confines of a tree stand platform. So years ago, I changed my stance to a very narrow one.

Second, by allowing you to find your own stance, you're not limited biomechanically. Each and every one of us has a specific way we walk, sit, move, and stand. Next time you're out and about, take note of how people stand. Yes, this may sound silly, but try it. You'll notice very few people stand with their feet shoulder-width apart. In fact, most of us stand with our feet relatively close together. This is our "natural stance." Being a good archer means being comfortable and natural. If that means your feet are closer than shoulder width, so be it.

Now that we have our stance, let's address the target. While we can go with whatever stance is natural (when facing the target it's best to stand at a right angle) 90 degrees to the target face. This will align our bow per-

pendicular to our target—no matter what type of target we're shooting (i.e., bag target, bale, animal, etc.).

Head

The most overlooked facet of shooting a bow is the head. In fact, I've never heard any other archery "expert" discuss the role of the head in shooting form. Odd when the head is central to making repeatable good shots.

When facing the target, your head should be straight up and down, without a tilt in one direction or the other. In other words, keep it level and still. If you lean your head over to meet the string, your form needs help. Try this: While looking forward, rotate and tilt your head at the same time. You'll notice your line of sight changes the more you tilt and rotate your head. This is counterproductive to good shooting form; it's not unlike trying to drive a car with your head tilted and cocked to one side.

Grip

We discussed the concept and importance of your grip when we tackled Beating Target Panic in Chapter seven. Remember, a bow is a physical extension of the

▲ The archer displays a typical stance. This stance is considered shoulder width or a bit wide. On the right, the archer displays a "narrow stance." The narrow stance mimics the natural manner people stand in everyday life.

▲ Elevated shots are difficult. Here, a bowhunter keeps his head square while executing a sharply downward angled shot.

shooter—an innate connection of machine and man, manifested via mechanical release, anchor point(s), and grip. In the big scheme of things, two distinct grips exist: the death grip and the relaxed grip.

Anchor Point

There's much to do about anchor points. Simply put, your anchor point is where you come to rest once at full draw. Throughout the years I've been shooting, I

▲ The "open grip," hands down, the most popular and worst grip in the archery game. Upon release of the arrow the archers grabs the bow introducing a egregious amount of torque on the bow leading to inconsistent and errant shots.

▲ Modified open grip. The grip is still technically "open," however, fingers placed on the front of the riser result in symmetrical pressure being exerted on the riser when the shooter "grabs" the bow upon arrow release.

▲ Even when dressed in full camo, your anchor points remain the same. This takes plenty of practice and long hours of training your mind to shoot the same no matter the situation.

have seen just about every conceivable anchor imaginable—and some that were unimaginable to that point. Because archery is such an individualized sport, I'm not sure there is a perfect anchor point. There are, however, some rules of thumb.

Most archers settle in somewhere at full draw around the side of their face with their bow string. This is the first anchor point. A second anchor is typically the tip of the nose or side of your nose on the string. If the string stretches well past the tip of your nose, your draw length is too long.

Finding a comfortable anchor is a matter of practicing until you find one that fits you. Something as simple as a string kisser button can make consistent anchoring a cinch. What is most important when looking for an anchor point is to make sure it is able to be repeated.

I once counseled an archer who was having trouble achieving consistent arrow groups. The archer was doing everything perfectly, from what I could tell, yet he was all over the target. Luckily, I noticed his release hand was slightly off their face at full draw; there was the slightest of gaps. I told him to hold tight when at full draw. Once he did so, I reached up and pushed his hand against his face. Within a few arrows, he was ringing the bull's eye on every shot. Problem solved.

▼ Multiple anchor points: An archer settles the string on the tip of his nose, corner of his mouth, and his thumb behind his neck. Multiple anchor points increase the probability of making each and every shot the same. Repeatability is the name of the game.

Follow Through

There has been plenty written about the archery follow through. For me, it is one of the simplest components of the shot. A good follow through is more or less the absence of a follow through. What? You'll never see a good golfer stop their swing the moment they contact the ball. The same is true of the perfect archery shot.

Think of a drawn bow as a stretched rubber band. When released, your bow hand and release hand should continue forward and backwards (respectively) ensuring a smooth follow through and well-placed shot.

Release

Without doubt, more has been written about "target panic," "buck fever," and "punching a trigger" than any other component of the archery shot sequence. Refer to Chapter Six for an in-depth review of this archery blight and its cure.

"Punching" the mechanical release trigger is a fast track to bad shots. Once you've settled into your anchor, gently squeeze. Contrary to popular belief, a stiff trigger is tougher to punch than a hair trigger. Also try moving the trigger back farther into your finger. Using your fingertip to trigger leads to punching.

Aiming

The previous discussion focused on the mechanics of the archery shot. We will now concentrate on those portions of the shot that aren't mechanical but mental. While it may seem rudimentary to the novice, aiming a bow isn't. Yes, the idea is to look through your peep sight, align the correct pin in the center of that window, put the pin on the target, and pull the trigger. Sounds simple enough.

Let me start this discussion by saying that contrary to popular belief, there are few archers who can hold a bow steady. Even the top target archers shake. The reason is simple: holding a bow at full drawn requires

▲ A bowhunter executes a shot from an elevated tree stand.

▲ Tripping the trigger with the fingertip leads to punching. Simply moving the trigger back one finger joint will significantly decrease your propensity to punch the trigger.

abnormal strength in muscles rarely taxed like they are when shooting a compound. Add to the mix that the bow is extended away from the body on a very long lever (the arm) and you've got a real challenge.

If you've ever painted with an extension pole, you'll understand what we are talking about here. While it is easy to get the paint on the wall, it is difficult to do so with any precision because the roller is out on the end of a very long lever. The pole in this case is the lever. The bow arm is the lever in the case of shooting.

If you're under the notion that you must hold your pin still to aim, you'll spend your entire archery career being disappointed. The best shooters in the world have learned how to manage their bow's movement when aiming. In fact, if you try and hold your bow steady by tensing up, you compound the problem.

Bows are best aimed when relaxed. Instead of fighting to keep the pin on the target, try this: When you are attempting to center your pin on the target, try to draw a small circle with the pin on the bull's eye. By doing so, you will relax your muscles as you move the bow in a very small increments versus trying to hold it steady on one spot. This helps relax the shot.

The World's Best Coaches Chime in on Increasing Your Effective Range

Colorado's Tim Strickland is one of the world's top teachers. An accomplished archer in his own right, Strickland has tutored Olympic archers as well as the world's top professionals. For increasing your effective range Strickland said, "Follow through is of paramount importance; archers make a fundamental mistake when shooting distances. The split second after release, their bow arm collapses, and the bow obstructs their line of sight to the target. The shooter attempts to peek around the limbs to see where they hit (or didn't). They just pulled their shot either left or right."

Strickland added that archers should "stay with the bow," referring to follow through. "Just as a golfer

One Eye or Two?

Physiologically speaking, monocular vision (closing one eye) affects your ability to aim a bow in the most efficient manner. Closing one eye results in the loss of stereoscopic binocular vision and diminishes the peripheral field of view.

Additionally, monocular vision results in approximately a 25 percent decrease in the size of the overall field of view. *Monocularity* is the absence of stereopsis (i.e., two images from two eyes being combined as one) and leads to a lack of depth perception.

The advantages of aiming with both eyes open are dramatic. With a complete field of view, you're able to acquire your target considerably quicker.

Monocular aiming eliminates a great deal of your peripheral vision, as well as limiting your ability to pinpoint an object's location accurately. Each eye sends the brain clues about the object's location in space. This is an important consideration in a hunting situation.

Envision an animal approaching from the left or right. In an attempt to limit movement, you draw, waiting for the animal to step into your sight window. With one eye closed and diminished peripheral vision, you're counting on it continuing along its travel path. However, if it changes course, you're out of luck.

Given the same scenario, and with both eyes open, you can now adjust and deliver an arrow appropriate for the changing conditions.

▶ Spot-and-stalking in open country and aiming with both eyes open. Aiming with both eyes open leads to a better field of view and depth perception.

Punch Drunk

There's been much written about "buck fever." For me, buck fever is the very same thing as target panic, or what target archers call punching the trigger. Call it what you will, any version of this plight results in only one thing: errant shots.

Bowhunters who punch their trigger are rarely accurate. Punching is typically a manifestation of folks who snap or drop shoot. The instant their sight pin crosses the target, they jab at the trigger. If this ails you, try this:

If you start your shot sequence with your pin above the target and drop down, reverse your routine. Start below the target and gently bring your pin up to the target (or vice versa). You'll find this new routine will minimize punching as your mind is now occupied with the new shot sequence.

To further minimize punching, move the trigger farther back in your finger. By doing so, it is impossible to use your fingertip to trip the trigger. These fingertip trips invariably lead to punching.

Finally, check your trigger tension. Contrary to popular belief, a stiff trigger is tougher to punch than a hair trigger. Increase the trigger's tension until you have to apply firm but smooth pressure to activate it.

continues their swing after hitting the ball, an archer likewise must follow through."

Follow through means allowing the bow arm to extend forward and the release arm to continue backward at release. "It's like you're holding a rubber band stretched out instead of a bow, cut the rubber and both arms move in opposite directions—that's follow through."

For improving hunting accuracy Strickland advocates using drop-away rests. "These are wonderful tools; they solve many shooting-form ills. Unlike their fixed-spring launcher counterparts, these rests really perform with ultrahigh performance bow setups. The arrow is on the rest for a shorter amount of time and is affected less by shooter glitches."

Georgia native Curtis Beverly has coached nearly twenty ASA Professional World Champions. Beverly said, "Archers get uncomfortable on longer shots because bow movement is exaggerated in their sight window; the target is smaller so you notice the pin moving more.

"Archers notice this movement and compound the problem by trying to hold the bow still by tightening up, but this makes it worse. You don't realize it, but your sight moves the same amount at shorter distances, too. However, you don't notice because the target fills the sight window."

Beverly recommends perfecting form at twenty yards. "Perfect each aspect of your shot by practicing at close targets. Once you're dialed-in and consistent, begin to move back slowly, two yards at a time. Get comfortable there, then move back another two yards. Repeat this and soon you'll have extended your comfort zone."

George Chapman has coached more than 350 world and national champions. Archery's Master Coach offers simple advice for archers attempting to extend their range: "Get a rangefinder."

Beyond the rangefinder, Chapman believes extending your effective range means being mentally prepared. "It's interesting how people are comfortable with that twenty-yard backyard pie-plate plink. However, move the target back a few yards and target panic sets in."

Chapman added, "It's like the guy who's afraid of heights. Put his tree stand on the ground and he's comfortable in it. Put that thing up about twenty feet in a tree, and he starts sweating. It's the same platform he was comfortable in on the ground; it's simply a change in elevation."

Chapman continued, "It's the same with shooting: the guy can stack the bull's eye all day at twenty, move him back to forty and his mind overloads and said 'too far.'" Chapman said "The shot sequence for that chipshot is the same as the forty; it's all between the ears."

According to Chapman, shooting an arrow is a relatively simple thing and should be kept that way. His advice is to "break it down into steps. 1) Get a comfortable stance; 2) draw; 3) settle into a comfortable and consistent anchor point; 4) focus on the target then gently squeeze the release; and 5) follow through. Don't make it any harder than it is."

Shots on High: Elevated Accuracy

Treestands are both a blessing and the bane of bowhunting whitetailers. Any number of variables dictates how successful you'll be when hunting aloft. Here's how to control some of these and increase your odds of scoring when hunting from on high:

Footloose

The most overlooked cog in the shooting machine is the feet. Tree stand platforms are compact, typically considerably narrower than an archer's stance. After spending the summer pounding bags in the backyard with a wide stance, the extra narrow stance demanded for treestand shots sneaks up and bites bowhunters at the worst time.

To remedy this, measure the standing platform of your favorite stand. During your next practice session, lay this measure out on the ground, limiting your stance to about six inches narrower. Once comfortable with this stance, you'll wonder how you ever made a treestand shot with your old wide stance.

Abby Normal

This may come as a shock, but all treestand shots aren't from a standing position. In fact, in many instances, the best ones are executed from a seated position.

To increase your versatility, devote one-third of your practice arrows to seated shots. Use an empty bucket flipped upside-down to mimic a treestand

---

A Word on Shot Distance

On occasion I have overheard a hunter say something similar to, "He was out way out there, but I had to let one fly because he was the biggest buck I've ever seen." As an ethical bowhunter, this should never be the case. The size of an animal's headgear should never dictate the distance we shoot. An intimate knowledge of your equipment and your shot abilities dictates the shot. Risking an unfamiliar shot is both inexcusable as well as unethical.

◀ An archer shooting at 3-D deer targets at 100 yards. Practicing at exaggerated distances greatly improves your efficiency at shorter distances, as you must refine your form to be accurate at these exaggerated distances.

seat. If your stands have rails, take those into account when practicing.

Cheap Seats

On occasion you'll hear someone brag about how high he hunts. Last I checked, there's no merit badge for these high-rise hunting antics. The fact is that most people miss from these exaggerated heights.

Try this—hunt as low as you're comfortable hunting. As your tree stand height decreases, the target size increases. Additionally, keep your hunting heights as consistent as possible. If using a climbing-style stand, mark your pull-up rope at your desired hunting height. Climb until your rope tells you that you're at the right height.

Acute, Obtuse, and Linear

Real-life shot angles are rarely broadside. However, well-intending archers thump their backyard targets broadside all summer long. When a real-world shot presents itself, (in a position other than broadside) ill-placed arrows often result.

Whether plinking bag targets, blocks, cubes, or 3-D deer targets, you should vary your practice angles. This is as simple as angling the target or moving your shooting position. A 3-D target, when shot in this manner, offers as real a shot scenario.

Cerebral Calisthenics

To stay sharp during the season, mentally practice shooting deer. To do so, simply imagine where your

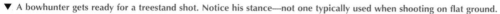

▼ A bowhunter gets ready for a treestand shot. Notice his stance—not one typically used when shooting on flat ground.

shot placement would be on a particular animal in front of you. Do this a few hundred times and you'll be surprised at how it becomes second nature.

One Shot Wonder

When hunting, you don't get multiple practice shots—you get *one* shot. Shooting dozens and dozens of practice arrows develops muscle memory and strong shooting muscles. However, it doesn't sharpen the mental shooting mind.

Try this: Shoot one arrow per day for a week. Place a target at an unknown distance and then go through your hunting shot sequence. If you can't deliver a kill shot, spend more time on the range until you can center-punch the kill zone on the first shot seven days in a row.

Selecting a Bow to Match Your Hunting Style

Dreaming of the perfect rig? When it comes to bows and accessories, remember that one size *doesn't* fit all. There are literally hundreds and hundreds of bow models out here to choose from. When considering a new bowhunting rig, make sure it fits your hunting and shooting style before laying down that hard-earned cash on your next launcher.

Treestands

Tree standers are confined by limited space. When space is tight, short bows with abbreviated axle-to-axle measures are the ticket offering the maneuverability to navigate difficult shots.

Tree Stand Sights

In terms of tree stand sights, try pendulums and fixed-pin setups.

Pendulums. Pendulums are still worth a look for those hovering above ground. The swinging pin adjusts for shot distance because the bow's tilted downward, taking some of the guesswork out of angled-shot distances.

Fixed-Pin. Typically a three-pin setup is all that's needed for Treestands. Three pins allow for shots to 60 yards (depending on how your sight is zeroed-in). Single-pin sights excel when dense coverage minimizes shot distances. The one-pin setup eliminates pin confusion (using the wrong pin).

Ground Blinds

Diminished overhead space challenges those giving it a go from the ground. Difficult to draw seated or

Make the Shot: Extend Your Effective Range

Every archer would love to be able to shoot another ten yards accurately. For decades now, the measure of accuracy was "hitting a pie plate at 20 yards." If we examine that statement, we realize how silly it is. A pie plate is a full 9 inches in diameter. Compare that to a whitetail's vitals, which are about 10 inches in diameter.

At a distance of 20 yards, most archers should be able to throw a rock and hit that. I mean, come on, *really?* Field archers shooting recurves can plaster the bull's eye at 100 meters (109.631 yards). So why is it we compound shooters have set the bar so low? I think the pie plate analogy must have been passed down for decades. I would venture to guess that it came from the recurve and longbow world.

Today's compounds are capable of fifty-cent piece-sized groups at 100 yards. Granted, there are few archers who are capable of shooting that group. Throughout the years, I have taken a bunch of heat over my activist stance on shooting distances. Anyone who has read my stuff knows that I am a proponent of shooting to extended distances as long as you are *competent* at those distances.

As I have previously mentioned, I have a 100-yard range in my yard. I routinely shoot to 100 yards when practicing. With that said, I would not shoot at an animal at 100 yards as too many factors can negatively affect that shot. But the point is that I practice to those distances to sharpen my shooting skills at shorter distances.

To improve your effective range, try this: Practice shooting 50 percent farther than your effective range. For instance, if your effective range is 40, shoot to 60. By doing so, you can stretch your effective range, and that 40-yarder turns into a chip shot.

kneeling shots at short distances are typically the shot du jure. Choose a lower draw weight bow with low mass weight to execute these awkward shots.

Ground Blind Sights

A rule of thumb is a ground blind sight can't be too bright because blinds are dark. Some hunters choose lighted sights to put the odds in their favor. Like a tree stand sight, the number of pins should be kept to a minimum as shots are routinely up close and personal.

Spot-and-Stalk

The perfect stalker has compact limbs and abbreviated axle-to-axle measure. An expansive brace height measure will offer forgiveness of shooter-induced error over exaggerated shot distances. Stout eccentrics translating into blistering speeds are mandatory for flat trajectories over rugged terrain.

Spot-and-Stalk Sights

Chasing animals on the ground is as exhilarating a proposition as there is. However, spot-and-stalk sights are very specialized because shots cover long distances. Five pins are the *minimum* you'll want in a stalking sight, while seven pin setups are perfect for those with a knack for converting shots at exaggerated distances.

Arrow Rests

Drop-aways

Drop-away arrow rests have become very popular in recent years. The reason is simple: they improve accuracy. Designs of just a decade ago were clumsy, and in most cases, incapable of falling out of the way fast enough to allow clearance as the arrow exited the bow.

Today's models are amazingly fast, silent, and deadly accurate. A quality drop-away minimizes shooter induced error by eliminating any arrow-to-rest contact as the arrow leaves the bow.

These are well-adapted for stationary hunting assignments, like treestands and ground blinds. For spot-and-stalk, keeping an arrow on these rests can be incredibly frustrating while crawling around.

Launchers

Some will argue launcher-style rests are the easiest to tune and are the most accurate. While debatable, launcher rests are best suited for Treestands and ground blinds when bow orientation is vertical.

Total Capture

These rests are the blue collar, meat-and-potatoes rests. Their lack of moving parts design is well-suited for any hunting situation.

Quivers

Regarded as the most "un-sexy" of accessories, quivers are indeed important. Any number is available, from hip- to bow-mounted and even backpack quivers. For most hunting applications, the standard detachable quiver is hard to beat.

However, while spot-and-stalk hunting, hip-mounted or backpack-style quivers are at their best. Both keep arrows within reach, while keeping arrows off the ground and out of harm's way.

Arrows

The aluminum versus carbon debate has raged for decades. Not one willing to get caught up in the fray, I recommend carbon over aluminum for any number of reasons—durability being the *best* reason to stuff your quiver with carbon.

Broadheads

Everyone has their favorite broadhead brand. However, putting brand loyalty aside, selecting the right *style* of broadhead is critical. Cut-on-contact, fixed-blade, and mechanicals are available in a dizzying array of cutting diameters and grain weights. For more information on broadheads, check out Chapter Eight.

My Eclectic Top 25 Tips for Bowhunters

Throughout the years of bowhunting, I've learned how to hunt the hard way by making every mistake and committing every possible error when out on the hunt. In an effort to help you avoid the same mistakes I've made, here are my twenty-five favorite tips on being a more successful bowhunter. They're in no particular order, as each has cost me an animal at one point or another.

1. **Chance Encounters.** You're trudging to your favorite stand and suddenly find yourself eye-to-eye with a giant set of antlers. After a minute long stare down, he bounds off. Make it a habit to have your release on while making these treks. You'll be ready when the shot presents itself.
2. **Fits Like a Muff.** Fumbling with clumsy-gloved hands on all-too important bow shots is frustrating. Use a hand muff instead of gloves to keep your hands warm when winter drives the mercury down. Shooting barehanded gives you a more accurate shot than shooting with gloved hands.

3. **Learning to Read.** Carbon shafts are the rage. In fact, most bowhunters now shoot them. While they're long on strength and accuracy, these black shafts fall short when attempting to "read" (the blood) shot placement. Crest arrows with light colors and fletch with white or yellow vanes make reading shafts simple.

4. **Who Turned Out the Lights.** Like it or not, most bow shots are in the first moments of dawn or the last fleeting minutes of daylight. Practice shooting 3-D targets (forget the bright white bag targets) in these low-light conditions and you'll quickly become acclimated to making deadly accurate low-light arrow deliveries.

5. **Under Cover.** Full-body harnesses are unattractive and cumbersome, but they'll save your life. Wear these life-savers over your base layer, then layer outerwear over that. You'll enjoy more freedom of movement when drawing on that big buck in winter's bulky clothing.

6. **Play Favorites.** Months prior to the archery opener, shoot all your broadheads. Cull errant arrows from your quiver. Shoot until you have six identically flying shaft/broadhead combos. Mark the vane of these first string shafts with an indelible marker to avoid confusing them with sub-performers.

7. **Shot Management.** Practice your shot sequence. Surprisingly, many bowhunters don't. When the shot presents, they're caught fumbling and rushing to launch an ill-advised shot. Practice getting into shot position, clipping your release, drawing, setting your feet, and executing. Remember, shooting from a tree stand or ground blind is continents away from the casual arrow lobs you've made in the backyard at that bag or foam critter. Targets of real fur and flesh will challenge your resolve.

8. **Have No Hang-Ups.** Learn to hunt from your tree stand with an arrow knocked and your bow in your lap. Bow hooks are great for hanging quivers, fanny packs, and binoculars, but they're no place for hunters who want to ground a whitetail. Many bowhunters have been busted while reaching for their hook hung bow.

9. **Don't Leave Home Without It.** Buy a range finder and use it. Make sure your outer layer of clothing has a pocket where your laser will be ready at a moment's notice. Pants pockets, fanny packs, backpacks, or bow hooks are no place for these when distance information is needed in a pinch.

10. **Landmark Decision.** While in your tree stand, use your rangefinder to mentally map out your effective range (how far you're comfortable shooting). Then use your laser to mark the distances to prominent landmarks within your shooting range. Repeat this until you can recite landmark distances sans the laser.

11. **Slip Into Something Comfortable.** You've got to layer in cold weather to stay warm, but a tightly wrapped hunter can hardly draw his bow, much less make an accurate shot. When settling into your stand, place your outerwear around the tree trunk in the order that you will put it on. Leave the front towards you and unzipped. Never take pull-over style outerwear to a tree stand. You won't be able to put it on without disconnecting your full-body harness.

12. **Height Matters.** Tree canopies cause bowhunting headaches. To be successful you must know how high to climb while remaining concealed and under the canopy. This is especially difficult when climbing in the dark. Place a screw-in bow hanger at your desired hunting height, and when your climber bumps it, you'll know you've arrived.

13. **It's a Long Way Back Down.** Keep your release wrapped around your bow's riser. Fumbling for a release that's in the bottom of a fanny pack or backpack usually results in a climb back down for a dropped release.

14. **You're Covered.** When hunting trees with branches or vines, tie your jacket over your bow prior to pulling it up. A jacket-draped bow eliminates branch and vine tangles on its way up.

15. **See Your Way Clear.** Clear shooting lanes are a must. Clearing lanes days (or minutes) before hunting alerts deer of your presence. Trim lanes as early as possible and trim the minimum needed to make unobstructed shots.

16. **Wrong Again.** Nothing's more frustrating than trying to pick the right climbing tree stand pin hole in the dark. When scouting, find a tree, adjust your stand, then climb it. If hunting that tree the next day, replace the pins back into the appropriate holes. If you select multiple trees prior to the season, jot down the pin positions for each tree. You'll be glad you did.

17. **Nose Bleed Section.** Sometimes I overhear bowhunters bragging about how high they hunt. The higher you climb, the tougher the shot. Acute downward shooting angles shrink the vital strike zone and increase shot distances. Contrary to

popular belief, hunt as *low* as you're comfortable. Nose bleed Treestands limit your success.

18. **Samsonite Gorilla.** You've saved for your fantasy out-of-state adventure only to find the airline baggage thugs have busted your bow in transit. Prior to leaving, find the nearest archery shop in the area you're traveling to. Should you need emergency assistance you'll know where to find it.

19. **Watch Your Step.** Ever wonder what it would feel like to slip and fall, catching each one of those tree steps in the gut on the way down? If you use screw-in tree steps, spend the extra $28 and buy six more pegs. Scrimping on steps by widely spacing them out will inevitably lead to falls. Install steps past your stand so you've a firm hand hold when climbing in and out. Less than five fins is a small price to pay to keep your guts where they belong.

20. **Go the Distance.** When practicing for the season opener, practice shots out to distances of 20 yards farther than the longest shot you're comfortable taking in the woods. You'll find your accuracy at shorter distances and confidence in the woods will improve.

21. **Get Tucked.** Rubber boots have become a bow-hunting mainstay. Take full advantage of them by tucking your pants down in them. Pant legs that brush against vegetation tip off weary deer of your presence in their neck of the woods.

22. **No Doze.** Quit using doe trails to access your tree stand. I can't count how many times I've hunted as a guest where the tree stand trail was an old doe trail. Notice I said "old," cause they're no longer a doe trial once you've made it yours, too.

23. **First Timers.** The best time to hunt a stand is not necessarily the first sit. Old timers swear by this wives' tale, but they're dead wrong. The best time to hunt a stand is when seasonal conditions and wind direction are right.

24. **Time's Up!** Don't make the mistake of sticking to trees or spots where you had success early in the bowhunting season. Remember, conditions have changed drastically along with the deer. Early season spots are useless later in the season.

25. **Hung Out to Dry.** The invention of the modern tree stand decades ago was a stroke of genius. However, I'm convinced critters have evolved and now include looking up for danger in their protective arsenal. Don't hang a tree stand out in the open; have something to break up your outline or you'll go bust every time.

Accuracy Improved: Bow Tuning 101

You can be the best shot in the woods, but if your bow is out of tune, you'll miss every time. A bow that's out of tune will leave you scratching your head. You won't be able to group field points much less broadheads. The best way to consistently drill dime-sized groups at 60 yards is to run your stick-and-string "through the paper."

Shooting an arrow through paper is relatively straight forward. As the arrow passes through the paper, it leaves a tear behind. By reading this tear, you're able to establish how well your bow is performing.

Many factors affect how well your bow strikes targets downrange. The basic premise behind consistent arrow groups is component synergy. The arrow rest, cams, limbs, nock, and string (among others) affect arrow flight. The trick to perfect tune is achieving Zen-like harmony.

Don't let that Zen reference spook you. Rest assured that a tightly tuned bow isn't that tough to achieve once you've successfully got a grasp on bow basics.

Getting Started

Find a spare piece of newspaper or butcher paper. Tape it over an old picture frame (after the glass and picture have been removed of course) or cut the bottom of a box out so you have the framework for your paper holder.

Place a target three to five feet behind the paper. Setup your target and paper so they're flat in front of you. You'll have to elevate both paper and backstop. You're now ready to shoot. Remember, you should be somewhere around 6 to 8 feet away from the target.

Note: Do *not* use your sights to shoot through the paper. Sight down your arrow shaft to make sure you're on the paper.

Once you've shot through the paper, check out your tear. This is where the fun begins. Paper tears reveal your bow's innermost tuning secrets. The ultimate goal is to achieve a perfect tear , which is commonly called a bullet hole.

Reading Tears

Ask any archer and they'll tell you that most of the intrigue in the archery game is being able to tinker with your gear. Fletching arrows, checking arrow spine, reserving strings, tuning broadheads, etc. are all labors of love for the hardcore archer. Archery is about tinkering.

THE BASICS OF BOW TUNING: TEAR CHART

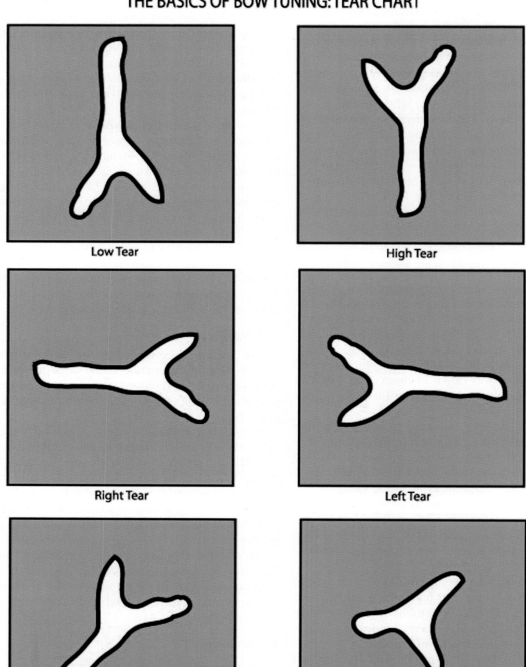

Low Tear

High Tear

Right Tear

Left Tear

Multidirectional Tear

Good Arrow Flight

◄ Various paper tears reveal any bow tuning issues as they visually report any ill-flying arrows.

Paper tuning is the tinkering archer's ultimate dream come true. While it may seem a bit overwhelming to a novice, rest assured you don't have to be an archery savant to get your bow to shoot tight groups.

There are a few "standard" tears you'll encounter. Here's a summary of those and the tuning culprit that'll keep you off target (refer to the tear chart).

NOTE: Before attempting to paper tune a bow, always make sure that you are shooting the right arrow spine. Choosing the right spine will typically eliminate 90 percent of tuning issues.

Horizontal Tear

A right- or left-handed horizontal tear results when the field point enters the paper from one angle and then the shaft and fletching enter from a different angle. Think of it as your arrow as flying sideways.

Don't panic. A horizontal tear means your rest tension is too tight or too loose. Adjust rest tension in one direction and shoot through the paper again. If your tear gets worse, you should adjust in the opposite direction. Keep adjusting until the tear is clean.

Right Tear

A right tear means your rest is too far to the right. Make small adjustments to the left until the tear turns into a bullet hole.

Left Tear

Just as a right tear indicates a rest too far to the right; a left tear indicates the rest is too far left. Make small adjustments to the right to remedy the problem.

Paths Less Traveled

Errant arrows can, at times, be caused by arrow shaft and vane clearance problems. Both the arrow shaft and/or vane can contact anything from the arrow rest to the cables. The easiest way to check clearance is to nock an arrow, then look down the shaft.

If there is a clearance issue, you should be able to spot it now. If you shoot and still suspect a clearance issue, spray your arrow with aerosol foot spray (the kind that leaves a powdery white residue). Any clearance issues will leave their mark on both arrow and offending bow components.

Cam Timing Issues

Cam timing is surrounded with much controversy and myth. No matter what type of bow you shoot (e.g., one-cam, twin-cam, hybrid, etc.), the cams must be in time. This simply means that both cams work in perfect unison.

It's best to check timing at full draw. To do so, watch the cams as they are drawn. They should both bottom out at the same time at full draw. If they do, you're in time. If they don't, you're not in time.

Getting a bow into time isn't that difficult—unless you have a bow press and some training, I'd recommend that you leave cam timing issues to your local pro shop.

Vertical Tear

Vertical tears can be either high or low. In most instances, these are the results of nock height adjustment or clearance issues. High vertical tears typically mean the rest is too high. Also, check rest tension, as it may be too tight. Low vertical tears mean the rest is too low. Check the rest tension. If your rest seems to be right, try moving your nock point either up or down.

If you cannot get a good tear following adjusting the rest, you should have a look at cam timing.

Multidirectional Tears.

These tears are most common and often misunderstood. The best way to conquer one of these is to start at one side (i.e., one direction of the tear, be it low, high, etc.), solve that issue, and then go from there.

Fix the left or right, then high or low, and then reshoot the paper. It is much easier this way, as you will be able to track what changes produced what results if you are only working on one issue at a time.

I'm in Tune

Once you've settled into your perfect bow tune, it's time to put your rig to the test on the range. After all, it's the tune that dictates accuracy either on the range or in the field. Here's how to assure your rig is hauling right.

Pace off three targets distances. Start at twenty, then go to thirty-five, and then fifty yards. Shoot six arrows each at these distances. Shoot at the same bull's eye each of the six times. Have another bow buddy stand behind you and take note of how your arrow is flying.

If you've done your tuning homework, your arrow should track true through the air and down to the target. You should also have near shaft-to-shaft groups at each distance. If you don't, shoot through the paper again and see how your tear is.

A tightly tuned bow will have you centering the bull's eye more times than not. Give these tips a try and you'll find that your shooting consistency will improve ten-fold.

SECTION 2
CROSSBOWS

SECTION 2

CROSSBOWS

XI. Introduction to Crossbows

*I*ntricate and complex socio-economic as well as environmental and biologically based factors have contributed extensively to the explosive rise of the crossbow. The availability of large, contiguous tracts of recreational property continues to decline annually as insidious urban and suburban sprawl continues to cast its dark shadow across the countryside. Once fertile farmlands and homesteads steeped in centuries of tradition have been consumed as parcels are dissected into tidy subdivisions and row housing.

As these expansive tracts vanish, so does the hunter's ability to pursue game via high-powered rifles. Center fire cartridges are slowly relinquishing their decades' long grip on hunters, succumbing to more sublime harvest modes that are primitive and less intrusive.

As herd management strategies via firearms evaporate, state and local wildlife biologists are forced to formulate new means to control rampantly increasing whitetail populations in non-traditional means. These management methods include turning to an unlikely hunting fraternity: that of the crossbow.

The interest and popularity of crossbow hunting has recently reached critical mass, as state after state adds the use of these ancient, primitive weapons to their hunting rosters. With their inclusion as an approved weapon, a flood of new revenue for both manufacturers, as well as state Department of Natural Resources, has been generated, replenishing previously exhausted coffers from a drastic downturn in license revenues.

Today, modern crossbow use is legal, to varying degrees, in twenty-nine states and throughout

◄ A modern crossbow hunter prepares for a shot while concealed by brush.

Canada—with more states to follow suit soon. Once considered by the archery "purists" as an unethical weapon, crossbow popularity has grown exponentially in recent years due in part to an aging hunting demographic.

Statistics reveal the average hunter's age is reaching the mid-fifty mark. Given the increasingly geriatric nature of the hunting population, compound bows are losing their preferred status among the hardcore archers. These hunters, due to physical constraints, are now opting for crossbows as their weapon of choice.

Market Data

The crossbow market is dynamic due to changing regulations on their use. For instance, in 2009 Pennsylvania, New Jersey, half of Michigan, and Texas added crossbow use to their deer seasons. The following year, Delaware, North Carolina, and Oklahoma did the same. New York added crossbows in 2011.

Providing a definitive number of crossbow hunters is a difficult task because states, (except Virginia), do not sell crossbow-only hunting permits. Crossbow permits are lumped under the general archery tags, or general hunting permits. Ohio, through a hunting survey, has estimated their crossbow hunting numbers fall between 140,000 and 160,000. When Michigan added a crossbow season in the lower half of the state in 2009, an excess of 52,000 crossbows were sold during the first week following the allowance.

Richard Bednar, President and CEO of TenPoint Crossbow Technologies, has been in the crossbow business for thirty years. Bednar, conservatively estimated a total of 2 million crossbows are in use today. This number is based on crossbow manufacturers' annual sales from the top five manufacturers: Excalibur, Horton, Barnett, Parker, and TenPoint. Bednar estimates top manufacturers' sales have increased from 25 to 40 percent per year since 2010. Bednar projects another 2 million additional crossbows will be sold over the course of 36 to 48 months as favorable crossbow hunting legislation is passed nationwide.

To the uninitiated, crossbows at a glance can be intimidating. Intimidating not in the classical way, but in a "wow, there's a lot going on with this thing" kind of way. What first strikes you is the array of "stuff"

▲ TenPoint Crossbow Technologies' Rick Bednar.

adorning the bow. There's the stock, which is mundane enough, but the limb setting is conspicuously at the "wrong" orientation. "Real" bows are, after all, a vertical affair and not prone to horizontal inclination. The trigger is positioned right where you'd expect to find it—centered and perched for action. Whether scope or pins appear, everything there is normal, too.

Making a Case for Crossbows

At a recent media event, a group of industry writers and editors gathered to evaluate new products from various outdoor manufacturers. The group included some pretty darn great outdoorsmen. In my group was one of the elder statesmen, a traditional longbow hunter and very well-respected writer whose been reporting on the sport for thirty years.

Our group's assignment was to visit each manufacturer's station and sit for a thirty-minute presentation. It seemed simple enough. When we arrived at a crossbow manufacturer's station, we were asked if we

▲ A crossbow hunter waits patiently against a tree trunk for passing game. Crossbows are very versatile hunting tools as they do not require drawing prior to the shot.

wanted to shoot one of their new models. Of course we did. Well, everyone except our traditionalist. After shooting several arrows, I noticed his absence at the shooting line. I politely asked him why he wasn't shooting the bows? He grumbled and mumbled something under his breath, shaking his head while walking away.

I was pretty sure I heard what he had said, but to make sure, I asked him to repeat it, only a bit louder so we all could glean something from his counsel. He blurted out, "I'm not shooting one of those damn things." Well, of course, I immediately jumped on that. I engaged him with a "why not?", which promoted him to go off on a tangent about how compounds and crossbows were the bane of the industry and were ruining it for all the *real hunters* (those who hunt with traditional gear). Wow.

Well, I waded in and kept the banter going with rapid questions about his position and why he believed

what he did. Needless to say, none of his answers held any water. He spewed one ignorant argument after another, negatively speaking about all forms of hunting other than his traditional stick-and-string bow. What a surprise that was. Here, this guy had been commenting on the sport of archery for years, yet held such a bias toward any hunting method other than traditional archery.

If he had his way, the only hunters allowed in the woods would be those who whittle their own bows from a fresh-cut limb and knapped their own arrowheads from flint, obsidian, or cherts they'd personally gathered.

I must admit that I held a similar opinion of crossbows for many years. I was of the opinion these weapons were designed for lazy and slob hunters (if they could be called hunters), those too lazy to learn the stick bow or compound. All that changed with one trip to the woods with a crossbow in hand.

I was invited on a crossbow hunt with one of the major bow makers. At the time, it was the last thing I wanted to do. After all—I was a *real* bowhunter. Well, after three days of blowing shot-after-shot, I realized these things weren't "guns" nor were they easily mastered. The fact is I never was able to get the bow on a deer because I kept hitting the tree stand rail . . . or making noise as I tried to maneuver the bow into position . . . or I couldn't find the animal in the scope or get a good post on the crossbow. . . . And so on and so on.

It was a humbling experience, and I'm here to tell you anyone who says a crossbow is easy to hunt with has never tried to hunt with one. There's nothing easy or automatic about them.

Oh, and my fellow media brother, who was so vocal about how terrible crossbows are, had never shot one—or a compound, for that matter. Yikes. And yet he knew *everything* about them and why they aren't *real* hunting weapons.

The sport of archery and bowhunting is a complex tapestry, a loose linen woven from many divergent threads, each representative of the many participants and disciplines in the game. Archery is a solo sport, however—one shared with others on a 3-D archery course, at the shooting line of an indoor event, or around a crackling campfire as tales are spun of the day's successes and failures.

Having providing first-hand commentary on the outdoor industry for nearly twenty years, I can honestly say that the industry moves at a glacier's pace. Rarely, if ever, can I recall a product, technique, or invention that has enjoyed overnight success.

That was until recently—when crossbows burst onto the scene as a relevant hunting weapon. This "bursting" of which I speak took a mere thousand years or so. Handicapped permits of yesterday have quickly given way to full-blown permits, and the dusty back room discussions of crossbows by the few ardent fans have turned to full-blown debates played out on the public forums.

In addition, crossbows and their discussions have become mainstays on the pages of some of the most influential hunting journals and magazines out there, such as *Outdoor Life*. While crossbows are definitely not new, having existed for an estimated 2,000 to 3,000 years, they are new to a hunting public searching for the next best thing.

▲ *Outdoor Life's* coverage of the crossbow boom. Cover reprint courtesy of *Outdoor Life* (Cover Photograph: Eddie Berman).

In fact, crossbows and their use have reached, what I would call, epidemic portions in a blink of an eye. Rarely can anything in the outdoor world be called "epidemic proportion." However, crossbows recently have become a burgeoning new market in the outdoor industry as states have rolled their use into regular hunting seasons. Once considered an unethical weapon, crossbow popularity has grown exponentially in recent years due to an aging hunting demographic.

As we touched on earlier, statistics reveal the average hunter age is fifty-four. Given the aging hunting population, compound bows are losing their favorite-weapon status among the hardcore. These hunters, due to physical and socio economic limitations, are now opting for crossbows as their weapon of choice.

States are rapidly adding crossbows to their regular seasons as a revenue generator as traditional license (i.e., archery tags) sales have stagnated and, in some instances, declined.

Crossbows use is also quickly becoming an additional herd management tool for local, state, and federal game managers eager to increase the management ability beyond marginally successful archery kills and the shrinking of firearm hunters.

Ripe for Up-Close-and-Personal Management

When asked to describe their reasons for hunting, most hunters will allude to their love of the outdoors and time away from the hectic pace that has become Corporate America. For many more, hunting provides the ability to put food on their family's table while enjoying the thrill of harvesting it. While the reasons for just getting out and hunting are numerous, one thread remains common throughout the experience—that of "getting close."

As we discussed in Chapter One, the availability of large, contiguous pieces of ground has become scarce as urban sprawl creeps outward, consuming farmlands and family homesteads with increasing veracity. As large tracts of land vanish, so does the ability of hunters to gun hunt.

As tracts shrinks, so does the opportunity to hunt with rifles capable of quickly covering several hundreds of yards. Center fire cartridge hunting has given way to more sublime tactics—that of stick and string or the recurve or compound bow. Typically, all that is needed to be successful using a bow and arrow is a parcel of land not much bigger than an acre or two.

In fact, in countless municipalities across the country, archery equipment is used by governments to reduce and eradicate unwanted and nuisance herds of deer that become public safety issues in metropolitan areas. So crossbows are capable of providing a safe, effective, and ethical deer herd management tool.

Recruiting New Bowhunters

Beyond their obvious advantages in assisting the handicapped hunt, crossbows are tremendous recruiting tools for new hunters. Crossbows are especially well-suited for young hunters and women who physically can't muster enough strength to pull a compound back.

With the use of the rope cocker, just about anyone can cock a crossbow. And if they can't cock a bow with the rope cocker, there are plenty of mechanical-winch-style cockers available that require very little physical strength.

For me, it is ridiculous for any hunter, whether compound or traditional archer, to say crossbows shouldn't be allowed in his or her woods. I am hopeful those who preach such intolerance never get injured—or, God forbid, get too old to physically draw their weapon (imagine that). Who are these people to decide who gets to hunt and how? The level of ignorance exhibited by those who spew such arguments knows no bounds, in my opinion.

Oddly enough, those young people who begin hunting at a young age typically continue on, converting from crossbow to compound bow. This conversion keeps new hunters coming into a sport dominated by geriatric consumers. Keep in mind, there are plenty of very well-organized anti-hunting groups out there trying to snuff out all hunting, everywhere. The more hunters, the stronger our voice will be when we speak out against them.

Common Crossbow Myths

As we've discussed, the advent of the internet has allowed old wives' tales, urban legends, and myths to propagate at an alarmingly rapid rate. It must be the immediate availability of information, albeit right or wrong, that sends these stories screeching across the bandwidths.

I read about a 1,300 pound pig named Hogzilla, that was killed by a teen wielding a handgun. It seems the youth saved a small town from certain destruction in the process. I read with interest about a world-record *typical* whitetail that weighed an amazing 400 pounds on the hoof and green scored right at 340 inches.

Then there's the one about the giant catfish, which is a resident of dams in the United States. You know the one—big enough to swallow a scuba diver whole as if he's a sugar-sprinkled human hors devour. This is great and entertaining reading, for sure. Factual? Of course not.

Growing up in Florida, I can't recall how many times friends swore they had friends who water skied in local lakes and fell off the skis. The stories always ended when the friends fell into a nest of copperhead snakes and were killed by hundreds of bites. Yikes, what a horrid way to go. I'm just glad it's not true.

▲ Rifles and crossbows have very little in common other than a stock and trigger.

So when it comes to the bona fide truth about crossbows, there's quite a bit of misinformation out there—most of which is propagated by those anti-crossbow folks who do not favor the use of crossbows during regular hunting seasons (or any season for that matter).

I'll try and debunk a few here for you.

Myth: Crossbows are guns. Therefore, they are not legal during archery seasons.

Fact: Oddly enough, crossbows are no more gun-like or rifle-like than any compound bow. When comparing a crossbow to a compound, negligible differences in ballistics can be found.

In fact, both send arrows downrange at around 300 feet-per-second on average. With the fastest of compound registering a meager 366 feet-per-second (PSE Omen).

Given these meager speeds, it's hard to imagine, even for minute, comparing crossbow ballistics and their subsequent arrow velocities with rifles whose speeds can eclipse the 4,200 feet-per-second mark (.220 Swift). So given the mathematical data, it is obvious the ballistics of a crossbow simply cannot compare to those of a rifle.

So while comparing crossbow to compound is valid, comparing crossbows to rifles isn't. The bottom line: crossbows share no ballistic similarities with firearms. Finally, the misconception that crossbows compare

▲ The PSE Omen is the fastest compound available, generating a blistering 366 feet-per-second at a ridiculous 27 inches of draw length and 60 pounds of draw weight.

▼ The PSE TAC-15 is the fastest production crossbow, delivering arrows downrange at an impressive 400-feet-per-second clip.

to rifles has led to their exclusion from some states' hunting seasons. However, with knowledge comes new opportunities as state after state adds crossbows to their hunting seasons.

Myth: Crossbows can hold rifle-type arrow groups out to one hundred yards.

Fact: Nothing makes me chuckle more than this one. I've found myself in the middle of discussions that have turned to this subject more than once. And in each instance, the conversation has turned ugly.

While crossbows are engineering marvels that shooting projectiles with amazing accuracy and consistency, they're not, I repeat, are *not* capable of holding tight groups out to a hundred yards. Under the most stringent of conditions, while shooting on an indoor range using weighted sandbags as a rest and a mechanically triggered release, one manufacturer was able to attain some pretty amazing groups. However, I've yet to witness a human capable of shooting a factory setup freehand with this type of accuracy.

While this type of over-the-top advertised accuracy sells more crossbows, it does nothing but frustrate the hunting public when they are unable to repeat such shooting feats. As always, keep in mind that a crossbow is a primitive, medieval weapon. Consider the hype before falling for such outrageous claims.

Myth: Crossbows are easy to use, and very little practice is needed to become proficient with them.

Fact: Having spent thousands of hours shooting both compounds, as well as crossbows, I can say the only real advantage a crossbow has over a compound is its ability to hold an arrow cocked in the ready-to-fire position.

Admittedly, crossbows generally take less time to master than vertical bows, however, it cannot be argued that shooting one is easy. Shooting a crossbow proficiently takes time and plenty of practice. Much like shooting a gun, proper breathing, target acquisition, and triggering are not skills acquired overnight or in a single practice session.

If shooting weapons with fixed sights or scopes were that simple, rifle matches would be a pretty boring affair. Remember, you will get as good as the amount of time you are willing to spend mastering your crossbow and its accessories.

Myth: Shooting a crossbow is fool-proof, requiring little or no skill.

Fact: Ask anyone who has ever spent a significant amount of time nestled behind a cocked crossbow string if crossbows are fool-proof and you'll get a resounding "heck no." The number of ways to mess a shot up is countless.

The myth must have been started by the anti-crossbows folks in an attempt to minimize them as hunting weapons. Think about it; a high-powered rifle is exponentially more powerful and accurate. So okay, how many times have you heard a story about a person missing an animal with a rifle? Plenty, I'm sure.

After explaining ad nauseum how crossbows simply do not compare in any way to rifles and their ballistics, it is easy to see why this statement is downright silly and meritless. As with any hunting weapon, crossbows require time behind them to become proficient, as well as accurate.

My experience has been that crossbows are easier to master than a compound bow. Only time behind the string can provide the experience and confidence to become good. Many mechanical issues can negatively affect a crossbow's accuracy. These include misaligned cocking of the string, stance, breathing, trigger squeeze, a rigid yet relaxed posture, consistent aiming, and repeatable follow through. Not to mention, a crossbower's needs to be able to judge distances correctly to get the proper trajectory to the target.

Myth: Crossbow hunters will deplete the deer herd due to their gun-like accuracy.

Fact: A crossbows trajectory is very comparable to that of a compound bow. Guns, centerfire rifles for instance, shoot bullets at over 3,000 feet-per-second. Compounds and crossbows, on the other hand, are hard-pressed to achieve 350 feet-per-second. Generating these meager terminal velocities offers less than optimal performance.

Arrow flight is degraded by several factors, including wind, humidity, elevation, and most importantly, shooter-induced error. As such, no crossbow shot by a human enjoys gun-like accuracy and certainly will not deplete an already over-populated deer herd.

Myth: Crossbows generate outlandish amounts of kinetic energy.

Fact: Math is math. The average crossbow generates roughly 80 to 100 ft-lbs. of kinetic energy. Now, by comparison, an *average* .30-30 hunting rifle generates more than 1,200 ft-lbs. of kinetic energy. As you can see, there is little comparison between powder-fired rifles and their kinetic energy and a crossbow's kinetic energy.

If a fair comparison was to be drawn, we would compare a crossbow to a compound bow. For instance, if we take a crossbow with an arrow weight of 420-grains (typical), which achieves a terminal velocity of 305 feet-per-second, and run it through our kinetic energy calculator, we find:

$$KE = mv^2/450{,}240$$
$$KE = (420)(305^2)/450{,}240$$
$$KE = 39{,}070{,}500/450{,}240$$

Kinetic Energy = **86.78 ft-lbs.**

In direct comparison, if we take a compound with an arrow weight of 350-grains (typical) and a terminal velocity of 335 feet-per-second and run it through our kinetic energy calculator, we find:

$$KE = mv^2/450{,}240$$
$$KE = (350)(335^2)/450{,}240$$
$$KE = 39278750/450{,}240$$

KE = 87.24 ft-lbs.

So in a real world comparison, our crossbow compared closely to the compound bow with regard to kinetic energy. Notice that neither, when compared to

▲ Barnett Crossbow.

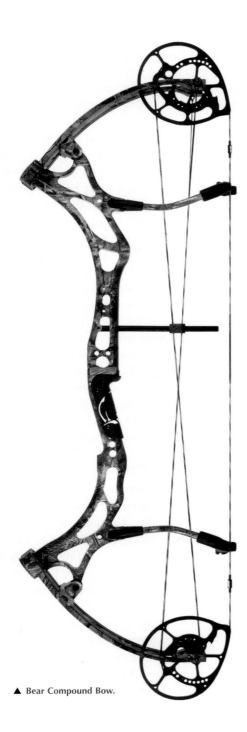

▲ Bear Compound Bow.

the rifle, can hold a candle to gunpowder-propelled projectiles.

Myth: Crossbows are the weapon of choice for poachers.

Fact: I'll be the first to admit that if you knew nothing about crossbows, and believed all the misinformation and hype out there about these weapons, this one would seem feasible. However, as we have seen, they are not gun-accurate, fast, nor capable of scaling large office buildings in a single bound. In fact, for poaching, they would be your *last* weapon of choice.

Crossbows are handicapped by their limited range, reducing poaching opportunities to around 35 yards. *Strike one.* They are a single-shot; should a poacher miss their first shot, they won't get another. *Strike two.* And finally, a crossbow does not have the knockdown power of a centerfire rifle, which grounds an animal where it stands. *Strike three!* I'm pretty sure a poacher wouldn't find it palatable to be following extended blood trails with flashlights (or their spotting Q-beam) at night.

Myth: A crossbow is not a bow.

Fact: This is a true statement—no arguing that. However, a compound is not a traditional bow, and a traditional bow is not a spear. And a spear is not a rock. I'm not too sure what we accomplish by making this comparison. If it is to prove that a crossbow is not a bow, and thus should not be allowed in the woods during archery season, you're spitting into the wind.

In the late 1960s and early '70s when compounds were introduced, no archery traditionalist considered them to be bows. In fact, the argument back then was considerably more heated. However, while a compound is not a recurve, it *is* a bow. And so is a crossbow technically. They are both powered by limbs, which are drawn and captured by the trigger—just as a mechanical release draws and captures the arrow and string of a compound.

Myth: Crossbow hunters are unethical because they do not practice. They wound more deer than they actually kill.

Fact: First of all, the assumption that crossbow users do not practice is pure supposition and has no factual foundation. There is no evidence to support this claim. In fact, most crossbow hunters are very accomplished hunters, many of whom have joined the crossbow ranks after converting from compound to crossbow. In fact, many have transitioned from recurve or longbow to compound and then to crossbow.

It has been my experience that archers are indeed much better and more disciplined hunters than rifle hunters. No offense to gun hunters, but the skill set required to get within a few yards of an animal to harvest it is definitely much larger than that of a gun hunter who must get within several hundred yards to take a shot.

Any number of factors must be taken into account when attempting to get spittin' close. These include scent control, attention to noise, visually blending in with the surroundings, managing your equipment in an efficient manner so as not to spook the animal while drawing on them, and remaining quiet at all costs. Judging distances correctly and placing a shot with a surgeon's precision all factor into the bowhunting scenario. Add to these environmental factors (cold, rain, sleet, snow, and blowing winds). Slipping close using traditional archery tackle sounds downright challenging, doesn't it?

Myth: Crossbow hunters are less ethical, dedicated, and proficient than conventional bowhunters.

Fact: This statement requires one to assume that conventional bowhunters in general are skilled experts who share a common passion and fervor and are inherently ethical hunters. At face value alone, that assumption cannot be supported. It is safer to assume and easier to support the argument that many conventional bowhunters would have greater success and more ethical hunts if they used crossbows.

Myth: Allowing crossbows will overcrowd the woods, decreasing the chances of success for the conventional bowhunter and will threaten the existence of, or at least the length of, archery-only seasons.

Fact: This is simply not true. Harvest data collected by states that include crossbows in their archery seasons show an increase in deer herds, not a decrease. In fact, many states now allow hunters to purchase additional tags to help decrease the herd numbers.

How Crossbows Work

No matter how we look at a crossbow, they're nothing more than a very simple mechanical machine. One that, interestingly enough, has changed very little in the multi-millennia since they first appeared on the scene in ancient times.

All crossbows have the same basic parts, or components. In their most rudimentary of forms, crossbows have: 1) a stock; 2) a riser; 3) cams (wheels on some, but if a recurve, no cams); 4) a trigger; and 5) strings and cables. These are all that's needed to launch an arrow downrange.

Ancient crossbows were designed to offer the user the most "power out" (i.e., arrow and bolt speed) with the least amount of "energy in" from the user. Unlike a traditional bow—one which must be drawn using relatively small muscles of the arms, shoulders, and to a lesser degree the back—the crossbow can be drawn using the largest muscles of the body: the back, legs, and buttocks. Additionally, with a cocking device, cocking a crossbow became very effortless, so much so that just about anyone can now cock one.

Another advantage medieval folks found with the crossbow was that it could be used by any person, no matter their physical size or strength. This is in contrast to the longbow, the power and arrow speed of which was directly dependent on the size of the user. Short users had slower arrows because they had smaller, shorter draw length bows. Meanwhile, larger archers had a distinct advantage with larger, longer draw length bows, faster arrows, and an expanded effective range.

The Physics of the Crossbow

If you boil a crossbow down to its most rudimentary function, you will notice that you have nothing but a very fancy spring. This spring is capable of letting loose via a trigger and nothing much more than that. You see, on a crossbow, the limbs are the "spring." They are capable of being put under tension just like a spring (which actually compresses). When a crossbow is drawn, the limbs are flexed and kinetic energy is stored in them. That kinetic energy is ready to perform work (fancy term in physics) when the energy is allowed to escape. (I hope the physicists out there will pardon my loose use of physics terminology.)

So if we've drawn our crossbow and engaged the trigger, we now have energy ready to be used at our whim. As the trigger is tripped, the string is released, free to travel forward, propelling the arrow down the arrow track and out of the bow as the limbs return to their resting position and original shape. As such, we have just converted the energy from our muscles (which we used to load energy into the machine) into energy sufficient to propel an arrow. Neat stuff.

The draw weight and the power stroke of a crossbow dictates the terminal speed of the arrow. *Draw weight* is the amount energy in pounds (typically expressed in foot pounds and on occasion in joules by mechanical engineers) that must be generated by the user to draw the bow to a fully drawn position (i.e., a ready-to-fire position). The *length of the power stroke*, typically described in inches, is the physical distance the arrow travels while still under the power (or influence) of the string. The longer the power stroke, the greater the distance the bow has to accelerate the arrow, and the higher the draw weight is (and the faster the arrow, which is described or expressed in meters-per-second).

Anatomy of the Modern Crossbow

The modern crossbow is a relatively simple mechanical machine—one much unchanged over the past few decades. Advances in crossbow technology have centered on materials science improvements and advancements. The limbs, for instance, have become considerably more reliable than those of just a decade ago. Older limbs were molded of fiberglass and mat. Today's limbs are laminated with carbon fiber to make them lighter, as well as more efficient, as the internal friction has been reduced.

Trigger assemblies have improved, as much of the engineering in the centerfire rifle has been transferred to crossbow triggers. Just a couple years ago, it was not uncommon to purchase a crossbow and discover a trigger pull of more than 9 pounds. Today's triggers are most commonly around 2.5 to 3 pounds of pull. Several manufacturers are currently working on adjustable triggers; in the next few years, we will see customizable triggers.

Stocks have seen their share of improvements, too. At one time, wood stocks dominated the market. Stocks today are almost all composites that take advantage of advances in injection molding.

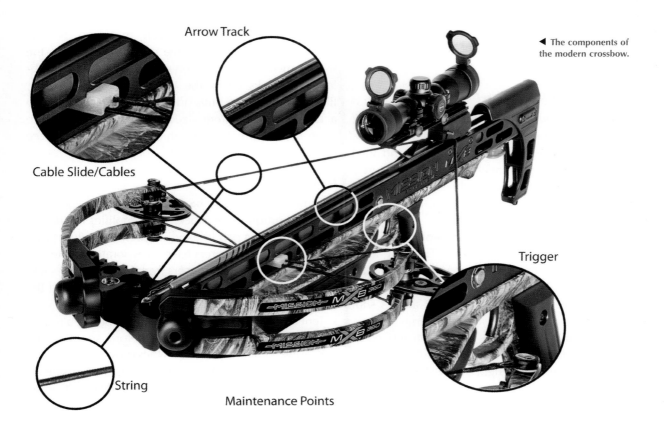

Arrow Track

◄ The components of the modern crossbow.

Cable Slide/Cables

Trigger

String

Maintenance Points

They have been rendered much lighter than their predecessors but are considerably stronger. Several manufacturers are developing carbon stocks that should be available soon. Strings and buss cables have been improved as man-made materials replace natural fibers prone to stretching, rapid wear, and diminished performance in adverse weather conditions.

All crossbows share common components, with a few exceptions. Here is an outline of the common components of the crossbow:

Riser

The riser is typically a machined or cast aluminum assembly to which the limbs are mounted. Risers vary in size and shape. Some are rather large, while others are little more than a set of limb pockets that accept the limbs. In recent years, manufacturers have attempted to reduce the physical size of the riser, as it is a major contributor to the overall mass weight of the crossbow.

Carbon fiber risers have been introduced recently. These molded risers allow the crossbow designer to shift the center of gravity rearward, making it much less front heavy and bettering the feel of the bow and its balance.

Arrow Track/Flight Track/Barrel

Sometimes referred to as the barrel or arrow track, the flight track is the foundation of the crossbow. Typically, these are extruded of aluminum and then machined to exacting tolerances. Some manufacturers actually mold the flight track and the stock as a single unit. While this simplifies manufacturing, it does make for a rather heavy design.

Recently, TenPoint Crossbow Technologies introduced a wrapped carbon flight track. The new track is lighter and stronger than comparable aluminum or molded tracks. Time will tell if the carbon track can withstand the rigors of thousands of arrows shot through these bows.

Precision Shooting Systems (PSE) introduced a crossbow without a flight track. Their PSE TAC series of crossbows utilizes full-length arrows that attach to the crossbow string via an arrow nock. The forward portion of the arrow is supported with an Escalade Sports Whisker Biscuit bristle-style arrow rest. By eliminating the flight track, the arrow leaves the bow with considerably less friction than those of tracked designs.

Trigger

Crossbow triggers are much like those of rifles. However, they do something rifle triggers don't—they hold an enormous amount of draw weight. When the crossbow is cocked and ready to shoot, the trigger mechanism actually captures the string, holding it until triggered. The problem is that the trigger must hold the string weight and be crisp and clean. This is not a simple task.

Most trigger mechanisms come with a safety and an anti-dry fire device, both of which add to the complexity of the assembly. As previously mentioned, crossbow triggers have improved exponentially in recent years as manufacturers have been able to modify them to accommodate all the requirements and still offer a nice touch and feel trigger.

Stock

Crossbow stocks are relatively mundane. Several styles exist, but they all have one purpose: offer the user something to hold onto and shoulder. Thumb-indexed stocks allow the user to grip a bit better, like a pistol. Some butts adjust to different lengths to accommodate different sized users. Cheek plates are often included that can be micro-adjusted for a more custom fit.

Fore Grip

Some molded stocks incorporate the front grip as an integral portion of the stock. This simplifies the design and eliminates a part (the individual forearm/fore grip). Almost all manufacturers have incorporated some type of flair or flange to keep users from inadvertently sticking their fingers into or onto the arrow track and the string.

TenPoint has even gone as far to incorporate a thumb safety that must be depressed before shooting the bow. This eliminates fingers in the arrow track. Barnett Crossbows incorporated a warning etched inside its scope reminding folks to keep their fingers out of the string's path.

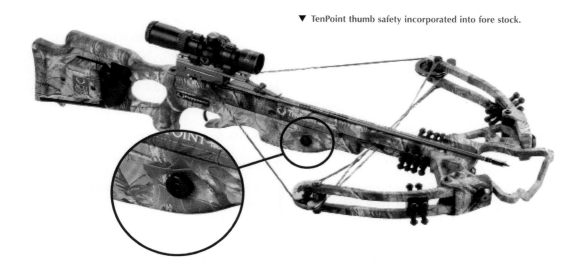

▼ TenPoint thumb safety incorporated into fore stock.

Limbs

The limbs are where the action is. They are responsible for storing the kinetic energy the cams, or eccentrics, transfer when the bow is drawn. Crossbow limbs vary greatly in design from manufacturer to manufacturer. Some are made using molded fiberglass, while others are made by laminating various materials together in layers and then cut and shaped to size.

Reverse Limbs

Several crossbow manufacturers mount their limbs in a reverse manner, which means they are oriented backwards. While this design is odd looking, it is also very efficient. Reverse limbs allow the bow to have a much longer power stroke. A longer power stroke means the arrow is on the bow longer. This permits more energy to transfer and results in faster arrow speeds. Reverse limbs also move the center of gravity backwards, making for delightfully balanced bows.

Draw Weight

Crossbows rely on heavy draw weights to propel arrows. Because their power strokes are very short, considerable draw weight is required to push the arrow. *Draw weight* is the amount of energy, in pounds, required to draw a crossbow string. Most crossbow draw weights range from 100 to 225 pounds.

Power Stroke

The power stroke is the distance the string travels from its cocked position to the at-rest position. Long power stroke bows are generally faster than their shorter counterparts because they transfer more energy into the arrow.

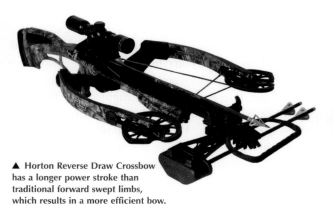

▲ Horton Reverse Draw Crossbow has a longer power stroke than traditional forward swept limbs, which results in a more efficient bow.

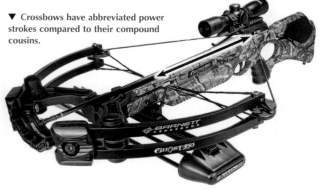

▼ Crossbows have abbreviated power strokes compared to their compound cousins.

Most crossbows have considerably heavier draw weights (usually 150 to 200 pounds) than compound bows. As such, some might think they develop more arrow speed than their compound cousins—that is, more draw weigh in, more power out (i.e., arrow speed). Well, not so fast (no pun intended)—remember what simple physics tell us:

Work (the crossbow pushing the arrow) = Force x Distance

This formula dictates that the amount of distance the force is applied to matters as much as the force applied. Crossbows, for the most part, have very abbreviated power strokes. This is due in part to the requirement of making them compact so they are maneuverable and not too unruly to use. Average crossbow power strokes fall somewhere between 10 and 14 inches. In comparison, compound bows have power strokes in the range of 17 to 23 inches.

Bowstring and Cables

The bowstring on a crossbow holds and launches the arrow. Most modern bowstrings are made of advanced man-made materials that do not stretch. In the past, crossbow strings had a problem stretching after being installed. When the bowstring stretches, it changes the timing and "tune" of the bow. Most crossbow manu-facturers now use prestretched strings with common bowstring materials that include Dacron B50 (stretch equals 2.6 percent), Spectra (a composite ultrahigh molecular weight polyethylene), Dyneema (high modulus polyethylene), Fast Flight S4 (high modulus polyethylene; stretch equals 1 percent), polyester, Kevlar (para-aramid synthetic fiber; stretch equals 0.8 percent), Vectran (a spun fiber of liquid crystal polymer).

Bowstring Serving

The point where the arrow nocks to the bowstring would wear very quickly, leading to failure if not served with an additional wrap of serving material. Serving materials are typically made of nylon.

Cam System

The basic cam system on a compound bow is made of a string, one or two eccentrics (cams), and one or two harnesses or cables. According to Robert Norton and his *Design of Machinery,* "In mechanical engineering, an eccentric is a circular disk solidly fixed to a rotating axle with its center offset from that of the axle (hence the word 'eccentric,' off center)." Some crossbows utilize round wheels, in lieu of "cams." These round wheels serve the same purpose as the cams with lobe profiles.

Cables

The cables are connected to the limb tips and cams (eccentrics). When the string is drawn, the cables take up and pay out cable. As they do, the limbs tips are pulled, flexing them. This flexing stores kinetic energy in the limbs, ready to be released and allowed to propel the arrow downrange.

Cable Slide

On most crossbows, the cables must be pulled downward to keep them from interfering with the travel of the string. They are typically housed in a slot in either the fore grip or in the flight track. Because they are pulled off-center, there is continuous upward tension on the string. The cable slide is designed to capture the cables and allow them to slide along the track with diminished friction. The cable slide keeps the cables from quickly wearing.

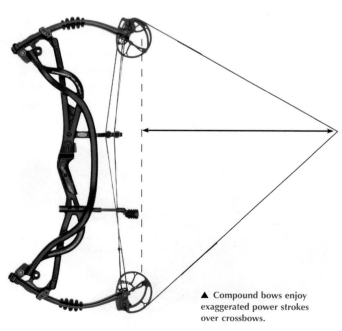

▲ Compound bows enjoy exaggerated power strokes over crossbows.

Cocking Device

Crossbows typically use very high draw weights (see *draw weight*) to propel to propel the arrow. As such, crossbows are very difficult, if not impossible, to cock by hand. A *cocking device* is a simple rope and pulley system that attaches to the bow's string and has two handles on it. The block-and-tackle-style system reduces cocking weight by about 50 percent. Cocking devices are superior to hand-cocking a crossbow as

▼ The TenPoint Crossbow Technologies hand cranking cocking system makes cocking a crossbow very easy for those hunters with limited physical strength.

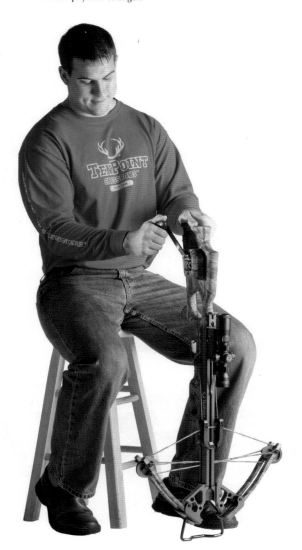

they allow for symmetrical cocking. That is, the string is symmetrically placed in the trigger assembly. When cocking a crossbow by hand, it is very easy to pull the string from somewhere other than the center. This results in the string being crocked and the arrow flying out of the bow cockeyed.

Crank-style cockers are also available. These are much like boat winches. The simple machine mounts to the bow and a handle is turned to crank the string back. Crank-style cockers are very popular with shooters who have limited physical capabilities as they reduce the draw weight even further through a gearing system.

Crossbow Arrows

There is an ongoing debate on what to call a projectile that is shot from a crossbow. Two distinctly different projectiles can be shot; they are 1) arrows and 2) bolts.

Crossbow bolts were designed in medieval times to penetrate the armor of soldiers on the battlefield. They are very short projectiles, void of fletching or vanes. They were constructed of metal and were very, very heavy.

Crossbow arrows, on the other hand, are relatively long projectiles with fletching or vanes and are relatively light in comparison to a crossbow bolt.

Modern crossbows do not shoot bolts. However, some manufacturers, especially arrow manufacturers, refer to arrows as bolts because many laypersons believe bolts are what crossbows shoot. The use of the word "bolt" was initiated by anti-crossbow people and organizations to distinguish crossbows from compounds and traditional bows. These people argued that since crossbows shot bolts and not arrows, they should not be considered for inclusion into archery deer seasons. To keep things simple: when referring to crossbow arrows, they should be called just that—arrows.

Weaver Rail

Most crossbow manufacturers mount a Weaver Rail in the top of the trigger housing. The Weaver Rail is designed to accept accessories, such as scopes. The Weaver Rail is a universally acknowledged standard mounting system.

Reverse Draw Crossbow

Every once in a while, an innovation comes along that changes the face of an industry. In the crossbow industry, that innovation was the reverse draw system. In the last fifty years, crossbows have become faster, quieter, smoother, and cooler than they used to be. It is safe to say that up until this time, there had not been any major crossbow design advancements since kings were defending their lands with cannons and swords.

Then came Jim Kempf's reverse draw design. Kempf, an avid deer hunter and self-taught engineer from Iowa, loves building things. He has always enjoyed designing crossbows. Kempf kept asking himself how he could design a smoother-shooting crossbow that was extra quiet. While sitting in a tree stand one day, waiting for a big buck to walk by, he decided to simply reverse the limb and riser arrangement so the bow string was at the leading edge, thus eliminating the brace height and maximizing the power stroke. Pulling the string into the curve of the limbs instead of away from it maximizes the power stroke and overall performance.

Most crossbows have a short power stroke, so a lot of draw weight is required to achieve enough kinetic energy and speed to bring down large animals. The reverse draw design developed by Kempf results in a generous power stroke, so an extreme amount of speed and kinetic energy can be achieved with less draw weight. With less draw weight comes a smoother-shooting, quieter crossbow.

The power stroke on reverse draw crossbows on the market today is as long as 19.75 inches, which is roughly 5 or more inches longer than a conventional crossbow. With that extra energy, a reverse draw crossbow only needs 100 to 125 pounds of draw weight to produce the same amount of energy as a crossbow with 150 to 200 pounds of draw weight. Because of the increased power stroke, improved speeds can be achieved when even more draw weight is added.

For example, a 165-pound reverse draw crossbow can produce arrow speeds beyond 400 feet-per-second and 160 pounds of kinetic energy. "I set out to create a smooth shooting crossbow that was user friendly, easy to shoot, fast, and accurate. The reverse draw design has solved many of the problems associated with crossbows including lots of noise and vibration," Kempf said.

Other benefits of the reverse draw design include a better balanced crossbow. "The riser on the reverse draw crossbow is centered and balanced in such a way that it is easier to shoot and more accurate than some designs. A centered riser is one of the advantages of this design," Kempf added.

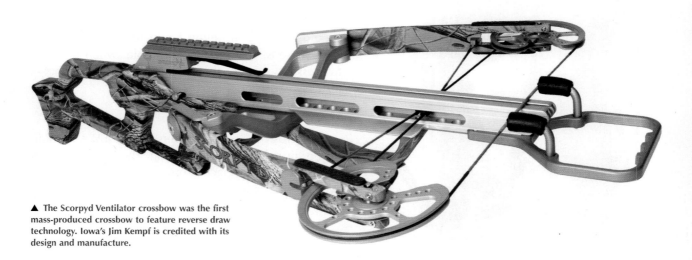

▲ The Scorpyd Ventilator crossbow was the first mass-produced crossbow to feature reverse draw technology. Iowa's Jim Kempf is credited with its design and manufacture.

Another advantage of the low poundage design of reverse draw crossbows is a smoother, crisper trigger with less trigger pull. Many crossbows have stiff triggers that are hard to pull, partially because there is so much weight resting on the trigger. Less draw weight equates to less trigger pull and a smoother trigger.

Since reverse draw crossbows don't require much draw weight to achieve great speeds, women, children, and older hunters who can't cock a conventional crossbow use a reverse draw crossbow. "An 80-pound reverse draw crossbow can shoot up to 310 feet-per-second and produce 75 pounds of kinetic energy. As a result, they can be fun for anyone to shoot because they are so quiet and user friendly. Kids are the future of this sport, and the reverse draw crossbow can help get kids involved in this sport," Kempf noted.

Many believe the reverse draw design is the crossbow design of the future. Many other crossbow companies in the industry have jumped on the band wagon and are licensing Kempf's patent and using the reverse draw design on their own bows. "Several companies are using our design, and I imagine more will do so in the future. The reverse draw design is truly unique and makes for an accurate crossbow, which is perfect for hunting and target shooting," Kempf explained.

When you look at the big picture, the reverse draw crossbow is still in its infancy. Kempf started designing and building them about a decade ago. It will be interesting to watch further reverse draw designs come into the market over the next decade as technology and innovation move forward in the crossbow industry.

Caveat Emptor! **Crossbow Speed Rating Conundrum**

"Blazing, paint peeling, blistering, top-fuel dragster, laser-like, hyper-super-duper fast, mind bogglingly speed," etc., etc., etc., blah, blah, blah. . . . Anyone whose spent any time at all looking at new crossbows has run into these manufacturers speed claims and their speed ratings. Without a doubt, speed ratings for bows are the most exaggerated claims in the outdoor industry.

Warning! For the crossbow novice, let the Latin *caveat emptor* be your guide. Caveat emptor means buyer beware. Wise counsel, indeed. Crossbows are typically speed-rated at the factory by the folks (the engineers) who designed and built them.

Unlike compound bows, with their International Bowhunting Organization (IBO) and Archery Manufacturer and Merchants Organization (AMO) standardized speed test methods, crossbows have no standardized speed testing. As a result, manufacturers post "overly optimistic" (as one archery industry insider described) performance data. Remember—caveat emptor!

Destroying Ourselves from the Inside Out

While attempting to collect photos for this book, I ran into a broadhead collector who, once he found out I was writing a book that included a section on crossbows, refused to help.

His argument was this: crossbows aren't real archery gear and their use should be outlawed. After spending a few minutes on the phone explaining that I was attempting to promote the entire sport of archery, he again refused to help.

I explained that I thought his archaic thought process was the root of how we are destroying ourselves as a group from within our own ranks. He said he didn't care and wouldn't "compromise his principles."

Folks, this is a perfect example of how we are destroying ourselves from within. His thought process draws lines in the sand between archers and weakens our ranks. I explained to him that I have no ill will toward the way he chooses to hunt (traditionalist) even though I would be equally entitled to condemn his archery equipment of choice. Instead, I choose to be tolerant of him and welcome him into the bowhunting fraternity with open arms as a fellow bowhunter.

XII. History of the Crossbow

On occasion, the crossbow is compared to a rifle, and rightly so. There are several striking similarities; however, what is fascinating is the modern gun was designed to *look like a crossbow*. That's right. The rifle was developed after the crossbow. This is a fact sometimes lost in discussions about crossbows.

In medieval times, the crossbow was designed to shoot projectiles, called bolts, through the armor of opposing forces. Modern crossbow design has not changed much since ancient times, but major improvement has been seen in the materials they are built from.

The exact origin of the crossbow cannot be pinpointed as it can be with compounds. This is because the crossbow dates back several millennia, in contrast to the compound bow, which saw its introduction in the late 1960s.

The earliest evidence of the existence of crossbows can be found in Europe. The crossbow here dates back to somewhere around the fifth century BC. In his work, Belopoeica, Heron of Alexandria described the "gastraphetes." Believed to have been invented around 400 BC, the gastraphetes was a large military crossbow. The gastraphetes was built from wood, animal horn, and sinew.

Then, a U-shaped extension was built onto the end of the bow, so the archer could place it against their stomach. These crude crossbows sometime exceeded fifteen feet in length and were capable of launching a forty-pound stone a distance of several hundred yards.

The ballista was another catapult-type weapon developed to launch implements at distant targets. The ballista was designed around Greek gastraphetes. However, it utilized two large levers with torsion springs for power. The ballista was powerful, capable of damaging building structures, thus allowing access by ground troops to fortresses. Smaller versions, capable of piercing body armor, were also developed and called "Scorpios."

An example of the importance of ballistae (plural of ballista) in Hellenistic warfare is the Helepolis, a siege tower employed by Demetrius during the Siege of Rhodes in 305 BC. Several Ballistae were placed at each level of the moveable tower. The large ballistae at the bottom level were designed to destroy the parapet and clear it of any hostile troop concentrations while the small armor piercing Scorpios at the top level sniped at the besieged. This suppressive shooting would allow them to mount the wall safely with ladders.

Crossbows were used in battle and warfare for centuries. Handheld bows proved to be more efficient, capable of shooting more arrows in a shorter period of time. However, longbows required years of practice to become proficient in their use. In contrast, the crossbow was capable of being a deadly, single-shot weapon after only a few days of training. Because they were slower to load and cock than the longbow, archers needed to develop a better system.

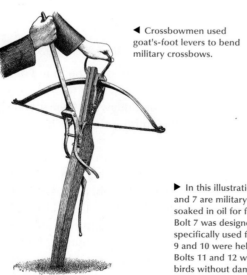

◀ Crossbowmen used goat's-foot levers to bend military crossbows.

▶ In this illustration, bolts 1, 2, 3, 4, 5, 6, and 7 are military bolts. Bolt 6 features tow soaked in oil for firing on ships and houses. Bolt 7 was designed for a slur bow. Bolt 8 was specifically used for killing deer, while bolts 9 and 10 were helpful in killing large birds. Bolts 11 and 12 were used for killing game birds without damaging the game itself.

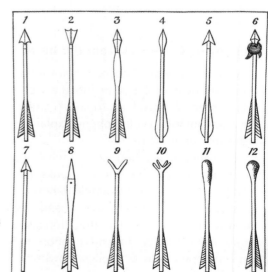

Crossbows evolved to use steel limbs, capable of massive draw weights and incredibly long effective shot distances when compared to longbows. The French are credited with the development of the crossbow *cranequin* and *windlass*. A cranequin was a toothed gear rod and a circular gear with a handle. One end of the cranequin attached to the string and was drawn by turning the hand to engage the gears. Often times, the crossbowmen was protected by a pavise (a long bow-man) while they drew their crossbows.

In Europe, armies utilized both mounted and unmounted crossbowmen in battle. These were inter-spersed with javeliners and archers and placed in the core of the battle formations. Crossbowmen were held in high esteem as professional soldiers, often with receiving higher rates of pay than other foot soldiers. The rank of commanding officer of the crossbowmen corps was one of the highest positions in many medi-eval armies, including those of Spain, France, and Italy. Crossbowmen were held in such high regard in Spain that they were granted status on par with the knightly class.

Flemish crossbowmen in the army of Richard Lionheart were so highly regarded that they were given two servants, two crossbows, and a pavise for protection. One of the servants' duties was to reload

the crossbows for the crossbowmen. A three-man team was capable of shooting up to eight shots a minute. A comparable single crossbowmen was able to shoot three shots per minute, however, they quickly tired and were less accurate than the three-man team.

Pay for crossbow mercenaries was considerably more than for longbow mercenaries. However, the crossbow did have drawbacks in battle. Their strings were subject to damage in wet conditions. In fact, the composite construction of the crossbow also proved to be a hindrance in battle. When it rained, the crossbow was subjected to string damage and the composites were subject to delaminating. Both led to catastrophic failure of the crossbow. The failure of the crossbow was demonstrated in Crecy in 1346, at Poitiers in 1356, and at Agincourt in 1415, where the French armies paid dearly for their reliance upon it. As a result, use of the crossbow declined sharply in France.

After the conclusion of the Hundred Years' War, however, the French largely abandoned the use of the longbow and, consequently, the military crossbow saw a resurgence in popularity. The crossbow continued to see use in French armies by both infantry and mounted troops until as late as 1520 when, as with elsewhere in continental Europe, the crossbow would be largely eclipsed by the handgun. Spanish forces in the New World would make extensive use of the crossbow, even after it had largely fallen out of use in Europe, with crossbowmen participating in Hernán Cortés's conquest of Mexico and accompanying Francisco Pizarro on his initial expedition to Peru. By the time of the conquest of Peru in 1532–1523, he would have only a dozen such men remaining in his service.

Later, mounted knights armed with lances proved ineffective against formations of pikemen (a *pike* is a very long thrusting spear used by the infantry). Pikemen were combined with crossbowmen whose bolts were designed to easily penetrate the mounted knights' heavy armor.

With the invention of the push-lever cocking device, crossbows could be used by soldiers on horseback. The advent of the crossbowmen mounted on horse-back led to the development of new cavalry tactics. These tactics included knights and soldiers advancing

◀ This crossbowman is mounted on a horse, holding a cranequin crossbow, and wearing a quarrel in his hat. Original illustration by P. Lonicerus, 1579.

▲ This was recreated based on an oil painting of the martyrdom of St. Sebastian, 1514. The man on the left is using a cranequin to wind up his crossbow. The man on the right is placing a bolt in his crossbow.

in triangular formations. The heaviest armored knights were placed on the point in front. Some of those on horseback would carry small, metal crossbows for up-close combat. In or around 1525, the military crossbow was replaced by gunpowder firearms, and the crossbow became a weapon of sporting hunters.

In China, the crossbow played an important role in the development of the society. Crossbow bolts dating back to the mid-fifth century have been discovered at a State of Chu burial site in Yutaishan, Jiangling County, Hubei Province.

To date, the earliest evidence of handheld crossbows was unearthed in burial tombs from the fifth century in Shandong. These artifacts were handheld crossbow stocks with bronze triggers. Earlier evidence of crossbows were discovered at Saobatang in the Hunan Province and were estimated to be from around the mid-fourth century.

China is credited by some for developing the first repeating crossbow. These relics were first mentioned in the *Records of the Three Kingdoms* and were found in 1986 in a tomb at Qinjiazui in the Hubei Province. These relics dated to the period of the fourth century also.

In Sun Tzu's influential book *The Art of War* (first appearance dated between 500 BC to 300 BC) refers to the characteristics and use of crossbows. *The Art of War* is an ancient Chinese military treatise attributed

to Sun Tzu (also referred to as Sun Wu and Sunzi)—a high-ranking military general, strategist, and tactician—and it was believed to have been compiled during the late spring and autumn period or early Warring States period.

Early records of crossbow use are rare and unreliable. However, the first such reliable record of crossbow use in Chinese warfare reveals an ambush that took place at the Battle of Maling in 341 BC. Documentation discloses that by around 200 BC, the crossbow was well-developed and widely used in China. Evidence points to the standardization of its parts by the Chinese government and mass production of parts by the government.

Relics of crossbows from 260 to 210 BC have been discovered among artifacts of soldiers of the Terracotta Army at a mausoleum of China's first emperor Qin Shi Huang. Historians also credit the Chinese with the development of the multi-bow arcuballista. Chinese armies additionally receive credit for developing the warfare technique of shooting behind themselves as they retreated. When on the battlefield, the Chinese army, with their superior crossbows, would feign retreat, drawing their adversaries in closer. Once close, they would shoot behind themselves. In modern China, crossbows are used by the police in lieu of guns, as guns are strictly prohibited in China.

In the Islamic world, the Crusaders used crossbows with great success against the Arab and Turkoman horsemen. Modified crossbows, capable of launching arrows great distances against advancing foot soldiers, were used by Islamic armies to defend their castles. During the Crusades, European armies ran up against Saracen composite bows. These crossbows were made of several varying materials including wood, animal antler or horn, and sinew. Each component was glued together into a composite material that was considerably stronger and more dependable than wood. These composites made the crossbows much more powerful and able to cast arrows considerably longer distances with better accuracy.

In Africa, crossbows were introduced to the natives by Portuguese adventurers. Crossbows were used by natives and are still used by native pygmy tribes for hunting. Poisoned arrows are common for hunting small game.

XIII. Shopping for a Crossbow

As I mentioned in Chapter One, crossbows are rapidly becoming hunting weapons of choice, not those of necessity. Once regarded a weapon of those hunters with special needs, crossbows are now mainstream hunting tools. If you're one of the many who would like to get into the game, now is a great time.

The crossbow bug has hit as state after state has incorporated these weapons into their hunting seasons. If it hit you and you're itching to get into the game, here's some tips to help put you get into the bow woods.

There are any number of factors to consider when shopping for your new bow. We're living in very economically stressful times. For most outdoorsmen, cash is a coveted commodity. But don't worry, there are several viable options out there.

When I'm asked by someone to recommend a crossbow, I always tell them there are many things to take into account—it's sort of like someone asking you to recommend a state for them to live in. Here are some aspects to consider when shopping for a crossbow.

Physical Limitation

In my opinion, this is the number one consideration when choosing a new crossbow. Crossbows come in every imaginable size and shape, each built to fulfill a specific niche in the market. If you're in good physical condition, then you will be able to use just about any crossbow out there. However, if you're not the perfect physical specimen (and who is?), consider those factors that may hinder your enjoyment of your new bow. These include cocking the bow and physically maneuvering it when in use.

There are three main ways to cock a modern crossbow: 1) manually by hand, 2) with a rope cocker, and 3) with a crank system.

Manually Cocking the Bow

For those out there with knuckles dragging on the ground, manually cocking the crossbow might be an option. I really don't recommend doing so because there are several drawbacks. First, if you're cocking a 200-pound bow, you'll be pulling two hundred pounds with your bare hands—while holding onto a relatively small string. I shake my head just thinking

about. I have manually cocked a bow on occasion (when I have forgotten my rope cocker), and let me tell you, it is not something anyone should do unless they have no other choice.

Besides being very uncomfortable, manually cocking a bow can result in a string that is cockeyed unless you grab the string exactly in the middle (which is not easily done). When you draw the string back on either side of the arrow track, the string will be captured unevenly. One side or the other will be longer or shorter. This is cause for concern. If the string is captured off-center, it will apply an uneven force to the arrow on launch. This uneven pressure will make the arrow leave the bow crocked. This aberration will continue downrange leaving you with an ill-flying and inaccurate arrow.

Manually cocking a bow does offer a couple of distinct advantages. For one, it is very fast. For those who can, all they have to do is merely reach down and yank the string back. This is opposed to attaching a rope cocker and pulling the bow back or installing a cranking device and manually cranking the bow back. You also do not have to depend on a cocking device, which may get left in a truck, in a bow case, or at your house.

Rope Cockers

Remember, crossbows are both heavy and difficult to cock. The standard default cocking mechanism is the rope cocker. *Rope cockers* are simply a length of rope with two handles and two hooks with integrated pulleys. Rope cockers typically reduce cocking poundage to half of the total draw weight. So if you're cocking a two hundred-pound bow, the rope cocker will require one hundred pounds of pull to cock using the rope cocker.

Rope cockers have several advantages. First, they are inexpensive and every crossbow comes with a standard rope cocker. These manufacturer-designed cockers are built specifically for the crossbow you purchase. In most instances, all you have to do is cut the rope to a length that fits you and your physical stature. Tall individuals typically leave the rope long to accommodate their height. Shorter individuals require a shorter rope length because a long rope will have them pulling the rope cocker above their eyes and chin.

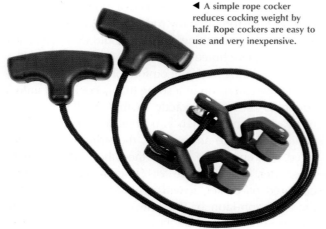

◀ A simple rope cocker reduces cocking weight by half. Rope cockers are easy to use and very inexpensive.

manufacturers have sleds instead of hooks). When the hooks are installed, reengage the reel and turn the crank handle until the string is drawn and locked in the trigger housing. Once cocked, remove the hooks and you're ready to go.

Cranks have several advantages. First and foremost, they are incredibly easy to operate. If you've ever used a boat winch, then you'll have no trouble operating one of these. Secondly, they require next to no physical strength to use. The typical crank requires about five to ten pounds of force to draw the string. Cranks also cock the string symmetrically every time. This is a huge advantage, as the crossbow will shoot the arrow every time in the same way.

There are a few drawbacks to cranks, though. Cranking devices are expensive. Some manufacturers install them permanently on the stock, however, and this adds to the price of the crossbow. Removable cranking devices are bulky and a pain to install each time you want to cock your bow. They, too, are heavy and must be carried with you. Lastly, they are slow. The gear reduction in them that enables them to easily crank back two hundred pounds makes cranking painfully slow. But, in reality, how often are you in a hurry to cock your bow?

Your Hunting Style

Crossbows are built to varying specifications

Spare rope cockers are typically priced at $35 (for a "tricked-out" model) or less. So losing one is tragic only if you're on a hunt in the middle of nowhere without one. Rope cockers draw the bow in a very symmetrical manner; they pull the string back with even tension on both side (as there are two string hooks). This cocks the bow symmetrically, with equal lengths of string locked into the trigger mechanism. This is advantageous because your arrow will leave the bow in an efficient manner, flying true and accurate. The real disadvantage to a rope cocker is that even though they reduce draw weight by 50 percent, pulling seventy-five or one hundred pounds is still difficult to those who are in less-than-perfect physical condition.

Cranking Devices

Most manufacturers offer some type of crossbow cranking device. These are nothing more than a miniature boat trailer winch. Their operation is very simple. To cock a bow using one, simply disengage the reel (spool) and pull the string hooks out. Once enough line is paid out, install the hooks on the string (some bow

▲ This Parker crossbow crank attaches externally to most common crossbows and helps the user cock the crossbow with little fuss.

to address all types of usage. It would be prudent for you to take a minute or two and jot down some of your requirements prior to stepping inside an archery pro shop. If you have an outline of what you'll be using the bow for, then you'll be better prepared to make an intelligent selection.

You should seriously consider what type of hunting you'll actually be doing. That is, How do you intend to use the crossbow and what for? Will you be hunting from a tree stand, ground blind, spot–and-stalking, etc.? If you're going to hunt from an elevated tree stand, the requirements are different than for ground blind usage.

If you tree stand hunt, do you hunt from climbing (portable) tree stands? Ladder stands? Fixed position?

Do you hunt from box blinds? Towers? Each of these has their own set of requirements. For those who hunt tree stands predominantly, short (overall length), compact crossbows are best.

Tree stands have limited room to move in, making them difficult to hunt from if you have a very longbow. You must also put the bow somewhere when it isn't in use (which is the majority of the time). Typically folks rest them in their laps. However, a large, bulky crossbow gets heavy lying in your lap for hours on end. Long crossbows are also difficult to swing and get into position for the shot. Keep in mind that you'll be in the open where the prying eyes of your quarry can easily detect any movement. One last note: short, compact bows are easily hauled up into the stand once there.

▲ A crossbow hunter slips along on a spot-and-stalk hunt. Spot-and-stalk hunting has recently regained popularity as it gets hunters out of trees and ground blinds and puts them on a level playing field with their quarry. Lightweight crossbows excel here.

▲ Tree stands offer crossbowers an advantage as they are able to elevate above the game and execute silent and deadly shots.

If you prefer hunting from a ground blind, you can get away with a larger crossbow because you have plenty of options of where to position it when not in use. Ground blinds are difficult for animals to see into; this affords you much greater mobility inside. Additionally, ground blinds allow you to post your crossbow on a shooting stick or some other type of rest. This means small, lightweight bows are not a necessity.

For the spot-and-stalkers out there, your needs differ. Typically, when spot-and-stalking, shot distances are increased. Additionally, you must be able to slip to within a reasonable shot distance. As such, a lightweight bow is best. However, longer shots require a more solid shooting platform. Heavier crossbows are much easier to aim and hold on target as they are less affected by the wind, user shake, etc. So I'm sure you

▲ Hunting from a ground blind with a crossbow has become extremely popular in recent years as these allow hunters to get up close to game while going unnoticed.

can see a conflict here. You need a lightweight bow that is heavy. What? This is a perfect example of how you must consider all factors, even though some may conflict. When choosing, you will have to compromise certain features to accommodate certain requirements you have.

Price

Prior to shopping for a crossbow, it's best if you decide on a budget. By doing so, you can limit your search to those bows that match your budget. This will eliminate quite a bit of shopping. There is no need to look at bows retailing for $1,200 if you've budgeted $500. Most crossbows come as packages—that is, they have a scope, quiver, rope cocker, and sometimes arrows and a sling. So in most instances, you'll need buy only a bow because accessories aren't needed,

which differs from the process involved when purchasing a compound bow (i.e., a sight, stabilizer, release, etc.), or dare I say, a rifle (i.e., scope mounts, scope, sling, etc.).

What to Buy?

I firmly believe you should buy a crossbow from a reputable manufacturer. Keep in mind that crossbows are a very significant investment. There are plenty of companies out there that manufacturer bows—and many others that buy crossbows from China, put their name on, and market them in the United States. Some are good, some aren't so good.

I recommend you research all of the various manufacturers prior to buying. Look into their warranties and service record. Most of this can be done online and in the various forums.

Be aware that there are manufacturers with very recognizable and storied names who build very poor products. A crossbow is only as good as the company who stands behind it. I will refrain from mentioning the brands that are great and the brands that aren't. Just do yourself a favor and look into each before deciding which one to take home with you.

Where to Buy?

The internet and eBay has changed the way hunters buy equipment. However, I want to impress upon neither as a good place to buy a crossbow. Now I'm sure I just infuriated the large box stores who sell online, but hear me out.

Let's say you buy a crossbow from an internet dealer and have a problem. In most cases, you'll be asked to ship the bow back to the retailer. This will be an über-costly proposition, as postage is ridiculous nowadays (typically about $55 one way from the post office and a bit more via UPS or FedEx). Not to mention, you'll be without your bow for quite some time. You're also trusting your costly investment to someone you've never met at a destination you've never or will ever see.

The same applies to buying on eBay. I'm not against shopping on eBay. I am, however, against buying a new bow (or used, for that matter) anywhere you cannot shoot it first prior to making your purchase. Buying a used bow online is a prescription for disaster. I have heard plenty of horror stories from folks who have bought bows online who suffered afterwards.

I urge you to visit a local full-service dealer. These independent dealers have your best interest at heart. They have established their businesses in your communities, and they aren't going anywhere. These full-service retailers are also great sources of information regarding brands and models that you may be interested in. They deal with the factories on a daily basis and know which brands are better and more reliable.

I also recommend you shoot every crossbow you are interested in prior to buying. There is relatively little chance you can select the right crossbow for you without first shooting it. Shoot them all, then compare each brand and model. Whittle down the field to the one that fits you best physically and budget-wise.

Even if you narrow your search to the specific make and model, I still would not recommend buying the bow online. Yes, you will save a few dollars, however, the dollars you save are not worth those you will lose dealing with a retailer who can only be reached via telephone or email. Local dealers are there for you when you need them.

One last word to the wise: should you shoot all the local dealers' bows, decide on a model, and then purchase it online, you're doing so at your own risk. Should you have an issue and try to take it to the local dealer, they will be less than thrilled about working on your bow. While none of these dealers would ever admit that, it is just the way it is.

I made this mistake a long time ago when buying a compound, and I paid dearly in the long run. I bought a popular bow from a large catalog house and saved $50 over the local dealer's price. When I took it in there for service, he was downright rude (he has since gone out of business). I asked him to have a look at it because I was having an issue with its tune. He said "Sure, but there is a $50 minimum on all services, and that includes looking at your bow." Touché. He'd lost out on the $50 in profit from selling me that bow and was hell-bent on making it back in service.

Let me state for the record: this pro shop's attitude was very unusual. I have never encountered anything like this since and have never had anything but pleasant experiences at local pro shops. In fact, local pro shops are owned by some of the best folks on Earth. Additionally, the people they have working there are the most knowledgeable technicians you'll find when it comes to archery equipment. Buying a bow from a local dealer is the equivalent of going to your doctor: You develop a personal relationship with them over time and they are always willing to help out no matter your predicament.

I would also not recommend buying from large box stores. Again, the retail price there will be lower than at the local pro shops. However, the "experts" and "techs" they have working there are typically not the best. This is, of course, not true of all large retailers, but in most cases, it applies.

I've been in these retailers before and heard the tech behind the counter giving directions to the local archery shop. Then he suggested the customer take his bow there to get it serviced. While many of you will disagree with me on this, I am relating to you my experience after being in the industry for decades.

Performance

You will be well-served to consider the performance metrics of each bow you consider buying. These include speed, shot noise, mass weight, and vibration. Also, look at the bow's fit and finish. While most people are enamored by really fast bows, speed is not the only necessity. Keep in mind that any bow that claims over-the-top speeds is a high-performance machine.

Remember: Physics dictates that to get that much speed out of a machine, something has to be compromised. In many cases, the bows that generate blistering top speeds are apt to be challenged to stay together too long. This is, of course, a general statement of what I have experienced over the years. "Speed" bows are much like top-fuel dragsters, built for short blasts of incredible performance yet less than reliable in the long run.

When shopping performance, keep in mind that manufacturers often fudge (lie about) their numbers. In fact, they fudge their numbers by a considerable amount. During my years of testing equipment, I have never found one bow that could attain the top speed printed on the outside of the box, the manual, or on the website. Never. As we've discussed in earlier chapters, these numbers are exaggerated by as much as 30 or 40 feet-per-second. Remember, "up to 400 feet-per-second" includes those speeds from 0 to 400 feet-per-second. So 300 feet-per-second falls in that "up to 400" range.

Mass weights of crossbows are also routinely exaggerated. Most bows weigh several ounces—and in some case, pounds—more than the advertised weight. I understand why they do this, but it seems blatantly dishonest.

Features

Prior to stepping into a pro shop, make certain you know what features you'd like. I highly recommend an anti-dry fire device. These keep you from triggering the bow when it doesn't have an arrow in it. Believe it or not, this happens often on bows without this device. Keep in mind that you must fire the bow to uncock it. Many an absent-minded user has pulled the trigger on a bow to uncock it without an arrow in it.

Firing a bow sans an arrow leads to immediate destruction of the crossbow, as the cams, limbs, and string literally explode. The anti-dry fire device keeps this from occurring. I have dry-fired a crossbow just once. After experiencing the horrific sound and feeling of unleashing all that stored energy on nothing, and having the bow come completely apart in my hands, I have never done it again.

Trigger

A nice trigger makes shooting a pleasant experience. A bad trigger makes shooting laborious. The only way to decide if you like a trigger or not is to shoot it. I once tested a crossbow that had a trigger that was advertised as "the best in business" (this was not the exact claim, but close). When checking it out, I found it had over a full inch of travel and horrible creep. It also took 10 pounds and 9 ounces to pull. A good trigger should have a pull of 2 to 3.5 pounds. It was almost like they knew their trigger was so horrible that they advertised it as the "best" in hopes of folks overlooking how bad it really was.

Quality of Components

As mentioned earlier, most crossbows come as a package with a scope, quiver, arrows, rope cocker, etc. When buying a package, make certain you check these accessories before finalizing your purchase. Never assume they are good to go without looking at them.

Scopes, for instance, can vary greatly when it comes to quality and clarity. Some package bows have a wonderful bow, but the scope is absolute junk. What good is a great crossbow that you can't aim because the scope is so bad? Likewise, a great crossbow can't shoot consistently if it is launching crappy arrows. Check the components and make sure they are quality pieces.

XIV. Crossbow Use Regulations

While crossbow use is becoming more prevalent as states ratify their use through legislative action, not all states approve of crossbow use. The following is provided as a guideline for each state and their general regulation regarding crossbow use.

Prior to using a crossbow in your state, check with local, state, and federal regulations regarding their use. The following is not provided or represented as an all-inclusive review of crossbow regulations.

Below is a summary of crossbow hunting regulations in the United States. This page is intended as a quick reference, and as such, there may be details about regulations in your state that are not mentioned here. Regulations change frequently from state to state. Please contact your local DNR (or equivalent) office for the latest information and regulations.

You may notice that for some states, I have simply provided a link. Please visit these websites to learn more about the rules and regulations in these states, as they are fairly detailed and specific.

Alabama

Crossbows are legal for all persons during the entire deer-hunting season. *http://www.outdooralabama.com*

Alaska

You may use a crossbow in any hunt that does not restrict weapons. "Certified bow hunters only," "bow and arrow only," or "muzzleloader only" hunts or areas specifically exclude other weapons, including crossbows. Scopes and other optical enhancement devices are not permitted. *http://www.state.ak.us*

Arizona

Crossbows are legal only by permit for disabled hunters. *http://www.gf.state.az.us*

Arkansas

Crossbows must have at least a 125-pound pull and a mechanical safety. Deer, turkey, and bear hunters are required to use arrowheads at least 7/8-inch wide. Poison may not be used on arrows. Magnifying sights may be used. Crossbows are not allowed for taking elk. *http://www.agfc.state.ar.us*

California

California law states that "a crossbow is not archery equipment and may not be used during the archery season." Unless you have a Disabled Archer Permit, crossbows may not be used during any archery season or during the general season when using an archery-only tag. *http://www.dfg.ca.gov*

Colorado

Crossbows are legal for all hunters during gun seasons and for handicapped hunters during archery season. *http://www.dnr.state.co.us*

Connecticut

Crossbows are legal only for disabled hunters by permit. *http://www.dep.state.ct.us*

Delaware

Allowed during all deer seasons. Crossbows used for deer hunting must have a minimum pull weight of 125 pounds, be manufactured after 1980, and have a mechanical safety. Crossbows may be equipped with a scope. It is unlawful to transport a crossbow on or within any vehicle while the crossbow is in the cocked position. Deer may be hunted with crossbows provided hunter orange is displayed when it is also lawful to hunt deer with a gun. Check with state regulations for additional details. *http://www.dnrec.state.de.us*

Florida

The Florida Fish and Wildlife Conservation Commission (FWC) passed a new rule that will extend zonal crossbow seasons by a month, thereby running concurrently with archery season. Check state regulations for additional details.

Crossbars are allowed during all deer seasons. Crossbows used for deer hunting must have a minimum pull weight of 125-pounds, be manufactured after 1980, and have a mechanical safety. Crossbows may be equipped with a scope. It is unlawful to transport a crossbow on or within any vehicle while the crossbow is in the cocked position.

Deer may be hunted with crossbows provided hunter orange is displayed when it is also lawful to hunt deer with a gun. *http://myfwc.com*

Georgia

Crossbows are legal in all seasons. *http://www. gohuntgeorgia.com*

Hawaii

Crossbows are legal by special disabled permit only. *http://www.hawaii.gov/dlnr*

Idaho

Crossbows are legal in big game seasons restricted to short-range weapons. They are permitted for use during archery season by disabled persons with a permit. *http://www.fishandgame.idaho.gov*

Illinois

Crossbows are legal for disabled hunters by permit only and hunters over the age of sixty-two with permits and tag. *http://www.dnr.state.il.us*

Indiana

Crossbows are legal hunting equipment during the late archery deer season for antlerless deer. Deer hunters may use crossbows to harvest deer of either sex only in the late archery season.
http://www.in.gov/dnr

Iowa

Crossbows are permitted for disabled hunters with a permit. Residents seventy and older may purchase a statewide antlerless deer license to hunt with a crossbow.
http://www.iowadnr.com

Kansas

Crossbows with a minimum draw weight of 125 will be allowed in regular firearms deer and turkey season. *http://www.kdwp.state.ks.us*

Kentucky

Crossbows may be used in designated weeks. See state regulations. Hunters using crossbows during a firearms deer season must follow all firearm season restrictions, zone guidelines, and hunting requirements in effect during firearms seasons. Crossbows are also permitted during muzzle-loader only season.

Disabled hunters with a permit may use a crossbow to hunt deer during the bow-only deer season. *http:// fw.ky.gov*

Louisiana

The Louisiana Department of Wildlife and Fisheries Commission now has the ability to establish a bow and arrow only season and a bow and arrow and crossbow season in special deer hunting seasons. *http://www. wlf.state.la.us*

Maine

A crossbow hunting license is required for hunters sixteen years of age or older to hunt bear with a crossbow during the bear hunting season or to hunt deer with a crossbow during the open firearm season on deer. A resident or nonresident ten years of age or older and under sixteen years of age may hunt with a crossbow if that person holds a valid junior hunting license (no crossbow license required). *http://www. maine.gov/ifw*

Maryland

Crossbows may be used to hunt only deer, with the exception of special crossbow permits for disabled hunters who may pursue all game legal for a vertical bow. All hunters may use crossbows for four weeks of archery season and four weeks of gun season. *http:// www.dnr.state.md.us*

Massachusetts

Crossbows are permitted for disabled hunters with a permit. *http://www.masswildlife.org*

Michigan

http://www.michigan.gov/dnr

Minnesota

Crossbows are permitted for disabled hunters with permit. *http://www.dnr.state.mn.us*

Mississippi

Crossbows are permitted for use in the archery season on state game land. Check state regulations for details. *http://www.mdwfp.com*

Missouri

Crossbows are classified as firearms and are permitted during firearms season. Disabled hunters with a permit may use a crossbow during archery season. *http://www.mdc.mo.gov/hunt*

Montana

Crossbows are legal during only gun season. There are no provisions for disabled hunters. *http://fwp. mt.gov/hunting*

Nebraska

In Nebraska, crossbows have been allowed as legal equipment during firearm seasons for decades. Starting in 1985, crossbows were allowed during the archery season for those with a permanent disability that prevented them from drawing a bow.

All restrictions on crossbows have been removed, including the disability provision and draw weight. Crossbows are legal archery equipment for big game (deer, antelope, elk, turkey, and bighorn sheep). *http:// www.ngpc.state.ne.us*

Nevada

Crossbows are legal for all during firearms season. *http://www.ndow.org/about/pubs/pdf/huntregs/ appbro/index.shtm*

New Hampshire

Crossbows are legal for all hunters with a crossbow hunting permit during firearms season. Disabled hunters may use a crossbow pursuant to disabled hunter regulations. *http://www.wildlife.state.nh.us*

New Jersey

http://www.state.nj.us/dep/fgw/njregs.htm

New Mexico

Crossbows are legal sporting arms for cougar, bear, deer, elk, pronghorn, javelina, Barbary sheep, persian ibex, oryx, turkey, and bighorn sheep. Hunters that qualify with a permanent mobility limitation may use crossbows to hunt waterfowl and upland game. Sights on crossbows shall not project light or magnify. *http:// www.wildlife.state.nm.us*

New York

Crossbows can be used during the regular firearms seasons in the Northern and Southern Zone, during the late muzzle-loading and bowhunting seasons, and during the January firearms season in Suffolk County. *http://www.dec.state.ny.us*

North Carolina

North Carolina allows the use of crossbows anytime bow and arrows are legal weapons. *http://www. ncwildlife.org/fs_index_04_hunting.htm*

North Dakota

Crossbows are not legal, except with a permit from the Game and Fish director. Contact the Department for additional information on crossbow regulations. *http://gf.nd.gov*

Ohio

Crossbows with a draw weight of no less than seventy-five lbs. and no more than two hundred lbs. are legal arms for archery, firearms, and muzzle-loader seasons. *http://www.dnr.state.oh.us*

Oklahoma

http://www.wildlifedepartment.com/huntregs.htm

Oregon

Crossbows are illegal. *http://www.dfw.state.or.us*

Pennsylvania

http://www.pgc.state.pa.us

Rhode Island

Crossbows are legal only for hunters who possess an official adaptive aid/crossbow permit obtained through the DEM division of licensing. *http://www.dem.ri.gov*

South Carolina

Crossbows are now allowed in archery seasons. *http://www.dnr.sc.gov*

South Dakota

Crossbows are legal for disabled hunters during archery season. *http://gfp.sd.gov/hunting/regulations/ default.aspx*

Tennessee

Crossbows are legal during archery, muzzle–loader, and firearms season. *http://www.state.tn.us/twra*

Texas

Where the open season is designated as "archery," only legal archery equipment that are specified as crossbows stated on the website may be used. *http://www.tpwd.state.tx.us*

Utah

Crossbows are legal only for disabled hunters by permit. *http://www.wildlife.utah.gov*

Vermont

Crossbows may be used by disabled hunters (with permit) for any game that may be taken by bow and arrow. *http://www.vtfishandwildlife.com*

Virginia

Crossbows are legal to use by any hunter. A crossbow license is required during an archery season. *http://www.dgif.state.va.us*

Washington

Crossbows are approved for use by qualifying archers with disabilities. *http://www.wdfw.wa.gov*

West Virginia

Class Y permit holders may hunt with a crossbow in established archery seasons. *http://www.wvdnr.gov*

Wisconsin

Crossbows are legal for disabled residents and non-residents under Class A, B, C, or crossbow permit and residents aged sixty-five and older. *http://www.dnr.state.wi.us*

Wyoming

Crossbows are legal during archery seasons and must have a ninety-pound minimum draw weight, shoot a sixteen-inch bolt, and cannot be cocked with a leverage-gaining device. *http://gf.state.wy.us*

XV. Hunting with a Crossbow

I'm flabbergasted at how many folks think hunting with a crossbow is easy. I think this a result of the anti-crossbow crowd preaching and lobbying against crossbow usage. These groups claim hunting with a crossbow is the same as gun hunting. As we have discussed in detail, this simply isn't true.

Whether you're a crossbow advocate or less than enthused, rest assured that crossbows are here to stay. Each year, thousands of loyal compounders and rifle hunters are making the conversion. There's any number of reasons for shouldering a crossbow. First and foremost, they are just plain fun to shoot and hunt with. If you're ready to take the plunge into the crossbow world, there are a few things to keep in mind when making the switch.

Different Strokes

Crossbows have abbreviated power strokes compared to their compound counterparts. As such, they require more draw weight to achieve efficient arrow speeds. Draw weights on crossbows typically range from 150 to 200 pounds. These heavyweights require mechanical cocking devices to draw. In hunting situations, this can be a detriment should the first shot on an animal be errant. Should you miss, chances are you won't get another try as re-cocking is neither a quick nor quiet affair.

Out Distanced

Most of us have heard the comparison of crossbows to guns. While widely purported by the anti-crossbow folks, it's a myth. Crossbows are primitive hunting weapons, and in most cases, a compound rig will outperform a crossbow.

Compound arrows weigh around 350-grains, while crossbow arrows tip the scales at an average of 425 to 450-grains. While the feet-per-second speeds are comparable, arrow trajectories are not. Crossbow arrows have considerably more drop than compounds

▲ Two crossbow hunters head out for an afternoon hunt.

▲ A crossbow hunter readies for the shot, an exciting moment for anyone who loves the thrill of the hunt.

and are typically less forgiving with their over-spined arrows.

Versatility

As a whole, crossbows are more versatile. Compounds are draw-weight and draw-length specific and sighted-in for one individual shooter. Crossbows can be sighted-in and used by any number of shooters.

In addition, once they have been cocked, anyone capable of holding the bow can shoot it. And, in most instances, crossbows are ambidextrous, so anyone, whether right- or left-handed, can enjoy shooting the same bow.

Physical Considerations

While crossbows have certain advantages, they're not without flaws. Most crossbows are physically heavy, making it a chore to lug them to and from hunting stands. They're also oddly balanced, with a completely unique feel from a rifle or compound, rendering them difficult to maneuver for the uninitiated.

When aiming a crossbow using a scope, your field of view is diminished over a traditional peep-and-compound pin-sight combination. Aiming with both eyes open on a compound affords a panoramic field of view, in contrast to the crossbow's claustrophobic tunnel vision view through a scope.

Ground Gainer

Crossbows do shine in several hunting situations. When assigned to ground-blind duty, they're particularly hard to beat. A ground blind's low overhead clearance has plagued almost every compounder who has spent time giving it a go from the ground.

In many cases, the upper limb has the frustrating tendency of contacting the blind's roof. Add to the mix the wingspan of the compound shooter, and fore and aft operating room rapidly becomes a treasured commodity.

In contrast, crossbows are bulky horizontally and not vertically tall, making them particularly well-suited for ground blinds. In addition, most crossbow shooters are efficient at shooting while sitting. Typically, a simple prop and seat make for a formidable crossbow shooting setup for ground blinds.

Crossbows excel in ground blinds for other reasons. For example, they need not be drawn during the heat of the hunt. When on a level playing field with your

▲ A crossbow hunter rattles for whitetail while hunting from the ground. Crossbows give ground hunters a distinct advantage as they do not have to be drawn like compounds.

quarry, staring eye-to-eye while drawing a compound may spook your game. Crossbows can be drawn long before an animal appears and can be held comfortably (and motionless) until the perfect shot presents itself.

Heavyweight Champ

Most crossbow novices will immediately notice how heavy the arrows are compared to compound arrows. Crossbow arrows typically weigh about seventy-five to a hundred grains more than their compound cousins.

With the added mass, crossbow arrows deliver considerably more kinetic energy to the target. This added oomph can mean the difference between a marginal shot resulting in marginal penetration or punching through for an ethical kill.

Business End

Whether compound or crossbow, if you're going to hunt, you'll need a compliment of broadheads. In most instances, getting broadheads to fly true out of a crossbow is more difficult than using a compound. As such, many crossbowers resort to mechanical broadheads.

While mechanical designs have progressed, they're still a compromise on performance. Mechanicals require more kinetic energy to deploy the blades upon impact, rendering them less efficient than their fixed-bladed counterparts.

While it may take a bit more tweaking to get fixed-blade heads to fly perfectly, do yourself and your game a favor and opt for these.

Up Close and In Your Face

Hardcore rifle hunters are blessed, for the most part, as they aren't harnessed to the confines of a climbing tree stand or musty ground blind. Rifle careers are often spent aloft in the comfort of box blinds with hissing kerosene heaters keeping toes from numbing and bones from rattling together.

▲ Hunting with a crossbow from an elevated tree stand takes some practice. Contrary to popular belief, it is nothing like hunting with a compound or a rifle.

Hey, I've spent countless hours shivering in a stand overlooking what appeared to be a promising plot of ground below. Well, too often, these spots have turned sour, leaving me to contemplate the origin of the universe or guessing how many yards it is to that stump or that funny colored rock over there.

Crossbow hunting, in direct contrast to rifle hunting, is an up-close-and-personal affair filled with emotional highs and lows and countless hours of boredom. You'll find yourself wondering why you're not home fixing the leaky gutter until you realize you're not home fixing the leaky gutter because you are hunting in an effort to avoid fixing the leaky gutter.

So as a rifle hunter, you've probably come to fancy the ability to "reach out and touch" animals at a distance. Well, when crossbow hunting, this just isn't going to happen.

My Crossbow Indoctrination

I've spent forty years pursuing game with various sticks and strings—at various times recurve, longbow, and compound—but I had never felt the urge or need to settle in behind a crossbow arrow. In fact, the thought of shouldering one of these mechanical albatrosses was an insult to my identity as a hardcore "bowhunter."

When it was introduced more than forty years ago, Holless Allen's controversial compound bow met strong, often violent opposition from bowhunting traditionalists. These traditional folks were hardcore hunters who saw the compound as an invasion into their hunting world with what they considered to be an unethical hunting weapon.

After all, using a traditional bow meant you would draw, aim, and shoot quickly and instinctively and sans the hoopla of a compound. There was no let-off with a traditional bow as there was with compounds. In fact, the bow became more difficult to draw as it was pulled farther back. And there were no sights! These compounds had sights that were, to most traditional people, much like "a rifle sight." And the let-off of the cams was definitely cheating as one could hold a bow at full draw much, much longer than it's heavily handicapped traditional relatives.

Now, contrast today's crossbow to those early compounds. They are easy to draw using a crank or rope cocker. They require no holding force and have an elaborate aiming system (a scope, in most cases). Oh, let's not forget their triggers. So it is easy to see how compound archers feel crossbows are unethical weapons, just as traditionalists thought compounds were so many years ago. But we all know how the opposition to compounds turned out. Today, they are the gold standard in archery hunting.

The Mississippi Delta

It's been four decades now, since the invention of the compound. And now the inclusion of crossbows in archery seasons infuriates modern traditionalists, which, ironically, include the compound crowd.

Admittedly, I was one of those compounds guys adamantly against the legalization of crossbows as hunting weapons. Now, I wasn't against their use by the handicapped hunters; I just didn't want these high-powered weapons poaching my deer in my woods.

That all changed when I was invited to hunt the black water swamps of the Mississippi Delta. When details of the hunt were disclosed, and I learned it was a crossbow hunt, I was apprehensive and more than a little skeptical. In fact, I made a few excuses so I wouldn't have to go and hunt with one of those crossbow things. But, ultimately, I went.

I had plenty of preconceived notions of my hunt. I figured I'd show up, shoot a couple range arrows, and head out and start piling the animals up under my stand. Really? After all, my thinking was that crossbows were easy to use and much like rifles. Wrong.

During the hunt, I spent hours waiting for my "easy" crossbow shot opportunity, but it never materialized. While spending time on the stand, I began to understand there were many dynamics unique to crossbows that were foreign to compounds and traditional gear.

What I learned in the Delta, and what's been confirmed on other crossbow hunts, is that hunting with a crossbow *isn't* easy. Nor is it remotely like hunting with a gun, as some critics would have you believe. In fact, the only distinct advantage I could find a crossbow provides over compounds is the string capture.

An Odd Dynamic

I'm often asked by other avid bowhunters what it's like to hunt with a crossbow. I always preface my remarks with, "You're not going to understand what

▲ Rattling from a position on the ground.

▲ Crossbowers ready their equipment for the hunt.

I'm about to tell you until you have actually tried one for yourself." Then I go into my dissertation on hunting with crossbows. For me, crossbows are *more* difficult to hunt with than compounds. Here's why.

Awkward Handling

Crossbows handle unlike compounds or rifles. Compounds and rifles have a wonderful balance. Their lines are geometrically pleasing and the center of gravity rests near the middle of each. Neither have appendages extending off them like crossbows have.

Crossbows are hindered by several design defects. To be efficient, they must have very stout limbs to provide enough kinetic energy to the arrow to propel it fast enough to kill. They must also have relatively long stocks to accommodate as long of a power stroke as possible. These long power strokes are still abbreviated compared to compounds.

Crossbows must be built in along two distinct lines: that of a stock and that a pair of outriggers, or limbs, mounted perpendicular to the stock. This setup lends itself to poor balance and horrible handling. So when aiming or handling the bow, the user is in a constant fight with the crossbow to control it.

Now, try and use this awkward handling machine in the confines of an elevated tree stand, one with a narrow standing platform and limited space. Crossbows require considerably more space to aim as you must find space for the limbs, which stick out side-to-side, and the stock, which protrudes forward. As you can imagine, you quickly run out of space to efficiently maneuver.

Weight

Crossbows are heavy. The average compound tips the scale at about four pounds. A rifle weighs between six and eight pounds. The typical crossbow, however, weighs around seven to eleven pounds. Also keep in mind that rifles and compounds are balanced neatly, while crossbows are not. Wielding this kind of awkward weight is counterproductive to ease-of-aiming.

Cocking

Crossbows must be cocked. No matter how easy they are to cock, in most instances, it's done on the ground. Anyone who has tried to cock a crossbow in a tree stand knows it is a tricky proposition—one I would not recommend trying. Rifles don't need to be cocked. Compounds require being drawn, of course, but this is a very natural movement and second nature to anyone who hunts with a compound.

The need for cocking a crossbow on the ground makes it a one-shot weapon. Not to mention, recocking a crossbow takes an enormous amount of movement and is very loud. Neither of these are conducive to attempting a second shot should you miss an animal with your first. You cannot simply slip another arrow in a compound and redraw or shuffle another cartridge into a rifle.

Carrying

Having to lug around a clumsy and awkward crossbow can be tiring. The end.

Forgiveness

Crossbows are very unforgiving weapons. Due to their short brace height (needed to maximize the length of the power stroke), an arrow is on the string for an extended period of time. During this time, any shooter-induced error will be multiplied by the crossbow, resulting in an errant shot.

Crossbow Hunting from Ground blinds

Elevated tree stands are the most popular method of hunting whitetail deer for many reasons. However, the average hunter is now fifty-four years old. For the older hunter, climbing a tree simply isn't an option.

Enter the ground blind. I have been told by a reliable source that ground blind sales now rival those of tree stands. I would imagine this is a reflection of the aforementioned average age of a hunter.

Advantages

Ground blinds have several distinct advantages over elevated tree stands. First and foremost, they don't expose a hunter to a fall scenario. Since they are on the ground, there is no place to fall to. Tree stands up twenty or more feet are dangerous. Should you fall from a tree stand, the results are never good. Of course, you should always be wearing your fall protection, but we won't go into that because this section is about hunting with crossbows.

Next, ground blinds are very easy to set up. In fact, it takes a matter of seconds to pop open a ground

▲ Erecting an AmeriStep ground blind is as easy as popping the blind open and securing the hubs. Most ground blinds open in a matter of seconds and secure as quickly.

▲ AmeriStep ground blind erected and secured.

blind. Now I understand when discussing "ground blinds," this encompasses a wide variety of styles including those you build using trimmings, blow downs, and anything that's readily handy. For now, I will keep my focus on commercially available pop-up ground blinds.

Another advantage with ground blinds is they can be erected anywhere. As long as you have, or can make, an opening large enough to place the ground blind, you can set it up. There is no reason to have to search for the perfect tree in which to place your tree stand. For me, this is the single greatest attribute of ground blinds. I have on plenty of occasions gone to the ground blind when an appropriate tree isn't available for climbing. A ground blind has many times saved the day for me when chasing animals.

Ground blinds also are great when inclement weather sets in. On occasion, you'll find yourself on the trail of a nice animal, only to have the weather turn rainy or worse. When this happens, hanging out in a tree stand simply isn't an option. Ground blinds shine when the sun doesn't, providing recluse from inclement weather.

Ground blinds also excel if you plan on videoing your hunt. They have roomy interiors, large enough to house both the hunter and the camera person. For this reason, ground blinds allow you to stretch out when

nothing is happening, unlike tree stands where real estate is at a premium.

Disadvantages

Now ground blinds do have their drawbacks. But if you know these prior to heading out, you can minimize them. First and foremost, ground blinds limit your ability to see. While most are designed with windows around the entire circumference, these cannot all be opened at once. When opening all the windows, you are silhouetted horribly inside. A ground blind will attract the stare of prying animal eyes; and if you have all the windows open, animals will easily pick you out.

Ground blinds can also be hot when the wind is idle and the sun is beating down on them. The sun also pulls the moisture from the ground; the moisture rises inside the blind, making it horribly humid. They can also be loud, amplifying any sound that is made inside of them. Think of a ground blind as a stereo speaker turned upside down. Any noise inside reverberates off the inside and is projected out of the windows.

Ground blinds, depending on brand and manufacturer, can be difficult to hunt out if you have a long wing span. This is especially noticeable when attempting to draw a compound bow. Tall hunters will find their bow hand is up against the front wall and their elbow is against the back wall, creating what is obvious not the best shooting scenario. The "shoot-through" windows (which are now so popular) in most cases really do affect your shot, no matter how much the manufacturer claims they won't.

Executing a shot from a ground blind can be exceedingly difficult. Remember, your shots are restricted by the window opening size and positioning. It's also restricted by where the animal is standing in relation to the openings. I have on plenty of occasions been unable to execute a shot from a ground blind because the window isn't lined up with the animal. This is especially true with a compound bow, which requires such a wide area to draw and aim in.

Crossbows, however, have a distinct advantage as they are considerably more compact at full draw. In many instances, you can simply navigate the crossbow into position to shoot, then get your eye behind the scope and trigger the arrow. Of course, you must make certain the limbs clear any obstacles that might get in the way of the shot. Having a limb hit a ground blind cross brace or anything else can be catastrophic.

Crossbow Hunting from Tree Stands

Hunting from an elevated tree stand with a crossbow can be exhilarating as well as frustrating. As mentioned previously, they provide several advantages for hunters. They also have several disadvantages too.

Advantages

Tree stands provide a crossbow hunter with an elevated platform from which they can see all that is going on around them. Elevated tree stands allow the hunter to observe how the animals in their immediate area move. It also allows them to determine if one buck is using the same area or trails on a consistent basis.

I'm often asked about my philosophy on hunting tree stands. In particular, folks want to know if I am able to go out to a new area, do a bit of scouting, and

▲ Navigating a crossbow in an elevated tree stand is not an easy task. Most hunters find it difficult until they've spent a few hours getting accustomed to the handling of the bow.

then hang a tree stand and bag a deer. This hardly ever happens.

For me, when I'm selecting a tree in a new area, the best I can hope for is to get inside a perimeter I think a target animal is traveling. That is, I feel I'm successful if I can make an educated guess as to where the deer will be and where they're going. Yes, on occasions I have been spot-on with my tree stand placement and scored the first time out. But in most cases, I fail to get anything. Anyone who tells you they can go out and scout an area, select a tree, and then hunt and score is being less than honest with you. No one I have ever met can do this all the time.

My goal when finding a tree is to establish a place where I can begin to narrow down my area once in the tree stand. With this new knowledge, I can then move my tree stand incrementally to slowly close the gap between me and the deer. It may take several sessions in a tree stand to get an idea of where to move to. In fact, this is almost always the case. It is for this reason I typically use climbing or portable climbing stands. They offer me the ability to move, scouting from the tree tops every time I change positions.

While using the chess analogy when discussing hunting is tired, it is applicable. In the game of chess, your first move never puts your opponent in checkmate. Instead, it takes plenty of maneuvering to get into position for a checkmate. This is so true of bowhunting. You make a best guess decision on the sign you find, then set up your stand (or ground blind). Then following each hunt, you move according to what you observe. Hopefully, in the end, after several position changes, you're able to close the gap and kill the animal you're hunting.

In addition to assisting you in narrowing down your hunting area, elevated tree stands afford you a bit more leeway with movement. If set up right, your tree stand should offer you some cover from an animal's eyes perhaps from the tree trunk placed between you and the animal or from climbing and slipping into the canopy. Both options offer a concealed spot to observe around your area without animals seeing you.

Tree stands also allow you to fool a deer's nose—not completely, but I'm confident you can get away with more scent-wise from a tree stand than a spot on the ground. If the breeze is blowing your scent and you are fifteen feet up, chances are that scent will be dispersed before it has a chance to filter down to the ground below. In a ground blind, though, your scent starts at nose level and remains there as it travels through the woods.

Disadvantages

On the down side, tree stand shots are never easy. With every foot you climb vertically, the target on the animal shrinks. The higher the climb, the more acute the shot angle. For those who like to climb above, say, fifteen feet, the target size is cut in half and grows smaller as you climb higher. Judging distances from an elevated perch is also very difficult, becoming more difficult as you climb higher and your perspective changes to one very unfamiliar. This is the reason companies offer angle compensating range finders. These have built-in inclinometers that measure the shot angle and adjust the target distance read out to provide the "real" distance to the target.

Hunting elevated is also considerably more physically demanding than hunting from the ground. Climbing up a tree is an athletic endeavor, one not suited for those who may not be in the best physical condition. It is a good idea to take a serious inventory of your health prior to attempting to climb. Not to mention, many times you'll be climbing in the dark, with inclement weather conditions that negatively affect the tree like snow, ice, and rain.

Portable climbing tree stands are also very noisy as you ascend and descend. If you are climbing in the early pre-dawn hours, the sound of bark crunching and falling to the forest floor below sends most animals hoofing into the next zip code as this is not a familiar sound for them, nor is the sight of a flashlight up twenty-feet in the air.

Tree stand hunters are also exposed to inclement weather, which quickly takes its toll on the body. The cold is especially hard on hunters above ground level. Tree stands provide no recluse from the wind and its chilling effects. While sitting in a tree stand, your entire body is exposed. By being exposed completely, the wind zaps the warmth from your body as it swirls around your entire exterior. This alone is why it is so hard to remain warm in an elevated tree stand.

Semipermanent tree stands, like lock-on style and ladder stands, require less physical exertion to climb, however, the more often they are used, the less effective they become as hunters rarely play the wind right each time out. Once your position has been discovered by animals, they will avoid the area.

Spot–and-Stalking with a Crossbow

The tactic of spot-and-stalk has regained favor over the past decade. Once a staple of hunters, it had been slowly abandoned with the advent and popularity of tree stands and now ground blinds. But when cable hunting shows depicted spot–and-stalking techniques, it slowly regained popularity.

For the crossbower, spot-and-stalking can be an exhilarating technique to ground great animals. It is also a very physically demanding technique, one not suited for the faint of heart. When spot-and-stalking

▲ Tactical spot-and-stalking with a crossbow is incredibly exciting. Slipping in close enough to game to harvest them is a challenge suited for the most skilled of woodsmen.

with a crossbow, several considerations must be taken into account.

First and foremost, when stalking with a crossbow, you must consider its physical weight. Walking, slipping, and crawling alone can be very exhausting—even for those in great physical condition. Add to the mix a heavy boat anchor and the task quickly becomes exponentially more difficult.

There are several accessories that can make the chore of lugging a crossbow along a bit easier. Notice I said "easier," not "easy." No crossbow is easy to carry over rugged and unruly terrain. However, if you plan on doing much stalking, you should take into account a crossbow's physical size and weight prior to making a purchase. There are several compact bows that can be handled with relative ease.

▲ A hunter traverses difficult terrain with his crossbow in hand.

XVI. Crossbow Accuracy

The modern crossbow is an incredible machine. It is capable of holding tight groups at mind-boggling shot distances. Crossbows are simple mechanical machines capable of uncanny accuracy. With the rarest of exceptions, crossbows can replicate the same shot over-and-over again. It is, after all, a machine.

So when folks (manufacturers) talk about how accurate a crossbow is, I'm always perplexed as to what they're talking about. This is due to the fact the crossbow isn't what makes errant shots; it's the human in the shot equation. In fact, it's the "man-to-machine" interface, specifically on the part of the shooter, that introduces shooting errors into the crossbow.

Becoming a great shot with a crossbow isn't that difficult. All you have to do is understand where the inconsistencies come from and minimize or eliminate these. Then consistency will be yours. While that may sound simple, can we really eliminate or minimize human error and attain shooting perfection. Sounds impossible, doesn't it?

A Better Shot

I channeled Mark Beck, former IBO World Crossbow Champion, and asked him to provide the basics of the

▲ Mark Beck, former IBO World Crossbow Champion and crossbow designer.

efficient crossbow shot. The crossbow design engineer outlined the fundamentals of the quintessential crossbow shot.

Beck identified five basic areas shooters should concentrate their attention on when attempting to develop a better shot. These are: 1) the grip; 2) the post hand; 3) trigger pull; 4) stance; and 5) the follow through.

Grip

Crossbows come in varying sizes and shapes. In fact, it seems there are as many different crossbow designs as there are shooters. There are plenty of options when it comes to grips, too—from narrow to fat and everything in between. Most crossbows today have some type of rear pistol grip, so that's where we will start.

According to Beck, you should center the base of your thumb on the back of the pistol grip. Beck said most people grab the pistol grip like a hammer or a hatchet. This grip leads to over-gripping the crossbow and sends arrows off course as the shooter induces unwanted torque.

When grabbing a grip in this manner, it is natural to squeeze tightly when releasing the arrow. Beck said "It's a natural reaction when releasing the shot to grab the grip like you're twisting the throttle of a motorcycle. By doing so, the shooter is subconsciously thinking they are steadying the shot, but they're not. Just the opposite; they're adding torque." Beck continued, "If you manhandle the grip or forearm, you'll torque the bow—*relax*."

Post Hand

For many, it's difficult to understand how much their front hand, or "post hand," contributes to shooting accuracy. While it may seem as if their front hand does little, this simply is not true. The post hand is the foundation for the forward section of the crossbow. In fact, the less control you have on the forward portion of the bow, the more errant your shots will be. When thinking of the forward hand, think of it as a pillar or foundation of the crossbow.

For any structure to be solid, it must have a sound foundation. For the crossbow shooter, this can only be achieved with a well-trained front post hand. Beck said, "Your front hand, or the 'post hand,' supports the bow—it doesn't manipulate or control it."

▲ A firm but gentle grip solidifies the hold and makes for good aiming.

Beck recommended an old, time tested traditional recurve bow shooting trick for the front hand: point your finger toward the target. "With your palm up, point your middle finger at the target, relaxing the hand," he instructed.

Beck warned against grabbing the forearm of the crossbow, as this leads to jerking the bow in one direction or another. Both negatively affect the way the arrow is delivered to the target. Beck explained, "Grabbing the forward stock with the post hand rolls the limbs over and pulls the shot."

Trigger Pull

Another important component of a solid crossbow shot is a quality trigger pull. For those rifle enthusiasts out there who use match grade triggers that are silky smooth and a delight to shoot, forget what those feel like. Crossbow trigger technology hasn't reached that level yet.

There is a distinct difference between a crossbow and rifle trigger. Crossbow triggers must hold the weight of the bowstring back in the ready-to-release position. As you can imagine, a two hundred-pound draw weight crossbow string lashed to a trigger makes for some binding issues, such as pulling forward on the trigger mechanism at around two hundred pounds. This puts a crossbow trigger at a distinct mechanical disadvantage.

Rifle triggers, however, are not holding any physical weight. They simply must overcome spring tension to fire. "A great trigger pull starts with a great trigger," said Beck. "Triggers should be smooth, with minimal creep and about three to four pounds of pull. Light triggers lead to punching while heavy triggers tense shooting muscles and spray arrows everywhere."

▲ A relaxed, open post hand keeps fingers clear of the string and cables and makes aiming effortless and torque-free.

Beck offered us an anatomy lesson when counseling on trigger pulls: "Your index finger has two points of articulation in it. These are joints where the finger can articulate or move. Pull the trigger using the middle of the finger—never the fingertip. Tip triggering involves two articulating finger joints. Triggering with the middle of the finger uses one joint, eliminating potential triggering variability."

Stance

A solid shooting foundation is vital to ultimate accuracy. The entire shooting fixture (your body) must align to support the bow. Beck advises, "Feet should be shoulder width; keep the bow close to your body, propped by the post hand with the forearm braced on the rib cage. Shift your weight slightly forward onto the front hip. After some experimenting, you'll find a natural feeling position supporting the bow using the entire body."

Follow Through

Beck said that follow through is crucial to the perfect shot sequence. "The perfect follow through is one void of body or head movement. The arrow rises and falls, with the shooter picking up the arrow in the scope and watching it strike the target."

Additional Advice for a Better Shot

Although Beck highlighted the five most important areas to focus on when trying to improve your shot, there are other aspects of the shot that you must also improve if you hope to become a more accurate bowhunter.

Trigger Feel

Triggers are rudimentary mechanical devices. As such, they operate in a repeatable, predictable manner. Because they are predictable, to shoot consistently, you must practice enough to be familiar with their pull and travel.

It is safe to say that no two crossbow triggers act the same. Each trigger has its own idiosyncrasies; each is as individual as the individual shooting the bow. It is simply silly to think we can pick up a crossbow, shoot a few arrows through it, and be good to go. It takes time and practice to learn a crossbow. Prior to heading out to hunt with one, ethical hunters will get to know their bow and its characteristics intimately.

When the opportunity comes to harvest an animal, they will do so in a methodical, well-practice manner, delivering a precise and deadly shot that terminates an animal in the fastest and most humane manner.

Hunters who pull their bows out the day before the season opener and shoot it once or twice to "see if it's still on" aren't ethical and should not hunt.

Use a Rest

Crossbows are as accurate as the shooter. If you miss your target, it is *you* who missed, not the crossbow. Crossbows are physically heavy, weighing more than twelve pounds (depending on brand and model). To compare, an average rifle that weighs around nine pounds (a military issue sniper rifle typically weighs around fourteen pounds).

For the most accurate shooting, I recommend you take a rest when shooting to maximize your accuracy. A good rest comes in all different shapes and sizes. They can be the railing on your tree stand, the bench in your shooting house, a backpack, or something as simple as a rolled up jacket. If you're a spot-and-stalk enthusiast or a ground blind hunter, a commercial shooting stick, monopod, or bipod are wonderful rests. If you shoot kneeling or sitting, then your thigh can be a solid prop.

Real-World Practice

Shooting in the backyard off a picnic table is great for thoroughly learning and understanding the idiosyncrasies of your crossbow. It is, however, not good practice for hunting. While in the field, shots rarely present themselves while you are in the correct shooting position. As such, your practice should include real-world shots. If you routinely hunt from an elevated tree stand, you should practice the different shot scenarios that may arise while hunting. These would include standing, sitting, leaning against a tree, etc.

▲ Using a post (something to rest the bow on while shooting) greatly improves accuracy. Here, a scrap piece of wood makes a great impromptu brace.

and down a tree or a tree stand exposes you to falling, and there is simply no reason to practice from exaggerated heights. Practicing these shots while at ground level will make them natural when you are above the ground.

During your practice sessions, you will discover things that would preclude your success in the field before they happen. For instance, you'll find that the new monopod you bought as a rest will not work in a tree stand, as there is no place to put the foot in a tree stand. It's better to discover these things now than when you're attempting to level your sights on a trophy animal in the field.

Sighting In

Modern crossbows all come with a scope or red-dot scope. It seems manufacturers have discovered crossbowers desire the entire package versus having to purchase them separately. I am of the opinion that as the sport matures, more top-shelf accessories will be available for users to purchase separately and install on their rigs themselves, much like compounds with their exhausting options for sights, rests, stabilizers, slings, vibration dampers, etc.

Your new crossbow (or old one for that matter) will require you to install the scope and sight it in. Now, this may sound a bit overwhelming for the newbie, but know that it is a very simple operation that requires little mechanical skill.

Follow the Directions

No matter the type of scope you have, whether red-dot, multi-reticle, illuminated, etc., they mount in similar manners. To simplify the installation, the best advice you can get is this: follow the manufacturer's instructions for its installation. Each scope has idiosyncrasies which must be tended to.

Nuts and Bolts

With your scope mounted according to the manufacturer's instructions, you're now ready to sight it in. Prior to getting all excited about tweaking your scope, word to the wise: read the instructions on how it adjusts. I can't tell you how many arrows I've lost thinking I know how the scope adjusts only to discover it is backwards from the last one I sighted in.

▲ This is a Bloodsport brand crossbow pod. The pod is designed to be mounted to the arrow quiver or sling mounting holes. The ball and socket design allows it to swivel for easy aiming. It may also be used as a forward vertical grip for a more natural shooting position and to keep the fingers out of the string.

While plenty of authors recommend you climb up in a tree stand to practice, I say don't bother. To practice these shots, simply set a tree stand on the ground next to a tree. Then practice these shots while on level ground. This does two things: First, it allows you to shoot hundreds of arrows without climbing up and down after a few shots. Second, it allows you to spend plenty of time in the stand safely getting used to hunting scenarios at heights. Repeatedly climbing up

▲ Mounting a scope is simple as long as you follow the directions.

Learn to Use Your Sight

The step-by-step instructions that follow will help you sight in your crossbow and make the most of your real-world practice.

1. Make sure your target is placed on a solid surface and that it is capable of stopping your arrow once it hits. Make certain that no one or nothing is beyond the target or within range of the bow. This means that you should have a clear zone that extends well beyond your target in case you launch an arrow past the target. This happens with regularity when sighting in a crossbow.

A quality target designed specifically for crossbows is a must. Do not use a target designed for compounds, as these will not stop crossbow arrows. Quality bag and foam targets are available. Make certain they say they are designed for crossbows.

2. Cock the crossbow according to the manufacturer's instructions. With an arrow installed, stand about ten yards from the target. Keep the crossbow pointed toward the target at all times. It is recommended that you use a prop or post (i.e., bench, shooting rest, prop, shooting stick, etc.) to sight in your scope as this provides a solid rest from which to shoot.

3. Put the crosshair of the sight in the center of the target. Gently squeeze the trigger.

4. Make certain to concentrate on a quality trigger pull. Repeat this with three arrows to get a grouping. Note: Your arrows should be very close to each other. If they are not, your shooting form is poor. You must achieve a tight grouping to move onto the next step.

5. With a tight grouping, adjust the scope according to the manufacturer's instructions for windage and elevation. Once you've made adjustments, shoot three more arrows.

6. Once you're hitting the bull's eye, move back to twenty yards. Adjust the scope until you're hitting the bull's eye at twenty yards. *Never* start at a distance beyond ten yards because you *will* miss the target. Once satisfied with your accuracy at twenty yards, move back to the distances you'd like to set the remaining reticle lines to.

Maintenance

Crossbows and their components receive an enormous amount of stress and strain when shot. They are small machines that exert an incredible amount of force to propel an arrow at amazing speeds. As I've mentioned before, I think of crossbows like I think of top-fuel dragsters. Top-fuel dragsters are built to run wide open for a very abbreviated amount of time. Once they have made their pass down the track, they are taken to the pits and rebuilt from head-to-toe. While crossbows aren't quiet that radical, they do require routine maintenance to keep them thumping arrows accurately.

Particular areas of interest to keep an eye on are: 1) the trigger; 2) strings and cables; and 3) the arrow track or arrow rail.

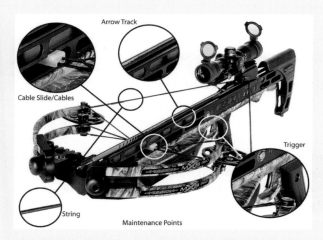

▲ Areas to keep an eye on when performing maintenance on your crossbow.

First, while the trigger is enclosed for the most part, it is prone to collect dust and dirt. Keeping triggers crisp and clean is as simple as referring to the manufacturer's manual for regular maintenance tips and suggestions. In most instances, this routine maintenance is nothing more than a visual inspection and the application of a light lube.

Strings and cable are the most common components that fail. Both of these are exposed to enormous forces, both at rest and while being drawn and shot. As such, they should be given the respect they deserve. This means regular inspection and lubing. I know of one manufacturer that recommends the string and cables be re-waxed every five shots. While this may be a bit extreme, you get the point. The strings and cables must be given love and attention.

I have personally had three strings break on my crossbows. One broke while it was in the case; the other two broke while the bow was at full draw. In every case, the result was traumatic. There is nothing pleasurable about having a bow string break. In fact, when the two strings broke during use, other parts and pieces of the bow blew off and went flying. One of the strings was getting a bit worn, and I really should have replaced it. The other one broke without notice.

Just as with the trigger maintenance, it is best to follow the manufacturer's recommendations for routine maintenance. This includes cleaning and waxing. Should a string or cable get dust or dirt on it, you *must* clean the string. These foreign objects get into the string and cut the individual fibers until the string ultimately fails.

Lastly, arrow tracks or rails receive plenty of friction as the arrow speeds down them and off to the target. Most arrow tracks are made of anodized aluminum. Anodized aluminum is a very hard and durable surface. However, graphite and carbon arrows are very abrasive. So it is common for these to wear the anodizing off the arrow track, making it rough.

To avoid this situation, apply lube as per the manufacture's recommendations. On crossbows with molded arrow tracks, it is of paramount importance you keep these well-lubed. The plastic used in molding is subject to wear as the arrows rub along them as they are fired. An unlubed plastic/composite track will groove quickly and may negatively affect the bows accuracy. As is always the case, follow the manufacturer's recommendations for cleaning and lubrication here.

Note: It is recommended you get familiar with the performance of the bow at close distances prior to attempting to set the distant reticle lines. It takes several shooting sessions to become familiar with trigger pull and the way the bow handles.

Understand Target Distances

When I first started shooting, many, many years ago, I struggled with hitting the target. If I had a target face at a given distance, once I zeroed in on it (after several arrows), I could consistently plow the bull's eye. It was just zeroing in on it that was the problem.

My early days were spent behind a recurve. To this day, I still shoot traditionally on a regular basis. As you know, recurves have no sights, no real arrow rests per se, and no trigger. The string is pulled by fingers and aiming is done instinctively. You must visually acquire your target, assume a balanced stance, draw the bow quickly, and release the arrow in a snap-like fashion.

With any of the hunting string sports—hunting with compounds, traditional recurves, longbows, or crossbows—judging distance is the single most important skill to acquire. In days gone by, hunters had to rely on their naked eye to meter their distance from their intended target. Those who judged distances poorly were typically skinny because they were rarely able to kill anything to eat.

▲ A laser rangefinder takes all the guess work out of difficult shots, both uphill and downhill.

When shooting a modern crossbow, judging distances is of paramount importance. Crossbows have limited ranges. No matter how "advanced and cutting-edge," they are still primitive weapons. The arrows are affected by aerodynamic drag and gravity. Aerodynamic drag slows the arrow's forward progress while gravity pulls the arrow toward the ground (and so the flight decays).

Any projectile has a flight path. Projectiles, in the classic sense of aerodynamics, are propelled by a force, the kinetic energy that has been stored in the limbs by the drawing of the bow. When shot, they continue along their flight path until their trajectory is degraded. It is this degradation of the flight path of the arrow you see as the arrow arcs.

Understanding this arc is what leads to a clear understanding of target distances. You see, as target distances increase, the arc of the arrow increases. Close targets, say to thirty yards, are struck prior to the arrow's trajectory degradating significantly. This is the reason targets are struck more accurately at shorter distances. The trajectory is flat and is not a huge consideration. However, as target distances increase, so does the arrow's arc.

Compensating for this is what makes longer shots more difficult than shorter shots. When looking through a crossbow scope, you see three or four graduated lines. Each line is a bit farther apart than the line directly above it. This is how the crossbow compensates for increasing target distances (or the arrow's arc). As the distance to the target increases, you must place the corresponding scope crosshair on the target. Farther targets require the bow be held at a higher angle, thus elongating the arrow's arc and ability to strike distant targets.

Plenty of rifle hunting converts are misled into believing crossbows shoot flat and therefore are capable of striking targets at exaggerated distances. After our previous discussion, it's obvious this is not the case. Additionally, many non-crossbow shooters feel crossbows are capable of exaggerated range. This is, again, not true because crossbows are very inefficient mechanical machines with very limited energy to propel the arrow over great distances.

Calculating Target Distances

Few bowhunters have an eye good enough to routinely judge the distance to the target. Any number of factors can complicate the process. For instance, when judging distance over a long distance with little or no visual landmarks (i.e., trees, rocks, streams, etc.), the eye has trouble determining the distance to the target. These landmarks allow the brain to calculate the distance to the near field object. The brain is capable of using the landmark as a reference point. That is, we typically know how big a tree is. With this as a reference point, the eye can project past the landmark and predict how far a distant object is by comparing it the closer known object.

When predicting distances in a confined area, multiple landmarks tend to confuse the eye and brain, and the opposite happens: you misjudge the distance due to optical overload. There is good news in all this, however. Modern rangefinders take all the guesswork out judging distances.

Rangefinders

These electronic gems fire a laser to the target, measure its reflectance, and calculate the distance to the object. And, I might add, they do so with uncanny accuracy. Typically rangefinders are accurate to within a foot or two if the target is easily attained.

I consider myself a really good judge of distances, having spent years shooting 3-D tournament archery. Even with hundreds of hours of practice judging distances on 3-D tournament courses, there always seems to be a target or two I misjudge—badly. And when I say misjudge, I mean I am capable of misjudging by several yards on a target that might be as close as twenty-five yards. In bow distances, this can be the difference between missing the vitals completely and a well-placed shot.

Laser rangefinders are inexpensive compared to a miss. Their prices range from as little as $100 for a

Calculating Arrow Speeds via Arrow Weight

Plenty of folks ask what affect increasing or decreasing the weight a crossbow arrow has on arrow speed. Well, there is a general rule of thumb for calculating this. To do so, you'll need to know your arrow's weight and its speed in feet-per-second (fps). Armed with these, you can calculate a change in arrow weight.

A crossbow's power or draw weight remains static for the most part unless you do some tweaking that in most cases will degrade your bow's performance, or worse, blow it up. So if the power is the same, we can take an arrow weight of say 420-grains and 305 fps of velocity.

420-Grains @ 305fps

$KE = mv^2/450,240$

$KE = (420)(305^2)/450,240$

$KE = 39,070,500/450,240$

$KE = 86.78$ ft-lbs.

We can now back the numbers out, and solve for "v," (or *velocity*), by plugging in some numbers as follows:
Subtract 50-grains (or however many grains lighter your arrow will be):

86.78 (our previous KE) $= 370v^2$ (our 420-grain arrow minus 50-grains)/450,240

$370v^2 = 39,071,827$

$v^2 = 105,599.53$

$v = 324.96$ fps

So we see a net increase in arrow speed of about ~20 fps.

For a heavier arrow, of say 50-grains, add 50 to our 420-grain arrow:

$86.78 = 470v^2/450,240$

$470v^2 = 39,071,827$

$v^2 = 83,131.546$

$v = 288.33$ fps

So we see a net decrease in arrow speed of about ~17 fps.

▲ Spinning an arrow in your palm will visually show you if they are straight.

base model to several hundred for models that have an elaborate array of bells and whistles.

The Mechanical Machine and Accuracy

As we have discussed, crossbows are mechanical machines capable of incredible accuracy. However, they are still mechanical machines that propel projectiles. As such, they are limited by their tolerances and build quality. Several mechanical things can affect arrow flight and your ultimate accuracy.

Wheel or Cam Timing

On those crossbows equipped with cams or wheels (recurve crossbows do not utilize wheels or cams), their "timing" can get out of sync. Crossbow wheels and cams are lashed or synced together via the cables.

When the bow is drawn, the wheels or cams rotate in perfect unison as the limbs flex. This concert of sorts loads the bow with the energy it will use to launch the arrow. These wheels or cams can get out of sync for various reasons. However, the most common is asymmetrical string or cable stretch.

Stings and cables are made of various fibers, some natural, some man-made. No matter which one is used, they both will stretch over time as they are under substantial tension. As they stretch, the wheels or cams rotate, making the bow become out of tune (i.e., the wheels or cams are not rotating together uniformly). This situation leads to different flexure rates of the limbs, and the arrow is launched awkwardly and errant arrow flight occurs.

Most manufacturers now engrave or mold (depending on wheel or cam material and coatings) timing marks on their wheels and cams. These marks allow the user to visually check whether the cams are rotating in time with each other. If your bow is equipped with such marks, it is best to check them on occasion to make sure everything is operating as the manufacturer meant it to. If you feel your bow is out of time, I highly recommend you visit a local pro shop and let a trained technician have a look at it.

Arrows

Crossbow arrows are made of either carbon or aluminum. Both materials, though very strong and sturdy, are capable of bending. That may sound logical for aluminum, but carbon arrows can bend, as well—especially when they are exposed to high temperatures (i.e., like those inside a car).

Beyond bending, variations in spine (the relative stiffness of an arrow) can lead to errant arrow flight. Variations in spine occur more often on carbon arrows. Aluminum arrows are extruded and typically have a very consistent seam and wall thickness. These constants in manufacturing make aluminum arrows a bit more consistent in flying than carbon models.

However, aluminum arrows are prone to bending and creasing when they come in contact with other arrows in a target. A bent or imperfect arrow can lead to poor target groups and should be checked often for straightness. If you suspect an arrow is compromised, set it aside to save yourself hours of frustration when

shooting. Flexing a carbon shaft prior to each shot will also allow you to check for splintering or any damage that might have occur in the previous shot.

Loosey Goosey

A modern crossbow has plenty of tiny fasteners that hold it together. These range from screws to bolts to cap heads to any number of other fasteners. Rest assured, if it can be tightened, it will come loose on a crossbow. Crossbows generate an enormous amount of vibration each time they are shot. As you can imagine, this will loosen hardware in short order. Always check all the hardware to make sure it is tight.

Arrow Retention Spring

An oft-overlooked portion of the shooting machine, the arrow retention spring is designed to place downward pressure on the arrow to keep it in place prior to the shot. On occasion, one can get a bit bent or moved off-center. Inadequate (or excessive) pressure can lead to errant arrows.

More Human Interaction

I often say that a compound or crossbow will shoot only as good as the individual who is behind the string. I firmly believe the skill level of that individual dictates the accuracy of the arrow. Earlier, World Champion

▲ Check arrow retention spring tension on occasion to ensure it is sufficient.

▲ Hand cocking a bow is painful as well as a good way to cock it crookedly.

Mark Beck led us through common human factors that affect the shot. Let's look at some other less common ways we humans can mess up our shooting.

Crooked Cocking

As a machine, crossbows are designed to work in perfect symmetry—the cams or wheels, the limbs, string and cables work in perfect concert with one another. In most instances, they do. However, if during the process of cocking the bow, the string is off-center, the bow will not launch the arrow straight. This happens most commonly when hand cocking (i.e., cocking the bow using your bare hands) the bow.

It can also occur when using a rope cocker or hand crank, as these are not immune to misaligning the string during cocking. Resolving this issue is relatively simple. Placing a mark on each side of the string where it intersects the arrow track while *at* rest allows the user to quickly visually check the uniformity of the string at full draw.

Depending on the color of your string, an indelible marker will work. If you have a darkly colored string, you can place a small amount of light color on each side to mark true center. Now, each time you cock the bow, you can check the marks and make sure the bow is cocking correctly.

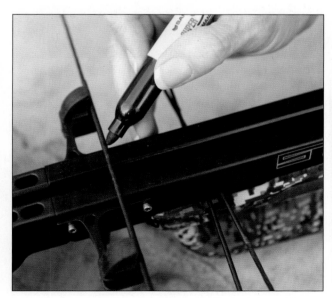

▲ Marking the string will give you a way to visually check the straightness or squareness of the string at full draw.

Canting the Bow

Crossbows are heavy and a bit on the clumsy side no matter how agile or nimble the manufacturer claims in their ads. As such, they are difficult to hold on target and steady. Compounding the problem is the fact they're front heavy and tipsy from side-to-side as the limbs protrude awkwardly outward.

For a crossbow to shoot consistently, it must be held level without any *canting*. Canting is defined as 1) angular deviation from a vertical or horizontal plane or surface; an inclination or slope. 2) a slanted or oblique surface; and 3) a thrust or motion that tilts something.

In real world application, if you're canting the bow with the one limb lower than the other, the bow will shoot to the left or right depending on the direction of the canting. If the bow is canted forward or upward, you will naturally shoot high or low.

To remedy canting, you can employ the use of a shooting stick or a prop, be it a commercially made prop or something as simple as a stick or limb. When hunting from an elevated tree stand, you should always use shooting rails because these provide a solid support for the bow. Make sure you pad them, as they get very loud when placing a crossbow on them prior to the shot.

The "P" Word—Practice

For years, anti-crossbow folks have promulgated the lie that crossbows shoot just like rifles. As we have seen—this simply is not true. Just as time on the range is required to become proficient with any weapon, the same time and repetition is required of crossbow users to become proficient with their equipment.

Each and every crossbow is unique. Time on the practice range is the only way to learn about your bow and become proficient enough to be an ethical hunter.

The Unforeseen

Any weapon—whether crossbow, compound, recurve, handgun, or longbow—is susceptible to becoming damaged. When used, they are subjected to significant abuse. When exposed to a hunting environment, they can quickly become compromised by the slightest of bumps against rocks, and tree branches, or they may be dropped.

I highly recommend you carry a couple practice arrows with you all the time. Prior to heading into the field, shoot a couple of these to make certain the bow is still on. Typically, one arrow is all you need, but carry a couple. Make sure these arrows weigh the same and are the same length and brand as your hunting arrows.

You should also give your bow a visual inspection prior to hunting. Visually inspect:

- Trigger for any obvious issues (like debris in the mechanism);
- Scope for level and tightness;
- Strings and cables for wear;
- Cams or wheels for debris, wear, or obstructions;

- Arrow track for any wear or obstructions (including burrs that will cut your string when released) Also make certain it is well-lubricated;
- Limbs for cracks or any deformation;
- Arrow retention spring for the proper tension;
- Broadheads for sharpness (when hunting);
- Arrows for tip tightness (or broadhead tightness), aligned nocks, and straightness;
- Scope batteries (for those scopes with red dots or illuminated reticles);
- Cocking device for wear (and to make sure you have it);
- Quiver (make sure you have it);
- Case (make sure you have it)

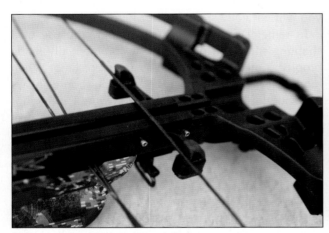

▲ Check strings and cables for wear and tear.

▲ Check field points for tightness prior to each shot.

▲ Check wheels, cams, and limbs for any signs of damage. If there are any, do not shoot the crossbow. Seek immediate professional crossbow help.

▲ Check broadheads for sharpness prior to each use. Never hunt with a dull broadhead.

▲ Check your cocking device for signs of wear. Having a rope cocker break while drawing a crossbow can be a very harrowing experience.

Mixed Cocktails

Bow manufacturers all build their bows around a specific arrow. That is, a specific arrow brand, length, and weight. The limbs, cams (or wheels), strings, and cables are all designed to match that arrow.

For these reasons, it is highly advantageous that you use the specific arrows the manufacturer recommends for their crossbows. By doing so, you extend the service life of your bow, and more importantly, allow it to operate at peak efficiency. Never mix arrow brands, models, weights, or lengths. If you do, you'll *never* get consistent target groups, and you'll damage your equipment in short order.

Replacing a String on a Recurve Crossbow

If using your cable stringer, place the loops of the cable stringer securely on the limb tips. Cock the bow using the cable stringer. Place the loop of the new string through the loop of the cable stringer and secure to the limb tip. (It is important to make sure the string loops are properly seated on the limb.) With assistance, you will need to slowly release the cable stringer by holding it securely in both hands while you have someone release the safety and then trigger of the bow.

Once the string and cable are in the resting position, you can remove the cable stringer. To ease this process, you can pull up slightly on the new string as if you were cocking the bow. This will allow the stringer to be easily removed. You may also use the string that you want to replace in the same fashion instead of using a cable stringer.

Source: barnettcrossbows.com

Popular Questions

In this section, I'd like to answer a few questions that prospective bowhunters and amateurs ask me frequently.

To Uncock or Not to Uncock?

Many bow hunters leave their crossbow cocked for lengthy periods of time. Is this a good idea? Well, no. When contemplating whether to uncock or not, consider that when left cocked, the limbs, strings, cams (or wheels), cam axles, cables, trigger mechanism, etc. are all left under inordinate amounts of stress.

If left cocked, crossbow components degrade over time. The limbs, for instance, slowly develop microfissures and stress cracks along their length (no matter what a manufacturer tells you to the contrary). Over time, these lead to splinters in the limbs or worse—complete limb failure. Leaving a bow cocked also degradates the limbs flexure, "tiring" them, leading to slower arrow speeds. Think of it like over-compressing a ballpoint pen spring. Once the pressure is relieved, the spring will not return to its original length. As such, the spring's ability to provide tension is compromised and performance is degradated.

Additionally, most states require your crossbow be uncocked when not in the field. In some states, this includes walking to and from your hunting spot. It also applies to crossbows when in transport. In other words, they must be uncocked (and in some states physically locked out) when not in the direct use of hunting.

What is the difference between a compound crossbow and recurve crossbow?

The difference between a compound and a recurve crossbow (or any archery bow) is that the compound bow incorporates a set of cams or wheels into the limb assembly. On the recurve bow, the string attaches directly to the limbs.

The benefit of the compound crossbow is it allows the user the ability to let-off (the reduction in draw weight by percentage when the wheels roll over from the action of drawing the string). A compound bow will let-off about 33 percent on current models, from a 150-lb draw weight to 75 lbs. when the wheels roll over. Not only is it easier for the user to cock a compound crossbow, but it is also produces less mechanical stress on the trigger mechanism. *Source: barnettcrossbows.com*

How Far is Too Far?

Crossbows are capable of sending lethal arrows downrange at exaggerated distances. However, while the crossbow may be capable of killing at protracted distances, are you? Some crossbowers may consider launching arrows at animals well beyond their effective range. These Hail Mary's rarely end in a harvest and, in most instances, they result in a miss or worse—a wounded animal.

Prior to heading to the field for your first hunt of the season, do yourself and the animals you hunt a favor. While practicing prior to the season opener, deter-

---

Uncocking a Crossbow Safely

Uncocking a crossbow can be challenging. To do so safely, it is recommended you shoot only an aluminum arrow tipped with a field point. *Never* attempt to uncock a crossbow by shooting with a broadhead attached.

For those who insist on shooting their arrow into the ground to uncock their bow, make certain you aim the arrow some distance away and out in front of you. Shooting an arrow directly into the ground in front of you can lead to serious injury and possibly death because they may deflect back at you.

Additionally, aluminum arrows bend when they strike anything hard in the ground. Once bent, they are easily identified as being damaged and can be taken out of service. Carbon arrows, however, can be damaged, and it not be readily apparent. The next time you attempt to shoot them, they may explode and cause serious injury or worse to you or bystanders.

One last note: It is highly recommended that you use a bag target to discharge an arrow from a cocked bow. This is considerably safer than shooting into the ground.

---

mine what distance you're comfortable shooting—the distance at which you're consistently deadly. So what does "consistently deadly" mean? Well, for me, it is the furthest distance you can always put an arrow in the kill zone. "Consistently" should mean 100 percent of the time.

If you're deadly nine out of ten shots, shorten the target distance and see if you're deadly there 100 percent of the time. Once you find that distance, limit your shots on game to this measure. Remember, an ethical hunter is the best ambassador for our sport and the future of it.

What do I do to extend the life of my bows synthetic cable/string system?

According to the Barnett website, lube wax should be applied to the flight track every five to ten shots. Lube wax should also be applied anywhere the cables make contact with the cable slide or Teflon tape, whichever is applicable, every twenty to thirty shots. To extend the life of your cables, it is important to apply lube wax to all non-served areas of the cables and string every 30 to 50 shots or when white fuzz begins to appear. If the crossbow has been exposed to excessive moisture, you may need to apply wax sooner.

SECTION 3
NEW PRODUCTS

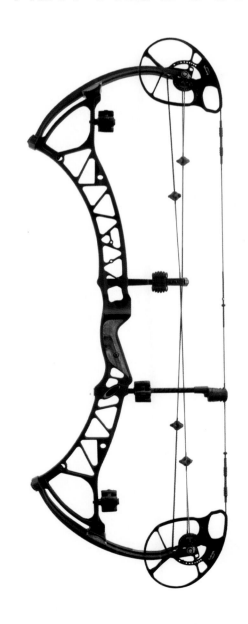

New Compounds 2013

Alpine Archery

Roxstar

Axle-to-Axle: 34½"
Speed: 330 fps (IBO)
Brace Height: 6½" with a 12" limb or 7½" with a 13" limb
Mass Weight: 4.5 lbs.
Draw Weights: 60 lbs. 70 lbs.
Draw Lengths: 28"–31" with a 12" limb or 29"–32" with a 13" limb
Cam: Velocitec 3G Cam
Limbs: Gordon composite limb, film dip finished in MO Infinity.
Cable Guard: New Fast Lane Roller Guide
Pocket: Split Point Limb Capture System with True Position Technology
Riser Color: Anodized Evolution camo
Grip: 1 piece rosewood
Let-Off: 80%
MSRP: $699
Durable camo anodized riser and accenting solid anodized components, capped off with Mossy Oak Infinity limbs. V3g Cam system with smooth draw force curve and 80% let-off.

Verdict

Axle-to-Axle: 31½"
Speed: 328 fps (IBO)
Brace Height: 6¾"
Mass Weight: 4 lbs.
Draw Weights: 60 lbs. 70 lbs.
Draw Lengths: 27"– 30"
Limbs: Gordon composite limb, film dip finished in RealTree APG
Cable Guard: Fast Lane Roller Guide
Pocket: Limb Vice Pocket Mounting System
Riser Color: RealTree APG
Grip: 2 piece rosewood
Let-Off: 80%
MSRP: $699.00
Reflexed forged riser with Limb Vice Pocket System that clamps the limb and pocket assembly against the riser to minimize noise, vibration, and recoil. Fast Lane Roller Guide is smooth and trouble free. An integrated offset quiver mount allows almost any quiver to be mounted back and out of the way. Pulse isolator string stop is fully adjustable and allows for fine tuning of centerline, as well as fore and aft movement. Comes with 416 stainless steel stabilizer insert.

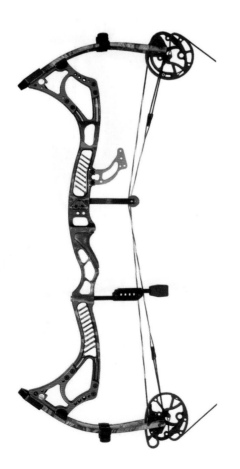

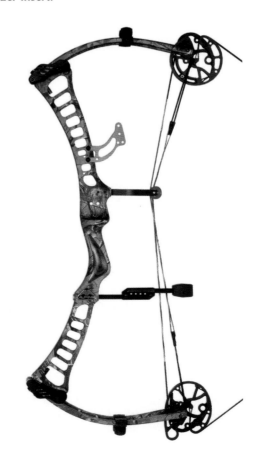

Bass Pro Shops

BPS RedHead Blackout

Axle-to-Axle: 32"
Speed: 333 fps (IBO)
Brace Height: 7"
Mass Weight: 3.8 lbs.
Draw Length: Adjustable between 26½" and 30½"
Let-Off: 80%
Finish Options: RealTree APG
MSRP: $599 (package)

The Throttle Cam Tech is the fastest and one of the most efficient single cams on the market. Rotating draw length modules adjust with a turn of a screw (a bow press is required). Limb mounted bearing assembly helps minimize cam lean. 6061 T6 aluminum riser is CNC machined to eliminate unnecessary weight and maximize strength. Short enough to maneuver deftly in ground blinds or tight treestands. 3-pin sight, Hostage arrow rest, 1-piece 5-arrow quiver, 5-inch stabilizer, string suppressor, peep sight, and sling.

Bear Archery

Domain

Axle-to-Axle: 33"
Speed: 322 fps (IBO)
Brace Height: 7"
Weight: 4 lbs.
Draw Length Range: 26"–31"
Peak Draw Weight: 50 lbs. 60 lbs. 70 lbs.
Let-Off: 80%
Finish Options: RealTree APG, Shadow Series,
Strings/Cables:
Retail: MAP $599.99
MAP $699.99 for Ready to Hunt Package
Trophy Ridge Whisker Biscuit
Trophy Ridge 4-Pin Sight
Trophy Ridge Stabilizer & Sling
Trophy Ridge Quiver
Peep Sight
Nock Loop
Compact for treestand or ground blind usage. Light enough to spot and stalk with while fast enough to harvest any North American game animal. Pre stretched.

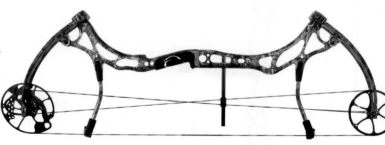

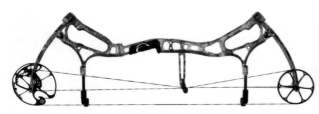

Empire
Axle-to-Axle: 32"
Speed: 330 fps (IBO)
Brace Height: 7"
Weight: 4 lbs.
Draw Length Range: 24"–31"
Peak Draw Weight: 50 lbs. 60 lbs. 70 lbs.
Let-Off: 80%
Finish Options: RealTree APG, Shadow Series, AP Snow/
Black, Green/Black, Red/Black
MAP $849.99
S13 Cam System and Max Preload Quad limbs power the
Empire. A 32-inch axle-to-axle length and a 7-inch brace
height make this bow the perfect mix of speed, forgive-
ness, and balance. Prestretched Contra-Band HP 8125
strings and 452X cables.

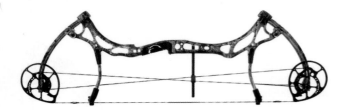

Method
Axle-to-Axle: 33"
Speed: up to 340 fps (IBO)
Brace Height: 6¾"
Weight: 4 lbs.
Draw Length Range: 26½"–31"
Peak Draw Weight: 50 lbs. 60 lbs. 70 lbs.
Let-Off: 75%
Finish Options: RealTree APG, Shadow Series,
MAP $649.99
A high-performance speed bow. A relatively long brace
height affords both speed as well as forgiveness. Pre-
stretched Contra-Band HP 452X strings and 452X cables.
MAP $749.99 for Ready to Hunt Package
RTH Package includes:
Trophy Ridge Whisker Biscuit
Trophy Ridge 4-Pin Sight
Trophy Ridge Stabilizer & Sling
Trophy Ridge Quiver
Peep Sight
Nock Loop

Motive 6 ▼
Axle-to-Axle: 32"
Speed: Up to 350 fps (IBO)
Brace Height: 6"
Weight: 4 lbs.
Draw Length Range: 25½"–30"
Peak Draw Weight: 50 lbs. 60 lbs. 70 lbs.
Let-Off: 75%
Finish Options: RealTree APG, Shadow Series, AP Snow/
Black, Green/Black, Red/Black
MAP $899.99
A short brace height bow with scorching speed. Bear
Synchronized Hybrid Cam System offers a smooth draw
cycle and efficiency. Pre Stretched Contra-Band HP 452X
strings and cables.

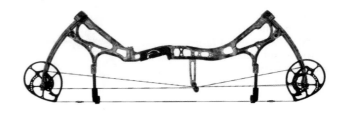

Motive 7 ▼
Axle-to-Axle: 32"
Speed: Up to 340 fps (IBO)
Brace Height: 7"
Weight: 4 lbs.
Draw Length Range: 26½"–31"
Peak Draw Weight: 50 lbs. 60 lbs. 70 lbs.
Let-Off: 75%
Finish Options: RealTree APG, Shadow Series, AP Snow/
Black, Green/Black, Red/Black
MAP $899.99
Much the same bow as the Motive 6, but with a more gen-
erous brace height measure of 7 inches promising a
smoother draw and more forgiveness. H13 Cams work
alongside Max preload quad limbs on a comfortable
32-inch axle-to-axle length. pre-stretched Contra-Band HP
452X strings and cables.

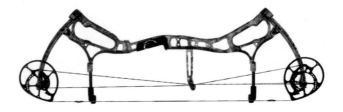

BowTech

Experience
Axle-to-Axle: 32"
Speed: 335 fps (IBO)
Brace Height: 7"
Draw Weights: 50 lbs. 60 lbs.
70 lbs.
Draw Length: 26½–31"
Kinetic Energy: 87 ft-lbs.
Effective Let-Off: 80%
Finish Options: Mossy Oak
Infinity, BlackOps
MSRP: $999
*Octane strings and cables,
Extinguish damping system,
carbon core limbs, Center
Pivot Extreme eccentrics, flex
guard cable guard. A large
brace height measure and
moderate arrow speeds make
this bow a shooter. It's smooth
drawing without the consider-
able "hump" in the draw cycle
that is commonly found on
speed bows.*

Darton

DS-600 ▶
Axle-to-Axle: 31³⁄₈"
Speed: 307–310 fps (IBO)
Brace Height: 7½"
Mass Weight: 4 lbs.
Draw Weights: 40 lbs. 50 lbs. 60
lbs. 70 lbs.
Draw Length: 25"–30"
Let-Off: 80%
Finish Options: Shadow Black,
Next Vista, Muddy Girl
MSRP: $421
*An economy priced bow suited
for the beginner or novice bow-
hunter. The large brace height
of this bow makes it very forgiv-
ing of shooter-induced form
errors. Its light mass weight will
be appreciated during long
hunts and where maneuverabili-
ty is required.*

DS-2800 ▶
Axle-to-Axle: 31¼"
Speed: 330–335 fps (IBO)
Mass Weight: 3.9 lbs.
Brace Height: 7"
Draw Weights: 40 lbs. 50 lbs. 60 lbs.
70 lbs.
Draw Length: 25"–30"
Let-Off: 80%
Finish Options: Shadow
Black, Next Vista, Muddy Girl
MSRP: $768
*A fast bow that is a manage-
able shooter, with a wide
7-inch brace height. Includes
Darton's draw stop modules
that enable shooters to tweak
the amount of cam let-off to
fit their shooting style. By
adding a draw stop adjustment module to the end of
the draw module you are
able to incrementally adjust
the effective let-off from
near 80% to 65%.*

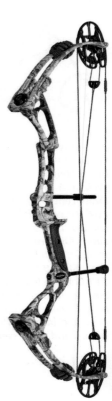

DS-3800 ▶
Axle-to-Axle: 33¹³⁄₁₆"
Speed: 340–350 fps (IBO)
Brace Height: 6"
Mass Weight: 4.1 lbs.
Draw Weights: 40 lbs. 50 lbs. 60
lbs. 70 lbs.
Draw Length: 25–31"
Let-Off: 80%–65% (effective let-off)
Finish Options: Target Red, Shadow
Black, Limited Edition, Next Vista,
Muddy Girl
MSRP: $947
*A versatile bow. The speed this bow
is capable of makes judging dis-
tance a less critical part of the
equation. Exclusive draw stop mod-
ules enable shooters to tweak the
amount of cam let-off to fit their
shooting style and to get the right
amount of performance form the
bow. Incrementally adjustable from
near 80% to 65%. dual sync cam
system is a Darton mainstay.*

DS-3900 ▶

Axle-to-Axle: 32⁷⁄₈"
Speed: 350–355 fps (IBO)
Brace Height: 5"
Mass Weight: 3.9 lbs.
Draw Weights: 40 lbs. 50 lbs. 60 lbs. 70 lbs.
Draw Length: 24"–30"
Let-Off: 80%
Finish Options: Shadow Black, Limited Edition, Next Vista, Muddy Girl
MSRP: $947

A pure speed bow with a 5-inch axle-to-axle measure. EET laminated quad limbs to power the latest design DualSync Cams for both maximum speed and efficiency. A compact 32⁷⁄₈-inch axle-to-axle, the DS-3900 has a comfortable, well balanced feel in the hand. Draw stop modules enable shooters to tweak the amount of cam let-off to fit their shooting style. By adding a draw stop adjustment module to the end of the draw module you are able to incrementally adjust the effective let-off from nearly 80% to 65%.

DS-4500

Axle-to-Axle: 38½"
Speed: 315–320 fps (IBO)
Brace Height: 7½"
Mass Weight: 4.0 lbs.
Draw Weights: 40 lbs. 50 lbs. 60 lbs. 70 lbs.
Draw Length: 26"–32"
Let-Off: 80%
Finish Options: Target Red, Shadow Black, Limited Edition, Next Vista, Muddy Girl
MSRP: $947

A long 38½-inch axle-to-axle bow with a higher 7½-inch brace height and longer draw lengths available up to 32 inches. Finger shooters will find the reduced string angle a plus. The reduced power stroke, resulting from the higher brace height, makes this bow an excellent choice when competing in tournaments. Adjustable draw stop modules that enable shooters to tweak the amount of cam let-off to fit their shooting style. By adding a draw stop adjustment module to the end of the draw module, you are able to incrementally adjust the effective let-off from near 80% to 65%.

Diamond

Core

Axle-to-Axle: 31"
Speed: 313 fps (IBO)
Brace Height: 7¼"
Mass Weight: 3.2 lbs.
Draw Weights: 40 lbs. 50 lbs. 60 lbs. 70 lbs.
Draw Lengths: 25"–30"
Finish Options: Mossy Oak Infinity
Let-Off: 80%
Package Includes: 3–pin sight
Arrow rest
Quiver
Wrist sling
Peep sight
String loop
MSRP: $499

The Core R.A.K. (Ready Aim Kill) is ready to shoot right out of the box. The Core R.A.K. comes with a package of factory installed, tuned, and tested accessories. Rotating module technology allows the adjustment of the bow's draw length and draw stop without the use of a bow press. carbon-rod string stop effectively silences shots by funneling the string's vibration to the bow's stabilizer.

Infinity Edge

Axle-to-Axle: 31"
Speed: Up to 308 fps (IBO)
Brace Height: 7"
Mass Weight: 3.1 lbs.
Draw Weight: 5–70 lbs.
Draw Length: 13"–30"
Let-Off: 75%
Finish Options: Mossy Oak Infinity
Package includes: 3-pin sight Arrow rest Quiver Wrist sling Tube peep sight String loop
MSRP: $399

An amazingly adjustable draw length and draw weight range, the Infinite Edge compound bow package from Diamond gives you maximum adjustability. A great bow for younger hunters, the Infinite Edge offers incredible adjustability to match an archer's development. Offering a versatility that makes it a great bow for well-rounded archers as well, this high performance bow features an incredible draw length range of thirteen to thirty inches and draw weight adjustment from five to seventy pounds.

Elite

Hunter

Axle-to-Axle: 31½"
Speed: 323–326 fps (IBO)
Brace Height: 7¾"
Weight: 4.3 lbs.
Draw Weights: 40 lbs. 50 lbs. 60 lbs. 65 lbs. 70 lbs. 80 lbs.
Finish Options: RealTree AP, RealTree APS, RealTree MAX-1, Ninja (Black)
MSRP: $899

The Elite features Winner's Choice bowstrings and cables, two-piece wooden grips, Cerakote firearm coating, symmetrical cam eccentrics for level nock travel, Delrin cable slide, two-track cams, and cold-forged then machined riser. Available in right-handed and left-handed models.

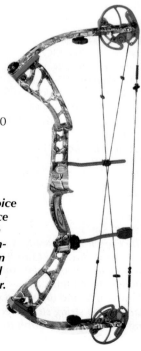

Hoyt

Carbon Element G3

Axle-to-Axle: 31½"
Speed: 332 fps (IBO)
Brace Height: 6 ¾"
Mass Weight: 3.6 lbs.
Draw Weight: 30–40, 40–50, 50–60, 55–65, 60–70, 70–80 lbs.
Finish Options: RealTree Xtra, RealTree MAX-1, Black Out, Bone Collector, Vicxen
MSRP: $1399

An exceptionally light compound constructed of hollow carbon tubes. CNC-machined aluminum components, XTS Pro Arc limbs, FUSE strings and cables, Pro Lock X-Lite pockets, Air Shox Technology, Stealth Shot and side plates grips. Available in right-handed and left-handed models.

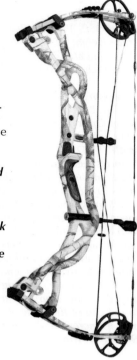

Carbon Matrix G3

Axle-to-Axle: 35 ½"
Speed: 327 fps (IBO) 337 fps @ 32"
Brace Height: 6 ¾" (XTS Pro ARC)7 ½" XTS 1000
Mass Weight: 3.8 lbs.
Draw Weight: 30–40, 40–50, 50–60, 55–65, 60–70, 70–80 lbs.
Hoyt Carbon Matrix G3 Xtra Camo Draw Lengths: RKT Cam & ½ 25.5–27", 27–29", 29–31"
RKT Cam & ½: 31.5–32"
Finish Options: RealTree Xtra, RealTree MAX-1, Half and Half, Black Out, Bone Collector, Vicxen, RealTree Snow, RealTree Pink
MSRP: $1399

A light compound built of hollow carbon tubes. CNC-machined aluminum components, XTS Pro Arc limbs, FUSE strings and cables, Pro Lock X-Lite pockets, Air Shox Technology, RKT Cam system, Stealth Shot and side plates grips. Available in right-handed and left-handed models.

Charger

Axle-to-Axle: 31"
Speed: 325 fps, 327 fps
Brace Height: 6¾", 7½"
Draw Weight: 30–40, 40–50, 50–60, 55–65, 60–70, 70–80 lbs.
Mass Weight: 3.8 lbs., 4.0 lbs.
Draw Lengths: Charger Cam & ½ 24–26½", 27–30"
Charger Cam & ½ 30½–31"
Limbs: ZRX, XTS 1000
Let-Off: 80%
Finish Options: RealTree Xtra, RealTree MAX-1, Half and Half, Black Out, Bone Collector, Vicxen, RealTree Snow, RealTree Pink
MSRP: $699
Package includes:
FUSE ProFire 3-pin sight
FUSE Banshee 4-arrow quiver
Whisker Biscuit
FUSE FlexBlade stabilizer
Hoyt bow sling
Peep sight and alignment tubing
Multilayer laminated limbs, Alpha Shox, Cam & ½ eccentrics system, Fuse custom strings, parallel split limbs, Pro fit custom grip, Prolock pocket, Stealth Shot and Tec Lite.

Spyder 34

Axle-to-Axle: 34" (XTS Pro ARC) 34½" (XTS 1000)
Speed: 330 fps, 340 fps (IBO)
Brace Height: 6¾", 7½"
Mass Weight: 4.0 lbs. 4.1 lbs.
Draw Weight: 30–40, 40–50, 50–60, 55–65, 60–70, 70–80 lbs.
Draw Lengths: RKT Cam & ½ 25.5–27", 27–29", 29–31" RTK Cam & ½ 31½"–32"
Let-Off: 80%
Finish Options: RealTree Xtra, RealTree MAX-1, Half and Half, Black Out, Bone Collector, Vicxen, RealTree Snow, RealTree Pink
MSRP: $899
RKT Cam, riser CNC-machined from aircraft-grade aluminum, XTS Pro Arc limbs, FUSE strings and cables (premium BCY material), Pro Lock X-Lite pocket, Air Shox technology, Stealth Shot and side plate grip. Available in right-handed and left-handed models. Also available in long-draw model (measures up to 32 inches in length).

Spyder 30

Axle-to-Axle: 30"
Speed: 330 fps
Brace Height: 6¾"
Mass Weight: 3.8 lbs.
Draw Weight: 30–40, 40–50, 50–60, 55–65, 60–70, 70–80 lbs.
Draw Lengths: RKT CAM & ½ 24.5–26", 26–28", 28–30"
Finish Options: RealTree Xtra, RealTree MAX-1, Half and Half, Black Out, Bone Collector, Vicxen, RealTree Snow, RealTree Pink
MSRP: $899
RKT Cam, riser CNC-machined from aircraft-grade aluminum, XTS Pro Arc limbs, FUSE strings and cables (premium BCY material), Pro Lock X-Lite Pocket, Air Shox technology, Stealth Shot, and side-plate grip. Available in right-handed and left-handed models.

Spyder Turbo

Axle-to-Axle: 34"
Speed: 340 fps
Brace Height: 6"
Mass Weight: 4.0 lbs.
Draw Weight: 30–40, 40–50, 50–60, 55–65, 60–70, 70–80 lbs.
Draw Lengths: RKT Cam & ½ 24.5–26", 26–28", 28–30"
Finish Options: RealTree Xtra, RealTree MAX-1, Half and Half, Black Out, Bone Collector, Vicxen, RealTree Snow, RealTree Pink
MSRP: $899
Riser CNC-machined from aircraft-grade aluminum, KT Cam, XTS Pro Arc limbs, FUSE strings and cables (BCY premium grade material), Pro Lock X-Lite pocket, Air Shox technology, and Stealth Shot.

Martin

Alien

Axle-to-Axle: 32"
Speed: Up to 335 fps (IBO)
Brace Height: 7"
Mass Weight: 3.5 lbs.
Draw Weights: 50 lbs. 60 lbs. 70 lbs.
Draw Lengths: 25½"–30½"
Finish Options: Next G1 Vista, Black Carbon, Bonz, Target Red, Skulz, FrostWhite
MSRP: $799.99
Nitro 3 Hybrid Cam, riser CNC-Machined from a solid block of 6061T6 aluminum, Power Tough limbs. Strings and cables are Hammer Head Strings Set with gore fiber, roto limb cup pivoting limb system eliminating forward or lateral movement, Martin carbon fiber STS, integrated VEM silencing arrow shelf to eliminate slapping of fall-away rest. SaddleBack Thermal Grip with slim ergonomic curve reduces torque and provides thermal protection from all weather conditions. Available right- or left-handed.

Blade X4

Axle-to-Axle: 31½"
Speed: Up to 315 (IBO)
Brace Height: 7"
Mass Weight: 3.75 lbs.
Draw Lengths: 26"–32"
Peak Draw Weight: 50 lbs. 60 lbs. 70 lbs.
Weight Adjustments: 35 lbs. from peak weight
Cams: Fury XT
Finish Options: Next G-1
MSRP: $349.99
Fury XT single cam, CNC-machined from a solid block of 6061T6 aluminum, Power Tough limbs, Strings and cables are Hammer Head Strings Set with Gore fiber, Roto Limb Cup Pivoting Limb System eliminating forward or lateral movement, Martin carbon fiber STS, Integrated VEM silencing arrow shelf to eliminate slapping from fall-away rest, custom target grip, Quad VEM vibration Vortex Escape Modules in specific locations to maximize their efficiency. Available in right-handed and left-handed models.

Mathews

Creed

Axle-to-Axle: 30"
Speed: 328 fps (IBO)
Brace Height: 7"
Draw Weight: 50–70 lbs.
Bow Weight: 3.85 lbs. (approximate)
Let-Off: 80%
Draw Lengths: 26–30" Half Sizes 26½–29½"
String/Cable String: 92¼" | Cable: 32¾"
Cams: SimPlex Cam
Riser Length: 26.50"
Finish Options: Black, Tactical, Lost
MSRP: $999
SimPlex cam (one cam design), GeoGrid riser, parallel limbs, reverse roller guard, walnut handle, harmonic dampers, string silencers, string stop, premium strings, and cables.

ZXT

Axle-to-Axle: 28"
Speed: Up to 326 fps (IBO)
Brace Height: 7³/₈"
Draw Weight: 40–70 & 65 lbs.
Bow Weight: 4.2 lbs. (approximate)
Draw Lengths: 24"–30" Half Sizes 24½–29½"
String/Cable String: 82⅞"
Cable: 30½"
Riser Length: 25⅝"
Cams: ZX
Let-Off: 80%
Finish Options: Black, Lost
MSRP: $799
ZX cam (one cam system), grid lock riser, SE6 Slim limbs, walnut grip, harmonic dampers, string suppressors, string stop, parallel limbs, reverse roller guard.

McPherson Series Monster

Chill

Axle-to-Axle: 30½"
Speed: Up to 333 fps (IBO)
Brace Height: 7"
Bow Weight: 3.90 approximate
Draw Weight: 50–70 lbs.
Draw Lengths: 23"–30" Half
Sizes: 23½"–29½"
Cams: Dyad Cam
String/Cable String: 60¾"
Cable: 28 1/8"
Riser Length: 23½"
Let-Off: 80%
Finish Options: Black, Tactical, Lost
MSRP: $999

The Chill is equipped with the DYAD AVS cam System which features dual perimeter weighted cams producing minimal post shot vibration and great speed. Combined with a reverse assist roller guard and a GeoGrid riser.

Obsession

Knightmare

Axle-to-Axle: 33½"
Speed: 342–350 fps (IBO)
Brace Height: 6³⁄₈"
Mass Weight: 4 lbs.
Draw Lengths: 23½"–30"
Let-Off: 80%
MSRP: $849

Smooth draw cycle but still provides strong feet-per-second performance. Narrow grip for torque-free shots; comes standard with America's Best strings and cables. Anti-torque cable guard, timing marks, and interchangeable draw length modules. Type 3 hard coat anodized.

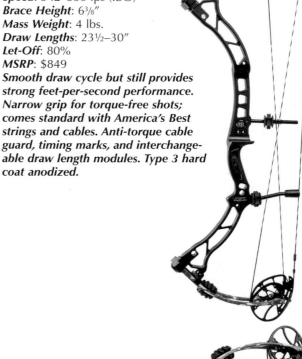

Mission

Ballistic

Axle-to-Axle: 30½"
Speed: 330 fps (IBO)
Brace Height: 7"
Mass Weight: 4.18 lbs.
Draw Weights: 50–70 lbs.
Draw Length: 26"–30"
Let-Off: 80%
Finish Options: Lost, Black
MSRP: $499

Zebra Hybrid strings and cables, AVS cam system, extruded riser, carbon-rod cable guard, string stop, and string silencers.

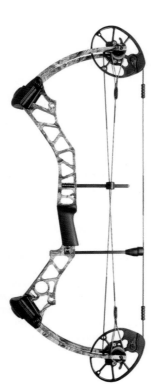

Lethal Force II

Axle-to-Axle: 33½"
Speed: 330–338 fps (IBO)
Brace Height: 7¼"
Mass Weight: 4 lbs.
Draw Lengths: 24½"–31"
Let-Off: 60%, 65%, 80%
MSRP: $849

Generous brace height, perfect for both hunting and 3-D tournaments. America's Best strings and cables, anti-torque cable guard, timing marks and interchangeable draw length modules. Type 3 hard coat anodized.

Sniper LT

Axle-to-Axle: 30¾"
Speed: 330–338 fps (IBO)
Brace Height: 7"
Mass Weight: 3.9 lbs.
Draw Lengths: 23½"–30"
Let-Off: 60%, 65%, 80%
MSRP: $849
Short axle-to-axle length with fast speeds. America's Best strings and cables, anti-torque cable guard, timing marks and interchangeable draw length modules. Type 3 hard coat anodized.

Parker

Eagle

Axle-to-Axle: 32"
Speed: 310 fps (IBO)
Brace Height: 7¾"
Mass Weight: 3.65 lbs.
Draw Weight: 50–60, 60–70 lbs.
Draw Length: 26"–31" (modules included)
String: Premium Stone Mountain String Tri-Color Twist 89¾"
Bus Cable: 33½"
Let-Off: 80%
Finish Options: Next G-1 Vista
MAP: $299.95 Bow Only
MAP: $349.95 Outfitter with Hostage Style Rest or Whisker Biscuit
Parallel limbs, single cam eccentric system, two-piece walnut grip, integrated sling, adjustable string suppressor, micro-lite pockets, machined riser, adjustable draw stops.

Prime

Defy

Axle-to-Axle: 31"
Speed: 335 fps (IBO)
Brace Height: 7¼"
Mass Weight: 4.1 lbs.
Draw Weight: 50 lbs. 60 lbs. 70 lbs.
Draw Length: 26" – 30"
Finish Options: Optifade Forest, Optifade Open Country, RealTree AP, Ice Blue, Ice Red, Jet Black
MAP: $949
Features the PCX cam and a forged 7000 series riser to provide a stable shooting platform. The ultra-fit rubber molded grip provides comfort and a consistent grip. Grips can be removed. 8190 BCY strings, extra-wide limbs, I-Glide Flex guard features a high-tensile spring steel that produces a more consistent and reliable system. It reduces cam movement by allowing cables to flex inward during the shot but clearing out of the way once the arrow is released.

Impact

Axle-to-Axle: 35"
Speed: 340 fps (IBO)
Brace Height: 6¼"
Mass Weight: 4.5 lbs.
Draw Weight: 50 lbs. 60 lbs. 70 lbs.
Draw Length: 26"–30"
Finish Options: Optifade Forest, Optifade Open Country, RealTree AP, Ice Blue, Ice Red, Jet Black
MAP: $949
Features the PCX cam and a forged 7000 series riser to provide a stable shooting platform. Like the Defy, the ultra-fit rubber molded grip provides comfort and a consistent grip. Grips can be removed. 8190 BCY strings, extra-wide limbs, I-Glide Flex guard features a high-tensile spring steel that produces a more consistent and reliable system. It also reduces cam movement by allowing cables to flex inward during the shot but clearing out of the way once the arrow is released.

One

Axle-to-Axle: 39¼"
Speed: 310 fps (IBO)
Brace Height: 7½"
Mass Weight: 4.6 lbs.
Draw Weight: 50 lbs. 60 lbs. 70 lbs.
Draw Length: 27½"–31½"
Finish Options: Blacked Out, Ice Blue, Ice Red
MSRP: $1,499

Features are similar to those of the Defy and the Impact PCT cam. Comes with a forged 7000 series riser to provide a stable shooting platform. Along with high performance, ultra-fit rubber molded grip provides comfort a consistent grip. Grips can be removed. 8190 BCY strings, extra-wide limbs, I-Glide Flex guard features a high-tensile spring steel that produces a more consistent and reliable system. It reduces cam movement by allowing cables to flex inward during the shot but clearing out of the way once the arrow is released.

Drive

Axle-to-Axle: 30½"
Speed: 318–326 fps (IBO)
Brace Height: 7½"
Weight: 4.6 lbs.
Draw Length: 26"–31½"
Peak Draw Weights: 50 lbs. 60 lbs. 70 lbs.
Let-Off: 75%
Finish Options: Mossy Oak Break-Up Infinity, Black Camo, Skullworks, Black
MSRP: $499

The most affordable bow in the PSE Pro Series X-Force line Planar Flex riser, drive cam with 6½ inches of draw length adjustment, 7½ inch brace height, and sting stop.

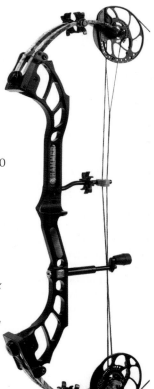

PSE

Dream Season DNA

Axle-to-Axle: 31"
Speed: 344–352 fps (IBO)
Brace Height: 6"
Weight: 3.7 lbs.
Draw Length: 26"–30"
Peak Draw Weights: 50 lbs. 55 lbs. 60 lbs. 65 lbs. 70 lbs.
Let-Off: 70%
Finish Options: Mossy Oak Break-Up Infinity, Black Camo, Skullworks, Black
MSRP: $899

The Dream Season DNA Compound Bow is constructed of ultra light and ultrastrong aluminum alloy. Featuring PSE Center Pull technology that places the arrow in the exact center of the bow for unparalleled tuneability and exceptional performance. The Core cam produces speeds up to 352 fps with a full 5 inches of draw length adjustment on the inner-cam.

Hammer

Axle-to-Axle: 32¼"
Speed: 327–335 fps (IBO)
Brace Height: 7"
Weight: 4.2 lbs.
Draw Weight: 50 lbs. 60 lbs. 70 lbs.
Draw Length: 26"–31"
Let-Off: 75%
Finish Options: Mossy Oak Break-Up Infinity, Black Camo, Skullworks, Black
MSRP: $749

From PSE's X-Force with the Hammer features a Planar Flex riser, the EVO™ cam with 6 inches of draw length adjustment, 7-inch brace height, and the Backstop 2.

Phenom

Axle-to-Axle: 36"
Speed: 321–329 fps (IBO)
Brace Height: 7"
Weight: 4.3 lbs.
Draw Length: 25½"–30"
Peak Draw Weights: 40 lbs. 50 lbs. 60 lbs. 70 lbs.
Let-Off: 75%
Finish Options: Blue, Red, Black, Skullworks, Mossy Oak Break-Up Infinity
MSRP: $649
Its design is forgiving with a 36-inch axle-to-axle length and 7-inch brace height. It features X-Technology, pivoting limb pockets, preloaded split limbs, the new Backstop 2, Planar Flex riser, and Raptor™ grip.

Sinister

Axle-to-Axle: 28"
Speed: 319–327 fps (IBO)
Brace Height: 7¼"
Weight: 3.9 lbs.
Draw Length: 25½"–30½"
Peak Draw Weights: 50 lbs. 60 lbs. 70 lbs.
Let-Off: 75%
Finish Options: Mossy Oak Break-Up Infinity, Black camo, Skullworks, Black
MSRP: $499
Very short axle-to-axle bow at 28 ATA. Large brace height of 7¼-inch minimizes string pinch on the arrow nock. Lightweight bow well-suited for any hunting situation, whether ground blinds, treestands, or spot-and-stalking.

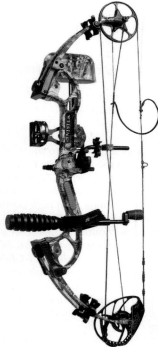

Prophecy

Axle-to-Axle: 32"
Speed: 332–340 fps (IBO)
Brace Height: 6"
Weight: 4.1 lbs.
Draw Length: 25"–30"
Peak Draw Weights: 50 lbs. 60 lbs. 70 lbs.
Let-Off: 75%
Finish Options: Mossy Oak Break-Up Infinity, Black camo, Skullworks, Black
MSRP: $699
Past parallel limbs, Planar Flex riser, and Backstop 2 are standard. Single-cam design.

Quest

Bliss

Axle-to-Axle: 31"
Speed: 290 fps @ 40 lbs. and 27" draw length
Brace Height: 7"
Weight: 4.05 lbs.
Draw Weight: 30–45 lbs. 45–60 lbs.
Draw Length: 23"–27"
Available in ½" increments
Finish Options: RealTree AP, G-Fade RealTree AP, G-Fade RealTree AP Pink
MAP: $399 for bow $499 for DTH (Designed To Hunt) Package
Features: Fluid SD cam eccentric system, forged then machined 60621 aircraft grade aluminum riser. DuraFuse finish and with string suppressors.

Drive

Axle-to-Axle: 33¼"
Speed: 330 fps (IBO)
Weight: 4.35 lbs.
Brace Height: 7"
Draw Weight: 50 lbs. 60 lbs. 70 lbs.
Draw Length: 26"–31" One inch adjustment per module
Finish Options: RealTree AP, Jet Black, G-Fade, G-Fade Mossy Oak Treestand
MAP: $699.99
Twin Track Flux Cam (modular design) with 1 inch of draw adjustment per module, I-Glide flex slide, forged machined 6061 aluminum riser, DuraFuse finish, adjustable string suppressor, meta speed studs, BowJax limb dampeners, pivoting limb pockets, BCY 452X strings and cables.

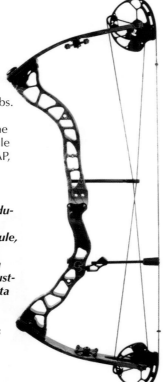

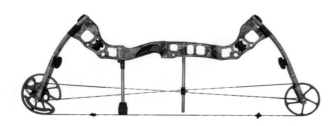

Ross Archery

XD (Xtreme Devastation)
Axle-to-Axle: 30½"
Speed: 320 fps (IBO)
Brace Height: 7½"
Mass Weight: 3.16 lbs.
Draw Weights: 40–50, 50–60, 60–70 lbs.
Draw Lengths: 26"– 31" in ½" increments
Let-Off: 80 %
Finish Options: Stealth Black, RealTree AP
MSRP: $524.95
DRT riser dampeners, Slim Line grip, and an amazingly light mass weight. Features dual-locking limb pockets, integrated string stop, and limb vibration dampeners.

Strother

Wrath SHO
Axle-to-Axle: 30³⁄₁₆"
Speed: Up to 335 fps (IBO)
Brace Height: 7³⁄₈"
Mass Weight: 4 lbs.
Draw Weight: 50 lbs. 60 lbs. 70 lbs. 80 lbs.
Draw Length: 27"–30"
Let-Off: 80%
Finish Options: RealTree AP Black, Predator 3-D Deception
MSRP: $839
Featuring the Badger Cam II with a smooth draw force curve. New lock and cradle limb pockets hold tolerances tight and pivot more outboard than other traditional limb designs. A uniquely designed carbon cable guard and string suppressor manage vibration after the shot. The very large brace height measure of 7⅜ inches makes this a real shooter.

Xpedition

Xplorer
Axle-to-Axle: 30½"
Speed: Up to 338 fps (IBO)
Brace Height: 7"
Mass Weight: (Approximate) 3.9 lbs.
Draw Weights: 50 lbs. 60 lbs. 65 lbs. 70 lbs.
Draw Lengths: 27"–30", Half sizes 27½"–29½"
Let-Off: 75%
Finish Options: RealTree AP Xtra, Molten Black
MSRP: $895
A deeply reflexed riser and X-Cell Cam eccentric system, providing good speed even with the long 7-inch brace height. A custom cable guard system manages the buss cable during and after the shot. An integrated string suppressor helps with vibration duties. At 30½ inches, ATA the bow is very compact.

X-Ring VI
Axle-to-Axle: 33½"
Speed: Up to 348 fps (IBO)
Brace Height: 6¼"
Mass Weight (Approximate): 4 lbs.
Draw Weights: 50 lbs. 60 lbs. 65 lbs. 70 lbs.
Draw Lengths: 27"–30"
Half Sizes: 27½"–29½"
Let-Off: 75%
Finish Options: RealTree AP Xtra, Molten Black
MSRP: $899
The X-Ring VI is a speed burner. The abbreviated brace height of six inches makes for a long power stroke, pushing arrows at a fast clip (348 fps). Draw length is adjustable in ½-inch increments. A custom cable guard system manages the buss cable during and after the shot. An integrated string suppressor helps with vibration duties.

X-Ring VII
Axle-to-Axle: 33½"
Speed: Up to 338 fps (IBO)
Brace Height: 7¼"
Draw Weights: 50 lbs. 60 lbs. 65 lbs. 70 lbs.
Draw Lengths: 28"–31"
Half Sizes: 28½"–30½"
Let-Off: 75%
Finish Options: RealTree AP Xtra, Molten Black
MSRP: $899.00
The X-Ring VII, with its wide 7¼-inch brace height is well-suited as a combo bow both for hunting as well as target archery (3-D). The axle-to-axle measure makes it easy to handle. The draw length is adjustable in ½-inch increments. A custom cable guard system manages the buss cable during and after the shot. An integrated string suppressor helps with vibration duties.

New Crossbows 2013

Arrow Precision

Firestorm II
Draw Weight: 165 lbs.
Speed: 375 fps
Mass Weight: 8.2 lbs.
Overall Length: 40½"
Width: 25¹⁹⁄₃₂" (uncocked) 19" (cocked)
Power Stroke: 14⅛"

Kinetic Energy: 137 ft-lbs. (with 20" carbon arrow with 100-grain tips), 148 lbs. (with 20" aluminums with 125-grain tips)
Trigger Pull: 2.4 lbs.
Finish Options: Next Vista Soft Touch Microprint
MSRP: $649.99
Includes: Weaver-style scope rail, 4x32 multi-reticle illuminated scope, quick-detach quiver, four carbon arrows, rope-cocking device, padded shoulder sling, eye protection, and assembly tools/hex keys.

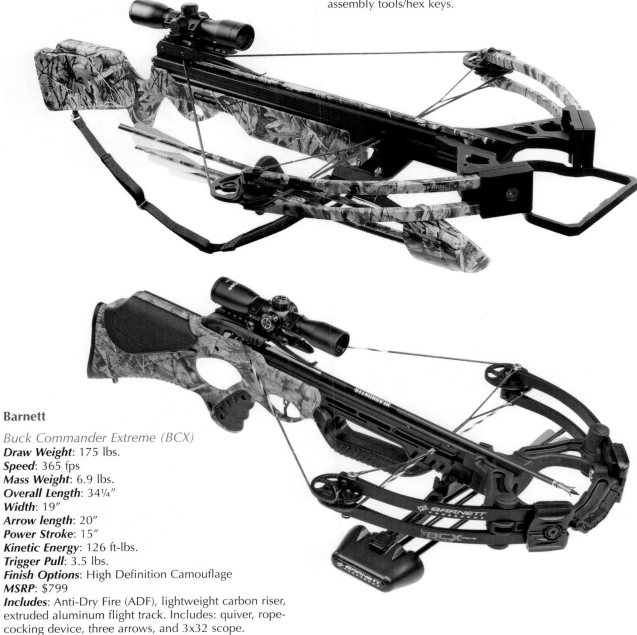

Barnett

Buck Commander Extreme (BCX)
Draw Weight: 175 lbs.
Speed: 365 fps
Mass Weight: 6.9 lbs.
Overall Length: 34¼"
Width: 19"
Arrow length: 20"
Power Stroke: 15"
Kinetic Energy: 126 ft-lbs.
Trigger Pull: 3.5 lbs.
Finish Options: High Definition Camouflage
MSRP: $799
Includes: Anti-Dry Fire (ADF), lightweight carbon riser, extruded aluminum flight track. Includes: quiver, rope-cocking device, three arrows, and 3x32 scope.

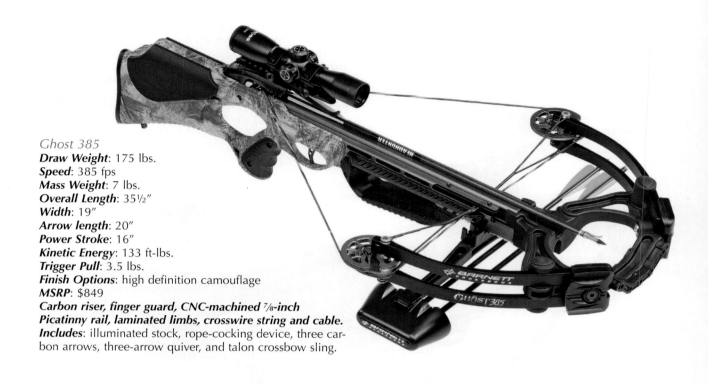

Ghost 385

Draw Weight: 175 lbs.
Speed: 385 fps
Mass Weight: 7 lbs.
Overall Length: 35½"
Width: 19"
Arrow length: 20"
Power Stroke: 16"
Kinetic Energy: 133 ft-lbs.
Trigger Pull: 3.5 lbs.
Finish Options: high definition camouflage
MSRP: $849
Carbon riser, finger guard, CNC-machined ⅞-inch Picatinny rail, laminated limbs, crosswire string and cable.
Includes: illuminated stock, rope-cocking device, three carbon arrows, three-arrow quiver, and talon crossbow sling.

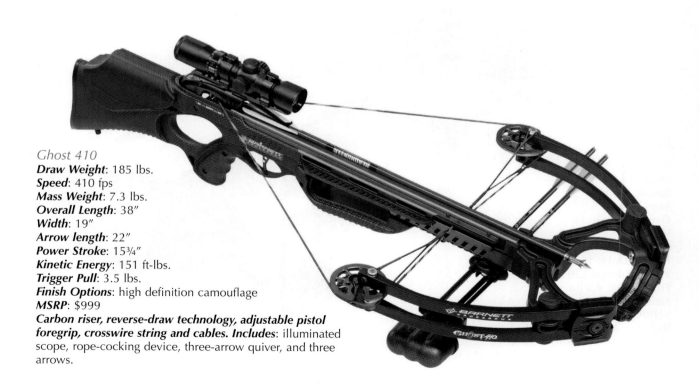

Ghost 410

Draw Weight: 185 lbs.
Speed: 410 fps
Mass Weight: 7.3 lbs.
Overall Length: 38"
Width: 19"
Arrow length: 22"
Power Stroke: 15¾"
Kinetic Energy: 151 ft-lbs.
Trigger Pull: 3.5 lbs.
Finish Options: high definition camouflage
MSRP: $999
Carbon riser, reverse-draw technology, adjustable pistol foregrip, crosswire string and cables. Includes: illuminated scope, rope-cocking device, three-arrow quiver, and three arrows.

BowTech

StrykeZone 350 BlackOps
Draw Weight: 135 lbs.
Speed: 350 fps
Mass Weight: 6.9 lbs.
Overall Length: 34³/₈"
Width: 19³/₁₆"
Power Stroke: 15½"
Kinetic Energy: 105 ft-lbs.
Finish Options: Black Ops
MSRP: $799
Creep-free trigger, one-piece molded stock, anti-dry fire device, string stops, and built-in Picatinny rail.
Included: quiver, sling, illuminated scope, five arrows.

Carbon Express

Intercept
Draw Weight: 185 lbs.
Speed: 360 fps
Mass Weight: 8.2 lbs.
Width: 17" (uncocked) 13½" (cocked)
6-Position AR style stock (13"–19")
Trigger Pull: 3 lbs.
Finish Options: Black Tactical
MSRP: $899
Included: Folding grips, foregrip bipods, adjustable foregrips, quick-detach scope mounts, compact flashlight w/quick-detach mount (flashlight not included), adjustable butt stock, compact crossbow case, and tactical single point shooting sling.

X-Force 350

Draw Weight: 165 lbs.
Speed: 300 fps
Arrows: 20"
Power Stroke: 12"
Kinetic Energy: 80 ft-lbs.
Finish Options: Black Tactical
MSRP: $299
Features and Included: Cast riser with rubber-coated foot stirrup for rugged dependability, heavy-duty compression molded limbs, Carbon Express PileDriver 20-inch cross-bolts with moon nocks, 4x32 six-point multi-reticle scope, trigger box safety system, and SilenTech™ coating for ultimate stealth and performance in the field.

Darton

Viper SS

Draw Weight: 170 lbs.
Speed: 340 fps
Mass Weight: 8.4 lbs.
Length: 35½"
Width: 17"
Power Stroke: 13½"
Bowstring: 36⅜"
Power Cables: 18¼"
Kinetic Energy: 102.7 ft-lbs.
Trigger Pull: 3 lbs.
Finish Options: Next Vista, Muddy Girl
MSRP: $799
Features: trackless barrel design, anti-dry fire safety, updated receiver with smoother trigger and safety, positive limb alignment system for greater accuracy, integrated riser/string suppressor system along with Darton's barrel dampener to reduce noise and vibration.
Pro Crossbow Package: Venom Scorpion scope, scope rings, Aeoforce II quiver, monopod package, cocking winch, rope cocker, crossbow case, and string wax/rail lube, three pak 22-inch glass surge arrows.

Hunter Crossbow Package: 4x32 scope, scope rings, Lynx black quiver, rope cocker, string wax/rail lube, and three pak 22-inch glass surge arrows.
Basic Crossbow Package: 4x32 scope, scope rings, Lynx black quiver, and rope cocker.
Starter Crossbow Package: 4x32 scope, scope rings, and Lynx black quiver.

Viper SS Xtreme
Draw Weight: 180 lbs.
Speed: 360 fps
Mass Weight: 8.4 lbs.
Length: 35½"
Width: 17"
Power Stroke: 13½"
Bowstring: 36¹/₁₆"
Power Cables: 18⁹/₁₆"
Kinetic Energy: 115 ft-lbs.
Trigger Pull: 3 lbs.
Finish Options: Next Vista, Muddy Girl
MSRP: $947
Features: Trackless barrel design, anti-dry fire safety, updated receiver with smoother trigger and safety, positive limb alignment system for greater accuracy, integrated riser/string suppressor system along with Darton's Barrel Dampener to reduce noise and vibration.
Pro Crossbow Package: Venom Scorpion scope, scope rings, Aeoforce II quiver, monopod package, cocking winch, rope cocker, crossbow case, string wax/rail lube, three pak 22-inch glass surge arrows.
Hunter Crossbow Package: 4x32 scope, scope rings, Lynx black quiver, rope cocker, string wax/rail lube, three pak 22-inch glass surge arrows
Basic Crossbow Package: 4x32 scope, scope rings, Lynx black quiver, rope cocker
Starter Crossbow Package: 4x32 scope, scope rings, Lynx black quiver

Excalibur

Matrix 355
Draw Weight: 240 lbs.
Speed: 355 fps arrow speeds obtained using 350-grain arrow and standard Matrix string.
Mass Weight: 5.4 lbs.
Overall Length: 34⁵¹/₆₄"
Arrow Length: 18"
Arrow Weight: 350-Grains
Power Stroke: 12¹³/₆₄"
Stock Type: Ergo-Grip
Finish: RealTree Xtra
MSRP: $949 (Lite Stuff Package Bow)
Features and Included: Ergonomic stock and pistol grip, power load limbs, quad-lock riser, Kolorfusion film dip process for rich graphics, molded cheek piece. Four-arrow quiver, four arrows, field points, rope-cocking device, 30 mm scope rings.

Matrix 380 Xtra
Draw Weight: 260 lbs.
Speed: 380 fps arrow speeds obtained using 350-grain arrow and standard Matrix string.
Mass Weight: 5.9 lbs.
Overall Length: 35^{19}/$_{32}$"
Arrow Length: 18"
Arrow Weight: 350-Grains
Power Stroke: 13^{7}/$_{64}$"

Stock Type: Ergo-Grip
Finish: RealTree Xtra
MSRP: $1,149.99 (Lite Stuff Package Bow)
Features: Ergonomic stock and grip, anti-dry fire device, de-cockable, Kolorfusion film dip process for rich graphics, molded cheek piece, integrated string suppressors. Four-arrow quiver, four arrows, field points, rope-cocking device, and 30 mm scope rings.

Horton

TRT Nitro
Draw Weight: 175 lbs.
Speed: 330 fps
Mass Weight: 6.5 lbs.
Overall Length: 37^{1}/$_{8}$"
Width: 20^{7}/$_{8}$"
Arrow Length: 20"
Power Stroke: 12½"
Finish: RealTree APG
MSRP: $599

Features: 7075 T6 forged aircraft-grade aluminum riser and a forged foot stirrup. Three layer laminated limbs, Gordon composite over-molded rubber grip and cheek piece. Sims LimbSaver NAVCOM Sound Stoppers dampen noise. Fully adjustable forearm and interchangeable butt plate. Adjustable length of pull from 13 to 14 inches (13.5 inches std.). Aluminum arrow track, CNC-aluminum sight bridge with Picatinny scope rail, anti-dry fire mechanism with ambidextrous safety, MIM Talon Ultra-Light trigger, synthetic string and cables. 4x32 multi-reticle scope, three-arrow quiver, and three 20-inch arrows.

Mission

Mission MXB-360
Draw Weight: Adjustable 100–160 lbs.
Speed: 360 fps
Mass Weight: 6.55 lbs.
Overall Length: 35"
Width: 19½"
Arrow Length: 22"
Power Stroke: 14"
Finish: Lost AT, Black
MSRP: $1,075 Hunter Package
Features: Zebra Hybrid string and cables, adjustable draw weight, fully assembled and in a case from the factory. MX-3 three-arrow quiver and three arrows. Choice of three Hawke brand scopes.

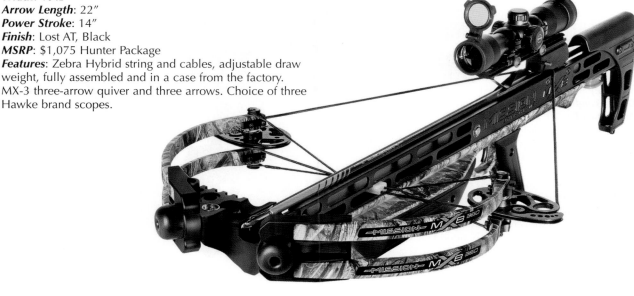

Parker

Blackhawk
Draw Weight: 160 lbs.
Speed: 320 fps
Mass Weight: 6.5 lbs.
Overall Length: 34¼"
Width: 20⅜"
Arrow Length: 20"
Power Stroke: 10¾"
Finish: Black
MSRP: $549

Feature: Split limbs, G2 bull-pup trigger, auto-engage ambidexterous safety, anti-dry fire device, vented forearm and safety finger flange, Red Hot string and cables. Illuminated multi-reticle scope, six Red Hot arrows, roller rope cocker, three Red Hot Crosspro 100 Broadheads, six 100 grams match weight field points, Red Hot sling, wax and lube kit, and soft crossbow case.

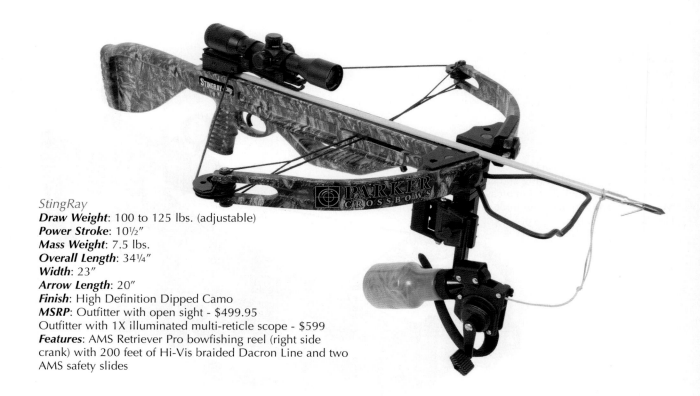

StingRay

Draw Weight: 100 to 125 lbs. (adjustable)
Power Stroke: 10½"
Mass Weight: 7.5 lbs.
Overall Length: 34¼"
Width: 23"
Arrow Length: 20"
Finish: High Definition Dipped Camo
MSRP: Outfitter with open sight - $499.95
Outfitter with 1X illuminated multi-reticle scope - $599
Features: AMS Retriever Pro bowfishing reel (right side crank) with 200 feet of Hi-Vis braided Dacron Line and two AMS safety slides

Patriot

F-14S

Draw Weight: 185 lbs.
Speed: 363 fps
Length: 37"
Width: 24"
Arrow Weight: 405 grams
Power Stroke: 14"
Finish Options: Next G-1 Vista
Mass Weight: 8.5 lbs.
MSRP: $799
Features: CNC-machined extended trigger mechanism, automatic safety, ambidextrous trigger and safety, anti-dry fire device, custom matched compression molded fiberglass limbs, CNC-machined aluminum riser and wheels, extruded and machined aluminum flight deck. Laser scope, quiver, four carbon arrows, carrying case, rope-cocking device, carrying sling, and lube wax.

PSE

Enigma
Draw Weight: 150 lbs.
Speed: 350 fps with 425-grain arrow
Mass Weight: 8.9 lbs.
Length: 40½" to 44¾"
Width: 20"
Axle-to-Axle: 17"

Power Stroke: 12¾"
Kinetic Energy: 116 ft-lbs.
Finish Options: Mossy Oak Break-Up Infinity, Skull Works
MSRP: $599
Features: X-Tech limbs, integrated Picatinny rail, adjustable stock, embroidered sling, side mounted quiver, 4x32 scope, four arrow quiver, four arrows, cocking rope, string wax, and rail lube.

TAC Elite
Draw Weight: 150 lbs.
Speed: 395–405 fps (425-grain arrow)
Mass Weight: 9 lbs.
Length: 41½"–45"
Width: 22" (measured from cam-to-cam)
Axle-to-Axle: 17" at brace
Power Stroke: 17¼"
Kinetic Energy: 155 ft-lbs. (425-grain arrow)
Finish Options: Black hard anodized aluminum for maximum durability.

MSRP: $1,499
Features: Fully adjustable stock, hard anodizing coating, fully CNC. machined riser, arrow barrel, trackless arrow system, AR-15 styling throughout, AR-15 style safety, crisp AR-15 style trigger, split limbs, integrated string stops, large stirrup styled bumpers. TAC case, scope, bipod, and three TAC arrows.

SA Sports Outdoors Gear

Ambush
Draw Weight: 150 lbs.
Speed: 285 fps
Mass Weight: 6.25 lbs.
Overall Length: 35″
Width: 28½″
Arrow Length: 16″
Stock Type: Ambidextrous, lightweight synthetic rear stock
Finish: Next G-1
MSRP: $329
Features: 4x32 multi-reticle scope, quick-detach quiver with four arrows, rope-cocking device, adjustable Weaver-style scope mount, ambidextrous auto safety, large boot-style foot stirrup, lightweight vented aluminum barrel, precision-machined aluminum wheels, integrated cable-string system, crank cocking device compatible (not included), ambidextrous lightweight synthetic rear stock, assembly tools and hex keys.

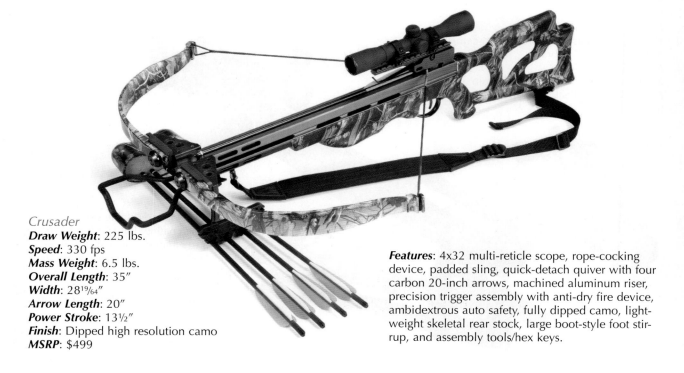

Crusader
Draw Weight: 225 lbs.
Speed: 330 fps
Mass Weight: 6.5 lbs.
Overall Length: 35″
Width: 28¹⁹⁄₆₄″
Arrow Length: 20″
Power Stroke: 13½″
Finish: Dipped high resolution camo
MSRP: $499

Features: 4x32 multi-reticle scope, rope-cocking device, padded sling, quick-detach quiver with four carbon 20-inch arrows, machined aluminum riser, precision trigger assembly with anti-dry fire device, ambidextrous auto safety, fully dipped camo, lightweight skeletal rear stock, large boot-style foot stirrup, and assembly tools/hex keys.

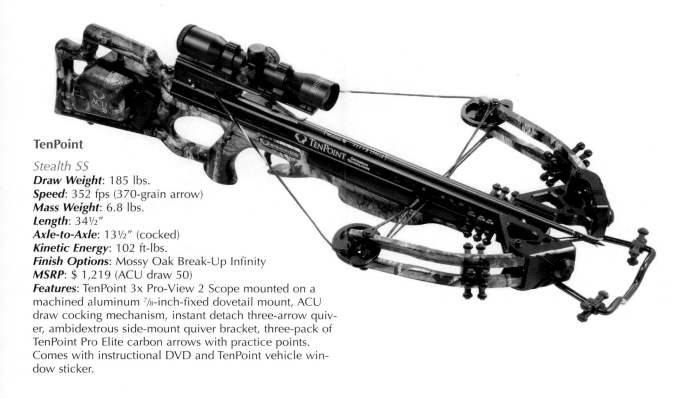

TenPoint

Stealth SS

Draw Weight: 185 lbs.
Speed: 352 fps (370-grain arrow)
Mass Weight: 6.8 lbs.
Length: 34½"
Axle-to-Axle: 13½" (cocked)
Kinetic Energy: 102 ft-lbs.
Finish Options: Mossy Oak Break-Up Infinity
MSRP: $ 1,219 (ACU draw 50)
Features: TenPoint 3x Pro-View 2 Scope mounted on a machined aluminum ⅞-inch-fixed dovetail mount, ACU draw cocking mechanism, instant detach three-arrow quiver, ambidextrous side-mount quiver bracket, three-pack of TenPoint Pro Elite carbon arrows with practice points. Comes with instructional DVD and TenPoint vehicle window sticker.

Tactical XLT

Draw Weight: 185 lbs.
Speed: 352 fps (370-grain arrow)
Mass Weight: 7.3
Axle-to-Axle: 13½" (cocked)
Kinetic Energy: 102 ft-lbs.
Finish Options: Black
MSRP: $1,419 (ACU draw)
Features: Aircraft-grade fluted aluminum barrel, TenPoint RangeMaster Pro Scope mounted on a machined aluminum ⅞-inch-fixed dovetail mount, ACU draw cocking mechanism, instant-detach three-arrow quiver, ambidextrous side-mount quiver bracket, six-pack of TenPoint Pro Lite carbon fiber arrows with practice points, BowJax crossbow noise dampening kit, GripGuard safety shield. Comes with instructional DVD, and TenPoint vehicle window sticker.

Vapor

Draw Weight: 165 lbs.
Speed: 360 fps (420-grain arrow)
Mass Weight: 6.8 lbs.
Cocked Width: 12$^{39}/_{64}$"
Axle-to-Axle: 12$^{39}/_{64}$"
Kinetic Energy: 121 ft-lbs.
Finish Options: RealTree APG
MSRP: $1,899 (ACU draw 50), $2,019 (ACU draw)
Features: PLT (Parallel Limb Technology) bow assembly and FSB (Functionally Superior Bullpup) stock, fitted with carbon fiber barrel, pistol grip, double-dipped camo film finish, integrated string stops, fore grip finger safety, anti-dry fire device, ambidextrous safety. RangeMaster Pro scope mounted on a machined aluminum $^7/_8$-inch-fixed dovetail mount, ACU draw cocking mechanism, instant-detach three-arrow quiver, ambidextrous side-mount quiver bracket, six-pack of TenPoint Pro V22 carbon fiber arrows with practice points, deluxe soft crossbow case, BowJax Crossbow Noise Dampening kit. Comes with instructional DVD and TenPoint vehicle window sticker.

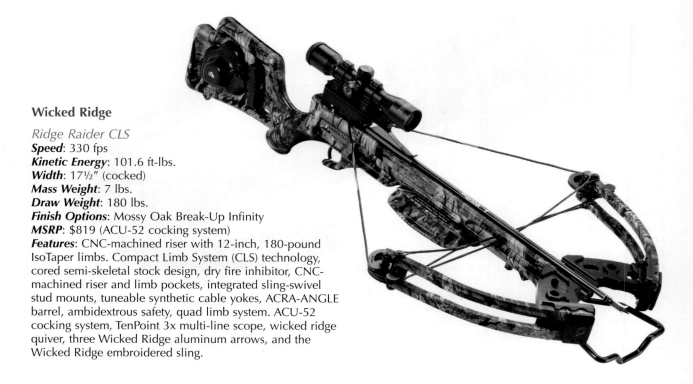

Wicked Ridge

Ridge Raider CLS
Speed: 330 fps
Kinetic Energy: 101.6 ft-lbs.
Width: 17½" (cocked)
Mass Weight: 7 lbs.
Draw Weight: 180 lbs.
Finish Options: Mossy Oak Break-Up Infinity
MSRP: $819 (ACU-52 cocking system)
Features: CNC-machined riser with 12-inch, 180-pound IsoTaper limbs. Compact Limb System (CLS) technology, cored semi-skeletal stock design, dry fire inhibitor, CNC-machined riser and limb pockets, integrated sling-swivel stud mounts, tuneable synthetic cable yokes, ACRA-ANGLE barrel, ambidextrous safety, quad limb system. ACU-52 cocking system, TenPoint 3x multi-line scope, wicked ridge quiver, three Wicked Ridge aluminum arrows, and the Wicked Ridge embroidered sling.

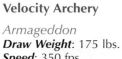

Velocity Archery

Armageddon
Draw Weight: 175 lbs.
Speed: 350 fps
Length: 35″
Mass Weight: 7.9 lbs.
Power Stroke: 15″
Kinetic Energy: 110 lbs.

Trigger Pull: 4 lbs.
Finish Options: Combat Black
MSRP: $499
Features: Split limbs, bull-pup stock, rubberized cheek pad and butt, integrated string stops, rubberized foot stirrup, custom foregrip, 4x32 red/green-reticle, quiver, three carbon arrows, rail lube, and cocking rope.

Defiant
Draw Weight: 150 lbs.
Speed: 325 fps
Mass Weight: 7.5 lbs.
Length: 33″
Axle-to-Axle: 18″ (cocked)
Power Stroke: 14½″
Kinetic Energy: 110 ft-lbs.
Trigger Pull: 4 lbs.
Finish Options: RealTree AP Xtra
MSRP: $429

Features and Included: Split limbs, bull-pup stock, rubberized cheek pad and butt, integrated string stops, rubberized foot stirrup, custom foregrip, 4x32 red/green-reticle, quiver, three carbon arrows, rail lube, and cocking rope.

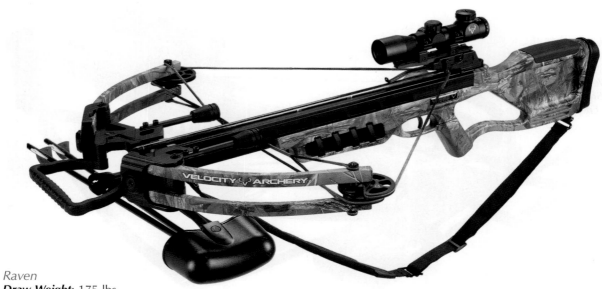

Raven
Draw Weight: 175 lbs.
Speed: 350 fps
Length: 35″
Mass Weight: 8 lbs.
Power Stroke: 15″
Kinetic Energy: 110 ft-lbs.
Trigger Pull: 4 lbs.
Finish Options: RealTree AP Xtra
MSRP: $499
Features and Included: Split limbs, bull-pup stock, rubberized cheek pad and butt, integrated string stops, rubberized foot stirrup, custom foregrip, 4x32 red/green-reticle, quiver, three carbon arrows, rail lube, and cocking rope.

New Arrows and Broadheads 2013

Arrows

Bass Pro Shops RedHead BlackOut X1 Pro Carbon

Features 2″ Blazer vanes and a straightness of ±0.001″ with a weight tolerance of ±0.5-grains and 100% carbon construction. Nocks installed and inserts included. $59.99–$109.99/12-pak

Bass Pro Shops RedHead BlackOut X3 Hunter

The BlackOut X3 Hunter features a straightness tolerance of ±0.003″ with the durability of 100% carbon. Comes with nocks installed and inserts included. Weight tolerance: ±2-grains and ships 32″ with 2″ vanes installed. $44.99–$79.99/12-pak

Bass Pro Shops RedHead BlackOut X5 Envy Carbon

100% carbon construction with 2″ Blazer vanes. Nocks installed and arrows shipped full length. Inserts included. Straightness ±0.005″ and weight tolerance of ±2-grains. $34.99–$59.99/12-pak

Beman ICS Crossbow Hunter

Designed specifically for big game, the ICS Crossbow Hunter features high-strength lightweight carbon which draws speed from high performance crossbows to aid in driving broadheads through big game for more pass-through impacts. ICS Crossbow Hunters combines super strong multi-laminate carbon with proven components systems for Beman's most advanced crossbow arrow ever. Lightweight ICS Crossbow Hunters shoots flatter and delivers deadly kinetic energy downrange with aerospace alloy inserts and front-of-center-enhancing brass inserts are available sold separately. Made in USA. $44.99/6-pak/fletched

Cabela's Outfitter Camo Carbon

Unidirectional, carbon-fiber core surrounded by high-strength composite fibers for durability and with a micro-smooth finish for quiet draws and easier removal from targets. A high-visibility, factory-installed cresting makes tracking this arrow in flight or at point of impact much easier. Available for draw weights 55/70 (400 spine weighing 8.6 gpi) and 65/80 (340 spine weighting 9.5 gpi). H nocks installed and HP inserts loose. $59.99/6-pak.

Carbon Express MAXIMA RED

The carbon Maxima RED is engineered with stiffer ends to contain and control dynamic spine to the center of the arrow, or the "red zone." Available in matched weight and spine 6- or 12-pack sets with a spine tolerance of ±0.0025". and weight sorting tolerance of ±1.0-grains. Straightness is ±0.0025" maximum measurement, not an average. Two dynamic spines cover bows from 40–92 lbs. $84.99/6-pak.

Carbon Express Mutiny Slasher

A highly polished finish allows for a quiet draw and easy removal from the target. Available in 6- or 12-pack sets sorted and matched by weight to ±2.0-grains with straightness to ±0.003". launchpad precision nocks, which deliver a controlled arrow release, better shaft alignment, and more consistent accuracy shot after shot. They also come with Carbon Express exclusive NRG-2 compact low-profile performance vanes for maximum arrow velocity and greater accuracy. $55/6-pak fletched.

Easton Aftermath

The reduced diameter multilayer carbon offers wind resistance for improved accuracy, and less friction for improved penetration on big game. Easton RPS inserts and orange H Nocks. Made in the USA. Spines available 500 (7.3 gpi), 400 (8.8 gpi), 340 (9.6 gpi), 300 (10.2 gpi). $44.99/6-pak fletched with 2" blazers to a pack.

Easton HEXX

Arrows feature preinstalled H Nocks, Microlite H inserts with a straightness of ±0.001" and a weight tolerance of ±1-grain with factory installed cresting. Offered in 480 spine weighing 6.3 gpi, 400 weighing 7.2 gpi, and 330 weighing 7.9 gpi. $93.99/6-pak.

PSE Carbon Force EXT Hunter

This small diameter and extra thick wall-high modular carbon shaft is ±0.001 straight; ½-grain per dozen; shafts consistent and spine matched within ±3-grains. Coated with PSE whisper coating for easy arrow pull. $199/12-pak.

Victory VAP (Victory Armour Piercing)

The VAP is a small diameter thick walled arrow for maximizing penetration with low-friction coefficients in flight and upon entry and exit of target animals. Small diameters also minimize in-flight aerodynamic drag and crosswind effects. The VAP is available in spines of 250 to 1,000 and with grains per inch varying from 5.2 (1000) to 9.7 (250). Straightnesses varying from ±0.001, 0.003 and 0.006. $140-$165/12-pak.

Broadheads

Barnett Gamecrusher

The 100-grain has a 1½" cutting diameter and utilizes a heavy-duty O-ring to ensure deployable blades remain in place until required to open in the target. $40/3-pak.

Clean Shot Hogzilla

A laser housed in the broadhead projects a beam out to the target. Put the laser on the target and release the string. The Hogzilla is designed for hogs and is made in the USA. Available in either 125- or 150-grain models. $99/2-pak.

Bass Pro Shops RedHead BlackOut

Fixed-blade design with German-made blades. Stainless steel ferrule promises strength, with 0.030" thick blades and a 1¹⁄₁₆" cutting diameter. $29.99/3-pak.

Crossbow Killzone

The 2-blade rear-deploying blades have 2-inch cutting diameter and are available in either 100 or 125-grains models. Practice blade included. $39.99/3-pak

Flying Arrow Archery Toxic

The Toxic is a coring broadhead with a cutting surface of 4.7". Stainless main blades with aircraft quality aluminum ferrule. 100-grain 3-pak retails for $45.

Fulton Precision Archery Ram Cat

Available in both 100- and 125-grain with solid one-piece stainless steel ferrule and chisel tip for cut-on-contact performance. Cutting diameters for 100-grain tape 1⅜" and 1½" for the 125. Blades are 0.032" thick 400-series stainless. $39/3-pak.

Innerloc Deep Slice

Designed for Easton Injexion arrows with a cutting diameter of 1¹⁄₁₆" at a weight of 100-grains. A thru-ferrule tip post insures broadhead integrity on the toughest of targets. $37.99/3-pak

Innerloc Falcon CLAW

The Falcon broadhead provides slicing action, and the CLAW is an appendage which slips behind the broadhead providing shock to small game. The CLAW vastly improves knockdown power on targets where pass-through's are not desired. $36.99/3-pak

Killzone 125

The Killzone 125 has rear deploying blades and a no-O-ring, rubber band design with a 2" cutting diameter and practice blade. Available with trophy tip or cut-on-contact tip. $39.99/3-pak

Low KE Killzone 100

The KE is designed for low poundage and short draw bows (and subsequently produces low kinetic energy). friction-fit blades deploy from the rear with a 1½" cutting diameter. $39.99/3-pak.

QAD Exodus

400 series stainless steel 1¼" cutting diameter blades sweep back over the shaft for better integrity. The 100-grain, 0.035" blade thickness and a cut-on-contact heads retail for $40/3-pak

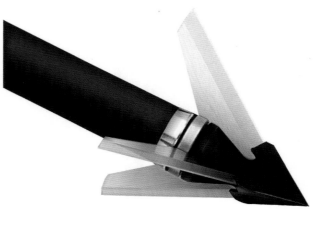

Rage Chisel Tip X-Treme

The incredibly aggressive tip is designed to split bone on errant shots. A 2⁵⁄₁₆" wound is huge with 0.035" thick stainless-steel blades. $49.99/3-pak.

Muzzy Trocar

Engineered for rugged use, the fixed-blade broadhead features a 0.035-inch-thick helix-blade design. A solid-steel ferrule, 1³⁄₁₆" cutting diameter, and is available in either 100- or 125-grain weights in standard configuration or Deep Six. $29.95/6-pak.

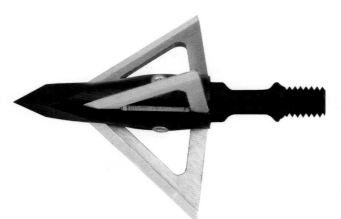

Rage Crossbow X

Designed for extra-fast crossbows. A 2″ cutting diameter with 0.035″ thick stainless-steel blades. The Crossbow X retails for $49.99/3-pak.

Rage Hypodermic

An exceptionally sharp, 1-piece, solid steel ferrule with hybrid-tip design. Deployable feature 0.035″ thick stainless steel with new shock collars that replace rubber bands. Includes practice head. $49.99/3-pak

Rage Xtreme 125

Designed like its 100-grain counterpart, the 125-grain features a ferrule with a very low ballistic coefficient, a 2.3″ cutting diameter, and a sweeping blade angle that maintains kinetic energy longer and penetrates deeper than any other broadhead. $49.99/3-pak.

Slick Trick Nuke

Known for fixed-blade broadheads, the Nuke is a 100-grain with 0.035″ rear deploying blades. Practice blade included. 1 13/16″ cutting diameter. $40/3-pak

Slick Trick VT100

The Viper Trick (VT) has 0.035″ stainless Lutz blades and a stainless ferrule. Available in both 100- and 125-grain, the VT features 1¹⁄₁₆″ cutting diameter with almost a full 2″ of blade surface. $30/3-pak.

Swhacker 2"

100-grain expandable 2-blade has 2" cutting diameter and 1" in-flight diameter. Stainless steel main blades are 0.032" thick and the point is case hardened. $33–$52/3-pak.

WASP Queen

For the ladies in the house, WASP Queen is pink. The Queen is built in both 75- and 100-grain weights. A razor-sharp ground tip insures good penetration with low poundage bows. Blades are 0.027" thick.

Trophy Take Ulmer Edge

Low flight profile, rear-deploying blades design. The 1½" cutting diameter head can be locked closed for practice without damaging blades. Stainless steel tip is rugged. $45–$50/3-pak.

New Sights, Rests, Releases, and Quivers 2013

Sights

Allen Company Peak Single Pin Wrapped Sight

0.019" wrapped fiber-optic single-pin design. Manufactured from solid aluminum with bright yellow optical aiming circle. Macro adjustable for windage and elevation. $49.

Axcel AXAT-DK HD-Pro

The new and improved HD-Pro has a micro-adjustable dovetail bracket and includes a Mathews Harmonic Damper. Available with 4, 5, or 7 pins in 0.010", 0.019" or 0.029" fiber size. Included with the sight is a universal quiver-mount bracket, making mounting your quiver easier. Compatible with 1¾" or 43mm diameter lenses. $239

APEX Gamechanger

An adjustable tension cam lock snugs the quiver to the bow's riser. Adjustable up and down. Soft touch tactical coating. Available in 5 arrow RealTree APG, 5-arrow Black, 5-arrow LOST, and 5-arrow Mossy Oak Infinity. $89.99

Archer's Xtreme AX Driver

A ranging style sight with a 0.019" single, fiber-optic pin design offering target sight accuracy with a precision vertical drive system and with key sight features that are required to make longer than average shots. Large sight housing offers an unmatched view of the target downrange. The fast and effective EDG Elevation Drive Gear system will allow the shooter to have pinpoint accuracy at any range. Second-axis gang adjustment with third-axis adjustable level system. $199.

Axion Soul Hunter

Weighing in at a mere 6 oz, this is designed for the hunter looking for the lightest weighted sight. CNC-machined with staggered mounting holes to fit any application. Independent windage and elevation adjustments with laser-etched adjustment lines. 2" aperture and 0.019" pins. Right and left-handed adaptable. $69.

APEX Bone Collector Gamechanger

Extra long fibers routed through the bracket increases durability and exposure to UV light. Soft-feel technical coating provides a quiet surface to reduce any unwanted noise. Ultra-fine click adjustment for windage and elevation. Level is illuminated with luminescent tape and is adjustable on the second and third-axis level with two vertical bars. Five 0.019" diameter pin. Available in black and camo dip. $148.

Axion VUE 400

CNC machined of 6061 aluminum for rugged and lightweight construction. Protected fiber-optics with a rheostat light and level. Solid lockdown windage and elevation with laser-engraved reference marks for sighting in your bow. 2" aperture with Glo Ring for ease-of-sighting. Pins available in 0.019" or 0.009" fiber. $129.

Axion VUE Micro Adjust

CNC machined of 6061 aluminum for rugged and lightweight construction. Protected fiber-optics with a rheostat light and level. Solid lockdown micro-adjust windage and elevation with laser engraved reference marks for sighting in your bow. 2" aperture with Glo Ring for ease of sighting. Pins available in 0.019" or 0.009" fiber. $149.

Black Gold Ascent Ambush

Ranger-style (movable) CNC-machined 6061 aluminum with one green 0.019" fiber-optic pin and oversized level. PhotoChromatic housing lightens and darkens for just the right amount of ambient light hitting the pin. 2x or 4x lens adaptable. Sculpted base with oversized clamping dovetails. $189

Black Gold Widow Maker

Micro-gang adjustable with rugged pins. Low-profile photo chromatic housing lightens and darkens to adjust pin brightness. CNC-machined 6061 T6 aircraft aluminum construction with 0.019" fiber-optic pins. $149

CBE Tek-Hybrid

A ranging style sight with a rapid drive elevation system for quick and precise vertical adjustment, a fiber management block with rheostat light for adjustable pin brightness and a rearview-sight tape display for making those fine, last minute adjustments without moving your bow. All Tek-Hybrid sights come standard with Rhino Pins and micro-adjustment. Available in 1-, 3-, and 5-pin housings. $189

Cobra Double Tine

Ranging style sight with no-tool windage and elevation adjustment with large, white aperture ring and adjustable third-axis bubble level. Rheostat light illuminates 0.019" pin. Fits right or left-handed bows. Available in black. $90

Copper-John Rut Wrecker

Carbon composite build with very wide bracket and structural supports in traditionally weak areas. A dovetail bracket makes adjustments easy. Available in 3- and 5-pins versions. Exceptionally light yet very rugged. Lost and Mossy Oak Infinity. $59

Fuse Carbon Blade

All-new Carbon Blade sights are equipped with an adjustable sight rail, built from a revolutionary Carbon Blade frame for strength and low mass weight. Third-axis leveling and hi-tech, bright, steel-encased 0.019" fiber pins in 3-, 5-, or 7-pin configurations are standard. Available in micro (M-Series) or standard (G-Series) gang adjust and in RealTree Xtra, AP, Max-1 and Black Out. $149

Fuse Pro Fire

12" of wrapped fiber-optics, precision-built metal pins deliver brightness to light up the target. Available in 3- or 5-pin configurations and comes standard in black. $39

PSE Slider II

Ranger-style sight with moving fiber-optic pin. Micro-adjust windage and adjustable third-axis level. All aluminum construction with rheostat UV light and phosphorescent sight ring. Lens compatible with 0.019" pin. Black. $69

Spot-Hogg Spark

An industry-first, lighted crosshairs with rheostat intensity, allow archers to quickly and easily adjust light concentration to better match natural lighting conditions. Lightweight 6061 aluminum construction. The wide sighting ring allows for the peep to be seen during low-light conditions. $189

G5 Optix Rock

Ambidextrous design with 100% CNC-machined aluminum construction. Metal pins in 0.019" and 0.010" fiber sizes. Micro-adjustable elevation and windage. Second-axis adjustable with 4-pin model available in Black, RealTree AP, Max-1, Lost Camo, Lost AT, Optifade Forest, and Optifade Open. 6-pin model available in Black, Max-1. $109–$139

Sword Centurian Hunter 2

Ranging style sight of CNC-machined T6061 aluminum construction with 2" aperture. Five pins available in 0.010", 0.019", or 0.029". LED light with approx 2" in elevation travel and third-axis adjustment. Preprinted yardage tapes. Available in right- or left-handed models. $209.99

Trijicon AccuPin AccuDial

A ranging style sight with unique triangular aiming tip points to your target, it does not obstruct it like traditional fiber-optic pins. Dual illumination system utilizes both fiber-optics and tritium for a very bright pin under any condition. A built-in transmission makes adjusting the sight simple and very smooth. $495

Trophy Ridge React

Features a tool-less sight system that, once calibrated at 20 and 30 yards, makes your 40-, 50-, and 60-yard pins mathematically impossible to be inaccurate. Constructed of copolymer; reversible sight mount with multiple mounting holes for versatility; (5) 0.019" fiber-optic pins; includes rheostat light and sight level. $139

TruGlo Archers Choice Range Rover Micro Adjust

The tool-less yardage block adjusts easily for quick, on the move yardage changes. An all-metal 0.019" sight pin is bright with a 1.8" inner aperture diameter. Glow-in-the-dark shooters's ring helps align peep sight. 40 pre-printed yardage labels help with sighting in. Adjustable for right or left-handed shooters. $119.99

TruGlo Rival FX

CNC-machined, ambidextrous sight is outfitted with interchangeable fiber design that permits swift, easy fiber replacement and color changes without disturbing the pin position. Illuminated level with luminescent tape, 2" inner diameter aperture, adjustable second-axis aperture, push-button light, and glow-in-the-dark ring. $139

TruGlo TSX Pro

Adjustably lighted, tool-less adjustment sight. Zero gap pins with extra long fibers routed through the housing for protection. CNC-machined of aircraft grade aluminum for durability. 1.8" aperture with bright glow ring for ease-of-sighting. Fits left or right handed shooters. 3-pin 0.019" diameter and 5-pin. Available in black or camo dip. $111

TruGlo TSX Pro Series Standard

Stainless steel tube-pin design keeps the fiber-optic safe. Tru Touch technical coating. 2″ inner aperture diameter with lightweight construction. Level is illuminated by luminescent tape with adjustable second and third-axis level with two vertical bars. CNC-machined. For right- or left-handed shooters. $62

TruGlo Tundra Series

Econ-priced series features high-end performance at a reasonable price. Bright fiber-optic pins are viewed through a wide, 1.8″ aperture. Level included to preclude canting the bow while aiming. Technical coating makes the sight soft to the touch. Adjustable for right- or left-handed shooters. $33

Quivers

Fuse Satori Streamline

This super lightweight quiver is built for those hunters on the move. Its minimalistic design is helium light and features a quick-detach design. Its long length grips arrows like a two piece without the bulk and is easily removed. Holds six arrows. $123

Fuse Switch

The Switch is capable of being changed from a 3- to a 5-arrow configuration to accommodate your hunting style. The module cover converts to accommodate the hunt. Low-profile design and modular grippers add to the quivers versatility. RealTree AP, Max-1, Black Out, or RealTree Xtra. $169

G5 Head-Loc

A flexible hood is quiet, lightweight, and has superior absorbing properties over traditional plastic. The low-profile design allows the quiver to sit close to the bow, improving shot balance and reducing the chances of catching branches while stalking through the woods. 6-arrow capacity. Tree mounting bracket included. $54.99

Kwikee Kwiver HI-5

The HI-5 mounting bracket allows for one-handed operation, either taking the quiver off or on. 6-inches of vertical adjustment allows the quiver to be moved for better balance on short limbed bows. Compatible with either carbon or aluminum. Available in 5-arrow capacity in Carbon Black, Lost, Mossy Oak Break-Up Infinity, RealTree APG. $65

PSE Flex 5

Lightweight flexible composite frame, dual grippers, movable frame mounting options. Quick-detach bracket for ease of operation. Mossy Oak Break-Up Infinity or Skullworks. $59

PSE X-5

A machined-aluminum frame with no moving parts to rattle and make noise during the shot. 2 mounting posts are easy to install and use. The PSE X Quiver will accept mechanical- or fixed-blade broadheads. Holds 5 arrows. Mossy Oak Break-Up Infinity. $99

Tightspot

Redesigned with foam-free hood and better arrow grippers to hold a range of arrows from the smallest to the largest. Weighs 10-ounces. Wrapped carbon-rod construction with independent arrow adjustment. Available in Matte Black, RealTree AP, RealTree APG, RealTree MAX-1, RealTree Xtra, Mossy Oak Infinity, Mossy Oak Treestand, Carbon Weave, and Lost. $139

Trophy Ridge Beacon

The frame is injection molded using ballistic copolymer. The hood houses four total non-game spooking green LEDs. Three LEDs are on the outside for maneuvering in the dark while one green LED is housed inside the hood for ease of arrow removal and insertion. $89

Trophy Ridge Torsion ▼

A universal quick-detach bracket for custom attachment according to arrow length. Rotates for ease of arrow access. Holds four arrows and is molded of ballistic copolymer for rugged use. Built in hood rope for hanging on a tree limb. $39

TruGlo Tru-Tec 5 ▲

Lightweight aluminum construction. Smooth, one-hand removal. Secure double-gripper design fits both carbon and aluminum arrows; mechanical and fixed broadheads. Mounting bracket is adjustable up/down with rubber hood insert to reduce noise. Threaded light mount accepts any TruGlo or Apex light. $69.99

Arrow Rests

Alpine Archery Whisperlite ▼

The Alpine Whisperlite is new and improved. This fall-away has improved sealed bearings for faster and smoother operation. Rest activation cord attaches to the buss cable for easy installation. Built-in arrow holder, independent windage, and elevation adjustment. $49.

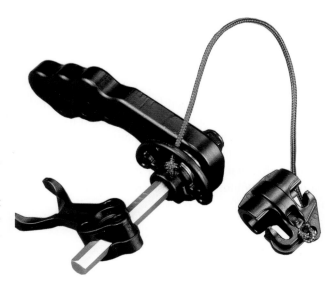

TruGlo Carbon XS ▲

Carbon construction makes this quiver light and tough. Cam-lock mounting system allows for smooth one-hand removal and moves the quiver tight against the bow riser for better balance and accuracy. The double arrow gripper design coupled with the rubberized arrow hood makes the Carbon XS perfect for both mechanical and fixed broadheads. $59

Axion Archery Pulse

The Axion Pulse automatic arrow rest guides arrows longer and retracts faster. The rest then resets itself to the up-right, ready position automatically. Provides maximum fletching clearance. Tested on bows shooting over 400 fps. Available in Black, Tactical, Mossy Oak Infinity, RealTree Xtra, and Pink. Right- or left-handed models. $189

Mathews Ultra Rest

The rest knows when to release and when to remain in the upright, ready-to-fire position. Rapid spring deployment ensures the rest drops away from the arrows path without interference. Features total fletching clearance, full arrow containment, and Mathews Harmonic Damping to remove excess vibration and noise. $139

G5 Halo Capture Rest

Equipped with independent adjustable launcher arms, this full capture rest can be adjusted to any size arrow shaft, including micro diameter arrows. The ambidextrous Halo Capture Rest features forward-flexing arms that spring out of the way of the arrows path for maximum forgiveness and accuracy. Available in Black. $49.99.

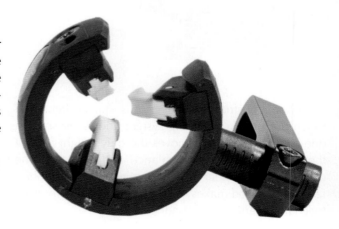

NAP Apache Carbon

Super quick operation along with 360-degree sound dampening mean whisper quiet operation, no matter what. The Apache does not require any wrenches or other tools to make adjustments; just set it and forget it. Laser graduations make fine tuning in the field a snap. Carbon black color only. Right-handed only. $119

Trophy Taker Smack Down Pro

An all-metal containment rest with variable attachment sights. Can be attached to the upper or lower limb or up or down the buss cable. Sealed ball bearing make for smooth operation. Built-in launcher dampeners for less noise and vibration and available in right or left-handed model. Black, RealTree AP, and Lost. $119

Schaffer Opposition

Bounce-back-free design cradles arrow when in the at-rest position and throughout draw cycle. Upon release, the grippers slide out of the way for total arrow clearance. Interchangeable side plates for Mathews, Hoyt, and PSE plus a Universal fit model. $159

TruGlo Carbon XS

Manufactured of lightweight carbon composite containment ring with a CNC-machined aluminum mounting bracket for strength in a light weight design. The launcher arms are piston activated, and there are no major moving components. $49

TruGlo Down Draft

A full containment drop away rest constructed of all aluminum. A stainless steel launcher arm with sealed bushings increases downward pressure during launch. This rest is laser-engraved so the shooter can make precise adjustments. The rest comes black in color and is available for right- or left-handed shooters. $59

Vapor Trail Limb Driver Pro V

Free-floating launcher blade at full draw allows initial arrow shock to be absorbed, resulting in truer arrow flight and more accuracy. Driver cord attaches to upper limb for immediate response after release. Can be used on either solid- or split-limb bows. $129.99

Vapor Trail Limb Driver Pro

New and improved Limbdriver Pro is operable from the top or bottom limb, increasing options for your personal setup preference. Available in Lost, RealTree APG, Mossy Oak Break-Up Infinity, and custom target colors (red, blue, silver, green, purple, and pink). $119

Xtreme Hardcore Gear V-Twin Capture Rest

Independent adjustable spring tension on each fluoro-polymer launcher allows for custom tuning of side and downward tension. CNC machined from billet aluminum. $89.95

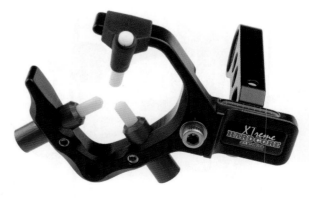

Releases

Cabela's Marksman

Adjustable length, trigger travel, and poundage. Precision-machined head assembly with Teflon-coated trigger and jaws. Spring loaded jaws and padded camo buckle strap. Made by industry leading Tru-Fire. Fits right or left hand. Made in USA. $59.99

Hot-Shot Nano

A full 30 percent smaller than most other releases. Lever link trigger results in less creep and a crisper trigger pull. Black leather stap. $79

Cobra Serpent EZ Adjust

Freely rotating dual caliper bow release with no-tool length adjustment. Padded RealTree camo buckle strap with forward mounted, fully adjustable trigger. $55

Jim Fletcher Insider

This loop-only style release resets after the shot and features a roller system for the ultimate in smooth performance with no trigger travel. The forward trigger helps gain back lost draw length when using the loop. Trigger is infinitely adjustable from heavy to hair trigger, and the hook is easily attached to the loop. Available with a deluxe leather buckle strap or a deluxe nylon strap with Velcro closure. Lifetime warranty. $75

Scott Exxus

Thumb trigger, three-fingered hand-held design with fully adjustable trigger tension and travel with fully rotational head. Interchangeable spring system for full range adjustment. Machined 440C stainless steel internal components with anti-wear/anti-friction titanium coating. Available in RealTree AP, black or red/black. $199

Scott Samurai

Features infinitely adjustable nylon-strap connector system, which offers torque-free performance. Offers infinite length adjustment and reduces torque, and the one-piece curved-trigger fits the contours of fingers. Buckle, hook, and loop models available in black only. $49

Scott Hero

Made specifically to fit the smaller hands and wrists of young (or women) shooters. The nylon strap connector offers easy and infinite length adjustment. Knurled-trigger for superior grip. Buckle model available in pink and blue. Hook and loop model available in pink and blue. $49

Timney Trigger

A double caliper features two jaws that open by pulling the trigger and close on the string by pushing the trigger forward. The hook features a single, open-faced prong that allows an archer to quickly connect to the bow string. It also engages by pushing the trigger forward and releases by pulling it. Both styles have sensitivity and length of pull adjustments. Timney releases attach to your wrist with leather straps adjusted by buckles. $93

Tru Ball Fang

Hook style release featuring a rubber insert in the trigger for improved feel. Two trigger options included in package: a straight trigger for more draw/speed and a relaxed trigger for greater comfort. The Fang also features a superior 2-screw trigger sensitivity setting provided by a separate trigger travel adjustment screw, and a separate trigger pressure setting screw with your choice of included varied weight springs. Black, Lost. $119

Tru-Fire Hardcore 4-Finger

T-handle style release, intended to be drawn with four fingers. An added metal tab opposite the hook allows connecting the release to the bowstring's D-loop to let it hang. The metal tab will keep the release from falling off. The machined aluminum head has a three-position adjustment mechanism, providing for 3-, 24- and 50-ounces of pressure needed to activate the thumb release. Trigger travel adjustment and adjustable lanyard. $129

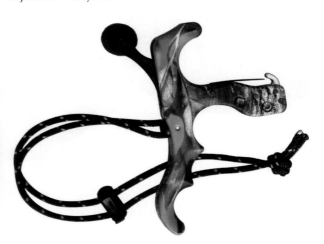

Tru Ball V-Lock Combo Max Hunter 3

Three-finger T-handle release that's attached to a wrist strap. So you get the draw feel of a T-handle, with the drawing power of your wrist. The release head has two jaws. There's a thumb bar on the handle that you push forward to open the jaws to attach the release to the bowstring, and you then push it again to release the string. The head swivels 360 degrees, so there's no chance of string torque. Straps come with Velcro or a buckle. MSRP Not Available.

Tru-Fire Hurricane Buckle Junior

The Hurricane Junior is designed for small hands. The wrist strap is smaller, so it can fit the smallest hands. It's adjusted by a buckle. The release also can be adjusted to shorten or lengthen the distance between the head and the wrist strap. The jaws on the Hurricane Junior's head are spring-loaded. You pull the trigger to open the jaws and connect the release to the string and then you pull the trigger again at full draw to release an arrow. $39

TruGlo Detonator

CNC-machined construction providing dependable, sturdy, worry-free performance. Stainless steel, wear-free single-jaw design is equipped with a streamlined magnetic open-hook design for fast loading and reloading and is perfect for string loops. 360° rotating head eliminates string torque for increased accuracy in the field. $79

TruGlo Nitrus

Stainless steel dual-caliper design with smooth trigger pull and micro-adjustable trigger for sensitivity and travel. The precision CNC-machined construction assures reliable, durable, worry-free performance. $59

TruGlo Speed Shot

90-degree pivoting connector system with torque-free 360-degree rotating head. Contoured, adjustable one-piece trigger and synchronized jaw design for smooth trigger pull. Compact dual-jaw design is perfect for string loops. CNC-machined aluminum construction. Available with micro-adjustable connector or torque-free rope connector. $49

SECTION 4
CURRENT PRODUCTS

Current Compounds

Alpine Archery

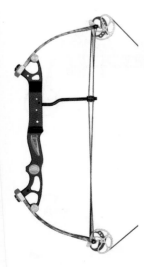

Rookie Youth Bow
Axle-to-Axle: 28"
Speed: N/A
Brace height: 6"
Mass Weight: 2.5 lbs.
Draw Weights: 10–35 lbs.
Draw Lengths:17"–23"
Cam: Radial Force A
Limbs: Bi-Flex composite limb, pink camo, or Bronze Camo
Cable Guard: Straight mounted carbon
Sight window: 8.25" single plane window with Alpine Rookie Medallion
Pocket: Mini Pocket Mounting System
Riser Color: Black powder coat
Grip: 2-piece rosewood
Let-Off: 65%
MSRP: $229
Features: A full 7 inches of draw adjustment and a peak weight of 35 pounds. Designed for the aspiring young bowhunter. Built to target ages 5 to 12 years.

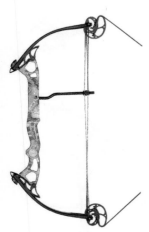

Ruckus
Axle-to-Axle: 30¾"
Speed: N/A
Brace Height: 6"
Mass Weight: 3 lbs.
Draw Weights: 50 lbs.
Draw Lengths: 22"–28"
Cam: Radial Force B
Limbs: Bi-Flex composite limb, black
Cable Guard: Straight mounted carbon
Sight Window: 8.25" single plane window with Ruckus medallion
Pocket: LX Pocket Mounting System
Riser Color: pink camo, or Mossy Oak Infinity camo
Grip: 2 piece rosewood
Let-Off: 65%
MSRP: $279
Features: Designed for ages 10 to 16. All CNC-machined components. Ruckus fitted with a wood grip and a pewter finished medallion.

Verdict
Axle-to-Axle: 31½"
Speed: 328 fps (IBO)
Brace Height: 6¾"
Mass Weight: 4 lbs.
Draw Weight: 60 lbs. 70 lbs.
Draw Length: 27"–30"
Cam: Velocitec 3G Cam
Limbs: Gordon composite limb, film dip finished in RealTree APG
Cable Guard: Fast Lane Roller Guide
Pocket: Limb Vice Pocket Mounting System
Riser Color: RealTree APG
Grip: 2 piece rosewood
Let-Off: 80%
MSRP: $649
Features: A reflexed forged riser, integrated offset quiver mount for optimal balance, adjustable string stop, 416 stainless steel stabilizer insert to the Verdict for positive and long lasting thread engagement for the stabilizer.

Bass Pro Shops

Kronik
Axle-to-Axle: 30¼"
Speed: 305 fps (IBO)
Brace Height: 7⅞"
Mass Weight: 3.5 lbs.
Draw Weights: 40 lbs.50 lbs. 60 lbs. 70 lbs.
Draw Length: 26"–30"
Let-Off: 80%
Kinetic Energy: N/A
Finish Options: RealTree APG
MSRP: $399
Features: CNC-machined aluminum riser, parallel limb technology, large draw length adjustment range, 3-pin sight, Hostage capture-style arrow rest, 5-arrow quiver.

RedHead Toxik
Axle-to-Axle: 32″
Speed: 320 fps (IBO)
Brace Height: 7″
Mass Weight: 3.8 lbs.
Draw Weights: 50 lbs. 60 lbs. 70 lbs.
Draw Length: 26½″–30½″
Let-Off: 80%
Kinetic Energy: N/A
Finish Options: RealTree APG

MSRP: $499
Features: CNC-machined aluminum riser, parallel limb technology, rotating cam module, no bow press draw length adjustments, 3-pin sight, Hostage capture-style arrow rest, 5-arrow quiver, 5″ stabilizer, wrist sling.

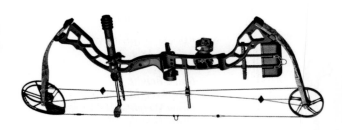

Bear Archery

Anarchy
Axle-to-Axle: 35.25″
Speed (IBO): 330 fps
Brace Height: 7.25″
Weight: 3.8 lbs.
Draw Length Range: 25″–31.5″
Peak Draw Height: 50 lbs. 60 lbs. 70 lbs.
Strings/Cables: Bear Contra-Band HP
Cable Slide: 4x4 Roller Guard
Let-Off: 80%
MSRP: $899.99
Features: Bear flat top cam; zero-tolerance limb pockets; stainless steel stabilizer brushing; customizable grip; dual arc offset string suppressors with added vibration-damping boots; available in black, camo, red, and green.

Domain
Axle-to-Axle: 33″
Speed (IBO): 322 fps
Brace Height: 7″
Weight: 4 lbs.
Draw Length Range: 26″–31″
Peak Draw Height: 50 lbs. 60 lbs. 70 lbs.
Strings/Cables: Contra-Band
Cable Slide: Slide
Let-Off: 80%
MSRP: $599.99
Features: All-new Bear E3 cam; offset string suppressors; zero-tolerance limb pockets; Idler Wheel with dual stainless steel sealed bearings; max preload quad limbs; available in camo.

Apprentice 2
Axle-to-Axle: 27.5″
Speed (IBO): 265 fps
Brace Height: 6.125″
Weight: 2.9 lbs.
Draw Length Range: 15″–27″
Peak Draw Height: 15 lbs. 60 lbs.
Strings/Cables: Contra-Band
Cable Slide: Slide
Let-Off: 70%
MSRP: $279.99
Features: Dual-rotating modular cam system; zero-tolerance limb pockets; Bear flared quad limbs; available in camo and pink camo.

Empire
Axle-to-Axle: 32″
Speed (IBO): 330 fps
Brace Height: 7″
Weight: 4 lbs.
Draw Length Range: 24″–31″
Peak Draw Height: 50 lbs. 60 lbs. 70 lbs.
Strings/Cables: Bear Contra-Band HP
Cable Slide: 4x4 Roller Guard
Let-Off: 80%
MSRP: $849.99
Features: All-new Bear S13 cam; stainless steel stabilizer brushing; customizable grip; zero-tolerance limb pockets; adjustable offset string suppressors; max preload quad limbs; lightweight Skeleton Idler Wheel with dual stainless steel sealed bearings. Available in black, camo, snow, red, and green.

Encounter
Axle-to-Axle: 30.5″
Speed (IBO): 310 fps
Brace Height: 7.75″
Weight: 3.7 lbs.
Draw Length Range: 27″–32″
Peak Draw Height: 50 lbs. 60 lbs. 70 lbs.
Strings/Cables: Contra-Band
Cable Slide: Slide
Let-Off: 80%
MSRP: $299.99
Features: Bear rotating-modular E2-cam; zero-tolerance limb pockets; string suppressor; Bear flared quad limbs; Idler Wheel with dual stainless steel sealed bearings; available in camo.

Legion
Axle-to-Axle: 30.5″
Speed (IBO): 318 fps
Brace Height: 7″
Weight: 4 lbs.
Draw Length Range: 26″–31″
Peak Draw Height: 50 lbs. 60 lbs. 70 lbs.
Strings/Cables: Contra-Band
Cable Slide: Slide
Let-Off: 80%
MSRP: $399.99
Features: Bear rotating-modular E2-cam; zero-tolerance limb pockets; dual arc offset string suppressors with added vibration-dampening boots; Bear flared quad limbs; Idler Wheel with dual stainless steel sealed bearings; available in camo.

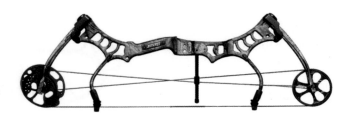

Home Wrecker
Axle-to-Axle: 28.625″
Speed (IBO): 280 fps
Brace Height: 7.25″
Weight: 3.2 lbs.
Draw Length Range: 22″–28″
Peak Draw Height: 40 lbs. 50 lbs.
Strings/Cables: Contra-Band
Cable Slide: Slide
Let-Off: 80%
MSRP: $399.99
Features: Bear single cam; dual arc offset string suppressors with added vibration-dampening boots; Bear flared quad limbs; axle-mounted weight dampeners; available in camo.

Method
Axle-to-Axle: 33″
Speed (IBO): 340 fps
Brace Height: 6.75″
Weight: 4 lbs.
Draw Length Range: 26.5″–31″
Peak Draw Height: 50 lbs. 60 lbs. 70 lbs.
Strings/Cables: Bear Contra-Band HP
Cable Slide: Slide
Let-Off: 75%
MSRP: $649.99
Features: All-new Bear H13 cam; zero-tolerance limb pockets; offset string suppressors; max preload quad limbs; available in black and camo.

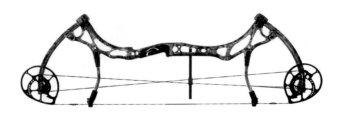

Motive 6

Axle-to-Axle: 32"
Speed (IBO): 350 fps
Brace Height: 6"
Weight: 4 lbs.
Draw Length Range: 25.5"–30"
Peak Draw Height: 50 lbs. 60 lbs.
70 lbs.
Strings/Cables: Bear Contra-Band
HP
Cable Slide: 4x4 Roller Guard
Let-Off: 75%
MSRP: $899.99
Features: All-new Bear H13 cam;
zero-tolerance limb pockets; stainless steel stabilizer brushing; customizable grip; adjustable offset string suppressors; max preload quad limbs; available in black, snow, camo, red, and green.

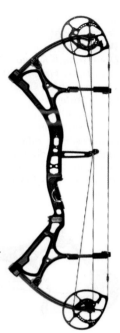

Outbreak

Axle-to-Axle: 29.25"
Speed (IBO): 308 fps
Brace Height: 7.25"
Weight: 3.5 lbs.
Draw Length Range: 16"–30"
Peak Draw Height: 15 lbs. 70 lbs.
Strings/Cables: Contra-Band
Cable Slide: Slide
Let-Off: 80%
MSRP: $299.99
Features: Dual-rotating modular cam system; zero-tolerance limb pockets; string suppressor, max preload quad limbs; available in camo.

Motive 7

Axle-to-Axle: 32"
Speed (IBO): 340 fps
Brace Height: 7"
Weight: 4 lbs.
Draw Length Range: 26.5"–31"
Peak Draw Height: 50 lbs. 60 lbs.
70 lbs.
Strings/Cables: Bear Contra-Band
HP
Cable Slide: 4x4 Roller Guard
Let-Off: 75%
MSRP: $899.99
Features: All-new Bear H13 cam;
zero-tolerance limb pockets; stainless steel stabilizer brushing; customizable grip; adjustable offset string suppressors; max preload quad limbs; available in black, snow, camo, red, and green.

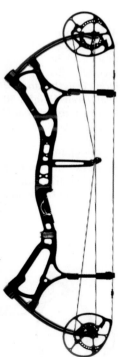

Siren

Axle-to-Axle: 31"
Speed (IBO): 300 fps
Brace Height: 6.75"
Weight: 3.8 lbs.
Draw Length Range: 22"–27"
Peak Draw Height: 40 lbs. 50 lbs. 60 lbs.
Strings/Cables: Contra-Band
Cable Slide: Slide
Let-Off: 75%
MSRP: $599.99
Features: Bear FH cam; zero-tolerance limb pockets; dual arc offset string suppressors; max preload quad limbs; Idler Wheel with dual stainless steel-sealed bearings; official bow of Realtree Girl; available in black and camo.

BowTech

Assassin ▶
Axle-to-Axle: 30¼"
Speed: 305 fps (IBO)
Brace Height: 7"
Mass Weight: 3.7 lbs.
Draw Weight: 40 lbs. 50 lbs. 60 lbs. 70 lbs.
Draw Length: 22½"–27"
Effective Let-Off: 65–80%
Kinetic Energy: 72.31 ft-lbs.
Finish Options: BlackOps, Mossy Oak Treestand
MSRP: $649
Features: Factory installed components include alloy peep, 4-pin TruGlo Apex Sight, wrist sling, BCY string loop, 1-piece five-arrow camo quiver, Hostage XL arrow rest, 4" stabilizer, and Dura-Flex string dampening. Rotating draw-length modules for ease of length adjustment. Binary cam system, carbon-rod string stop, Octane factory string and cables, carbon string stop, and solid limbs.

Destroyer LE ▶
Axle-to-Axle: 32³/₈"
Speed: 350 fps (IBO)
Brace Height: 6"
Mass Weight: 4.12 lbs.
Draw Weights: 60 lbs. 70 lbs.
Draw Length: 25"–30"
Effective Let-Off: 80%
Kinetic Energy: 95.22 ft-lbs.
Finish Options: BlackOps
MSRP: $849
Features: Limited number production run, HardCore split limbs, OverDrive Binary eccentrics system, FLX-Guard, forged riser, Octane factory strings, and carbon-rod string stop.

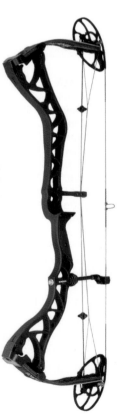

Heartbreaker
Axle-to-Axle: 30¼"
Speed: 305 fps (IBO)
Brace Height: 6¾"
Mass Weight: 3.7 lbs.
Draw Weight: 40 lbs. 50 lbs. 60 lbs.
Draw Length: 22½"–27"
Let-Off: 65–80%
Kinetic Energy: 72.31 ft-lbs.
Finish Options: BlackOps, Heartbreaker, Mossy Oak Infinity, Mossy Oak Treestand, Razzberry
MSRP: $699

Features: Designed for female shooters. Factory installed components include 4-pin sight, quiver, arrow rest, stabilizer, peep sight, nock loop, and sling. Rotating draw length modules for ease of length adjustment. Binary cam system, carbon-rod string stop, Octane factory string and cables, carbon string stop, and solid limbs.

▼ BowTech Heartbreaker

Insanity.

Insanity CPX
Axle-to-Axle: 32"
Speed: 355 fps (IBO)
Brace Height: 6"
Draw Weights: 50 lbs. 60 lbs. 70 lbs. 80 lbs.
Draw Length: 25½"–30"
Effective Let-Off: approx 80%
Kinetic Energy: 98.0 ft-lbs. at 70 lbs.
Finish Options: Mossy Oak Treestand, Alternate finishes include Mossy Oak Infinity, Gore Optifade Forest or Open Country, RealTree APG HD, and BlackOps. Target colors AnoRock Onyx and Inferno. All finishes except Mossy Oak Treestand include black limbs.
MSRP: $999
Features: CPX Technology, HardCore Limbs, OverDrive Binary eccentrics system, FLX-Guard, forged riser, Octane factory strings, carbon-rod string stop, split-buss cable, and 2-piece wood grip.

Insanity CPLX (Long Draw)
Axle-to-Axle: 35"
Speed: 340 fps (IBO)
Brace Height: 7"
Draw Weights: 50 lbs. 60 lbs. 70 lbs. 80 lbs.
Draw Length: 27½"
Kinetic Energy: 89.9 ft-lbs. at 70 lbs.
Effective Let-Off: approx 80%
Finish Options: Mossy Oak Treestand, Alternate finishes include Mossy Oak Infinity, Gore Optifade Forest or Open Country, RealTree APG HD, and BlackOps. Target colors AnoRock Onyx and Inferno. All finishes except Mossy Oak Treestand include black limbs.
MSRP: $1,049
Features: CPX technology, HardCore limbs, OverDrive Binary eccentrics system, FLX-Guard, forged riser, Octane factory strings, carbon-rod string stop, split-buss cable, 2-piece wood grip.

C.P. Oneida Eagle Bows

Hawk

Axle-to-Axle: 40"
Brace Height: 6"–6.375"
Weight: 3.2 lbs.
Draw Length Range: 22"–25"
Peak Draw Height: 25 lbs. 45 lbs.
Let-Off: 55–75%
MSRP: $875.00
Features: Designed to meet the needs of small-framed adults, women, and youth who have a short draw length, the Hawk provides speed and deep penetration while keeping with Oneida's smooth draw and easy let-off; available in Autumn Orange, Next Gen G-1 camo, and flat black; optional packages available.

Osprey

Axle-to-Axle: 43"–44"
Brace Height: 6.5"–8"
Weight: 3.4 lbs.
Draw Length Range: 25"–31.5"
Peak Draw Height: 35 lbs. 55 lbs.
Let-Off: 60–80%
MSRP: $745.00
Features: Built from a new lightweight, durable casting, the Osprey offers a wide range of poundage and let-off selections; fast drawing, quick-pointing bow is designed to make the "snap shot" that most bow-fisherman are presented with; available in Red Reaper.

Kestrel

Axle-to-Axle: 42"–43"
Brace Height: 6.125"–7.375"
Weight: 3.8 lbs.
Draw Length Range: 25"–31"
Peak Draw Height: 25 lbs. 45 lbs. 35 lbs. 55 lbs. 50 lbs. 70 lbs.
Let-Off: 65–80%
MSRP: $1,395.00
Features: Designed to be smaller and faster than any other previous adult model in Oneida history; available in Next Gen G-1 camo and flat black; optional packages available.

Talon

Axle-to-Axle: 43"–44"
Weight: 3.4 lbs.
Brace Height: 6.5"–8"
Draw Length Range: 26"–32"
Peak Draw Height: 25 lbs. 45 lbs. 35 lbs. 55 lbs.
Let-Off: 55–75%
MSRP: $875.00
Features: Built from a new lightweight, durable casting; offers a wide range of poundage and let-off selections; comes with an assortment of interchangeable modules for easy draw-weight and let-off adjustment; available in Next Gen G-1 camo and flat black; optional packages available.

Concept Archery

Believer
Axle-to-Axle: 33¹/₁₆″
Speed: 312 fps (IBO)
Brace Height: 8¹/₈″
Mass Weight: 4.3 lbs.
Draw Weights: 30 lbs. 40 lbs.
50 lbs. 60 lbs. 70 lbs.
Draw Length: 25″–30″ in ¹/₂″
increments
Let-Off: 99%
Kinetic Energy: N/A
Finish Options: God's
Country Early Season
MSRP: $774.99
Features: Unique 99% let-off
bow with solid limbs. String
stop, CNC-machined riser
and cams. Upper and lower
string speed nocks, LimbSaver
string decelerator, power ring
cable guard dampener, Teflon
cable slide, string leech.

C32
Axle-to-Axle: 31 9/16″
Speed: 314 fps (IBO)
Brace Height: 6⁵/₈″
Mass Weight: 3.5 lbs.
Draw Weights: 30 lbs. 40 lbs.
50 lbs. 60 lbs. 70 lbs.
Draw Length: 24″–30″ in ¹/₂″
increments
Let-Off: 99%
Kinetic Energy: N/A
Finish Options: Next G1
MSRP: $699.99
Features: Unique 99% let-off
bow with solid limbs. Available
in pink carbon fiber limbs &
pink marble riser. Power ring
cable guard dampener (black),
Teflon cable slide, string leech.
Available in right-handed mod-
els only (allow 4 to 6 weeks for
delivery).

Believer G1
Axle-to-Axle: 33¹/₁₆″
Speed: 312 fps (IBO)
Brace Height: 8¹/₈″
Mass Weight: 4 lbs.
Draw Weights: 30 lbs. 40 lbs.
50 lbs. 60 lbs. 70 lbs.
Draw Length: 25″–30″
Let-Off: 99%
Kinetic Energy: N/A
Finish Options: Next G1
MSRP: $774.99
Features: Unique 99% let-off
bow with solid limbs. String
stop, CNC-machined riser
and cams. Upper and lower
string speed nocks, LimbSaver
string decelerator, power ring
cable guard dampener, Teflon
cable slide, string leech.

C99
Axle-to-Axle: 35³/₈″
Speed: 310 fps (IBO)
Brace Height: 7⁵/₈″
Mass Weight: 4.1 lbs.
Draw Weights: 30 lbs. 40 lbs.
50 lbs. 60 lbs. 70 lbs.
Draw Length: 25″–32″ in ¹/₂″
increments
Let-Off: 99%
Kinetic Energy: N/A
Finish Options: Next G1
MSRP: $749.99
Features: Unique 99% let-off
bow with solid limbs. Larger
idler wheel, in-line black wal-
nut grip, LimbSaver products:
power ring cable guard damp-
ener (black), Teflon cable slide,
string leech.

Mini 29

Axle-to-Axle: 29"
Speed: 318 fps (IBO)
Brace Height: 7⅞"
Mass Weight: 3.9 lbs.
Draw Weights: 30 lbs. 40 lbs. 50 lbs. 60 lbs. 70 lbs.
Draw Length: 23"–30" in ½" increments
Effective Let-Off: 99%
Kinetic Energy: N/A
Finish Options: Next G1 Early Season
MSRP: $764.99
Features: Arrowhead cut-outs in riser, upper and lower string speed nocks, LimbSaver products: string decelerator, power ring cable guard dampener, Teflon cable slide, string leech.

Diamond Archery

Atomic

Axle-to-Axle: 24"
Speed: 191 fps (IBO)
Brace Height: 6"
Mass Weight: 1.9 lbs. (bow only)
Draw Weights: 6–29 lbs.
Draw Length: 12"–24"
Effective Let-Off: N/A
Kinetic Energy: 20.66 ft-lbs.
Finish Options: Pink and Blue Atomic Limbs
MSRP: $229
Features: Youth bow with rotating modules for ease of draw length adjustable. Wide range of draw weights accommodates shooters of all sizes and strength. Anti-backout limb bolt system, solid limbs. 3-pin TruGlo Apex sight, Hostage XL arrow rest, 3-arrow quiver, 3 carbon arrows.

P50

Axle-to-Axle: 33¹⁄₁₆"
Speed: 312 fps (IBO)
Brace Height: 6¹³⁄₁₆"
Mass Weight: 3.9 lbs.
Draw Weights: 30 lbs. 40 lbs. 50 lbs. 60 lbs. 70 lbs.
Draw Length: 24"–30" in ½" increments
Effective Let-Off: 99%
Kinetic Energy: N/A
Finish Options: Next G1
MSRP: $709.99
Features: Unique 99% let-off bow with solid limbs. LimbSaver products: power ring cable guard dampener (black), Teflon cable slide, string leech.

Core

Axle-to-Axle: 31"
Speed: 313 fps (IBO)
Brace Height: 7¼"
Mass Weight: 3.2 lbs.
Draw Weights: 40–70 lbs.
Draw Length: 25"–30"
Effective Let-Off: 80%
Kinetic Energy: 76.16 ft-lbs.
Finish Options: Mossy Oak Infinity
MSRP: $499
Features: Rotating modules, solid limbs, carbon-rod string stop, 3-pin Apex sight, Octane Hijack arrow rest, Octane DeadLock Lite quiver, comfort wrist sling, alloy peep, BCY string loop, and a 5-inch Ultra-Lite Octane stabilizer.

Deadeye
Axle-to-Axle: 32″
Speed: 343 fps (IBO)
Brace Height: 6⅛″
Mass Weight: 3.9 lbs.
Draw Weights: 60 lbs. 70 lbs.
Draw Length: 26½″–30½″
Effective Let-Off: 80%
Finish Options: Mossy Oak Infinity, BlackOps
MSRP: $749
Features: FLX-Guard, 7-layer laminated solid limbs, carbon-rod string stop, 4-pin sight, Octane Hijack Hostage arrow rest, Octane DeadLock Lite quiver, comfort wrist sling, alloy peep, BCY string loop, and a 5-inch Ultra-Lite Octane stabilizer.

Diamond Infinite Edge
Axle-to-Axle: 31″
Speed: 310 fps (IBO)
Brace Height: 7″
Draw Weights: 5–70 lbs.
Draw Length: 13″–30″
Mass Weight: 3.1 lbs.
Effective Let-Off: N/A
Kinetic Energy: N/A
Finish Options: BlackOps, Pink Blaze, and Mossy Oak Break-Up Infinity
MSRP: $399
Features: Solid limbs, Octane DeadLock Lite quiver, 3-pin Apex sight, Hostage XL arrow rest, tube peep sight, and BCY string loop.

Diamond Outlaw
Axle-to-Axle: 32″
Speed: 330 fps (IBO)
Brace Height: 7″
Mass Weight: 3.8 lbs.
Draw Weights: 50 lbs. 60 lbs. 70 lbs.
Draw Length: 26½″–30½″
Effective Let-Off: 80%
Kinetic Energy: 84.66 ft-lbs.
Finish Options: Mossy Oak Treestand
MSRP: $599
Features: Rotating modules, solid limbs, carbon-rod string stop, 3-pin Apex sight, Octane Hijack arrow rest, Octane DeadLock Lite quiver, comfort wrist sling, alloy peep, BCY string loop, and a five-inch Ultra-Lite Octane stabilizer.

Fugitive
Axle-to-Axle: 32″
Speed: 337 fps (IBO)
Brace Height: 6½″
Mass Weight: 3.8 lbs.
Draw Weights: 60 lbs. 70 lbs.
Draw Length: 26″–30″
Effective Let-Off: 80%
Kinetic Energy: 88.28 ft-lbs.
Finish Options: Mossy Oak Infinity, BlackOps
MSRP: $649
Features: FLX-Guard, 7-layer laminated solid limbs, carbon-rod string stop, 4-pin sight, Octane Hijack Hostage arrow rest, Octane DeadLock Lite quiver, comfort wrist sling, alloy peep, BCY string loop, and a 5-inch Ultra-Lite Octane stabilizer.

Elite Archery

Answer
Axle-to-Axle: 33½″
Speed: Up to 340 fps (IBO)
Brace Height: 7″
Mass Weight: 4.1 lbs.
Draw Weights: 40 lbs. 50 lbs. 60 lbs. 70 lbs. 80 lbs.
Draw Length: 27″–30″ in ½ increments
Let-Off: N/A
Kinetic Energy: N/A
Finish Options: RealTree Max-1, RealTree APS, RealTree AP, Anodize Red, Anodize Black, Anodize Blue
MSRP: $899
Features: Cerakote-performance coating, Winner's Choice strings and cables, 2-piece grip, string stop, integrated vibration dampening, and solid limbs.

GT500

Axle-to-Axle: 34⅞"
Speed: 332–336 fps (IBO)
Brace Height: 7⅛"
Mass Weight: 4.1 lbs.
Draw Weights: 60–90 lbs.
Draw Length: 27"–31"
Let-Off: N/A
Kinetic Energy: N/A
Finish Options: Ninja, RealTree Max-1, RealTree APS, RealTree AP
MSRP: $799
Features: Cerakote-performance coating, Winner's Choice strings and cables, 2-piece grip, string stop, integrated vibration dampening, and solid limbs.

Pulse

Axle-to-Axle: 34⅛"
Speed: Up to 342 fps (IBO)
Brace Height: 6"
Mass Weight: 4.3 lbs.
Draw Weights: 50 lbs. 60 lbs. 70 lbs.
Draw Length: 26"–30" in ½" increments
Let-Off: 80%
Kinetic Energy: N/A
Finish Options: Ninja, RealTree Max-1, RealTree APS, RealTree AP, Cosmic Orange, Slime, Blue Fliptone
MSRP: $849
Features: Cerakote-performance coating, Winner's Choice strings and cables, 2-piece grip, string stop, integrated vibration dampening, and solid limbs

Hunter

Axle-to-Axle: 31½"
Speed: Up to 334 fps (IBO)
Brace Height: 7¾"
Mass Weight: 4.3 lbs.
Draw Weights: 40 lbs. 50 lbs. 60 lbs. 65 lbs. 70 lbs. 80 lbs.
Draw Length: 27"–31"
Let-Off: N/A
Kinetic Energy: N/A
Finish Options: Ninja, RealTree Max-1, RealTree APS, RealTree AP
MSRP: $799
Features: Cerakote-performance coating, Winner's Choice strings and cables, 2-piece grip, string stop, integrated vibration dampening, and solid limbs

Pure

Axle-to-Axle: 36"
Speed: Up to 343 fps (IBO)
Brace Height: 7"
Mass Weight: 4.1 lbs.
Draw Weights: 50 lbs. 60 lbs. 65 lbs. 70 lbs. 80 lbs.
Draw Length: 27"–31½" in ½" increments
Let-Off: N/A
Kinetic Energy: N/A
Finish Options: RealTree Max-1, RealTree APS, RealTree AP, Anodize Red, Anodize Black, Anodize Blue
MSRP: $899
Features: Cerakote-performance coating, Winner's Choice strings and cables, 2-piece grip, string stop, integrated vibration dampening, and solid limbs.

Tour

Axle-to-Axle: 38"
Speed: Up to 328 fps (IBO)
Brace Height: 7⅛"
Mass Weight: 4.3 lbs.
Draw Weights: 50 lbs. 60 lbs. 65 lbs. 70 lbs.
Draw Length: 27"–32" in ½" increments
Let-Off: N/A
Kinetic Energy: N/A
Finish Options: RealTree Max-1, RealTree APS, RealTree AP, Anodize Red, Anodize Black, Anodize Blue
MSRP: $899
Features: Cerakote-performance coating, Winner's Choice strings and cables, 2-piece grip, string stop, integrated vibration dampening, and solid limbs.

Z28

Axle-to-Axle: 32½"
Speed: Up to 320 fps (IBO)
Brace Height: 7¾"
Mass Weight: 4 lbs.
Draw Weights: 60–90 lbs.
Draw Length: 27"–30"
Let-Off: N/A
Kinetic Energy: N/A
Finish Options: Ninja, RealTree Max-1, RealTree APS, RealTree AP
MSRP: $799
Features: Cerakote-performance coating, Winner's Choice strings and cables, 2-piece grip, string stop, integrated vibration dampening, and solid limbs.

XLR

Axle-to-Axle: 36½"
Speed: Up to 316 fps (IBO)
Brace Height: 8½"
Mass Weight: 4.25 lbs.
Draw Weights: 50–90 lbs.
Draw Length: 27"–28½"
Let-Off: N/A
Kinetic Energy: N/A
Finish Options: Ninja, RealTree Max-1, RealTree APS, RealTree AP
MSRP: $799
Features: Cerakote-performance coating, Winner's Choice strings and cables, 2-piece grip, string stop, integrated vibration dampening, and solid limbs.

Hoyt

Alpha Elite

Axle-to-Axle: 36"
Speed: 321 fps (ATA)
Brace Height: 7"
Mass Weight: 4.4 lbs.
Draw Weights: lbs.
Draw Length: 26"–31½"
Let-Off: N/A
Kinetic Energy: N/A
Finish Options: RealTree AP, RealTree Max-1, Blackout, Half and Half, RealTree Snow, RealTree Pink, custom red, custom blue, custom black, pearl white, pink, orange, cobalt blue, jet black, green, red fusion, fusion
MSRP: $1,250
Features: Cam & ½, Fuse string and cables, X-Lite ProLock pocket, shoot-thru technology, multilayer lamination, AlphaShox, and split limbs.

Contender

Axle-to-Axle: 38⁵/₈"
Speed: 315 fps (ATA)
Brace Height: 7¹/₈"
Mass Weight: 4.6 lbs.
Draw Weights: 30–40 lbs. 40–50 lbs.
50–60 lbs. 60–70 lbs.
Draw Length: 24"–30½"
Let-Off: N/A
Kinetic Energy: N/A
Finish Options: RealTree AP, RealTree
Max-1, Blackout, Half and Half,
RealTree Snow, RealTree Pink, custom
red, custom blue, custom black, pearl
white, pink, orange, cobalt blue, jet
black, green, red fusion, and fusion
MSRP: $1,049
Features: A relatively neutral riser
geometry, the split limb equipped
Contender is a forgiving shooter with
its large brace height. Multilayered
limbs and Hoyt's proven cam and ½
power system deliver smooth draw
and good nock travel. Alpha Shox rubber dampeners enhance vibration control.

Pro Comp Elite

Axle-to-Axle: 37⁷/₈"
Speed: 305 fps (ATA)
Brace Height: 8¹/₈"
Mass Weight: 4.8 lbs.
Draw Weights: 30–40 lbs. 40–50 lbs.
50–60 lbs. 60–70 lbs.
Draw Length: 24½"–32"
Let-Off: N/A
Kinetic Energy: N/A
Finish Options: Blackout, Half and
Half, RealTree Snow, RealTree Pink,
fusion, red fusion, green, orange,
cobalt blue, jet black, pearl white,
pink
MSRP: $1,350
Features: Cam & ½, Fuse string and
cables, X-Lite ProLock pocket, shoot-
thru technology, multilayer lamination,
AirShox.

Pro Comp Elite XL

Axle-to-Axle: 40⁵/₈"
Speed: 315 fps (ATA)
Brace Height: 8"
Mass Weight: 5 lbs.
Draw Weights: 30–40 lbs. 40–50
lbs. 50–60 lbs. 60–70 lbs.
Draw Length: 25"–32"
Let-Off: N/A
Kinetic Energy: N/A
Finish Options: RealTree Xtra,
RealTree Max-1, Blackout, Half and
Half, RealTree Snow, RealTree Pink,
custom red, custom blue, custom
black, pearl white, pink, orange,
cobalt blue, jet black, green, red
fusion, fusion
MSRP: $1,450
Features: Cam & ½, Fuse string and
cables, X-Lite ProLock pocket,
shoot-thru technology, multilayer
lamination, AirShox.

Prohawk

Axle-to-Axle: 32"
Speed: 308 fps (ATA)
Brace Height: 7¼"
Mass Weight: 4 lbs.
Draw Weights: 20–30 lbs. 30–40
lbs. 40–50 lbs. 50–60 lbs. 60–70
lbs.
Draw Length: 23"–30"
Let-Off: N/A
Kinetic Energy: N/A
Finish Options: RealTree Xtra,
RealTree Max-1, Blackout, Half
and Half, RealTree Snow, realtree
pink, custom red, custom blue,
custom black, pearl white, pink
MSRP: $599
Features: AlphaShox, Cam & ½,
Fuse custom string and cables, split
limbs, Pro Fit custom grip, X-Lite
ProLock pockets, Tec-Lite.

Ruckus

Axle-to-Axle: 29¾"
Speed: 281 fps (ATA)
Brace Height: 6¾"
Mass Weight: 2.8 lbs.
Draw Weights: 10–40 lbs.
20–50 lbs.
Draw Length: 18"–28"
Let-Off: N/A
Kinetic Energy: N/A
Finish Options: RealTree AP,
RealTree Max-1, Blackout,
RealTree Pink
MSRP: $399
Features: Includes Fuse ProFire
3-pin sight, Fuse Banshee
4-arrow quiver, Whisker Biscuit
arrow rest. Alpha Shox, Fuse
string and cables, split limbs,
Tec Lite riser, and Versa Flex
draw length technology.

Vantage Elite Plus

Axle-to-Axle: 40½"
Speed: 309 fps (ATA)
Brace Height: 8⅛"
Mass Weight: 4.8 lbs.
Draw Weights: 30–40 lbs. 40–50 lbs.
50–60 lbs. 60–70 lbs.
Draw Length: 25"–31½"
Let-Off: N/A
Kinetic Energy: N/A
Finish Options: RealTree AP,
RealTree Max-1, Blackout, Half and
Half, RealTree Snow, RealTree Pink,
custom red, custom blue, custom
black, pearl white, pink, orange,
cobalt blue, jet black, green, red
fusion, fusion
MSRP: $1,349
Features: Cam & ½, Fuse string and
cables, shoot-thru technology,
multilayer lamination, and
AlphaShox.

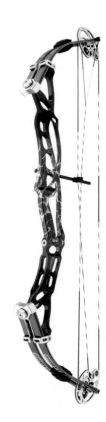

Tribute

Axle-to-Axle: 45"
Speed: 274 fps (ATA)
Brace Height: 8"
Mass Weight: 4.8 lbs.
Draw Weights: 30–40 lbs. 40–50
lbs. 50–60 lbs. 60–70 lbs.
Draw Length: 26"–34"
Let-Off: N/A
Kinetic Energy: N/A
Finish Options: RealTree Xtra,
RealTree Max-1, Blackout, Half and
Half, RealTree Snow, RealTree Pink,
fusion, red fusion, green, orange,
cobalt blue, jet black, pearl white,
pink
MSRP: $899
Features: AlphaShox, Fuse strings
and cables, split limbs, Pro Fit cus-
tom grip, ProLock pocket, and Tec
Lite riser.

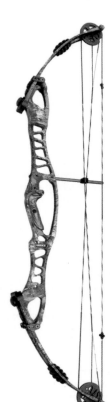

Vector 32

Axle-to-Axle: 32"
Speed: 330 fps (ATA)
Brace Height: 6¾"
Mass Weight: 4 lbs.
Draw Weights: 30–40 lbs. 40–50
lbs. 50–60 lbs. 55–65 lbs. 60–70
lbs. 70–80 lbs.
Draw Length: 24½"–30"
Let-Off: N/A
Kinetic Energy: N/A
Finish Options: RealTree AP,
RealTree Max-1, Blackout
MSRP: $949
Features: Multilayer lamination
limbs, AlphaShox, Cam & ½, Fuse
custom strings and cables, in-line
roller cable guard, Pro Fit custom
grip, X-Lite ProLock pocket, Silent
Shelf technology, Tec Lite riser,
Stealth Shot.

LimbSaver

DeadZone-30
Axle-to-Axle: 30″
Speed (IBO): 325 fps
Brace Height: 6.75″–7.25″
Weight: 3.9 lbs.
Draw Length Range: 25″–30″ (dependent on cam size)
Peak Draw Height: 50 lbs. 60 lbs. 70 lbs.
Let-Off: 80%
MSRP: N/A
Features: H.E.A.T. Modular Cam; draw length adjustable cams; pivoting camo-limb pockets; JBK custom bow strings and cables; fall-away arrow rest pad; arrow-impact strip; Teflon cable slide; available in camo.

DeadZone-32
Axle-to-Axle: 32″
Speed (IBO): 330 fps
Brace Height: 6.875″–7.125″
Weight: 4.5 lbs.
Draw Length Range: 25.5″–30.5″ (dependent on cam size)
Peak Draw Height: 50 lbs. 60 lbs. 70 lbs.
Let-Off: 80%
MSRP: N/A
Features: H.E.A.T. Modular Cam; draw length adjustable cams; camo-dipped limb pockets; JBK custom bow strings and cables; fall-away arrow rest pad; arrow impact strip; Teflon cable slide; available in camo.

DeadZone-36
Axle-to-Axle: 36″
Speed (IBO): 325 fps
Brace Height: 7.75″–7.875″
Weight: 3.8 lbs.
Draw Length Range: 27.5″–32.5″ (dependent on cam size)
Peak Draw Height: 50 lbs. 60 lbs. 70 lbs.
Let-Off: 80%
MSRP: N/A
Features: H.E.A.T. Modular Cam; rock-solid riser design; draw length adjustable cams; JBK custom bow strings and cables; fall-away arrow rest pad; arrow impact strip; Teflon cable slide.

Proton
Axle-to-Axle: 32″
Speed (IBO): 335 fps
Brace Height: 7″
Weight: 3.8 lbs.
Draw Length Range: 25″–30″ (dependent on cam size)
Peak Draw Height: 50 lbs. 60 lbs. 70 lbs.
Let-Off: 80%
MSRP: N/A
Features: 3-phase H.E.A.T. cams; posi-lock seven-position poundage adjustment system; laminated limb sets; torque-

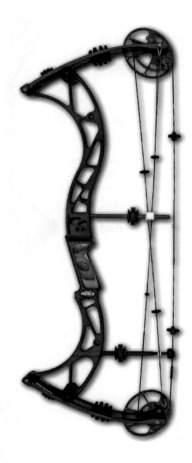

free hardwood grip; limb-pocket dampener; LimbSaver super leeches; string decelerator; cable rod dampener; available in camo.

SpeedZone-34
Axle-to-Axle: 34″
Speed (IBO): 350 fps
Brace Height: 5.5″–5.875″
Weight: 3.8 lbs.
Draw Length Range: 25″–30″ (dependent on cam size)
Peak Draw Height: 50 lbs. 60 lbs. 70 lbs.
Let-Off: 80%
MSRP: N/A
Features: H.E.A.T. Modular Cam; draw length-adjustable cams featuring hyperdrive speed module; String decelerator system; available in camo.

Martin Archery

Alien
Axle-to-Axle: 32"
Speed (IBO): 335 fps
Brace Height: 7"
Weight: 3.5 lbs.
Draw Length Range: 25.5"–30.5"
Peak Draw Height: 50 lbs. 60 lbs.
70 lbs.
Limb Type: Twin
MSRP: N/A
Features: Nitro 3 Hybrid Cams;
Carbon Stealth STS; CNC-machined
solid aluminum riser; three VEM
vibration vortex modules; saddle-
back thermal grip; Martin Cable
Containment System (CCS); thread-
ed steel stabilizer insert; Silent
Hunter arrow shelf; available in
Vista, Bonz, Skulz, black, red, and
white.

Blade X4
Axle-to-Axle: 31.5"
Speed (IBO): 315 fps
Brace Height: 7"
Weight: 3.75 lbs.
Draw Length Range: 25"–31"
Peak Draw Height: 70 lbs.
Limb Type: Twin
MSRP: $379.00
Features: Hybrix 3.0 Cams; CNC-
machined solid aluminum riser;
adjustable brace height and grip
angle; custom grip; dual-carbon
fiber STS string suppressor;
PowerTough limbs; Silent Hunter
arrow shelf; available in Vista.

Bengal
Axle-to-Axle: 31"
Speed (IBO): 320 fps
Brace Height: 7"
Weight: 3.8 lbs.
Draw Length Range: 25"–31"
Peak Draw Height: 50 lbs. 60 lbs.
70 lbs.
Limb Type: Single
MSRP: $499.99
Features: Fury XT Single Cam;
Carbon Stealth STS; CNC-
machined solid block aluminum
riser; PowerTough limbs; saddle-
back thermal grip; Quick-lock sta-
bilizer mount; Silent Hunter arrow
shelf; available in Vista, Bonz,
Skulz, black, red, and white.

Nemesis35
Axle-to-Axle: 35"
Speed (IBO): 335 fps
Brace Height: 7"
Weight: 3.8 lbs.
Peak Draw Height: 50 lbs.
60 lbs. 70 lbs.
Draw Length Range: 26"–31"
Limb Type: Twin
MSRP: N/A
Features: Nitro 3 Hybrid Cams;
Carbon Stealth STS; three VEM
vibration vortex modules; CNC-
machined solid aluminum riser;
saddleback thermal grip; Martin
Cable Containment System
(CCS); threaded steel stabilizer
insert; Silent Hunter arrow shelf;
available in Vista, Bonz, Skulz,
black, red, and white.

OnzaXT

Axle-to-Axle: 33.25"
Speed (IBO): 330 fps
Brace Height: 7"
Weight: 4 lbs.
Draw Length Range: 25.5"–31"
Peak Draw Height: 50 lbs. 60 lbs. 70 lbs.
Limb Type: Single
MSRP: $649.99
Features: Nitro 3 Hybrid Cams; Carbon Stealth STS; CNC-machined solid block aluminum riser; saddleback thermal grip; Quick-Lock stabilizer mount; PowerTough limbs; Silent Hunter arrow shelf; available in Vista, Bonz, Skulz, black, red, and white.

Phantom X4

Axle-to-Axle: 32.5"
Speed (IBO): 315 fps
Brace Height: 7"
Weight: 3.85 lbs.
Draw Length Range: 26"–32"
Peak Draw Height: 70 lbs.
Limb Type: Twin
MSRP: N/A
Features: Fury XT single cam; CNC-machined solid block aluminum riser; saddleback thermal Grip; Quick-lock stabilizer mount; Silent Hunter arrow shelf; available in Vista.

Pantera

Axle-to-Axle: 34"
Speed (IBO): 320 fps
Brace Height: 7"
Weight: 4.1 lbs.
Draw Length Range: 25.5"–32"
Peak Draw Height: 50 lbs. 60 lbs. 70 lbs.
Limb Type: Single
MSRP: $549.00
Features: Fury XT Single Cam; Carbon Stealth STS; CNC-machined solid block aluminum riser; saddleback thermal grip; PowerTough limbs; cloaked (camo) cams; Quick-Lock stabilizer mount; Silent Hunter arrow shelf; available in Vista, Bonz, Skulz, black, red, and white.

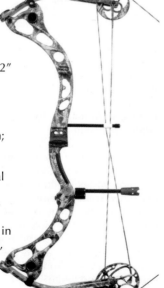

Prowler

Axle-to-Axle: 30"
Speed (IBO): 320 fps
Brace Height: 7"
Weight: 3.4 lbs.
Draw Length Range: 24.5"–30.5"
Peak Draw Height: 50 lbs. 60 lbs. 70 lbs.
Limb Type: Single
MSRP: N/A
Features: Fury XT Single Cam; PowerTough limbs; Quick-Lock stabilizer mount; saddleback thermal grip; Silent Hunter arrow shelf; available in Vista, Bonz, Skulz, black, red, and white; right-hand model only.

ScepterV

Axle-to-Axle: 40"
Speed (IBO): 330 fps
Brace Height: 7"
Weight: 4.4 lbs.
Draw Length Range: 27"–32"
Peak Draw Height: 50 lbs. 60 lbs. 70 lbs.
Limb Type: Single
MSRP: N/A
Features: Nitro 3 Hybrid Cams; Carbon Stealth STS; CNC-machined solid aluminum riser; custom target grip; nine stabilizer mounts; threaded steel stabilizer insert; PowerTough limbs; Silent Hunter arrow shelf; available in Vista, Bonz, Skulz, black, red, and white.

Seeker

Axle-to-Axle: 33"
Speed (IBO): 340 fps
Brace Height: 5.75"–7.75"
Weight: 4.6 lbs.
Draw Length Range: 27"–32"
Peak Draw Height: 50 lbs. 60 lbs. 70 lbs.
Limb Type: Single
MSRP: N/A
Features: Hybrix 3.0 cams; PowerTough limbs; CNC-machined solid aluminum riser; adjustable brace height and grip angle; custom grip; dual-carbon fiber STS string suppressor; Silent Hunter arrow shelf; available in Vista, Bonz, Skulz, black, red, and white.

Threshold

Axle-to-Axle: 36.75"
Speed (IBO): 310 fps
Brace Height: 7"
Weight: 3.4 lbs.
Draw Length Range: 23.5"–31" (depending on mode)
Peak Draw Height: 40 lbs. 50 lbs. 70 lbs.
Limb Type: Single
MSRP: $233.39
Features: M-Pro cams; interchangeable modules for adjustable draw weight; Mantis rest; twist lock six-arrow quiver; fiber-optic striker sight; 75% let-off; right-handed models only; available in Vista.

Mathews

Helim

Axle-to-Axle: 30"
Speed: Up to 332 fps (IBO)
Brace Height: 7"
Mass Weight: 3.5 lbs.
Draw Weights: 40–70lbs.
Draw Length: 26"–30" half sizes 26½"–29½"
Let-Off: 80%
Kinetic Energy: N/A
Finish Options: Black, Lost
MSRP: $959
Features: Helim Cam and QCA; Geo Grid Lock riser, SE6 Composite SlimLim, parallel limbs, Reverse Sphere Lock pivoting limb cup system, reverse assist roller guard, Walnut SlimFit in-line grip, Harmonic Stabilizer Lite, Dead Endstring stop, string grub, Mathews Harmonic Damper, Monkey Tail, Genuine Mathews string and cables, ball bearing idler wheel.

Genesis Pro
Axle-to-Axle: 35½"
Speed: N/A fps (IBO)
Brace Height: 7⅝"
Mass Weight: 2.95 lbs.
Draw Weights: 15–25 lbs.
Draw Length: Up to 30"
Let-Off: 0%
Kinetic Energy: N/A
Finish Options: Lost
MSRP: N/A
Features: composite limbs, Mathews Genuine bowstring, molded competition grip, quick replacement rest, aluminum idler wheel, and ball bearing idler wheel.

Mini Genesis
Axle-to-Axle: 29½"
Speed: N/A fps (IBO)
Brace Height: 6⅛"
Mass Weight: N/A
Draw Weights: 6–12 lbs.
Draw Length: 14"–25"
Let-Off: 0%
Kinetic Energy: N/A
Finish Options: Mini Genesis Pink 2, Mini Genesis Blue 3, Mini Genesis Red, Mini Genesis Black 3, Lost
MSRP: N/A
Features: composite limbs, Mathews Genuine bowstring, molded competition grip, quick replacement rest, aluminum idler wheel, and ball bearing idler wheel.

Jewel
Axle-to-Axle: 28"
Speed: 325 fps at 60 lbs. and 29" draw length
Brace Height: 6⅜"
Mass Weight: 3.6 lbs.
Draw Weights: 40 lbs. 45 lbs. 50 lbs. 55 lbs. 60 lbs.
Draw Length: 22"–29"
Let-Off: 80%
Kinetic Energy: N/A
Finish Options: Lost, Black, Pink, Teal
MSRP: $999
Features: Perimeter Weighted Jewel cam, grid lock riser, SE5 Composite limb system, parallel limb design, SphereLock pivoting limb cup system, limb turret, reverse assist roller guard, Mathews Genuine Bowstring, SlimFit in-line grip, Harmonic Stabilizer Lite, Harmonic damping system, string suppressors, Dead End string stop, Monkey Tails, string grub, and ball bearing idler wheel.

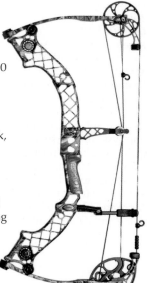

McPherson Series Monster

Chill
Axle-to-Axle: 30½"
Speed: Up to 333 fps (IBO)
Brace Height: 7"
Mass Weight: 3.9 lbs. (approximate)
Draw Weights: 50–70 lbs.
Draw Length: 23"–30"
Let-Off: 80%
Kinetic Energy: N/A
Finish Options: Black, Lost
MSRP: $999
Features: DYAD cam system, Geo Grid lock riser, Reverse Assist Roller Guard, focus grip, Harmonic Stabilizer Lite, Dead End string stop, string grub, Monkey Tail, Genuine Mathews string, and cables.

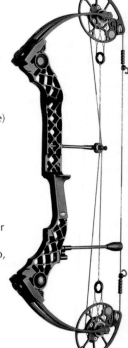

M5

Axle-to-Axle: 33"
Speed: Up to 360+ fps
Brace Height: 5"
Mass Weight: 4.5 lbs.
Draw Weights: 50 lbs. 60 lbs. 70 lbs. 80 lbs.
Draw Length: 24½"–30" (24½"–29½" in half sizes)
Let-Off: 65% and 80%
Kinetic Energy: N/A
Finish Options: Lost
MSRP: $999
Features: Advanced vectoring system, quad V-lock limbs, grid lock riser, Walnut SlimFit grip, Harmonic stabilizer, Harmonic damping system, Dead End string stop, string grub, roller guard.

M7

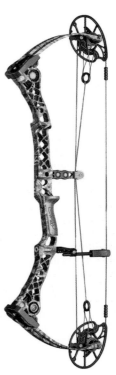

Axle-to-Axle: 33"
Speed: Up to 344+ fps
Brace Height: 7"
Mass Weight: 4.4 lbs.
Draw Weights: 50 lbs. 60 lbs. 70 lbs. 80 lbs.
Draw Length: 26½"–32" (26½"–31½" in half sizes)
Let-Off: 65% and 80%
Kinetic Energy: N/A
Finish Options: Lost
MSRP: $999
Features: Advanced vectoring system, quad V-lock limbs, grid lock riser, Walnut SlimFit grip, Harmonic stabilizer, Harmonic damping system, Dead End string stop, string grub, roller guard.

M6

Axle-to-Axle: 33"
Speed: Up to 354+ fps
Brace Height: 6"
Draw Weights: 50 lbs. 60 lbs. 70 lbs. 80 lbs.
Draw Length: 25½"–30½" (25½"–30½" in half sizes)
Mass Weight: 4.45 lbs.
Kinetic Energy: N/A
Let-Off: 65% and 80%
Finish Options: Lost
MSRP: $999
Features: Advanced vectoring system, quad V-lock limbs, grid lock riser, Walnut SlimFit grip, Harmonic stabilizer, Harmonic damping system, Dead End string stop, string grub, roller guard.

Monster MR8

Axle-to-Axle: 33"
Speed: Up to 333 fps (IBO)
Brace Height: 8"
Mass Weight: 4.45 lbs.
Draw Weights: 50–80 lbs.
Draw Length: 27½"–32½"
Let-Off: 80%
Kinetic Energy: N/A
Finish Options: Lost
MSRP: $999
Features: Advanced vectoring system, quad V-lock limbs, grid lock riser, Triple Damper roller guard, Walnut SlimFit grip, Harmonic stabilizer, Harmonic damping system, Dead End string stop, string grub.

Safari

Axle-to-Axle: 33"
Speed: 350 fps @ 85 lbs. with 425-grain arrow
Brace Height: 6"
Mass Weight: 4.8 lbs.
Draw Weights: 85 lbs. or 70 lbs.
Draw Length: 25½"–31" (25½"–30½" in half sizes)
Let-Off: 65% & 80%
Kinetic Energy: N/A
Finish Options: Black
MSRP: $2,100
Features: Advanced vectoring system, quad V-lock limbs, Honeycomb Core technology, integral grip with African wood inlays, Harmonic stabilizer, Harmonic damping system, Dead End string stop, string grub, roller guard.

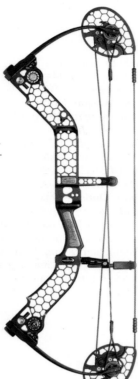

Z9

Axle-to-Axle: 30"
Speed: Up to 312 fps (IBO)
Brace Height: 8¾"
Mass Weight: 4 lbs.
Draw Weights: 40 lbs. 50 lbs. 60 lbs. 65 lbs. 70 lbs.
Draw Length: 27"–32" (27½"–31½" in half sizes)
Let-Off: 80%
Kinetic Energy: N/A
Finish Options: Lost
MSRP: $899
Features: Z9 cam, grid lock riser, SE5 composite limb system, limb turret, parallel limbs, reverse assist roller guard, SlimFit in-line grip, SphereLock pivoting limb cup system, Harmonic stabilizer, Dead End string stop, string grub, Mathews Harmonic damping system, Monkey Tail, Genuine Mathews string and cables, string suppressors.

Z7 Magnum

Axle-to-Axle: 32"
Speed: Up to 340 fps (IBO)
Brace Height: 6⅜"
Mass Weight: 4.25 lbs.
Draw Weights: 40 lbs. 50 lbs. 60 lbs. 65 lbs. 70 lbs.
Draw Length: 24"–30"
Let-Off: 80%
Kinetic Energy: N/A
Finish Options: Lost
MSRP: $999
Features: ZX cam & QCA, grid lock riser, SE5 composite limb system, parallel limbs, reverse assist roller guard, SlimFit in-line grip, SphereLock pivoting limb cup system, Harmonic stabilizer, Dead End string stop, string grub, Mathews Harmonic damping system,, Monkey Tail, Genuine Mathews string and cables, string suppressors.

ZXT

Axle-to-Axle: 28"
Speed: Up to 326 fps (IBO)
Brace Height: 7⅜"
Mass Weight: 4.2 lbs. approximate
Draw Weights: 40–70 lbs. 65 lbs.
Draw Length: 24"–30"
Let-Off: 80%
Kinetic Energy: N/A
Finish Options: Black, Lost
MSRP: $799
Features: ZX cam, Geo grid lock riser, SE6 Composite SlimLim, parallel limbs, reverse assist roller guard, Walnut SlimFit in-line grip, Harmonic Stabilizer Lite, Dead End string stop, string grub, Mathews Harmonic damping system, Monkey Tail, Genuine Mathews string and cables, string suppressors.

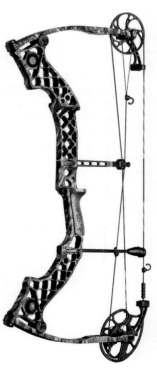

Mission

Craze
Axle-to-Axle: 28"
Speed: Up to 306 fps (IBO)
Brace Height: 7½"
Mass Weight: 3.6 lbs.
Draw Weights: 15–70 lbs.
Draw Length: 19"–30"
Let-Off: 80%
Kinetic Energy: N/A
Finish Options: Lost AT, Black, White Marble, White Tiger, Green marble, Green Tiger, Pink Marble, Pink Tiger, Pink Camo, Gator
MSRP: $299
Features: Carbon-rod cable guard, extruded riser, D-Amplifiers, Zebra Hybrid string and cables, composite grip.

Rally
Axle-to-Axle: 37"
Speed: Up to 300 fps (IBO)
Brace Height: 7¼"
Mass Weight: 4 lbs.
Draw Weights: 26–70 lbs.
Draw Length: 22"–30"
Let-Off: Up to 75%
Kinetic Energy: N/A
Finish Options: Lost AT, Black, White Marble, White Tiger, Green marble, Green Tiger, Pink Marble, Pink Tiger, Pink Camo, Gator
MSRP: $499
Features: Opti-Mod cam, carbon-rod cable guard, extruded riser, D-Amplifiers, Zebra Hybrid string and cables, composite grip.

Menace
Axle-to-Axle: 31"
Speed: N/A fps (IBO)
Brace Height: 7¼"
Mass Weight: 2.95 lbs.
Draw Weights: 16–52 lbs.
Draw Length: 17"–30"
Let-Off: Up to 70%
Kinetic Energy: N/A
Finish Options: Lost AT, Black, White Marble, White Tiger, Green marble, Green Tiger, Pink Marble, Pink Tiger, Pink Camo, Gator
MSRP: $269
Features: Universal cam, carbon-rod cable guard, extruded riser, D-Amplifiers, Zebra Hybrid string and cables, composite grip.

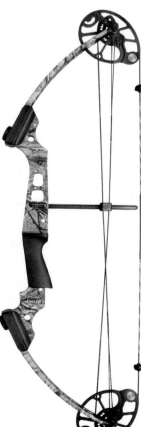

Venture
Axle-to-Axle: 30¼"
Speed: Up to 321 fps (IBO)
Brace Height: 7⅛"
Mass Weight: 3.96 lbs.
Draw Weights: 35–70 lbs.
Draw Length: 26"–31½"
Let-Off: 80%
Kinetic Energy: N/A
Finish Options: Lost, Black, Pink Camo
MSRP: $499
Features: Voyager single cam, roller cable guard, Zebra Hybrid string and cables, string suppressors, Dead End string stop, CNC-machined riser, composite grip.

Parker

Buckshot Extreme
Brace Height: 6½"
Speed: N/A
Draw Weights: 15–29 lbs. 30–45 lbs.
Draw Length: 17–26"
Mass Weight: 2.75 lbs.
Kinetic Energy: N/A
Axle-to-Axle: 28"
Let-Off: 80%
Finish Options: Film-dipped camo
MSRP: $199
Features: Synprene Grip, solid limbs, carbon-rod cable guard, integrated sling.

Sidekick Extreme
Brace Height: 7⅝"
Speed: Up to 270 fps
Draw Weights: 20–40 lbs. 40–60 lbs.
Draw Length: 18–28"
Mass Weight: 3.25 lbs.
Kinetic Energy: N/A
Axle-to-Axle: 31"
Let-Off: 80%
Finish Options: Next G-1
MSRP: $299
Features: Machined aluminum riser, string suppressor, integrated braided wrist sling, extreme parallel limbs, full 10 inches of draw length adjustment without the aid of a bow press (only an Allen Key is required to change draw lengths from 18 to 28 inches with half inch increments in between). Walnut finished two-piece grip.

Python
Brace Height: 7"
Speed: 325 fps
Draw Weights: 50–60 lbs. 60–70 lbs.
Draw Length: 26–30" (modules included)
Mass Weight: 4.25 lbs.
Kinetic Energy: N/A
Axle-to-Axle: 30"
Let-Off: 80%
Finish Options: RealTree Advantage Timber
MSRP: $599
Features: Extreme parallel limb design, two-piece deep walnut finish grip, tunable string suppressor, integrated sling, Python high performance single cam, tunable draw stop, split limbs with Fulcrum pocket system, roller cable guard, Premium Stone Mountain string, riser machined aluminum, deluxe roller cable, speed bearings, sealed bearing, and roller guard.

Velocity
Brace Height: 7¼"
Speed: 315 fps
Draw Weights: 50–70 lbs.
Draw Length: 26–31"
Mass Weight: 4.15 lbs.
Kinetic Energy: N/A
Axle-to-Axle: 30⅛"
Let-Off: 80%
Finish Options: RealTree Advantage Timber
MSRP: $399
Features: Extreme parallel limb design, two-piece deep walnut finish grip, tunable string suppressor, integrated sling, Python high performance single cam, tunable draw stop, split limbs with Fulcrum Pocket system, roller cable guard, Premium Stone Mountain string, riser machined aluminum, deluxe roller cable, speed bearings, sealed bearing. and roller guard.

Prime

Centroid LR

Brace Height: 7"
Speed: 332 fps (IBO)
Draw Weights: 50 lbs. 60 lbs. 70 lbs.
Draw Length: 27"–31"
Mass Weight: 4 lbs.
Kinetic Energy: N/A
Axle-to-Axle: 34¼"
Let-Off: N/A
Finish Options: RealTree AP, Jet Black
MSRP: $899
Features: Parallel cam technology, forged 7000 series riser, laminated limbs, Shield Service Program, Gore fiber string and cables, Ti-Glide Titanium Flexing Cable System.

Shift LR

Axle-to-Axle: 30"
Speed: 332 fps (IBO)
Brace Height: 7"
Mass Weight: 3.7 lbs.
Draw Length: 26"– 30"
Draw Weight: 50 lbs. 60 lbs. 70 lbs.
Let-Off: 80%
Finish Options: RealTree AP, Jet Black
MAP: $899
Features: Like the Centroid LR, the Shift LR has Parallel Cam Technology, forged 7000 series riser, laminated limbs, a Shield Service Program, Gore fiber string and cables, and a Ti-Glide Titanium Flexing Cable System.

PSE

Bow Madness 3G

Brace Height: 7"
Speed: 330–322 fps (IBO)
Draw Weights: 50 lbs. 60 lbs. 70 lbs.
Draw Length: 25"–30"
Mass Weight: 4.3 lbs.
Kinetic Energy: N/A
Axle-to-Axle: 33⅛"
Let-Off: 75%
Finish Options: Mossy Oak Break-Up Infinity
MSRP: $799
Features: Preloaded past parallel split limbs, Planar Flex riser, Backstop 2, Madness Pro single-cam system. Field Ready (FR) package includes: Aries sight, Whisker Biscuit rest, FlexTech stabilizer, Mongoose quiver, PSE Neoprene sling, peep sight, nock loop, True-Fire Hurricane release, Supreme bowcase, and a four-pack of PSE X-Weave arrows.

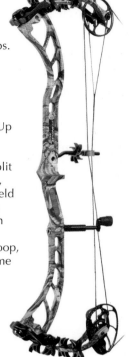

Brute X

Brace Height: 7¼"
Speed: 320–312 fps (IBO)
Draw Weights: 50 lbs. 60 lbs. 70 lbs.
Draw Length: 25"–30"
Mass Weight: 4.7 lbs.
Kinetic Energy: N/A
Axle-to-Axle: 31"
Let-Off: 75%
Finish Options: Mossy Oak Break-Up Infinity
MSRP: $599
Features: Preloaded X-Tech™ split limbs, machined riser, pivoting limb pocket system and the Madness Pro™ cam allow for ½-inch" adjustments with PSE's posi-lock inner-cam, StingStop, multiple sight mounting holes, and Raptor grip. Field Ready (FR) package includes: Gemini sight, Whisker Biscuit rest, FlexTech stabilizer, Mongoose quiver, PSE Neoprene sling, peep sight, nock loop, True-Fire Hurricane release, Supreme bowcase, and a 4 pack of PSE X-Weave arrows.

Chaos AD

Axle-to-Axle: 32¼"
Speed: 298 fps @ 28" draw length
Brace Height: 6¼"
Mass Weight: 3.2 lbs.
Draw Weights: 40 lbs. 50 lbs. 60 lbs.
Draw Length: 16½"–28"
Let-Off: 75%
Kinetic Energy: N/A
Finish Options: Black camo
MSRP: $379
Features: Adaptable cams allow eight full turns on the limb bolt. Preloaded 12-inch split limbs. Ready to Shoot (RTS) package includes Gemini sight, Whisker Biscuit rest, Mongoose quiver, peep wheel, and nock set.

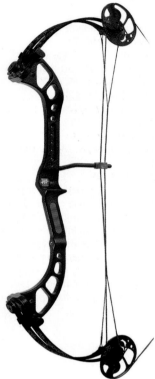

Discovery 2

Axle-to-Axle: 31½"
Speed: N/A
Brace Height: 6½"
Mass Weight: 2.7 lbs.
Draw Weights: 20 lbs.
Draw Length: to 30"
Let-Off: 0%
Kinetic Energy: N/A
Finish Options: Mossy Oak Infinity, blue, red
MSRP: $179
Features: The Discovery 2 cam design ramps up to reach the bow's peak weight then holds a constant draw weight up to a 30-inch draw, making it the perfect bow for youth and adults alike.

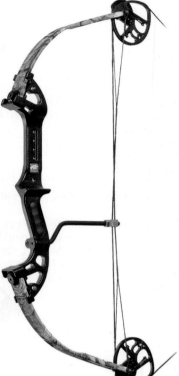

Chaos One

Axle-to-Axle: 30½"
Speed: 312–320 fps @29" draw length
Brace Height: 6¾"
Mass Weight: 3.4 lbs.
Draw Weights: 40 lbs. 50 lbs. 60 lbs.
Draw Length: 24"–29"
Let-Off: 75%
Kinetic Energy: N/A
Finish Options: Black camo, Skullworks, black, pink camo
MSRP: $299
Features: Designed for small frame shooters. Preloaded 12-inch split limbs, and HP single-cam system.

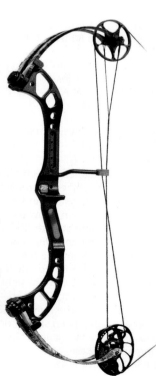

Dream Season DNA

Axle-to-Axle: 31"
Speed: 352–344 fps (IBO)
Brace Height: 6"
Mass Weight: 3.7 lbs.
Draw Weights: lbs.
Draw Length: 26"–30"
Let-Off: 70%
Kinetic Energy: N/A
Finish Options: Black, Skullworks, Mossy Oak Break-Up Infinity, black camo
MSRP: $899
Features: Center pull technology that places the arrow in the exact center of the bow for unparalleled tuneability and exceptional performance. Core cam produces speeds of up to 352 fps and has 5 inches of draw length adjustment on the inner cam. Centerlock 2 Limb Pockets, flex cable slide, and Backstop 2.

Drive

Axle-to-Axle: 30½"
Speed: 326–318 fps (IBO)
Brace Height: 7½"
Mass Weight: 4.6 lbs.
Draw Weights: 50 lbs. 60 lbs. 70 lbs.
Draw Length: 26"–31½"
Let-Off: 75%
Kinetic Energy: N/A
Finish Options: Black, Skullworks, Mossy Oak Break-Up Infinity, black camo
MSRP: $499
Features: The most affordable X-Force bow features Planar Flex riser, drive cam with 6½ inches of draw length adjustment, 7½-inch brace height and the StingStop.

Freak MAX

Axle-to-Axle: 38"
Speed: 354–346 fps @ 32" draw length
Brace Height: 7⅛"
Mass Weight: 4.6 lbs.
Draw Weights: 60 lbs. 70 lbs. 80 lbs.
Draw Length: 28"–32"
Let-Off: 75%
Kinetic Energy: N/A
Finish Options: Mossy Oak Break-Up Infinity, Black Camo, Skullworks, Black
MSRP: $949
Features: Extra long draw bow. EVO cam, Centerlock 2 pockets, flex cable guard, X-Tech limbs, Backstop 2 limb damper, America's Best string and cables, tuning and alignment marks, slim grip, split limbs.

EVO Max

Axle-to-Axle: 32¼"
Speed: 345–337 fps (IBO)
Brace Height: 6"
Mass Weight: 4.2 lbs.
Draw Weights: 50 lbs. 60 lbs. 65 lbs. 70 lbs.
Draw Length: 25"–30"
Let-Off: 75%
Kinetic Energy: N/A
Finish Options: Black, Skullworks, Mossy Oak Break-Up Infinity, black camo
MSRP: $849
Features: EVO cam, Centerlock 2 Pockets, flex cable slide, X-Tech limbs, Backstop 2 limb damper, America's Best string and cables, tuning and alignment marks, slim grips, pre-loaded split limbs.

Hammer

Axle-to-Axle: 32¼"
Speed: 335–327 fps (IBO)
Brace Height: 7"
Mass Weight: 4.2 lbs.
Draw Weights: 50 lbs. 60 lbs. 70 lbs.
Draw Length: 26"–31"
Let-Off: 75%
Kinetic Energy: N/A
Finish Options: Black, Skullworks, Mossy Oak Break-Up Infinity, black camo
MSRP: $749
Features: Planar flex riser, EVO cam, Brute X pockets, X-Tech limbs, Backstop 2 limb damper, America's Best string and cables, tuning and alignment marks, split limbs, slim grip.

Mini Burner

Axle-to-Axle: 26½"
Speed: 261–253 fps @ 26" draw length
Brace Height: 7"
Mass Weight: 2.5 lbs.
Draw Weights: 20 lbs. 29 lbs. 40 lbs.
Draw Length: 16"–26"
Let-Off: 70%
Kinetic Energy: N/A
Finish Options: Mossy Oak Break-Up Infinity, blue, pink camo
MSRP: $199
Features: Flexible twin-cam system switches from constant peak weight to "Grow With You" draw length adjustments, all without a bow press. The Mini SF technology limb assembles like a solid limb with all the bend capabilities of a split limb.

Revenge

Axle-to-Axle: 29⅝"
Speed: 340–332 fps (IBO)
Brace Height: 6¼"
Mass Weight: 4.2 lbs.
Draw Weights: 50 lbs. 60 lbs. 70 lbs.
Draw Length: 24½"–30"
Let-Off: 75%
Kinetic Energy: N/A
Finish Options: Black, Skullworks, Mossy Oak Break-Up Infinity, black camo
MSRP: $649
Features: Drive cam, Bow Madness pockets, X-Tech limbs, Backstop 2 limb damper, Planar Flex riser, tuning and alignment marks, slim grips.

Omen Max

Axle-to-Axle: 33⅝"
Speed: 366–358 fps @ 27" draw length
Brace Height: 5½"
Mass Weight: 4.3 lbs.
Draw Weights: 60 lbs.
Draw Length: 27"
Let-Off: 70%
Kinetic Energy: N/A
Finish Options: Black, Skullworks, Mossy Oak Break-Up Infinity, black camo
MSRP: $949
Features: UF cam, Centerlock 2 pockets, flex cable slide, X-Tech limbs, Backstop 2 limb damper, America's Best string and cables, tuning and alignment marks, slim grips, preloaded split limbs.

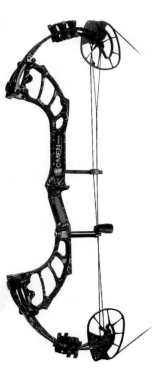

Phenom

Axle-to-Axle: 36"
Speed: fps (IBO)
Brace Height: 7"
Mass Weight: 4.3 lbs.
Draw Weights: 40 lbs. 50 lbs. 60 lbs.
Draw Length: 25½"–30"
Let-Off: 75%
Kinetic Energy: N/A
Finish Options: Blue, red, black, Mossy Oak Break-Up Infinity, Skullworks
MSRP: $649
Features: Mini EVO cam, Brute X limb pockets, Backstop 2 limb damper, X-Tech limbs, tuning and alignment marks, split limbs.

Prophecy

Axle-to-Axle: 32"
Speed: 340–332 fps (IBO)
Brace Height: 6"
Mass Weight: 4.1 lbs.
Draw Weights: 50 lbs. 60 lbs. 70 lbs.
Draw Length: 25"–30"
Let-Off: 75%
Kinetic Energy: N/A
Finish Options: Mossy Oak Break-Up Infinity, black camo, Skullworks, black
MSRP: $699
Features: Brute X Pockets, Limb dampers, tuning and alignment marks, slim grip, AMP cam (single-cam system).

Stiletto

Axle-to-Axle: 29¾"
Speed: 320–312 fps @ 27" draw length
Brace Height: 6"
Mass Weight: 4 lbs.
Draw Weights: 40 lbs. 50 lbs. 60 lbs.
Draw Length: 23"–27½"
Let-Off: 75%
Kinetic Energy: N/A
Finish Options: Mossy Oak Break-Up Infinity, Skullworks, Black Camo, Pink Camo
MSRP: $699
Features: Mini EVO cam, Bow Madness pockets, X-Tech limbs, Backstop 2 limb damper, Planar Flex riser, tuning and alignment marks, split limbs, slim grips.

Rally

Axle-to-Axle: 33¾"
Speed: 308–300 fps (IBO)
Brace Height: 7½"
Mass Weight: 4.5 lbs.
Draw Weights: 50 lbs. 60 lbs. 70 lbs.
Draw Length: 18"–30"
Let-Off: 70%
Kinetic Energy: N/A
Finish Options: Mossy Oak Break-Up Infinity, Black
MSRP: $299
Features: OP Cam system, rally pockets, limb dampers, tuning and alignment marks, slim grip. Engineered for maximum adjustability with 14-inch of draw length adjustment. Limb bolts can be adjusted a full ten turns.

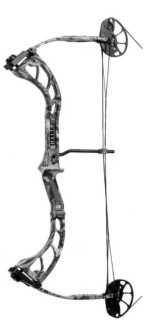

Stinger 3G

Axle-to-Axle: 33"
Speed: 314–306 fps (IBO)
Brace Height: 7¾"
Mass Weight: 4.7 lbs.
Draw Weights: 50 lbs. 60 lbs. 70 lbs.
Draw Length: 25½"–30½"
Let-Off: 75%
Kinetic Energy: N/A
Finish Options: Mossy Oak Break-Up Infinity, Black Camo, Skullworks, Black
MSRP: $299
Features: HP cam (single-cam system), rally pockets, limb dampers, tuning and alignment marks, slim grips, machined aluminum riser, posi-lock inner cam for easy draw length adjustment, parallel limbs, and a shooter-friendly 7¾-inch brace height.

Supra Max
Axle-to-Axle: 37¼"
Speed: 332–324 fps (IBO)
Brace Height: 7"
Mass Weight: 4.5 lbs.
Draw Weights: 40 lbs. 50 lbs.
60 lbs.
Draw Length: 25½"–30"
Let-Off: 75%
Kinetic Energy: N/A
Finish Options: Red, blue,
black, Mossy Oak Break-Up
Infinity
MSRP: $849
Features: Mini EVO cam,
Centerlock 2 pockets, X-Tech
limbs, Backstop damper, limb
dampers, America's Best string
and cables, tuning and align-
ment marks, slim grip.

Quest

Bliss
Axle-to-Axle: 31"
Speed: 290 fps (IBO)
Brace Height: 7"
Mass Weight: 4.05 lbs.
Draw Weights: 30–45 lbs.
45–60 lbs.
Draw Length: 23"–27"
Let-Off: 80%
Kinetic Energy: N/A
Finish Options: RealTree AP
MSRP: $399–$499
Features: Fluid SD cam, forged
machined 6061 aluminum riser,
DuraFuse finish, string suppressor,
solid limbs.

Vendetta DC
Axle-to-Axle: 34"
Speed: 330–322 fps (IBO)
Brace Height: 7"
Mass Weight: 4.3 lbs.
Draw Weights: 50 lbs. 60 lbs. 70 lbs.
Draw Length: 26½"–32"
Let-Off: 75%
Kinetic Energy: N/A
Finish Options: Black, Skullworks,
Mossy Oak Break-Up Infinity, black
camo
MSRP: $699
Features: Drive cam, Bow Madness
pockets, X-Tech limbs, Backstop
damper, limb dampers, tuning and
alignment marks, slim grip.

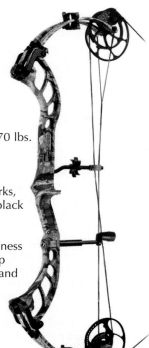

Drive
Axle-to-Axle: 33¼"
Speed: 330 fps (IBO)
Brace Height: 7"
Mass Weight: 4.3 lbs.
Draw Weights: 50 lbs. 60 lbs.
70 lbs.
Draw Length: 26"–30"
Let-Off: 80%
Kinetic Energy: N/A
Finish Options: G-fade RealTree
AP, G-Fade Mossy Oak Treestand
MSRP: $699–$799
Features: Twin-Track Flux cam,
I-Glide Flex, forged machined
6061 aluminum riser, DuraFuse
finish, adjustable string suppres-
sor, G5 Meta Speed Studs,
BowJax limb dampeners.

Rogue

Axle-to-Axle: 31"
Speed: 312 fps (IBO)
Brace Height: 7½"
Mass Weight: 4.2 lbs.
Draw Weights: 50 lbs. 60 lbs. 70 lbs.
Draw Length: 26"–30½" (½" increments)
Let-Off: 80%
Kinetic Energy: N/A
Finish Options: RealTree AP, Jet Black
MSRP: $399–$529
Features: Fluid cam, forged machined 6061 aluminum riser, DuraFuse finish, string suppressor, solid limbs.

Ross

Crave DRT 33.5

Axle-to-Axle: 33½"
Speed: 335 fps (IBO)
Brace Height: 6½"
Mass Weight: 4 lbs.
Draw Weights: 50 lbs. 60 lbs. 70 lbs.
Draw Length: 27"–31"
Let-Off: 80%
Kinetic Energy: N/A
Finish Options: Stealth Black, RealTree AP
MSRP: $749
Features: Machined riser, slim line grip, dual-locking limb pockets, 2-track dual sync cam system, modular draw length adjustment, integrated limb stop, sealed bearings, Winner's Choice string and cables, lifetime warranty.

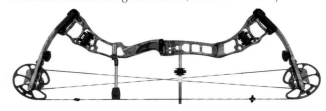

Torrent

Axle-to-Axle: 31"
Speed: 322 fps (IBO)
Brace Height: 7"
Mass Weight: 4.2 lbs.
Draw Weights: 50 lbs. 60 lbs. 70 lbs.
Draw Length: 25½"–30" (½" increments)
Let-Off: 80%
Kinetic Energy: N/A
Finish Options: RealTree AP, G-Fade RealTree AP
MSRP: $499–$599
Features: Fluid cam, I-Glide, forged machined 6061 aluminum riser, DuraFuse finish, string suppressor, G5 Meta Speed Studs, BowJax limb dampeners, solid limbs.

HIT

Axle-to-Axle: 36½"
Speed: 332 fps (IBO)
Brace Height: 7"
Mass Weight: 4.12 lbs.
Draw Weights: 50 lbs. 60 lbs. 70 lbs.
Draw Length: 27"–31"
Let-Off: 80%
Kinetic Energy: N/A
Finish Options: Stealth Black, RealTree APG
MSRP: $749
Features: Machined riser, slim line grip, dual locking lib pockets, two-track dual sync cam system, modular draw length adjustment, integrated limb stop, sealed bearings, Winner's Choice string and cables, lifetime warranty.

Just Like Dad's
Axle-to-Axle: 27"
Speed: 282 fps (IBO)
Brace Height: 7"
Mass Weight: 2.96 lbs.
Draw Weights: 20–50 lbs.
Draw Length: 18"–28"
Let-Off: 80%
Kinetic Energy: N/A
Finish Options: Stealth Black, RealTree APG
MSRP: $379
Features: Machined riser, slim line grip, rotating-modular draw length adjustment, LimbSaver anti-vibration products, lifetime warranty.

XD
Axle-to-Axle: 30½"
Speed: 320 fps (IBO)
Brace Height: 7½"
Mass Weight: 3.16 lbs.
Draw Weights: 50 lbs. 60 lbs. 70 lbs.
Draw Length: 25"–30"
Let-Off: 80%
Kinetic Energy: N/A
Finish Options: Stealth Black, RealTree APG
MSRP: $524
Features: DRT riser dampeners, machined riser, slim line grip, modular draw length adjustment, integrated limb stop, lifetime warranty.

Strother

Hope
Axle-to-Axle: 34"
Speed: 342 fps (IBO)
Brace Height: 6½"
Mass Weight: 3.75 lbs.
Draw Weights: 40–60 lbs.
Draw Length: 24"–25½"
Let-Off: 80%
Kinetic Energy: N/A
Finish Options: Black Death, Predator 3-D Deception, RealTree AP
MSRP: $849
Features: Badger cam, super-glide cable slide, split limbs, ZT Loc-N-Cradle limb pockets.

Moxie
Axle-to-Axle: 37½"
Speed: 330 fps (IBO)
Brace Height: 7⅜"
Mass Weight: 4.3 lbs.
Draw Weights: 40–80 lbs.
Draw Length: 28"–32"
Let-Off: 80%
Kinetic Energy: N/A
Finish Options: Black Death, Predator 3-D Deception, RealTree AP
MSRP: $839
Features: Like the Hope, the Moxie has a Badger cam, super-glide cable slide, split limbs, ZT Loc-N-Cradle limb pockets.

SX Rush

Axle-to-Axle: 33³/₈″
Speed: 345 fps (IBO)
Brace Height: 6³/₈″
Mass Weight: 4.25 lbs.
Draw Weights: 50–80 lbs.
Draw Length: 27″–30″
Let-Off: 80%
Kinetic Energy: N/A
Finish Options: Predator 3-D Deception, RealTree AP Black
MSRP: $799
Features: Similar to other Strother bows, the SX Rush has a Badger cam, super-glide cable slide, split limbs, ZT Loc-N-Cradle limb pockets.

Winchester

Destiny SS

Axle-to-Axle: 31½″
Speed: 305 fps
Brace Height: 7¼″
Mass Weight: 2.75 lbs.
Draw Weights: 9–56 lbs.
Draw Length: 17″–30″
Let-Off: N/A
Kinetic Energy: N/A
Finish Options: RealTree Pink
MSRP: $349
Features: 2-piece rubber grip, 2-piece wooden grip, speedsters, LimbSavers, Winchester Archery hat. ready-to-shoot package: 3-pin fiber-optic sight, arrow rest, quiver, sling, peep sight.

Wrath

Axle-to-Axle: 32″
Speed: 330 fps (IBO)
Brace Height: 8″
Mass Weight: 4 lbs.
Draw Weights: 40–80 lbs.
Draw Length: 27″–31½″
Let-Off: 80%
Kinetic Energy: N/A
Finish Options: Black Death, Predator 3-D Deception, RealTree AP
MSRP: $839
Features: Like the SX Rush, the Wrath comes equipped with a Badger cam, super-glide cable slide, split limbs, ZT Loc-N-Cradle limb pockets.

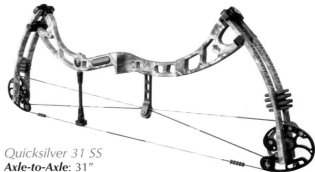

Quicksilver 31 SS

Axle-to-Axle: 31″
Speed: 325+ fps
Brace Height: 7¼″
Mass Weight: 3.8 lbs.
Draw Weights: 40–70 lbs.
Draw Length: 27″–30″
Let-Off: N/A
Kinetic Energy: N/A
Finish Options: Proveil Reaper Woods
MSRP: $399
Features: Two-piece rubber grip, two-piece wooden grip, speedsters, LimbSavers, Winchester Archery hat.

Quicksliver 34 SS

Axle-to-Axle: 34″
Speed: 330 fps
Brace Height: 7″
Mass Weight: 3.9 lbs.
Draw Weights: 40–70 lbs.
Draw Length: 27″–30″
Let-Off: N/A
Kinetic Energy: N/A
Finish Options: Proveil Reaper Woods
MSRP: $399
Features: 2-piece rubber grip, 2-piece wooden grip, speedsters, LimbSavers, Winchester Archery hat.

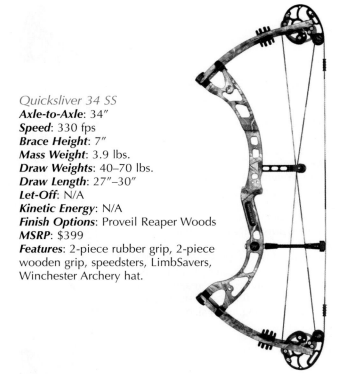

Thunderbolt SS

Axle-to-Axle: 31½″
Speed: 305 fps
Brace Height: 7¼″
Mass Weight: 2.75 lbs.
Draw Weights: 9–56 lbs.
Draw Length: 17″–30″
Let-Off: N/A
Kinetic Energy: N/A
Finish Options: Next G-1 Vista
MSRP: $299
Features a Ready-to-Shoot Package: 3-pin fiber-optic sight, arrow rest, quiver, sling, and peep sight. 2-piece rubber grip, speedsters, LimbSavers, Winchester Archery hat.

Tracker SS

Axle-to-Axle: 31¼″
Speed: 315 fps
Brace Height: 7¼″
Mass Weight: 4 lbs.
Draw Weights: 40–70 lbs.
Draw Length: 27″–30″
Let-Off: N/A
Kinetic Energy: N/A
Finish Options: Proveil Reaper Woods
MSRP: $399
Features: Similar to the Quicksilver bows, the Tracker SS also includes a two-piece rubber grip, two-piece wooden grip, speedsters, LimbSavers, Winchester Archery hat.

Vaquero

Axle-to-Axle: 32″
Speed: 320 fps
Brace Height: 7¼″
Mass Weight: 4.1 lbs.
Draw Weights: 40–70 lbs.
Draw Length: 27″–30″
Let-Off: N/A
Kinetic Energy: N/A
Finish Options: Proveil Reaper Woods
MSRP: $399
Features: Two-piece rubber grip, two-piece wooden grip, speedsters, LimbSavers, Winchester Archery hat.

Current Crossbows

Arrow Precision

Blaze II
Draw Weight: 150 lbs.
Speed: 345 fps
Mass Weight: 8 lbs.
Length: 33″
Width: 18½″
Power Stroke: 14½″
Kinetic Energy: N/A
Trigger Pull: 2.5 lbs.
Finish Options: Film-dipped camo
MSRP: $499
Features: Manual safety, innovational compression molded limbs, foot stirrup, Weaver-style scope rail, padded sling, 4x32 illuminated scope, quick-detach quiver with 4 carbon arrows, rope-cocking device, string suppressor system to reduce noise and vibration; eye protection and assembly tools/hex keys included; adjustable vertical foregrip for extra stability.

Inferno Blitz
Draw Weight: 150 lbs.
Speed: 285+ fps
Mass Weight: 7.37 lbs.
Length: 33″
Width: 28½″
Power Stroke: 12½″
Kinetic Energy: N/A
Trigger Pull: N/A
Finish Options: Film-dipped camo
MSRP: $299
Features: Multi-reticle illuminated 4x32 scope, quick-detach quiver with 4 arrows, rope-cocking device, adjustable Weaver-style scope mount, auto safety, boot-style foot stirrup, padded sling, vented aluminum barrel, ambidextrous, lightweight synthetic rear stock, eye protection, assembly tools/hex keys.

Inferno Fury
Draw Weight: 175 lbs.
Speed: Up to 235 fps
Mass Weight: 5.85 lbs.
Length: 34½"
Width: 26½"
Power Stroke: 10½"
Kinetic Energy: N/A
Trigger Pull: N/A
Finish Options: Film-dipped camo
MSRP: $219
Features: 3 multi-range red dot sight range sight, quick-detach quiver with 4 arrows, padded shoulder sling, adjustable Weaver-style scope mount, ambidextrous, auto safety, boot-style foot stirrup, ambidextrous rear stock; eye protection and assembly tools/hex keys included.

Inferno Hellfire
Draw Weight: 165 lbs.
Speed: 375+ fps
Mass Weight: 8.2 lbs.
Length: 40½"
Width: 25 39/64"
Power Stroke: 14¹³/₆₄"
Kinetic Energy: N/A
Trigger Pull: N/A
Finish Options: Next Vista
MSRP: $369
Features: Machined aluminum riser, precision trigger assembly, anti-dry fire equipped, ambidextrous, auto safety, eye protection included, comfort grip, Weaver-style scope mount, 4x32 multi-reticle illuminated scope, rope-cocking device, padded sling, quick-detach quiver, carbon 20-inch arrows, boot-style foot stirrup, assembly tools/hex keys.

Wildfire
Draw Weight: 225 lbs.
Mass Weight: 7.3 lbs.
Speed: 345+ fps
Length: 39½"
Width: 36¼"
Power Stroke: 16½"
Kinetic Energy: N/A
Trigger Pull: N/A
Finish Options: Next G1 Soft Touch Microprint
MSRP: $579
Features: Machined aluminum riser, anti-dry fire equipped, precision trigger assembly, ambidextrous, auto safety, 4x32 multi-reticle illuminated scope, rope-cocking device, quick-detach quiver with four carbon arrows, padded sling, boot-style foot stirrup; eye protection and assembly tools/hex keys; and adjustable Weaver-style scope mount, noise reduction dampener system.

Barnett

Ghost 350
Draw Weight: 175 lbs.
Speed: Up to 350 fps
Mass Weight: 7.5 lbs.
Length: 37"
Width: 24"
Power Stroke: 12"
Kinetic Energy: 116 ft-lbs.
Trigger Pull: N/A
Finish Options: RealTree APG
MSRP: $599
Features: Carbon riser, metal injection molding trigger system, crosswire strings, whiplash cams, anti-dry fire. Includes quiver, three 20-inch headhunter arrows, 3x32 illuminated scope and cross rope-cocking multi-tool.

Ghost 400
Draw Weight: 185 lbs.
Speed: 400 fps
Mass Weight: 8.2 lbs.
Length: 38"
Width: 24"
Power Stroke: 15¾"
Kinetic Energy: 151 ft-lbs.
Trigger Pull: N/A
Finish Options: Carbon Black
MSRP: $1,119
Features: Carbon riser, AVI technology molded over laminated limbs which reduces noise and vibration, aluminum flight track, crosswire strings, whiplash cams, ADF Trigger (anti-dry fire), MIM (Metal Injection Molding) trigger system. Includeds quiver, three arrows, 3x32 scope, sling, rope-cocking device .

Penetrator Carbon Lite
Draw Weight: 175 lbs.
Speed: 375 fps
Mass Weight: 8 lbs.
Length: 37"
Width: 24"
Power Stroke: 15"
Kinetic Energy: 133 ft-lbs.
Trigger Pull: N/A
Finish Options: Film-dipped camo
MSRP: $749
Features: Carbon Riser, ADF Trigger (anti-dry fire), and MIM trigger system. Includeds quiver, three arrows, rope-cocking device, 3x32 scope.

Quad 400

Draw Weight: 150 lbs.
Speed: 345 fps
Mass Weight: 9 lbs.
Length: 37″
Width: 26¾″
Power Stroke: 15½″
Kinetic Energy: 112 ft-lbs.
Trigger Pull: N/A
Finish Options: Film-dipped camo
MSRP: $399
Features: High-density gas-assist composite stock (a first in the industry), a thumbhole grip, and a 15½-inch power stroke are combined with a parallel limb design producing arrow speeds of over 345 fps. Includes quiver, 3 arrows, 4x32 scope or premium red dot.

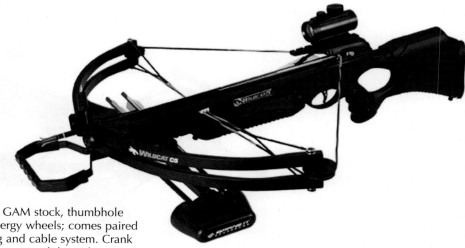

Wildcat C5

Draw Weight: 150 lbs.
Speed: 320 fps
Mass Weight: 8.5 lbs.
Length: 35¼″
Width: 26¾″
Power Stroke: 13″
Kinetic Energy: 97 ft-lbs.
Trigger Pull: N/A
Finish Options: Black
MSRP: $349
Features: Lightweight composite GAM stock, thumbhole grip, vented quad limbs, high energy wheels; comes paired with paired with Crosswire string and cable system. Crank compatible. Includes quiver, 3 arrows, red dot sight.

Vengeance

Draw Weight: 140 lbs.
Speed: 365 fps
Mass Weight: 7.9 lbs.
Length: 34¼″
Width: 24″
Power Stroke: 18″
Kinetic Energy: 126 ft-lbs.
Trigger Pull: N/A
Finish Options: Black
MSRP: $899
Features: Carbon Lite Riser with reverse draw technology, split limbs, anti-dry fire, safety, composition stock. Includes quick-detach quiver, three 22-inch arrows, and an illuminated 3x32 multi-reticle scope, rope-cocking device .

BowTech

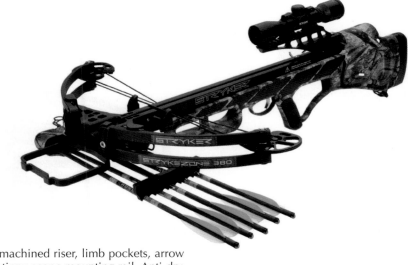

StrykeZone 350
Draw Weight: 135 lbs.
Speed: 350 fps
Mass Weight: 6.9 lbs.
Length: 34³/₈″
Width: 19³/₁₆″
Power Stroke: 15½″
Kinetic Energy: 105 ft-lbs.
Trigger Pull: N/A
Finish Options: BlackOps, Mossy Oak
MSRP: $749
Features: Extruded foot stirrup, split limbs, machined riser, limb pockets, arrow track, composite stock with pistol grip. Picatinny scope mounting rail. Anti-dry fire device and integrated safety. Includes five arrows, quick-detach quiver, multi-reticle scope, cocking aid, detachable carrying sling, string stops.

StrykeZone 380
Draw Weight: 160 lbs.
Speed: 380 fps
Mass Weight: 6.9 lbs.
Length: 35″
Width: 19½″
Power Stroke: 15½″
Kinetic Energy: N/A
Trigger Pull: N/A
Finish Options: BlackOps, Mossy Oak
MSRP: $799
Features: Extruded foot stirrup, split limbs, machined riser, limb pockets, arrow track, composite stock with pistol grip. Picatinny scope mounting rail. Anti-dry fire device and integrated safety. Includes five arrows, quick-detach quiver, multi-reticle scope, cocking aid, detachable carrying sling, string stops.

Carbon Express

Covert CX-1
Draw Weight: 185 lbs.
Speed: 330 fps
Mass Weight: 8.2 lbs.
Length: 32½″
Width: 22″
Power Stroke: 14″
Kinetic Energy: 105 ft-lbs.
Trigger Pull: N/A
Finish Options: Mossy Oak Break-Up
MSRP: $499
Features: Quick-detach, 3-arrow quiver, 3 Carbon Express Maxima Hunter 20-inch arrows, rope-cocking device, lighted scope with red/green illuminations for varying light conditions. Rail lubricant and practice points are included.

Covert CX-2

Draw Weight: 200 lbs.
Speed: 385 fps
Mass Weight: 8.9 lbs.
Length: 36"
Width: 22½"
Power Stroke: 14½"
Kinetic Energy: 142 ft-lbs.
Trigger Pull: 5 lbs.
Finish Options: Mossy Oak Treestand
MSRP: $599

Features: Bull-pup ergonomic stock, anodized aluminum CNC-machined flight rail, fully adjustable forearm and grip. Rubber coated 1-piece aluminum foot stirrup. Universal 7/8" Weaver-style scope mount. Anti-dry fire device. Includes 4x32 multi-reticule lighted scope, quick-detach 3-arrow quiver, three 20-inch Maxima Hunter carbon arrows with moon nocks and practice points, rail lubricant, universal rope-cocking unit.

Covert SLS

Draw Weight: 185 lbs.
Speed: 355 fps
Mass Weight: 8.3 lbs.
Length: 36"
Width: 17"
Power Stroke: 13"
Kinetic Energy: 119 ft-lbs.
Trigger Pull: N/A
Finish Options: Mossy Oak Obsession
MSRP: $599

Features: CNC-machined aluminum riser, all-metal trigger and safety, anti-dry fire mechanism, compact bull-pup stock positions the trigger mechanism 4-inch forward, aluminum alloy cams, 9-inch multi-position adjustable Picatinny rail system, fully adjustable. Includes 4x32 Pro Deluxe Lighted Scope, Quick-detach quiver, three arrows, rope cocker, rail lubricant, and practice points.

X-Force 350

Draw Weight: 165 lbs.
Speed: 300 fps
Mass Weight: N/A
Length: N/A
Width: N/A
Power Stroke: 12"
Kinetic Energy: 80 ft-lbs.
Trigger Pull: N/A
Finish Options: Black
MSRP: $399

Features: Tactical stock, safety, aluminum cams, rubber coated stirrup. Includes quiver, three arrows, 4x32 scope, rail lubricant, three practice points.

X-Force 400

Draw Weight: 175 lbs.
Speed: 310 fps
Mass Weight: 7.65 lbs.
Length: 30½"
Width: 26¼"
Power Stroke: 12"
Kinetic Energy: 85 ft-lbs.
Trigger Pull: N/A
Finish Options: Mossy Oak Break-Up
MSRP: $399
Features: A compact crossbow designed for tight spaces. Package includes 4x32 scope, quick-detach quiver, three 20-inch arrows and cocking device.

Darton

Fireforce

Draw Weight: 185 lbs.
Speed: 400 fps
Mass Weight: 8.4 lbs.
Length: 38"
Width: 24¼"
Power Stroke: 17¼"
Kinetic Energy: 142 ft-lbs.
Trigger Pull: 3 lbs.
Finish Options: Next G-1 Vista, Muddy Girl
MSRP: $1,031
Features: DualSync cams, trackless barrel design, anti-dry fire safety, rifle style safety mounted on the barrel, riser/string suppressor system and barrel dampener, split limbs, extruded foot stirrup, pistol grip stock, machined riser and barrel/track. Various accessory packages available.

Serpent

Draw Weight: 170 lbs.
Speed: 335 fps
Mass Weight: 8.4 lbs.
Length: 35½"
Width: 22"
Power Stroke: 13"
Kinetic Energy: 99.7 ft-lbs.
Trigger Pull: N/A
Finish Options: Next G-1 Vista, Muddy Girl
MSRP: $694
Features: Trackless barrel design, anti-dry fire safety, positive-limb alignment system, riser/string suppressor system, barrel dampener. Various accessory packages available.

Terminator
Draw Weight: 165 lbs.
Speed: 340 fps
Mass Weight: 7.5 lbs.
Length: 35″
Width: 24″
Power Stroke: 14″
Kinetic Energy: 102.7 ft-lbs.
Trigger Pull: N/A
Finish Options: Next G-1 Vista
MSRP: $526
Features: Anti-dry fire safety, barrel dampener, split limbs, extruded stirrup, pistol grip. Various accessory packages available.

Excaliber

2500 Apex
Draw Weight: 90 lbs (40 lb also available)
Speed: 220 fps
Power Stroke: 11.8″
MSRP: $549.99
MSRP: $484.99 (40 lb)
Features: Extended stirrup; rear aperture target sight; fiber-optic front sight; metallic blue finish.

6845 Axiom SMF
Draw Weight: 175 lbs.
Speed: 305 fps
Power Stroke: 14.5″
Weight: 5.8 lbs.
Length: 37.5″
Arrow Length: 20″
Arrow Weight: 350-grains
Stock Type: Traditional
MSRP: $599.99
Features: Sold exclusively as a kit; Synthetic Main Frame (SMF); matching multiplex crossbow scope with mounting hardware; rope-cocking aid; 4-arrow quiver; four FireBolt arrows complete with field points; available in Realtree camo.

Equinox 6770, 6772, 6776, 6790

Draw Weight: 225 lbs.
Speed: 350 fps
Weight: 6.4 lbs.
Length: 38.4"
Arrow Length: 20"
Arrow Weight: 350-grains
Power Stroke: 16.5"
Stock Type: Thumbhole
MSRP; 6790: $769.99
6770: $949.99
6772: $999.99
6776: N/A
Features (all models): Ambidextrous cheek piece; tapped to accept Excalibur's scope and quiver mounts; fiber-optic sight; available in Realtree camo

6770: Vari-Zone multiplex crossbow scope; mounting rings and base; four arrow quiver and mounting bracket; rope-cocking aid
6772: Shadow-Zone multiplex green or red illuminated reticle crossbow scope; mounting rings and base; 4-arrow quiver and mounting bracket; rope-cocking aid
6776: new Multi red dot sight with reflex technology for lighted electronic sighting system; 4-arrow quiver and mounting bracket; rope-cocking aid

Exomax 6760, 6762, 6766, 6780

Draw Weight: 225 lbs.
Speed: 350 fps
Weight: 6.5 lbs.
Length: 39.5"
Arrow Length: 20"
Arrow Weight: 350-grains
Power Stroke: 16.5"
Stock Type: Traditional
MSRP: 6780: $729.99
6760: $929.99
6762: $969.99
6766: N/A
Features (all models): Recurve limb design; ambidextrous cheek piece; drilled and tapped to accept optional scope and quiver mounts; available in Realtree camo
6760: Vari-Zone multiplex crossbow scope; mounting rings and base; four arrow quiver and mounting bracket; rope-cocking aid

6762: Shadow-Zone multiplex green or red illuminated reticle crossbow scope; mounting rings and base; four arrow quiver and mounting bracket; rope-cocking aid
6766: new Multi red dot sight with reflex technology for lighted electronic sighting system; 4-arrow quiver and mounting bracket; rope-cocking aid

6733 Ibex SMF

Draw Weight: 175 lbs.
Speed: 305 fps
Weight: 5.9 lbs.
Length: 36.3"
Arrow Length: 20"
Arrow Weight: 350-grains
Power Stroke: 14.5"
Stock Type: Thumbhole
MSRP: $649.99
Features: Sold exclusively as a kit; Synthetic Main Frame (SMF); matching multiplex crossbow scope with mounting hardware; quiver and mounting bracket; 4 arrows and target points; quick-detach sling studs; drilled and tapped to

accept Excalibur's scope and quiver mounts; rope-cocking aid; available in Realtree camo.

6754 Eclipse XT LSP
Draw Weight: 200 lbs.
Speed: 330 fps
Weight: 6.3 lbs.
Length: 37.4"
Arrow Length: 20"
Arrow Weight: 350-grains
Power Stroke: 15.5"
Stock Type: Thumbhole
MSRP: $929.99

Features: S5 sound and vibration control system; matching cheek piece; package includes Shadow-Zone scope and mounting hardware; four firebolt arrows and target points; quiver mounting bracket and a matching quiver; available in black carbon.

3500 Matrix 355 Tact-Zone
Draw Weight: 240 lbs.
Speed: 355 fps
Weight: 5.4 lbs.
Length: 34.8"
Arrow Length: 18"
Arrow Weight: 350-grains
Power Stroke: 12.2"
Stock Type: Ergo-Grip
MSRP: $949.99
Features: Compact recurve technology; PowerLoad limbs; Ergo-Grip stock; Quad-Loc riser; Tact-Zone scope (with 30 mm rings); 4-arrow quiver (with bracket); four Diablo arrows, four 150-grain field points; rope-cocking aid; available in Realtree Xtra camo.

3800 Matrix 380 Xtra Tact-Zone
Draw Weight: 260 lbs.
Speed: 380 fps
Weight: 5.9 lbs.
Length: 35.6"
Arrow Length: 18"
Arrow Weight: 350-grains
Power Stroke: 13.1"
Stock Type: Ergo-Grip
MSRP: $1,149.99
Features: Compact recurve technology; self contained Guardian™ anti-dry fire system with a built-in release; Tact-Zone Scope (with 30mm rings); cheek piece; R.E.D.S. suppressors; a 4-arrow quiver (with bracket); four Diablo arrows; four 150-grain field points; rope-cocking aid; available in Realtree Xtra camo

3900 Matrix 380 Blackout Tact-Zone
Draw Weight: 260 lbs.
Speed: 380 fps
Weight: 5.9 lbs.
Length: 35.6"
Arrow Length: 18"
Arrow Weight: 350-grains
Power Stroke: 13.1"
Stock Type: Ergo-Grip
MSRP: $1,149.99
Features: Compact recurve technology; self contained Guardian™ anti-dry fire system with a built-in release; Tact-Zone Scope (with 30mm rings); cheek piece; R.E.D.S. suppressors; a 4-arrow quiver (with bracket); 4 Diablo arrows; four 150-grain field points; rope-cocking aid; available in black carbon

Phoenix 2240, 6720, 6722, 6726
Draw Weight: 175 lbs.
Speed: 305 fps
Weight: 6.3 lbs.
Length: 37.5"
Arrow Length: 20"
Arrow Weight: 350-grains
Power Stroke: 14.5"
Stock Type: Traditional
MSRP; 2240: $569.99
6720: $749.99
6722: $799.99
6726: N/A
Features (all models): Drilled and tapped for Excalibur's scope and quiver mounts; fiber-optic sight; available in Realtree camo

6720: Vari-Zone multiplex crossbow scope; mounting rings and base; 4-arrow quiver and mounting bracket; rope-cocking aid
6722: Shadow-Zone multiplex green or red illuminated reticle crossbow scope; mounting rings and base; four arrow quiver and mounting bracket; rope-cocking aid
6726: New multi red dot sight with reflex technology for lighted electronic sighting system; 4-arrow quiver and mounting bracket; rope-cocking aid

Pixel
Draw Weight: 40 lbs.
MSRP: $469.99
Features: Introductory/learner crossbow

Vixen II 6700, 6710
Draw Weight: 150 lbs.
Speed: 285 fps
Weight: 5.9 lbs.
Length: 35.5"
Arrow Length: 20"
Arrow Weight: 350-grains
Power Stroke: 13.5"
Stock Type: Traditional
MSRP: $729.99
Features: Drilled and tapped for Excalibur's scope and quiver mounts; Vari-Zone multiplex crossbow scope; mounting rings and base; 4-arrow quiver and mounting bracket; rope-cocking aid; available in Realtree camo and Realtree camo pink.

Vortex 2260, 6750, 6752, 6756
Draw Weight: 200 lbs.
Speed: 330 fps
Weight: 6.3 lbs.
Length: 37.4"
Arrow Length: 20"
Arrow Weight: 350-grains
Power Stroke: 15.5"
Stock Type: Thumbhole
MSRP; 2260: $669.99
6750: $849.99
6752: $899.99
6756: N/A
Features (all models): Drilled and tapped for Excalibur's scope and quiver mounts; fiber-optic sight; available in Realtree camo.

6750: Vari-Zone multiplex crossbow scope; mounting rings and base; 4-arrow quiver and mounting bracket; rope-cocking aid.
6752: Shadow-Zone multiplex green or red illuminated reticle crossbow scope; mounting rings and base; 4-arrow quiver and mounting bracket; rope-cocking aid.
6756: New Multi red dot sight with reflex technology for lighted electronic sighting system; 4-arrow quiver and mounting bracket; rope-cocking aid.

Horton

Fury
Draw Weight: 160 lbs.
Speed: 360 fps
Mass Weight: 8.1 lbs.
Length: 35½"
Width: 17½"
Power Stroke: 15⅜"
Kinetic Energy: N/A
Trigger Pull: N/A
Finish Options: RealTree APG
MSRP: $899
Features: Reverse Draw technology, CNC-machined cams, laminated limbs, Viper-X string with stumper arms, CNC-machined Picatinny rail sight bridge with anti-dry fire mechanism, spring-loaded ball detent arrow retention, ergonomic stock with interchangeable recoil pads, Monte

Carlo cheek rest and grip, MIM Talon™ trigger with two-sided safety. includes multirange 4x32 scope, 5-arrow quiver, rope-cocking sled, and 3 arrows.

Havoc 150

Draw Weight: 150 lbs.
Speed: 300 fps
Mass Weight: 8.3 lbs.
Length: 34½"
Width: 17½"
Power Stroke: 13"
Kinetic Energy: N/A
Trigger Pull: N/A
Finish Options: RealTree APG
MSRP: $799
Features: Reverse draw technology, CNC-machined riser and barrel, CNC-machined cams, CNC Picatinny rail sight bridge with anti-dry fire mechanism, Spring-loaded ball detent arrow retention system, lightweight ergonomic stock with interchangeable recoil pads, accommodates EZ7 dovetail cocking mechanism (not included), ambidextrous Monte Carlo cheek rest, foot stirrup. Includes added boot-grip ridges, Viper X String, MIM Talon ultralight trigger with dual-sided safety.

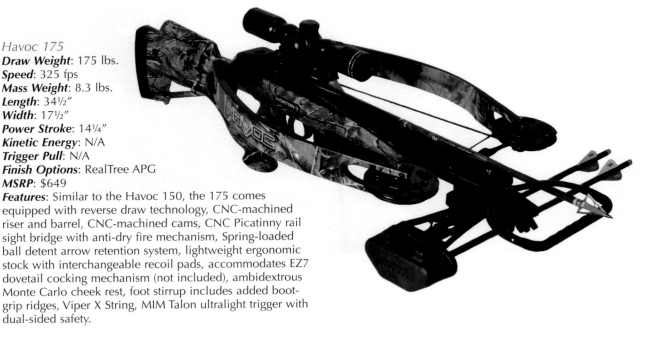

Havoc 175

Draw Weight: 175 lbs.
Speed: 325 fps
Mass Weight: 8.3 lbs.
Length: 34½"
Width: 17½"
Power Stroke: 14¼"
Kinetic Energy: N/A
Trigger Pull: N/A
Finish Options: RealTree APG
MSRP: $649
Features: Similar to the Havoc 150, the 175 comes equipped with reverse draw technology, CNC-machined riser and barrel, CNC-machined cams, CNC Picatinny rail sight bridge with anti-dry fire mechanism, Spring-loaded ball detent arrow retention system, lightweight ergonomic stock with interchangeable recoil pads, accommodates EZ7 dovetail cocking mechanism (not included), ambidextrous Monte Carlo cheek rest, foot stirrup includes added boot-grip ridges, Viper X String, MIM Talon ultralight trigger with dual-sided safety.

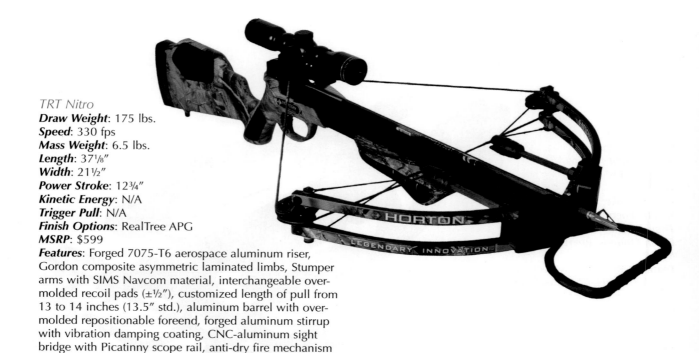

TRT Nitro
Draw Weight: 175 lbs.
Speed: 330 fps
Mass Weight: 6.5 lbs.
Length: 37⅛"
Width: 21½"
Power Stroke: 12¾"
Kinetic Energy: N/A
Trigger Pull: N/A
Finish Options: RealTree APG
MSRP: $599

Features: Forged 7075-T6 aerospace aluminum riser, Gordon composite asymmetric laminated limbs, Stumper arms with SIMS Navcom material, interchangeable over-molded recoil pads (±½"), customized length of pull from 13 to 14 inches (13.5" std.), aluminum barrel with over-molded repositionable foreend, forged aluminum stirrup with vibration damping coating, CNC-aluminum sight bridge with Picatinny scope rail, anti-dry fire mechanism with ambidextrous safety, MIM Talon ultralight trigger, high performance synthetic string and cables. Also Includes multi-range 4x32 scope, 3-arrow quiver, three arrows, sound-stoppers, cocking sled.

Mission

MXB-360
Draw Weight: 100, 125, 160 lbs.
Speed: Up to 360 fps
Mass Weight: 6.55 lbs.
Length: 35"
Width: 19½"
Power Stroke: 14"
Kinetic Energy: N/A
Trigger Pull: N/A
Finish Options: Lost AT/Black
MSRP: $899

Features: The bow riser doubles as the foothold, eliminating the extra weight of a stirrup. Adjustable draw weight is controlled by adjusting the limb bolts. String and cables are changeable without a bow press. Bow comes preassembled. Synthetic tactical stock and split limbs. Hawke 3x32 MAP wire reticle, Non-illuminated, three Mission arrows (half-moon metal nock, 22-inch long, custom weighted for optimal performance), Mission MX-3 quiver, Mission crossbow case.

Parker

Bushwhacker

Draw Weight: 150 lbs.
Speed: 285 fps
Mass Weight: 7 lbs.
Length: 32″
Width: 23⅜″
Power Stroke: 11″
Trigger Pull: N/A
Finish Options: RealTree Max-4
MSRP: $379–$449

Features: Entry level bow. Ultralight weight design, aggressive stock styling, G2 trigger, auto-engage ambidextrous safety, anti-dry fire device, vented forearm, RealTree Max-4 camo limbs with black stock. Includes Scope, 4-arrow quick-detach quiver, four arrows with field points, and rope cocker.

Challenger

Draw Weight: Adjustable 125–150 lbs.
Speed: 275–300 fps
Mass Weight: 5.5 lbs.
Length: 31¾″
Width: 21¼″
Power Stroke: 10¼″
Kinetic Energy: N/A
Trigger Pull: N/A
Finish Options: Film-dipped camo, Pink
MSRP: $429–$499

Features: Advanced split-limb technology, G2 bull-pup trigger, auto-engage ambidextrous safety, auto-engage anti-dry fire mechanism, vented forearm with safety-finger flange, red hot string. Includes quiver, rope cocker, scope and 4 arrows.

Concorde

Draw Weight: 175 lbs.
Speed: 300 fps with 20″ 400-grain carbon arrow
Mass Weight: N/A
Length: 34½″
Width: N/A″
Power Stroke: 9.6″
Kinetic Energy: N/A
Trigger Pull: N/A
Finish Options: Next Vista Soft Touch
MSRP: $1,199

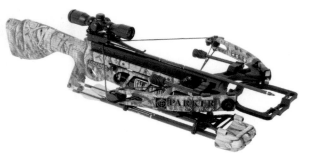

Features: Pushbutton autococking and uncocking using integrated CO2 bottle. Cocking and uncocking takes two seconds. String suppressors, solid limbs, pistol grip stock, machined riser. Includes 4-arrow quick-detach quiver, six arrows with field points, illuminated multi-reticle scope or pinpoint scope, roller-rope cocker, red hot Crosspro 100 broadheads, red hot crossbow sling, red hot wax and lube kit and red hot soft crossbow case.

Enforcer

Draw Weight: 160 lbs.
Speed: 300 fps 20″ 400-grain arrow
Mass Weight: 7 lbs.
Length: 32″
Width: 24″
Power Stroke: 11″
Kinetic Energy: N/A
Trigger Pull: N/A
Finish Options: RealTree Max-4
MSRP: $429-$499
Features: Aggressive stock styling, G2 trigger, auto engage ambidextrous safety, anti-dry fire device, vented forearm. Includes quiver, rope cocker, scope, four arrows.

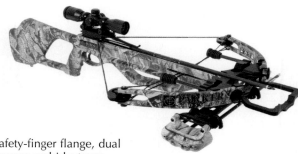

Hornet Extreme

Draw Weight: 165 lbs.
Speed: 315 fps 20″ 400-grain arrow
Mass Weight: 7.5 lbs.
Length: 32″
Width: 21¼″
Power Stroke: 11¾″
Kinetic Energy: N/A
Trigger Pull: N/A
Finish Options: Next Vista Soft Touch
MSRP: $649- $939
Features: Thumbhole pistol grip design, vented forearm with safety-finger flange, dual string suppressors, red hot string and cable, G2 Trigger, auto-engage ambidextrous safety, anti-dry fire device. Includes quiver, rope cocker, scope, 4 arrows.

Thunderhawk

Draw Weight: 160 lbs.
Speed: 320 fps
Mass Weight: 6.5 lbs.
Length: 34¼″
Width: 20³/₁₆″
Power Stroke: 10¾″
Kinetic Energy: N/A
Trigger Pull: N/A
Finish Options: Film-dipped camo
MSRP: $549–$849
Features: Advanced split-limb technology, G2 bull-pup trigger, auto engage ambidextrous safety, auto-engage anti-dry fire mechanism, vented forearm with safety-finger flange, red hot string. Includes quiver, rope cocker, scope, 4 arrows.

Tornado F4

Draw Weight: 165 lbs.
Speed: 340 fps w/ 20" 400-grain arrow
Mass Weight: 8 lbs.
Length: 35½"
Width: 20¾"
Power Stroke: 12¼"
Kinetic Energy: N/A
Trigger Pull: N/A
Finish Options: Film-dipped camo
MSRP: $849–$1,189
Features: Advanced split-limb technology, G2 bull-pup trigger, auto-engage ambidextrous safety, auto-engage anti-dry fire mechanism, vented forearm with safety-finger flange, red hot string. Includes quiver, rope cocker, scope and four arrows.

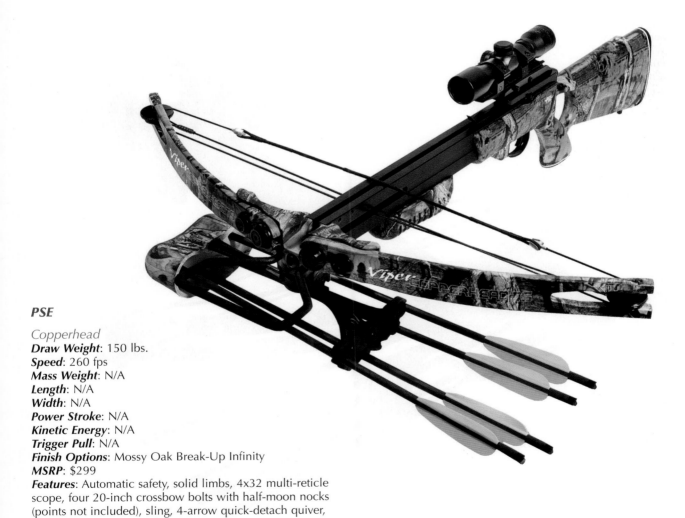

PSE

Copperhead
Draw Weight: 150 lbs.
Speed: 260 fps
Mass Weight: N/A
Length: N/A
Width: N/A
Power Stroke: N/A
Kinetic Energy: N/A
Trigger Pull: N/A
Finish Options: Mossy Oak Break-Up Infinity
MSRP: $299
Features: Automatic safety, solid limbs, 4x32 multi-reticle scope, four 20-inch crossbow bolts with half-moon nocks (points not included), sling, 4-arrow quick-detach quiver, four carbon arrows, cocking rope.

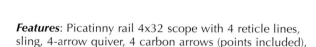

Enigma
Draw Weight: 150 lbs.
Speed: 350 fps with 425-grain arrow
Mass Weight: 8.9 lbs.
Length: 44¾"
Width: 20"
Power Stroke: 12¾"
Kinetic Energy: 116 ft-lbs.
Trigger Pull: N/A
Finish Options: Mossy Oak Brea-Up Infinity, Skullworks
MSRP: $599
Features: Split limbs, adjustable tactical-styled stock, machined riser and cams, Picatinny rail 4x32 scope with 4 reticle lines, sling, 4-arrow quiver, 4 carbon arrows (points included), cocking rope, wax-stick rail lube.

Reaper
Draw Weight: 185 lbs.
Speed: 310 fps (425-grain arrow)
Mass Weight: N/A
Length: N/A
Width: N/A
Power Stroke: N/A
Kinetic Energy: 86 ft-lbs.
Trigger Pull: N/A
Finish Options: Mossy Oak Break-Up Infinity
MSRP: $399

Features: Picatinny rail 4x32 scope with 4 reticle lines, sling, 4-arrow quiver, 4 carbon arrows (points included), cocking rope.

Smoke

Draw Weight: 180 lbs.
Speed: 330 fps with 425-grain arrow
Mass Weight: 9.15 lbs.
Length: 36½"
Width: 24¼"
Power Stroke: 14"
Kinetic Energy: 102 ft-lbs.
Trigger Pull: N/A
Finish Options: black
MSRP: $699
Features: AR-15 styling stock, split limbs, 5-position folding front grip, machined riser, 4x32 scope, quiver, 4 arrows, sling, cocking rope, rail lube, flashlight.

TAC Elite

Draw Weight: 150 lbs.
Mass Weight: 9 lbs.
Speed: 395–405 fps
Length: 45"
Width: 17" at brace
Power Stroke: 17¼"
Kinetic Energy: 155 ft-lbs.
Trigger Pull: N/A
Finish Options: Hard anodized Black
MSRP: $1,499
Features: CNC-machined components (risers, barrel, trigger housing), fully adjustable stock, split limbs, integrated string stops, ventilated barrel, pistol grip, flip-up scope covers, TAC Scope, case, bipod, tree TAC arrows.

TAC Ordnance

Draw Weight: 150 lbs.
Speed: 395–405 fps (425-grain arrow)
Mass Weight: 7.2 lbs. without lower and accessories
Length: 34¾" unmounted
Width: 22" measured cam-to-cam
Power Stroke: 17¼"
Kinetic Energy: 155 ft-lbs.
Trigger Pull: N/A
Finish Options: Hard anodized Black
MSRP: $1,299
Features: CNC-machined components (risers, barrel, and trigger housing), fully adjustable stock, split limbs, integrated string stops, ventilated barrel, pistol grip, flip-up scope covers, TAC Scope, case, bipod, tree TAC arrows.

Toxic
Draw Weight: 150 lbs.
Speed: 325 fps (425-grain arrow)
Mass Weight: 9.4 lbs.
Length: 39″
Width: 22¼″
Power Stroke: 11″
Kinetic Energy: 100 ft-lbs.
Trigger Pull: N/A
Finish Options: Mossy Oak Break-Up Infinity, Skullworks
MSRP: $499
Features: Automatic safety, split limbs, Picatinny rail, 4x32 multi-reticle scope, four 20-inch crossbow bolts with half-moon nocks (points not included), sling, 4-arrow quick-detach quiver, 4 carbon arrows, cocking rope.

SA Sports Outdoor Gear

Fever
Draw Weight: 175 lbs.
Speed: 240 fps
Mass Weight: 4.85 lbs.
Length: 31″
Width: 27″
Power Stroke: N/A
Kinetic Energy: N/A
Trigger Pull: N/A
Finish Options: Film-dipped camo
MSRP: $199
Features: Lightweight recurve laminated limb-style bow, 4x32 multi-reticle scope, quick-detach quiver with four arrows, padded shoulder sling, adjustable Weaver-style scope mount, fully dipped camo pattern, ambidextrous auto safety, large boot-style foot stirrup, compact ambidextrous rear stock, rope-cocking device; eye protection and assembly tools/hex keys included.

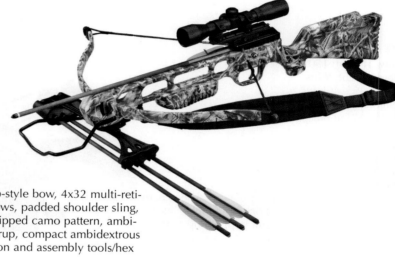

Ripper
Draw Weight: 185 lbs.
Speed: 340 fps
Mass Weight: 7.75 lbs.
Length: 35″
Width: 28″
Power Stroke: 13½″
Kinetic Energy: N/A
Trigger Pull: N/A
Finish Options: Film-dipped full coverage camo
MSRP: $499
Features: Quad limb compound, 4x32 multi-reticle scope, rope-cocking device, padded sling, quick-detach quiver with four carbon 20-inch arrows, machined aluminum riser and wheels, precision trigger assembly, anti-dry fire equipped, ambidextrous auto safety, skeletal rear stock, large boot-style foot stirrup, assembly tools/hex keys included.

Vendetta
Draw Weight: 200 lbs.
Speed: 375+ fps
Mass Weight: 8.5 lbs.
Length: 38½"
Width: 19" cocked
Power Stroke: 14"
Kinetic Energy: N/A
Trigger Pull: 3.5 lbs.
Finish Options: Next G1
MSRP: $599
Features: Anti-dry fire protection, ambidextrous auto safety, machined aluminum riser, integrated step-through-style foot stirrup, illuminated multirange 4x32 scope, quick-detach quiver with 4 carbon arrows, rope-cocking device, padded shoulder sling, machined aluminum radical cam, assembly tools/hex keys included.

Scorpyd

Telson 130
Draw Weight: 130 lbs.
Speed: 385 fps
Mass Weight: N/A
Length: 37½"
Width: 16¾"
Power Stroke: 19¾"
Kinetic Energy: 132 ft-lbs.
Trigger Pull: ~3 lbs.
Finish Options: Camo
MSRP: $899

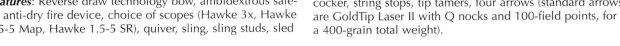

Features: Reverse draw technology bow, ambidextrous safety, anti-dry fire device, choice of scopes (Hawke 3x, Hawke 1.5-5 Map, Hawke 1.5-5 SR), quiver, sling, sling studs, sled cocker, string stops, tip tamers, four arrows (standard arrows are GoldTip Laser II with Q nocks and 100-field points, for a 400-grain total weight).

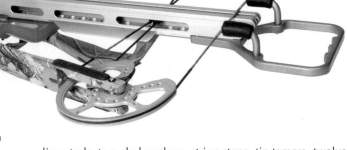

Ventilator
Draw Weight: 150 lbs.
Speed: 400 fps
Mass Weight: N/A
Length: 35¾"
Width: 12¾"
Power Stroke: 18½"
Kinetic Energy: 140 ft-lbs.
Trigger Pull: ~3 lbs.
Finish Options: Camo, Silver
MSRP: $1,349 and up
Features: Patented reverse draw technology, Kempf Tech trigger assembly, anti-dry fire, MIM trigger components, manual safety, forged riser, Barnsdale laminated limbs, titanium fasteners, folding stock, vented barrel, vented stock, MIL spec Type III anodized, scope choice, quiver, sling, sling studs, two sled cockers, string stops, tip tamers, twelve arrows (standard arrows are GoldTip Laser II with "Q" nocks and 100-grain field points, for a total weight of 400-grains).

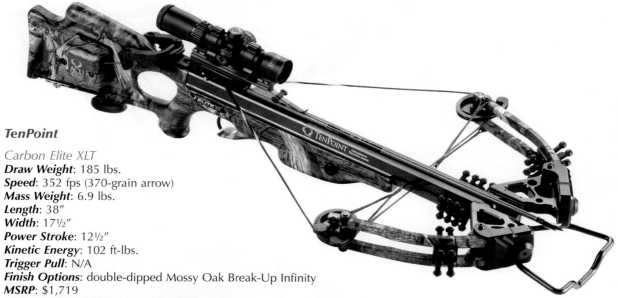

TenPoint

Carbon Elite XLT
Draw Weight: 185 lbs.
Speed: 352 fps (370-grain arrow)
Mass Weight: 6.9 lbs.
Length: 38"
Width: 17½"
Power Stroke: 12½"
Kinetic Energy: 102 ft-lbs.
Trigger Pull: N/A
Finish Options: double-dipped Mossy Oak Break-Up Infinity
MSRP: $1,719
Features: TenPoint's RangeMaster Pro scope mounted on a machined aluminum ⅞-inch-fixed dovetail mount, ACU draw cocking mechanism, instant-detach, 3-arrow quiver, ambidextrous side-mount quiver bracket, six-pack of TenPoint Pro Elite carbon fiber arrows with practice points, deluxe soft crossbow case, TenPoint's exclusive BowJax crossbow noise dampening kit, GripGuard safety shield, owner's instructional DVD, TenPoint vehicle window sticker.

Carbon Fusion CLS
Draw Weight: 185 lbs.
Speed: 364 fps (370-grain arrow)
Mass Weight: 7.2 lbs.
Length: 38½"
Width: 20½"
Power Stroke: 13"
Kinetic Energy: N/A
Trigger Pull: N/A
Finish Options: Double-dipped Mossy Oak Break-Up Infinity
MSRP: $1,819
Features: Similar to the Carbon Elite XLT, the Carbon Fusion CLS includes TenPoint's RangeMaster Pro scope mounted on a machined aluminum ⅞-inch-fixed dovetail mount, ACU draw cocking mechanism, instant-detach, 3-arrow quiver, ambidextrous side-mount quiver bracket, 6-pack of TenPoint Pro Elite carbon fiber arrows with practice points, deluxe soft crossbow case, TenPoint's exclusive BowJax crossbow noise dampening kit, GripGuard safety shield, owner's instructional DVD, TenPoint vehicle window sticker.

Carbon Xtra CLS
Draw Weight: 185 lbs.
Speed: 364 fps (370-grain arrow)
Mass Weight: 7.3 lbs.
Length: 38 $^{51}/_{64}$"
Width: 20½"
Power Stroke: 13"
Kinetic Energy: N/A
Trigger Pull: N/A
Finish Options: RealTree APG
MSRP: $2,719
Features: This bow takes the best of TenPoint's Carbon series and combines them into one bow. This package includes laminated wood stock, TenPoint's RangeMaster Pro scope mounted on a machined aluminum ⁷/₈-inch-fixed dovetail mount, ACU draw cocking mechanism, instant-detach 3-arrow quiver, ambidextrous side-mount quiver bracket, claw sling, six-pack of TenPoint Pro Elite carbon fiber arrows with practice points, Six-pack of TenPoint Pro Elite Premium Hunter carbon fiber arrows equipped with NAP Spitfire 100-grain broadheads and lighted nocks, TenPoint airline-approved compact travel and storage case, deluxe soft crossbow case, SteddyEddy telescoping light-weight aluminum monopod, TenPoint carekit, including the premium Microlon precision oiler, string wax and conditioner, flight rail and trigger lube, TenPoint's exclusive BowJax crossbow noise dampening kit, string dampening system (SDS), GripGuard safety shield, owner's instructional DVD, TenPoint vehicle window sticker.

GT Flex
Draw Weight: 180 lbs.
Speed: 297 fps (370-grain arrow)
Mass Weight: N/A
Length: N/A
Width: N/A
Power Stroke: 13¼"
Kinetic Energy: N/A
Trigger Pull: N/A
Finish Options: Mossy Oak Break-Up Infinity
MSRP: $719
Features: Recurve crossbow. TenPoint's 3x Pro-View 2 scope mounted on a machined aluminum ⁷/₈-inch-fixed dovetail mount, ACU draw cocking mechanism, instant-detach 3-arrow quiver, 3-pack of TenPoint aluminum arrows with practice points, owner's instructional DVD, TenPoint vehicle window sticker.

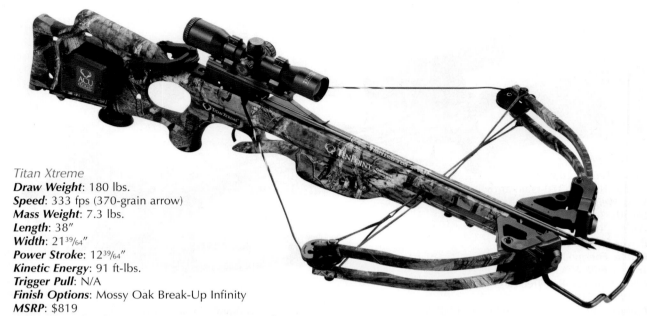

Titan Xtreme
Draw Weight: 180 lbs.
Speed: 333 fps (370-grain arrow)
Mass Weight: 7.3 lbs.
Length: 38"
Width: 21$^{39}/_{64}$"
Power Stroke: 12$^{39}/_{64}$"
Kinetic Energy: 91 ft-lbs.
Trigger Pull: N/A
Finish Options: Mossy Oak Break-Up Infinity
MSRP: $819
Features: TenPoint's 3x Pro-View 2 scope mounted on a machined aluminum ⅞-inch-fixed dovetail mount, ACU draw cocking mechanism, instant-detach 3-arrow quiver, 3-pack of TenPoint aluminum arrows with practice points, GripGuard safety shield, owner's instructional DVD, TenPoint vehicle window sticker.

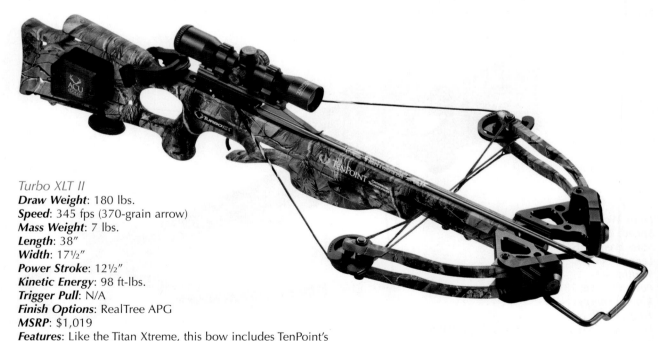

Turbo XLT II
Draw Weight: 180 lbs.
Speed: 345 fps (370-grain arrow)
Mass Weight: 7 lbs.
Length: 38"
Width: 17½"
Power Stroke: 12½"
Kinetic Energy: 98 ft-lbs.
Trigger Pull: N/A
Finish Options: RealTree APG
MSRP: $1,019
Features: Like the Titan Xtreme, this bow includes TenPoint's 3x Pro-View 2 scope mounted on a machined aluminum ⅞-inch-fixed dovetail mount, ACU draw cocking mechanism, instant-detach 3-arrow quiver, 3-pack of TenPoint aluminum arrows with practice points, GripGuard safety shield, owner's instructional DVD, TenPoint vehicle window sticker.

Wicked Ridge

Invader

Draw Weight: 180 lbs.
Speed: 315 fps
Mass Weight: N/A
Length: N/A
Width: 17½" cocked
Power Stroke: N/A
Kinetic Energy: 92.6 ft-lbs.
Trigger Pull: 3.5 lbs.
Finish Options: Double dipped Mossy Oak Break-Up Infinity
MSRP: $499–$549

Features: Compact limb system, CNC-machined riser, ACU-52 integrated self-retracting rope-cocking system, ambidextrous safety, dry fire inhibitor, quiver, TenPoint 3x multi-line scope, ACRA-ANGLE barrel, tunable synthetic cable yokes, quad limb system, Wicked Ridge instant-detach quiver, safety engineered fore grip, PowerTouch trigger, semi-skeletal stock design, integrated sling-swivel stud mounts, CNC-machined aluminum riser and pockets.

Raider CLS

Draw Weight: 180 lbs.
Speed: 330 fps
Mass Weight: lbs.
Length: N/A
Width: 17½" cocked
Power Stroke: N/A
Kinetic Energy: 101.6 ft-lbs.
Trigger Pull: 3.5 lbs.
Finish Options: Double dipped Mossy Oak Break-Up Infinity
MSRP: $799

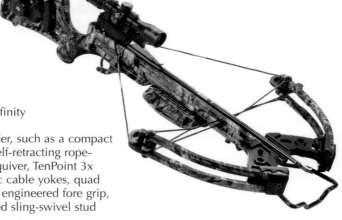

Features: This bow includes features similar to the Invader, such as a compact limb system, CNC-machined riser, ACU-52 integrated self-retracting rope-cocking system, ambidextrous safety, dry fire inhibitor, quiver, TenPoint 3x multi-line scope, ACRA-ANGLE barrel, tunable synthetic cable yokes, quad limb system, Wicked Ridge instant-detach quiver, safety engineered fore grip, PowerTouch trigger, semi-skeletal stock design, integrated sling-swivel stud mounts, CNC-machined aluminum riser, and pockets.

Warrior HL

Draw Weight: 175 lbs.
Speed: 300 fps
Mass Weight: N/A
Length: N/A
Width: N/A
Power Stroke: N/A
Kinetic Energy: 84 ft-lbs.
Trigger Pull: 3.5 lbs.
Finish Options: Double dipped Mossy Oak Break-Up Infinity
MSRP: $399, $449

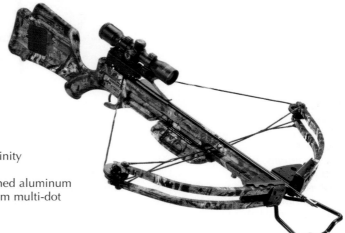

Features: D-75 string and cables, HL limbs, CNC-machined aluminum wheels, TenPoint's 3x multi-line scope or Ridge-Dot 40mm multi-dot scope, dry fire inhibitor, PowerTouch trigger.

Winchester

Blaze SS
Draw Weight: 155 lbs.
Speed: 325+ fps
Mass Weight: N/A
Length: N/A
Width: 17½"
Power Stroke: 12½"
Kinetic Energy: 100 ft-lbs.
Trigger Pull: N/A
Finish Options: Proveil Reaper Buck
MSRP: $899
Features: Split limbs, machined riser and limb pockets, integrated string stops, extruded foot stirrup, rope cocker, pistol grip stock, molded cheek pad, speedsters, limb savers, matching quiver with offset bracket, Winchester archery hat.

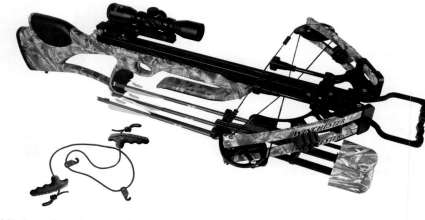

Bronco SS
Draw Weight: 150 lbs.
Speed: 315+ fps
Mass Weight: N/A
Length: N/A
Width: 18"
Power Stroke: 11½"
Kinetic Energy: N/A
Trigger Pull: N/A
Finish Options: Next G1 Vista
MSRP: $899
Features: Split limbs, machined riser and limb pockets, integrated string stops, extruded foot stirrup, rope cocker, pistol grip stock, molded cheek pad, speedsters, limb savers, matching quiver with offset bracket, Winchester archery hat.

Stallion SS
Draw Weight: 165 lbs.
Speed: 340+ fps
Mass Weight: 7.7 lbs.
Length: N/A
Width: 17½"
Power Stroke: 12½"
Kinetic Energy: 115 ft-lbs.
Trigger Pull: N/A
Finish Options: Proveil Reaper Buck
MSRP: $899
Features: Split limbs, machined riser and limb pockets, integrated string stops, pistol grip stock, molded cheek pad, speedsters, limb savers, matching detachable four-bolt quiver with offset bracket, Winchester archery hat, dual sudden-stop string dampeners, rope cocker.

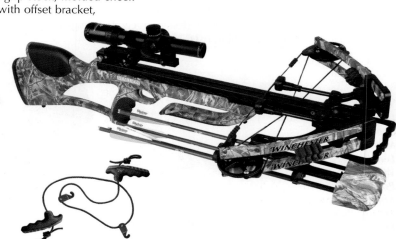

Current Arrow Shafts

Arrow Dynamic Nitro Stinger XLT
Straightness: ± 0.001
Tip Diameter: 0.328"
Nock Diameter: 0.261"

Length: Uncut 32"
Spine: 325°
GPI: 5.0
MSRP: $159.95/12-pak.

Beman Classic MFX
Micro-diameter MFX carbon construction
Extremely durable PhotoFusion™ wood-grain finish
X Nock installed
Brass HIT and Regular insert included

Break-off insert included
Straightness: ± 0.003"
Weight tolerance: ± 2-grains
MSRP: $69.99/12-pak.

Beman ICS Bowhunter
High-strength ICS C2 carbon
Straightness: ± 0.006"
Weight Tolerance: ± 2-grains
Direct-fit Super Nocks installed

CB inserts included
Fletched with 2" XPV vanes
Sizes: 300 (9.5 gpi), 340 (9.3 gpi), 400 (8.4 gpi), and 500 (7.3 gpi)
MSRP: $89/12-pak.

Beman ICS Hunter
Accurate and durable
Straightness: ± 0.006"
Weight tolerance: ± ± 2-grains

Installed Direct-Fit SuperNock®
CB Inserts
2" Vanes
MSRP: $49.99/6-pak.

Beman ICS Hunter Junior
For bows with draw weights under 40 lbs.
High-strength C2 carbon composite shaft with Pre installed Super Nock

CB insert
3" vanes
Weight: 7.3 gpi
MSRP: $41.99/6-pak.

Beman ICS Hunter Pro Carbon
Realtree® PhotoFusion™ cam weave
Microlite™ S Nocks installed
ViBrake Hot Tail inserts included
2" Blazer® Vanes

Straightness: ± 0.002"
Weight Tolerance: ± 2-grain
Sizes: 340 (8.8 gpi), 400 (8.1 gpi)
MSRP: $59.99/6-pak.

Beman ICS Speed
ViBrake Hot Tail inserts
Multilayer carbon fiber
Nocks and inserts included
Straightness: 0.003"

Weight tolerance: ± 2-grains
Sizes: 340 (8.1 gpi)
400 (7.2 gpi)
MSRP: $89.99/12-pak.

Beman MFX Bone Collector Carbon
Patented micro-diameter carbon construction
HIT® inserts
X-Nocks installed

Straightness: ± 0.003"
Weight tolerance: ± 2-grains
Sizes: 340 (9.5 gpi), 400 (9 gpi)
MSRP: $59.99/6-pak.

Cabela's Outfitter Arrow
N-Fused™ Carbon technology
Constructed using innovative carbon nanotubes
High Performance™ inserts enhance head-to-shaft alignment
Recommended field-point size: 9/32" or 18/64"
Arrows are full length

Draw weight: (340) 65–80 lbs.; (400) 55–70 lbs.
Length: (340) 31 3/8"; (400) 30 7/8"
Diameter: (340) 0.2865"; (400) 0.2833"
Straightness: ± 0.003"
Weight tolerance: ± 2-grains
MSRP: $59.99/6-pak.

Carbon Express Amped XS
Diamond-coat finish for easy target removal
Composite construction
70-grain cone tip

Designed for low poundage or youth bows
Sizes: 280 (12.8 gpi)
MSRP: $47.99/6-pak.

Carbon Express Flu Flu
Great for bird and small game hunting
Carbon composite construction
4.5" full feathers

Length: 31"
Size: 350
MSRP: $16.99/per arrow

Carbon Express Game Slayer
Carbon Express 20" 2219 Crossbow Bolts
Moon Nock
Made from 7001-T6 alloy

Pre-fletched
457-grains with 100-grain (point sold separately)
MSRP: $39/3-pak

Carbon Express Mach 5
Lightest and fastest hunting arrow in the Carbon Express line
Advanced 100% pure carbon construction
Diamond-coat finish for smoother draw
Tunable nocks

Fletched with 2" Predator vanes
Straightness tolerance: ± 0.0025"
Weight tolerance: ± 1.0-grain
Sizes: 250 (7 gpi), 350 (8.1 gpi)
MSRP: $69.99/6-pak.

Carbon Express Maxima Blue Streak
Buff Tuff® Plus
Diamond Weave
Dual Spine Weight Forward™
2" Tiger Blazer® vanes/Tiger wraps

BullDog™ collar
Straightness: ± 0.001"
Weight tolerance: ± 1.0-grains
Sizes: 150 (7.1 gpi), 250 (8 gpi), 350 (8.9 gpi)
MSRP: $89.99/6-pak.

Carbon Express Maxima Blue Streak (typesetter, use photo A)
Dual Spine Weight Forward™ technology
Diamond Weave carbon cross-weave material delivers unparalleled spine consistency
BuffTuff® finish

2" Fusion® vanes for greater broadhead accuracy.
Weighted precision insert
Straightness: + 0.0025"
20" or 22" 6-paks with 100-grain field points
MSRP: $64.99/6-pak.

Carbon Express Maxima Hunter
Buff Tuff® Plus carbon weave construction
BullDog™ nock collar
Dual Spine Weight Forward™

Straightness: ± 0.0025"
Weight tolerance: ± 1.0-grains
Sizes: 250 (8 gpi), 350 (8.9 gpi)
MSRP: $159.99/12-pak.

Carbon Express Maxima Hunter KV
Made with a layer of Kevlar
Dual Spine Weight Forward™ technology
BuffTuff® Plus carbon weave construction

BuffTuff® finish with Mossy Oak® Break Up® pattern
Straightness: ± 0.0025″
20″ or 22″ 6-paks with 100-grain field points
MSRP: $67/6-pak.

Carbon Express Mayhem
Carbon
Straightness: ± 0.004″ max
Total Weight: 20″ weighs 423-grains (with 100-grain point)
Total Weight: 22″ weighs 449-grains (with 100-grain point)
Diameter: 0.458″

Length: 20″ and 22″
Fletching: 3″ Vanes
Nock Type: flat back and half-moon included
MSRP: $44.99/6-pak.

Carbon Express Mayhem
Buff Tuff K-3 construction
Bulldog™ neck collars
Straightness tolerance: ± 0.0035″

Weight tolerance: ± 1.0-grain
Sizes: 250 (8.9 gpi), 350 (9.8 gpi)
Mossy Oak Break-Up camo/black
MSRP: $124.99/12-pak. (shafts)

Carbon Express Mayhem Hot Pursuit
Designed for women
K-360°™ weave technology
360° spine
Carbon Express built-in weight forward™ technology
2″ Fusion™ Vanes

BullDog™ nock collars
Straightness: ± 0.0035″
Weight tolerance: ± 1.0-grain
Size: 150 (8 gpi)
MSRP: $74.99/½ doz.

Carbon Express Mayhem Hunter
Built-in weight-forward design
Super-tough carbon arrow finish
Blazer vanes
BuffTuff Plus K-360° Weave

Sizes: 250 (8.9 gpi), 350 (9.8 gpi)
MSRP: $74.95/6-pak.

Carbon Express Piledriver Hunter
Bulldog™ nock collars for strength and durability
Straightness: ± 0.003"

Weight tolerance: ± 2.0-grains
Sizes: 250 (9.7 gpi), 350 (10.4 gpi)
MSRP: $84.99/12-pak. shafts

Carbon Express Release Bolt
Designed for shots into ground when unloading a cocked crossbow
Made from 100% woven-wrapped layered fiberglass
Built to withstand ground impacts

Special point keeps arrow from penetrating deep into the ground
Steel point to withstand hard or frozen ground
Designed for hundreds of release shots
MSRP: $11.99/per bolt

Carbon Express The Crush
Diamond-Coat finish delivers smoother release
2" Raptor vanes
BullDog™ nock collars

Straightness: ± 0.003"
Weight Tolerance: ± 1.0-grains
Sizes: 250 (8.7 gpi), 350 (9.5 gpi)
MSRP: $54.99/6-pak.

Carbon Express Thunderstorm
Designed for youth
Carbon-composite construction
Designed for draw weights from 30 to 50 lbs.
Fletched with ™Predator vanes
29" length

Includes all internal components, including a tunable, press-fit nock
8.3-grains per inch
Arrows are 29" in length
MSRP: $44.99/6-pak.

Easton ACC Pro Hunter
Straightness: ± 0.002"
Weight tolerance: ± 0.5-grains
Black, microsmooth 9 micron finish

Now incorporates X-Nock
Sizes: 300, 340, 390, 440
MSRP: $160/12-pak. shafts

Easton Axis N-Fused
N-Fused carbon nanotubes
Ultra-small diameter
Microsmooth finish
HIT® insert, chamfer stone, installation tool, and HIT epoxy included
Hidden Insert Technology

X-Nocks installed
2" Blazer® vanes
Straightness: ± 0.003"
Weight Tolerance: ± 2-grain
Sizes: 340 (9.5 gpi), 400 (9 gpi)
MSRP: $64.99/6-pak.

Easton Axis Realtree N-Fused
N-Fused carbon nanotubes
Ultra-small diameter
Microsmooth finish
HIT® insert, chamfer stone, installation tool, and HIT epoxy included Hidden Insert Technology

X-Nocks installed
2" Blazer® vanes
Straightness: ± 0.003"
Weight Tolerance: ± 2-grain
Sizes: 340 (10.3 gpi), 400 (9.8 gpi)
MSRP: $69.99/6-pak.

Easton Bloodline N-Fused
Small diameter, lightweight shaft
High-performance for hunting or target
Carbon nanotube N-Fused® fibers
Factory-crested, pre installed red H-Nocks

Straightness: ± 0.003"
Weight Tolerance: ± 1.0-grains
Sizes: 330 (8.7 gpi), 400 (7.7 gpi), 480 (6.8 gpi)
MSRP: $89.99/12-pak. shafts

Easton Carbon Injexion
Small diameter, lightweight shaft
High-performance for hunting or target
Carbon nanotube N-Fused® fibers
Factory-crested, Pre installed red H-nocks

Straightness: ± 0.003"
Weight Tolerance: ± 1.0-grains
Sizes: 330 (8.7 gpi), 400 (7.7 gpi), 480 (6.8 gpi)
MSRP: $89.99/12-pak. shafts

Easton Carbon Ion
Designed for the lower-poundage, shorter draw length archer
Small diameter shafts
Reduced wind drift
Enhanced penetration
Factory-crested

2" Blazer® vanes
Blue H-Nocks installed
HP inserts included
Straightness: ± 0.003"
Sizes: 500 (7.3 gpi), 600 (6.4 gpi)
MSRP: $49.99/6-pak.

Easton Flatline Superlite
Multilayer wrapped carbon fibers lend strength
Black, smooth matte finish
Pre installed MicroLite nocks
Included MicroLite inserts

Straightness: ± 0.003"
Weight tolerance: ± 2-grains
Sizes: 340 (8.2 gpi), 400 (7.4 gpi)
MSRP: $59.99/6-pak.

Easton Genesis V2 Blue
Approved by NASP for tournament use
Made of 7075 aerospace alloy
Guaranteed straightness: ± 0.005"

Weight tolerance: ± 2.5%
Length: 29.5"
MSRP: $31.99/6-pak.

Easton Genesis V2 Orange
Approved by NASP for tournament use
Made of 7075 aerospace alloy
Guaranteed straightness: ± 0.005"

Weight tolerance: ± 2.5%
Length: 29.5"
MSRP: $31.99/6-pak.

Easton Premium Finish XX75 Camo Hunter
Shaft Weight: ± 1%
Diameter Tolerances: ± 0.0003"
Spine Tolerances: ± 0.0005"
Straightness: ± 0.002"
Fletched with three 4" plastic vanes

High-grade 7075 aluminum alloy shafts
Hard-anodized PermaGraphic for durability
Super UNI Nock and Super UNI Bushing
Sizes: 2117, 2213, 2216, 2314, 2315, 2413
MSRP: $89.99/12-pak.

Easton ST Axis Full Metal Jacket N-Fused Camo
Ultra-high strength N-FUSED® carbon core sheathed in full metal jacket
X-Nocks installed
Deep Six insert
Chamfer stone
Installation tool

HIT epoxy included
Straightness: ± 0.002"
Weight Tolerance: ± 2-grains
Sizes: 340 (11.3 gpi), 400 (10.2 gpi)
MSRP: $74.99/6-pak.

Easton ST Axis N-Fused Deep Six

Ultra-high strength N-FUSED® carbon core sheathed in full metal jacket
X-Nocks installed
deep six insert

Chamfer stone
Installation tool
HIT epoxy included
Sizes: 340 (11.3 gpi), 400 (10.2 gpi)
MSRP: $74.99/6-pak.

Easton XX75 Camo Hunter

Straightness: ± 0.002"
Shaft weight: ± 1%
Diameter Tolerance: ± 0.0003"
Fletched with 4" PlastiFletch aluminum inserts

High-grade 7075 aluminum alloy shafts
Super UNI brushing system and nock
4-color camo finish
Sizes: 2117, 2213, 2216, 2314, 2315, 2413
MSRP: $74.99/12-pak.

Easton XX75 Gamegetter

Straightness: ± 0.003"
Fletched with 4" vanes
Hard-anodized, 7075-T9 aluminum alloy arrows

Full-diameter taper swage
RPS insertSizes: 340 (11.7 gpi), 400 (12 gpi), 500 (10.6 gpi)
MSRP: $54.99/12-pak.

Excalibur Diablo Illuminated Crossbow Arrows

Diablo carbon arrows equipped with Burt Coyote's Lumenok
Activated by accelerative force
Provides illuminated path to targets
MSRP: $69.99/3-pak

Fred Bear Lit'l Brave
24" fiberglass youth arrows
3" plastic vanes

Steel target points
MSRP: $5.99/3 pak

Gold Tip Expedition Hunter
Each Expedition Hunter arrow is hand-weighed to within ±2-grains
Ultrasonic coating system for a smoother, cleaner finish
Shaft length: 32"

Straightness: ± 0.006"
Standard with GT Series nock inserts
RealTree APG™ finish
Sizes: 5575 (8.5 gpi), 7595 (10.9 gpi)
MSRP: $84.99/12-pak.

Gold Tip Expedition Hunter Pre Cut
Each Expedition Hunter arrow is hand-weighed to within ±2-grains
Ultrasonic coating system for a smoother, cleaner finish
Shaft length: 27", 28", 29", 30"

Straightness: ± 0.006".
Standard with GT Series nock inserts
RealTree APG™ finish
Sizes: 5575 (8.5 gpi), 7595 (10.9 gpi)
MSRP: $54.99/12-pak.

Gold Tip Kinetic Hunter
Small diameter
Built with all premium components
Straightness: ± 0.006"

Weight tolerance: ± 2-grains
Sizes: 400 (9.5 gpi), 300 (10.4 gpi)
MSRP: $56.99/6-pak.

Gold Tip Kinetic XT
Hard-hitting, small diameter hunting shaft
Straightness: ± 0.003"

Weight tolerance: ± 0.5-grains
Sizes: 400 (9.5 gpi), 300 (10.4 gpi)
MSRP: $74.99/6-pak.

Gold Tip Pro Hunter
One of the most consistent graphite hunting arrows in the world.
Straightness tolerance: ± 0.001"
Weight tolerance: ± 1-grain per dozen

Shaft Length: 32"
Standard GT Series nock and inserts.
Sizes: 5575, 7595 (weights vary)
MSRP: $79.99/6-pak.

Gold Tip Pro Hunter RealTree
Straightness: ± 0.001"
Weight Tolerance: ± 1-grain

Complete with GT Series nock and inserts
MSRP: $259.99/12-pak. shafts

Gold Tip Velocity Hunter
100% pure carbon shafts weigh 25–30-grains less than standard shafts
Multilayer carbon construction
Standard Accu-Lite Lite nocks (8.3-grains) and Accu-Lite

inserts (11.4-grains)
Straightness: ± 0.006"
Weight tolerance: ± 2-grains
Sizes: 300 (8.5 gpi), 400 (7.4 gpi)
MSRP: $84.99/12-pak.

Horton Lightning Strike Aluminum
Matched-Weight™ crossbow arrows
7075-T9 aluminum alloy for optimal balance and accuracy

20" shaft with plastic vanes
Straightness: ± 0.003"
MSRP: $39.99/6-pak.

PSE Carbon Force Black Mamba
The Black Mamba uses a stainless steel insert and a stainless steel insert collar for added FOC weight and durability
9.2 gpi
Straightness: ± 0.003"

10.5-grains per inch weight tube for a total weight of 19.7-grains per inch
Shafts come full length with inserts and collars loose, nocks installed
MSRP: $111.99/12-pak. shafts

PSE Carbon Force Bow Madness Radial X- Weave
Designed with input from the Drury Outdoors Team
Radial X Weave Technology
A computer process wraps individual carbon fibers to create a weave pattern

Straightnes: ± 0.003"
Weight Tolerance: ± 5-grains
Arrows are full length with loose inserts
MSRP: $99.99/12-pak. shafts

PSE Carbon Force Desperado
Designed for youth bows
High-grade carbon cut to length with target points installed

Available in 26″, 28″, and 30″ lengths
Recommended bow weight not exceed 50 pounds
MSRP: $64.99/12-pak.

PSE Carbon Force EXT Hunter
Small diameter and extra thick wall-high modular carbon shaft
Straightness: ± 0.001″ straight
Weight tolerance: ± ½-grain per dozen shafts

Coated with PSE whisper coating for easy arrow pull
PSE uses exclusive Fast Recovery System (FRS) technology in building each arrow
All shafts are spine aligned for easy and accurate fletching
MSRP: $199/12-pak. shafts

PSE Carbon Force Radial X-Weave Predator
Radial X Weave process
Straightness: ± 0.005″

Weight tolerance: ± 5-grains per dozen
Fletched with 2″-Blazer® vanes
MSRP: $129.99/12-pak.

PSE Carbon Force Radial X-Weave Pro
Radial X Weave technology
Straightness: ± 0.001″
Computer process wraps individual carbon fibers to create a weave pattern
Shafts are full length with inserts loose and nocks installed

Fletched arrows are full length with inserts loose and nocks installed
Arrows are fletched with either 4″ Duravanes or Blazer vanes
MSRP: $119.99/12-pak.

Redhead Blackout X1 Pro Carbon
Straightness: ± 0.001″
Weight tolerance: ± 0.5-grains
100% carbon construction
2″ Blazer vanes

Ships with nocks installed
Inserts included
Shipped full length (32″)
Sizes: 340 (8.7 gpi), 400 (8 gpi)
MSRP: $109.99/12-pak.

Redhead Blackout X3 Hunter Carbon
Straightness: ± 0.003″
100% carbon for durability and smooth penetration
Ships with nocks installed

Inserts included
Weight Tolerance: ± 2-grains
Sizes: 340 (8.7 gpi), 400 (8 gpi)
MSRP: $79.99/12-pak.

Redhead Blackout X5 Envy Carbon
100% carbon construction
Nocks ship installed
Inserts are included

Straightness: ± 0.005"
Weight Tolerance: ± 2-grains
Sizes: 340 (8.7 gpi), 400 (8 gpi), 500 (7.2 gpi)
MSRP: $34.99 - MSRP: $59.99/6-pak.

Redhead Carbon Supreme Hunter
Front of Center (FOC) Fusion technology
Front ⅔ of arrow is heavier BuffTuff™ with Realtree Hardwoods Green® HD™

Straightness: ± 0.003."
Weight tolerance: ± 1-grain
Shipped full length 32 ½"
MSRP: N/A

Victory VAP
The VAP (Victory Armor Piercing)
Ultra small diameter and thick walled
100% high modular core
100% hand fletched

Bohning "F" nocks.
Straightness: ± 0.001",0.003",0.006"
Sizes: 6.1–9.7 gpi
MSRP: $149/12-pak.

Victory VForce
Bohning blazer nocks and inserts
Made with the highest quality carbon composite fibers available.
100% hand fletched

Standard V-Force Arrows are sorted to ± 0.5 of-grain weight per dozen on all 300, 350, and 400 sizes, ± 3-grains weight tolerance on 500 and 600 per dozen.
MSRP: $109/12-pak.

Victory VooDoo Bolt
Ultra small diameter shaft
Rail Ryder Technology
2 contact points on rail

Sizes: 20", 22", 24"
Includes AAE Max Hunter vanes and Penetrator broadhead adapter
MSRP: $59.99/6-pak.

Victory XBolt
Made with 100% carbon
Brass insert
Half-moon nocks (also available with a flat nock)
Made with the highest quality carbon composite fibers

Smooth polished finish
Duravane vanes
Available with 92- or 110-grain brass inserts
MSRP: $459.99/12-pak. shafts

Current Broadheads

American Broadhead Company Super Sonic
0.036"-thick blades
1⅛" cutting diameter
420 grade stainless steel construction
Cut-on-contact fixed bald design
85, 100, 125-grain weights
$39.99/3-pak

Arrowdynamic Solutions Guillotine 125-grain
Eliminates need for meat destroying chest shot
Designed for quick and lethal head or neck shot
Great broadhead for turkey
4" x 4" cutting diameter
125-grains
$39.99/3-pak

Arrowdynamic Solutions Guillotine 100-grain
Eliminates need for meat destroying chest shot
Designed for quick and lethal head or neck shot
Great broadhead for turkey
2.5" x 2.5" cutting diameter
125-grains
$39.99/3-pak

Carbon Express F-15 Dual Blade Fixed Broadhead
The only side-by-side, dual fixed-blade broadhead available
Six devastating razor-sharp edges
100-grains
1⅛" cutting diameter
$39.99/3-pak

Carbon Express F-15 Expandable
Dual side-by-side cutting blades
Six total cutting edges
Metal Injection Molded
1-piece ferrule constructed of 440 stainless steel
0.030″ thick blades
1⅜″ cutting diameter
$39.99/3-pak

Carbon Express XT 4
1-piece main blade construction
Curved cutting blade surface for greater penetration
Back of main and bleeder blade are sharpened for greater damage
0.058″ blade thickness
100-grains
1⅛″ cutting diameter
$19.99/3-pak

Clean Shot Hogzilla Killa'
Disposable battery pack for up to 100 shots
Internal laser beam is adjustable up-and-down
1¼″ cutting diameter
Quick target acquisition with or without sight pins
Weight adjustable: 125-grain (with standard tip) and 150-grain (with large tip) included in package.
Single Pack Includes:
(2) Spot-On® laser hogzilla killa' broadheads
(1) Bow mounted magnet
(2) Disposable batteries
(6) Hunting blades
(2) Standard hollow point tips
(2) Large hollow point tips
complete instruction sheet
$99.99/2-pak

Clean Shot Hollow Point

Tip works like a core drill removing a 0.25" caliber size hole
1¼" cutting diameter
100, 125, 150-grains
$39.99/3-pak

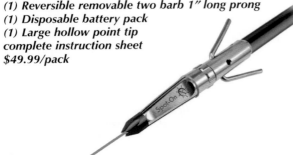

Clean Shot Spot on Bowfish Assassin

Automatic laser activation
Eliminates Snell's law on light refraction in water
Quick target acquisition
Disposable battery for up to 100 shots
Standard removable double barb 1-inch long, fold-over prong for quick release of fish
Package Includes:
(1) ⁵⁄₁₆" Spot-On® laser bowfish assassin point
(1) Laser activation bar
(1) Adjustable magnet slide
(1) Reversible removable two barb 1" long prong
(1) Disposable battery pack
(1) Large hollow point tip
complete instruction sheet
$49.99/pack

Eastman Outfitters Shocker Small Game Point

Varmint point or stump shooting
Spring arms designed to snag on grass or brush for easy arrow location
100-grains
$12.99/2-pak

Easton Deep Six Field Point

Secure point-to-insert connection
40 threads per inch (TPI)
25% more thread engagement than 8–32 threads
100-grains
$8.99/6-pak

Easton V3 Expandable Varmint Point

Head has field point profile in flight
Opens on impact
Blades are replaceable
100-grains
$21.99/2-pak

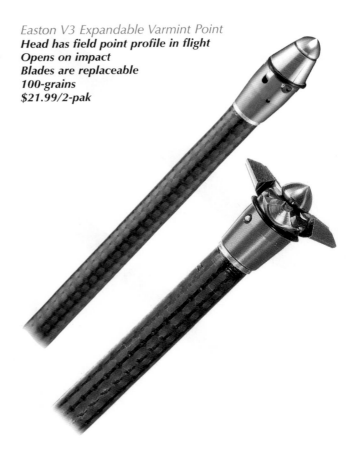

Excalibur Boltcutter
Constructed entirely from stainless steel
150-grains
1¹⁄₁₆″ cutting diameter
$37.99/3-pak

Fulton Precision Archery Ramcat
Lobes on tip minimize wind planing
0.032″ blades cut in any direction
1-piece stainless body construction
$34.99/3-pak

Excalibur X-Act
Mechanical blades open to cut on impact
Clip-Loc blade control uses no O-rings or bands
100-grains
¹⁷⁄₁₆″ cutting diameter
$44.99/ 3-pak

Hartcraft Exchange
Utilizes one ferrule
Five different blade configurations
All blade options are 100% stainless steel and 0.030″ thick
Blades: Trophy I (100-grains/1⅛″ cutting diameter); Trophy II (100-grains/1½″ cutting diameter); Thumper (100-grains/1⅛″ cutting diameter); Lil Thumper (100-grains/1⅛″ cutting diameter) Lopper (125-grains/2⅜″ cutting diameter). Master Pak including all blades option, 3-per set.
$144.95

Game Vector Tracking System

No effect on arrow flight due to its totally balanced light weight design
Designed to aid the archery hunter in successful game recovery
38-grains
Can be reused
Over 48-hour battery life
Up to two-mile range
Does not require special arrows
Use with any broadhead or expandable
Price per unit: N/A

G5 Montec Crossbow

1-piece stainless steel construction
Easy to install design
Strong, multi-tapered blades
cut-on-contact nose
Easy-to-sharpen edges
Available in 100 and 125-grains
$34.99/3-pak

G5 Montec

Cut-on-impact nose ensures deep penetration
Multi-tapered blades
Available in 85, 100, 125-grains
1-piece MonoFlow™ technology
Sizes: 85, 100, 125-grains (1", 1¹⁄₁₆", 1⅛" cutting diameter)
$34.99/3-pak

G5 Pre-Season Montec Practice Point

Crafted using solid, 1-piece MonoFlow™ technology.
Points have rounded edges
Rust-resistant coating
Sizes: 85, 100, 125-grains
$29.99/3-pak

G5 Small Game

Field-point flight
Three talon-like prongs
Prongs flip the arrow upward on impact with the ground
Dispatches down-sized critters with a megadose of shock-and-tear trauma
Sizes: 100-grains, 125-grains
$24.99/3-pak

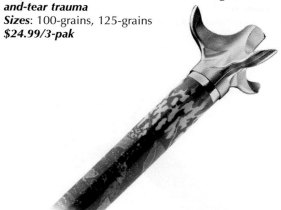

Grim Reaper Razorcut Whitetail Special

Mechanical 3-blade design
2" cutting diameter
Ideal for whitetail-sized game
Great for higher kinetic energy bows
Includes practice head
100-grains
$39.99/3-pak

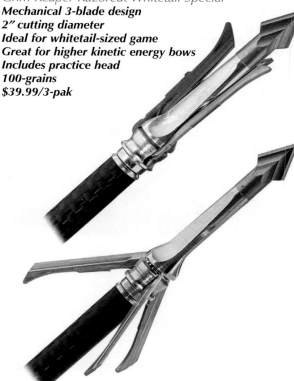

G5 Tekan

Blade deployment requires less than 3 lbs. of energy
1-piece stainless steel ferrule
½" cut-on-contact point
1½" cutting diameter
$39.99/3-pak

Grim Reaper Razortip

Trocrazor tip features 3 mini razors in hardened steel tip
No deflection design
LockNotch blade retention system provides quick and smooth blade expansion
No O-rings or rubber bands
Maxx Edge blades
0.035" blades
1⅜" cutting diameter
$39.99/3-pak

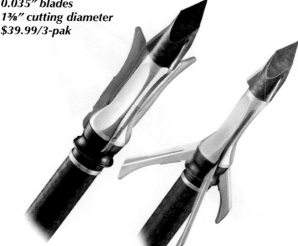

Innerloc Carbon Tuner
Exclusive Blade alignment technology
Center-locking system
Endur-edge tempering
Three-blade design
1¹⁄₁₆" cutting diameter
100-grains
$36.99/3-pak

Magnus Stinger
Stainless steel blades
Replaceable main blade can be re-sharpened
Durable ferrule made of aircraft-grade aluminum
Diamond tip on main blade
Spin tested for accuracy
1¹⁄₁₆" cutting diameter
$29.99/3-pak

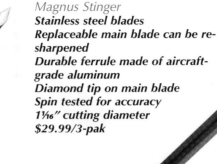

Innerloc Falcon
Blade alignment technology
Center-locking system
Tune with a simple twist of the tuning stud
Endur-edge blades
Three-blade design
1" cutting diameter
$39.99/3-pak

Magnus Stinger Buzzcut
Serrated main blade
Spin tested
Cut-on-contact diamond tip
4-blade design
1¼" cutting diameter
100-grains
$34.99/3-pak

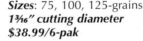

Magnus Bullhead
0.048" stainless steel blades
Replaceable blades can be resharpened
One set of replacement blades in every pack
100-grains (2¾" cutting diameter), 125-grains (3¾" cutting diameter)
$39.99/3-pak

Muzzy 3-Blade
Hardened steel Trocar Tip
Blade system switches from hunting blades to practice blades in seconds
Blades interlock in aluminum ferrule for additional stability
Vented 0.020" stainless steel blades
Sizes: 75, 100, 125-grains
1³⁄₁₆" cutting diameter
$38.99/6-pak

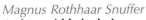

Magnus Rothhaar Snuffer
1-piece tri-blade design
Made of carbon steel that's been copper brazed and heat treated to 44C Rockwell hardness
Lifetime guarantee
$39.99/6-pak

Muzzy 4-Blade
Hardened steel Trocar tip
Blade system switches from hunting blades to practice
blades in seconds
Blades interlock in aluminum ferrule for additional stability
Vented 0.020" stainless steel blades
Sizes: 90, 100, 125-grains
1" and 1⅛" cutting diameter
$38.99/6-pak

Muzzy Phantom
4-blade design
0.040" main blades
0.028" bleeder blades
1⅛" cutting diameter
$29.99/3-pak

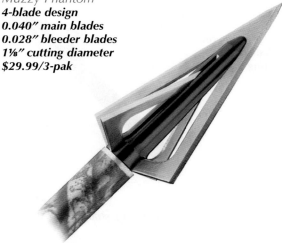

Muzzy Crosskill
Designed for crossbows
3-blade ultra-compact design
0.025" thick blades
1³⁄₁₆" cutting diameter
Trocar Tip
$34.99/3-pak

Muzzy Phantom Fred Eichler Signature Series
Cut-on-contact Tonto-style tip
Blades are easily resharpened
1⅛" cutting diameter
125-grains
$39.99/3-pak

Muzzy MX-3
Hardened steel Trocar Tip
1¼" cutting diameter
Blades interlock in aluminum ferrule for additional stability
Vented 0.025" stainless steel blades
$26.99/3-pak

Muzzy Quick-Release Fish Head
Stainless steel Trocar cutting point
Dual barbs prevent fish from spinning off
2 turns of the tip and reverse barbs for easy fish removal
$9.99/per head

Muzzy SG-X
Designed for small game
Trocar tip with spring-loaded arms
Stainless steel body
100-grains
$17.99/3-pak

NEET Small Game Stopper
Fits easily behind field point or broadhead
Prevents deep penetration
Adds shocking power to impact
$9.99/6-pak

New Archery Products Razorcaps
Laser welded
Stainless steel blades
Cut-on-contact design
Sizes: 100, 125, 200-grains
$44.99/3-pak

New Archery Products Bloodrunner 2-Blade
Fixed-blade and mechanical technologies
Stainless steel blades are 0.035" thick
2¹⁄₁₆" cutting diameter
$39.99/3-pak

New Archery Products Bloodrunner 3-Blade
Fixed-blade and mechanical technologies
Stainless steel blades are 0.035" thick
1½" cutting diameter
$39.99/3-pak

New Archery Products Big Nasty Deep Six Series
Shaft forward design
deep six technology
Arrow shaft acts as the ferrule
All-steel broadhead
1⅜" cutting diameter
Sizes: 100-grains
$39.99/3-pak

New Archery Products Hellrazor Crossbow
All-steel
1-piece cut-on-contact design
1⅛" cutting diameter
100, 125-grains
$39.99/3-pak

New Archery Products Killzone Trophy Tip
Trophy Tip®
Two-blade rear-deploying broadhead
2" cutting diameter
Spring-clip design
100-grains
$39.99/3-pak

New Archery Products Killzone
Two-blade, rear-deploying mechanical
Uses no rubber bands or O-rings
Spring-clip design
2" cutting diameter
Sizes: 100-grains
$39.99/3-pak

New Archery Products Spitfire 3
Microgrooved, low-drag Slimline ferrule
Cut-on-impact hardened carbon steel Trophy Tip®
Three-blade surgical-steel design
Unique snap-locking blade-retention system with no O-rings or rubber bands
1½" cutting diameter
Sizes: 85, 100, 125-grains
$39.99/3-pak

New Archery Products Killzone Deep Six Series
Two-blade, rear-deploying mechanical
Deep Six technology
Uses no rubber bands or O-rings
Spring-clip design
2" cutting diameter
100-grains
$39.99/3-pak

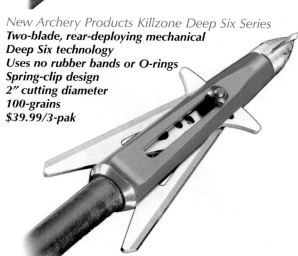

New Archery Products Spitfire Crossbow
Flight, spin, and high-speed tested
1½" cutting diameter
125-grains
$39.99/3-pak

New Archery Products Spitfire Edge
Trophy Tip®
Microgrooved SlimLine® ferrule
Straight/serrated blade design
1¾" cutting diameter
100-grains
$39.99/3-pak

New Archery Products Spitfire Maxx Deep Six Series
Three-blade design
Deep Six Technology
1¾" cutting diameter
Trophy Tip®
$39.99/3-pak

New Archery Products Thunderhead Edge
Exclusive straight/serrated blade technology
Offset blades
Trophy Tip® point
Microgrooved ferrule
100-grains
1⅛" cutting diameter

New Archery Products Thunderhead Razor
Three-blade design
1⅛" cutting diameter
Offset blade alignment
Trophy Tip® point
100-grains
$34.99/3-pak

Octane Thug
Crossbow uncocking/release arrow
Piston equipped
Designed to be shot into ground repeatedly without damage
$29.99/per bolt

New Archery Products Thunderhead Crossbow
1³⁄₁₆" cutting diameter
125-grains
$39.99/6-pak

Rage 2-Blade
Rear-deploying SlipCam™
Chisel point
ShockLock™ blade-retention system
Black, anti-friction chisel points
Red-anodized ferrules
100-grains
Practice head included
2" cutting diameter
$39.99/3-pak

Rage 3-Blade
Rear-deploying SlipCam™
Chisel point
ShockLock™ blade-retention system
Black, anti-friction chisel points
Red-anodized ferrules
100-grains
Practice head included
1½″ cutting diameter
$39.99/3-pak

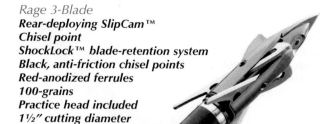

Rage Chisel 3-Blade
Rear-deploying SlipCam™
Chisel point
ShockLock™ blade-retention system
Black, anti-friction chisel points
Red-anodized ferrules
100-grains
1½″ cutting diameter
$39.99/3-pak

Rage 40KE
Designed for short draw lengths
Light draw weights generating less than 40ft lbs. of kinetic energy
SlipCam™ technology
1½″ cutting diameter
100-grains
$39.99/3-pak

Rage Crossbow
HexFlat™ design
No rubber bands
Reliable cam deployment, rear deployment
Machined aircraft-grade aluminum body
Practice broadhead included
¾″ in-flight diameter
1¾″ cutting diameter
$39.99/3-pak

Rage Chisel 2-Blade
Rear-deploying SlipCam™
Chisel point
ShockLock™ blade-retention system
Black, anti-friction chisel points
Red-anodized ferrules
125-grains
2″ cutting diameter
$39.99/3-pak

Rage Titanium
All-titanium ferrule
0.039″ stainless steel
Instant-cut tip
Rear-deploying 0.035″
Blades expand at impact
Minimum cutting diameter of 2″
In-flight diameter of ¾″
100-grains
$79.99/3-pak

Rage Turkey 2-Blade
Deploys from rear
Machined aircraft-aluminum body
HexFlat™ design for stable flight
Stainless steel instant-cut tip
Includes a free practice head
2¼" cutting diameter
100-grain
$39.99/ 3-pak

Redhead Blackout Expandable 100
Expandable two-blade design
Microgrooved SlimLine® ferrule
Hardened Trophy Tip®
Razor-sharp Diamize® stainless steel blades
2" cutting diameter
100-grains
$29.99/3-pak

Rage Turkey 3-Blade
Deploys from rear
Machined aircraft-aluminum body
HexFlat™ design for stable flight
Stainless steel instant-cut tip
Includes a free practice head
1¾" cutting diameter
100-grain
$39.99/ 3-pak

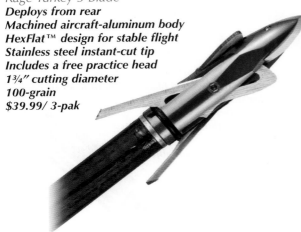

Redhead Blackout Expandable
Expandable two-blade design
Microgrooved SlimLine® ferrule
Razor-sharp Diamize® stainless steel blades
2" cutting diameter
100-grains
$29.99/3-pak

Rage X-Treme
2.3" cutting diameter
Shock Collar
Designed for use with bow draw weights 60 lbs. and up
$44.99/3-pak

Redhead Blackout FXD
1-piece cut-on-contact broadhead
Stainless steel construction
Photon-welded fixed blades
1⅛" cutting diameter
100-grains
$29.99/3-pak

Redhead Gator
Cut-on-contact broadhead
In-flight diameter of ⅞″
Free-floating blades deploy from the rear at impact
2″ Cutting diameter
100-grains
$29.99/3-pak

Rocket Aeroheads Meat Seeker 2-Blade
Piston Hammer deploys the blades without lever or cams
Chisel tip for maximum penetration
Non-barbed design blades
Deploys blades without lever or cams
100-grains
2″ cutting diameters available
$39.99/3-pak

Reign
Main blade has swivel action.
Metal Injection Molded ferrule
Cut-on-contact tip
100-grains
$24.99/3-pak

Rocket Aeroheads Meat Seeker 3-Blade
Piston Hammer deploys the blades without lever or cams
Chisel tip for maximum penetration
Non-barbed design blades
Deploys blades without lever or cams
100-grains
1½″ cutting diameters available
$39.99/3-pak

Rocket Aeroheads Hammerhead
Improved tip-to-ferrule and blade-to-ferrule connections
Long ferrule design
2″ cutting diameter
$24.99/3-pak

Rocket Aeroheads Miniblaster
Slim, lightweight broadhead
1¾″ cutting diameter
$24.99/3-pak

Rocket Aeroheads Sidewinder
1½″ cutting diameter
Three-blade design
Rubber band closure
$24.99/3-pak

Rocket Aeroheads Steelhead
Solid steel, titanium-nitride-coated, one-piece ferrule
Machined chisel tip
1⅛″ cutting diameter
100-grains
$29.99/3-pak

Sanford Innovations ExpanDead
Rear blade deployment
1½″ cutting diameter
O-Ring Pivot System
Lock-Arm™ technology locks blades
$43.99/3-pak

Satellite Field Points
Sizes: 75, 90, 100, 125-grains
$5.99/12-pack.

Sanford Innovations Bloodshot
100% solid steel construction with replaceable blades
Cut-on-contact tip with 2.25″ of combined cutting surface
2 main-blade design with 0.040″ blade thickness
Blade-Overlock™ technology
Quadra-Blade™ design with 4 equal points
$38.99/3-pak

Satellite Silk Arrow Tip
Eases shaft removal from all types of foam targets
Sizes: 100, 125-grains
$14.99/½ /12-pack.

Saunders Bludgeon Small Game Head
Great for stump shooting
Flies accurately
Virtually indestructible
Sizes: 85, 100, 125-grains
$12.99/4-pak

Saunders Combo Point
Reduces 3-D target damage
50% longer for less drag and greater
stability than standard field points
$7.49/12-pack.

Slick Trick
4 blades
Super-short 1-piece
Rhinosteel™ ferrule
Alcatraz Bladelock™
4 sharp Lutz Solingen®
German blades
1" cutting diameter
0.035" blade thickness
(0.030" for 85-grain model)
$29.99/3-pak

Slick Trick Grizz Trick
1⅛" cutting diameter
100-grains
$29.99/3-pak

Slick Trick Razor Trick
4-blades with a cutting diameter of 1¼"
Super steel ferrule is stronger than titanium
0.035" Lutz Mercedes blades
Sizes: 100, 125-grains
$29.99/3-pak

Slick Trick X-Bow Trick
Designed for crossbows
0.035" stainless steel Lutz Mercedes blades
4-edge, bone splitting tip
Cutting diameter 1⅛"
175-grains
$29.99/3-pak

Steel Force Phat Head
Nearly indestructible with a blade thickness of 0.080"
1" cutting diameter on main blade
¾" 2-piece bleeder blade
Short aluminum ferrule
100-grains
Four-blade design
$35.99/3-pak

Swhacker
Mechanical broadhead
High-carbon steel tip
2 small wing blades for cutting
through hair, hide, and bones
2 long, ultra-sharp main blades
that open upon impact
Sizes: 100, 125-grains
(2" cutting diameter)
$34.99/3-pak

Steel Force Premium Lock-Down
Premium Lock-Down design
Four-blade design
Durable 0.048" blades
Stainless steel broadhead
Sizes: 100, 125-grains (1"and 1³⁄₁₆"
cutting diameter)
$35.99/3-pak

Tight Point Shuttle
T-Lock blade-to-ferrule connection
Non-vented blades
Ferrule heat treated steel
1⅛" cutting diameter
$34.99/3-pak

Steel Force Sabertooth
Serrated blades
Graphite-impregnated blade coating reduces friction
1" cutting diameter
$37.99/3-pak

Trophy Taker Terminal T-Lock
T-Lock blade-to-ferrule connection
Non-vented blades
Ferrule heat-treated steel
1¹⁄₁₆" cutting diameter
$34.99/3-pak

Tru-Fire T1
Replaceable fixed-blade head
Ferrule machined from a solid piece of steel
Aggressive tip creates an unsealable hole
1⅛″ cutting diameter
0.032″-thick stainless steel blades
100-grains
$34.99/3-pak

Wasp Archery Z-Force Rear Deploy
Unique ball-bearing system
1⅝″ cutting diameter
Solid steel ferrule
Three-blades design
100-grains
$39.99/3-pak

Viking
Designed to Falcon Principle of Aerodynamics
Solid, non-vented blades
Cutlery grade stainless steel
Can be sharpened
Sizes: 100, 125, 150, 180, 200-grains
Pricing varies according to custom setup

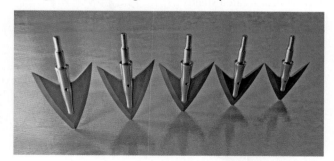

Wasp Boss SST 100
Designed to handle speeds topping 300 fps
Stainless smart tip (SST), heat-treated, stainless steel, cut-on-impact, chisel point tip
Shortened aerodynamic ferrule
0.027″ stainless steel blades
Blades aligned with cutting edges on tip for top penetration
1⅛″ cutting diameter
$37.99/3-pak

Wasp Archery Queen
Designed for lower poundage bows
1″ cutting diameter
0.027″ stainless steel blades
Stainless smart tip
Superior flight characteristics
Includes two sets of replacement blades
75-grains
$34.99/3-pak

Wasp Jak-Hammer SST
1¼″ cutting diameter
100-grains
0.036 blade thickness
Pre-aligned stainless smart tip (SST)
Blades fold forward in flight; retained by O-ring
$34.99/3-pak

Current Sights, Rests, and Quivers

Allen Equalizer II
3 metal fiber-optic pins
Sight pin rack is adjustable for windage and elevation
Clear sight pin guard
Brass inserts for all mounting screws
MSRP: $19.99

Allen Intruder II Aluminum
Machined-aluminum bracket, post, and sight-rack
Molded smoke-sight pin guard
3 metal-body fiber-optic pins
MSRP: $22

Allen Firebrand
4-pin extended fiber sight for increased brightness
Pin light for low light conditions
All aluminum pin rack and bracket
Macro-adjustable pin rack
Level included
MSRP: $44

Allen Peak Single Pin
Wrapped fiber design
Manufactured from solid aluminum
Yellow optical-aiming circle
Macro-adjustment for windage and elevation
MSRP: $39.99

Allen Three Pin
Extended fiber for brighter pins
Precision metal pins
Manufactured from solid aluminum
Macro and micro-adjustment
MSRP: $21.99

Apex AG1203 Tundra
Ultra-tough composite construction
Tru Touch soft-feel technical coating
Innovative pin design improves sight picture and protects fibers
Quick and easy fiber replacement
Aperture has 1.8" inner diameter
0.019" pins
Large circular field of view
Includes level
Reversible bracket for greater vertical adjustability
Glow-in-the-dark shooter's ring
Adjustable for left- and right-handed users
Adjustable light included
MSRP: $29.99

Apex AG1514 Accu-Strike
Weight: 5 ounces
Extra long fibers routed through bracket for increased durability and exposure to Ultra-light
Tru Touch soft-feel technical coating
Innovative pin design allows for quick and easy fiber replacement
Micro push-button light included
CNC-machined
1.8" inner diameter
Reversible bracket for greater vertical adjustability
Glow-in-the-dark shooter's ring
Adjustable for left- and right-handed users
MSRP: $92

Apex AG2211 Atomic Rover
Extra long, protected, wrapped fiber
Aperture has a 1.8" inner diameter
Adjustable with one hand
Glow-in-the-dark shooter's ring helps align peep sight
Vertical adjustment allows it to fit virtually all bows
Level with two vertical bars
Level is illuminated by luminescent shooter's ring
Adjustable for left- and right-handed users.
Micro push-button light
MSRP: $123

Apex AG2701 Nano Dot

Steady Dot™ technology
Precise aiming dot approximates a 0.010" dot for faster target acquisition
Dual-color rheostat allows for multiple brightness settings in both green and red
Optics and mounting bracket designed specifically for archery
Precision, micro-adjustable bracket
Vertical adjustment accommodates virtually all bows
Soft-feel technical coating
Glow-in-the-dark shooter's ring
Glow-in-the-dark yardage tape.
Water-resistant and shock-resistant
Unlimited eye relief
Adjustable for left- and right-handed users
MSRP: $172

Apex BC1204 Bone Collector

Compact design (3.8 ounces)
Composite construction
Adjustable for left- and right-handed users
Micro push-button light included
0.019" diameter pins
MSRP: $45

Apex AG4314 Axim

Extra long, fully protected wrapped fibers
Micro, stainless steel tubes protect fibers
Soft-feel technical coating
Ultrafine click adjustment for windage and elevation
Tool-less design
Laser markings for windage, elevation, and pin adjustments
Aperture has 1.8" inner diameter
Glow-in-the-dark shooter's ring
Adjustable for left- and right-handed users
Micro push-button light
MSRP: N/A

Apex BC1514 Bone Collector Accu Strike

Lightweight design
TRU FLO™ fiber design
Extra long fibers routed through bracket for increased durability and exposure to Ultraviolet light
Aperture has 1.8" inner diameter
Adjustable for left- and right-handed users
Micro push-button light
All metal construction
Glow-in-the-dark shooter's ring
MSRP: $74

Apex BC4514 Bone Collector Sight Fixed Bracket

Extra long, fully protected wrapped fibers
Micro, stainless steel tubes protect fibers
Aperture has 2.0" inner diameter
Micro push-button light
Ultrafine click adjustment for windage and elevation
Laser markings for windage, elevation, and pin adjustments
Adjustable for left- and right-handed users
Tool-less design
Micro push-button light
Glow-in-the-dark shooter's ring
MSRP: $123

Archer Xtreme Carbon Carnivore

Machined from 6061T6 billet
Wrapped in 100% 3K carbon fiber-cloth bands
3K carbon bracket ridge for unmatched strength
Vibration-absorbing rubberized clear coat
Zero-gap
Center core pin stainless steel pin tubes
Five 0.019" x 11" super-flex fibers
EZ Tech tool-less micro-pin-adjustable system
Fiber harness system maximizes light transmission
Laser marked for precision windage and elevation adjustments
Tool-less lockdown knobs for fast in-field adjustments
2nd axis gang adjustment
third-axis leveling system
2" aperture, ambidextrous
MSRP: $279

Archer Xtreme Driver 1

Available in 0.019" single pin or four-pin system (20" of fiber-optic)
Multi-adjustable elevation positioning
Micro-elevation and horizontal adjustments
Vertical tape location accepts digital yardage tape
Center core pin stainless steel tube pins
2nd Axis gang adjustment with third-axis adjustable level
Laser marking for horizontal and elevation adjustments.
Precision micro-adjustment for horizontal and elevation
Machined 6061T6 aluminum construction from solid billet
MSRP: $179.99

Archer Xtreme Driver 4

AX Arc Xtreme available in four-pin system
Multi-adjustable elevation positioning for maximum adjustment
Micro-elevation and horizontal adjustments
Vertical tape location accepts digital yardage tapes or personal marks
AMO standard sight mounts with quiver mounting holes.
Center core pin stainless steel tube pins
4x0.019" ultra super-flex fiber-optic in alternating green and yellow alternating
2nd axis gang adjustment with adjustable 3rd-level axis
RH/LH adjustable by reversing bracket and replacement of bubble to top of pin guard.
Laser marking for horizontal and elevation adjustments
Precision micro-adjustment for horizontal and elevation
Machined 6061T6 aluminum construction from solid billet
MSRP: $199.99

Archer Xtreme Headhunter
three-pin x 0.019" ultra super-flex fiber-optic in green, red, and yellow
2" sight housing for maximum field of view in low light conditions
Bottom LED deployment for easy access and elimination of fibers in low light (light included)
Gang adjustment system for both horizontal and elevation adjustment
LH adjustable by reversing bracket and replacement of bubble to top of pin guard
Laser marking for horizontal and elevation adjustments
MSRP: $65

Archer Xtreme Titanium XT
Titanium 2" sight housing for maximum field of view
Adjustable 2nd and 3rd axis
TBR titanium bracket-ridge system for ultimate strength
HV fiber guard ring system for peep to housing alignment
Fiber-harness bracket system allows maximum light for each pin
5" ultra super-flex fiber-optics
2nd axis gang adjustment with third-axis adjustable level system
Easy-set micro-adjustments with tool-locking knobs
Laser markings for horizontal and elevation adjustments
Precision micro-adjustments
MSRP: $299

Archer Xtreme Primal XD
Fully machined 6061T6 aluminum construction from solid billet
Low-light accuracy
Exclusive fiber-harness system
Center core pin technology
five-pin design with 0.019" fibers
Ambidextrous
MSRP: $189

Axion GLX Gridlock
Adjustable light and level included
Easy windage and elevation adjustments
Laser-etched adjustment lines
Two-inch pin guard with Glo Ring
CNC Machining for a custom Gridlock look
Right- or left-hand adaptable
Pins available in 0.019" or 0.009" fiber
Additional pins available
MSRP: $139

Axion GLX Gridlock Micro Pro Series
Adjustable light and level included
Mathews Lite Harmonic Stabilizer
Tool-less micro-adjustments
Laser-etched adjustment lines
Two-inch pin guard with Glo Ring
Detailed CNC Machining for a custom Gridlock look
Right- or left-hand adaptable
Pins available in 0.019" or 0.009" fiber
Additional pins available
MSRP: $139

Black Gold Rush 5 Pin Camo
PhotoChromatic shell meters light
Interchangeable fluorescent sight ring for quick and positive peep alignment even in low light
Optional Big Dog pin guard for use with oversized peeps 3, 4, or 7-pin models all metal 0.019" diameter
MSRP: $111–$141

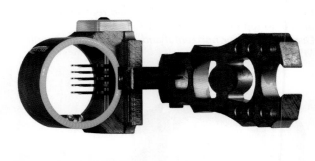

Black Gold Ascent 3 Pin Head
PhotoChromatic shell meters light
Lock on third-axis prevents movement
Adjustable level
2X or 4X lens adaptable
54 sight tapes included
First axis adjustment keeps sight dialed in at long ranges
Oversized clamping dovetails
MSRP: $219

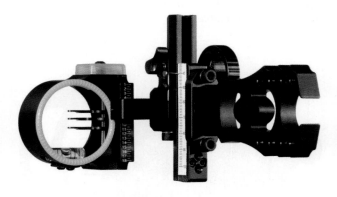

Black Gold Surge 5 Pin Camo
PhotoChromatic shell meters light
2nd axis adjustable level
Delrin® "Hush Wheels" for smoother adjustment and quieter operation
2X or 4X lens adaptable (custom shop) makes target easier to see
adjustable 1st and 2nd axis
Two-piece machined pins are four-way micro-adjustable
Inch Wheel micro-adjustment
Interchangeable fluorescent rings for quick, reliable peep alignment even in low light
MSRP: $200–$230

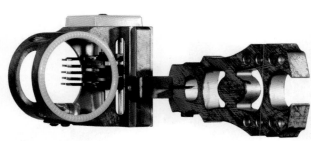

Black Gold Vengeance 5 Pin Dovetail

PhotoChromatic shell meters light
Oversized (40% larger) adjustable 2nd axis level
Delrin® "Hush Wheels" for smoother adjustment and quieter operation
Lockable 3rd axis prevents any movement
2X or 4X lens adaptable (Custom Shop) makes target easier to see
Full 1st, 2nd, and 3rd axis adjustability
2-piece machined pins are 4-way micro-adjustable micro-horizontal and -vertical gang adjustment
Inch Wheel micro-adjustment
Optional Big Dog pin guard for use with oversized peeps
Interchangeable fluorescent guard ring
MSRP: $247–$277

Copper John Mark-1

CNC-machined components
3rd axis adjustable bubble level
Bright orange pin guard highlight for rapid peep alignment
Speed gap technology
IronClad fiber-optics
Extra long, ultra-protected fibers for super bright aiming points
RH/LH convertible
Dual Mount windage bracket for super wide adjustment window
Laser-engraved components for increased precision
Pre-drilled to accept AfterBurner light
MSRP: $89.99 (5-pin)

Copper John GraveDancer

CNC-machined components
Bubble level
Bright orange pin guard highlight for rapid peep alignment
Speed gap technology; zero-pin gap leaving room to spare on even the fastest bows
EasyGlide Technology
Extra long, ultra-protected fibers for super bright aiming points
Ambidextrous for RH/LH shooters
MSRP: $69

Copper John Mark-2

CNC-machined components
3rd axis adjustable bubble level
Bright orange pin guard highlight for rapid peep alignment
IronClad fiber-optics
Extra long, ultra-protected fibers for super bright aiming points
RH/LH convertible
Dual Mount windage bracket for super wide adjustment window
Laser-engraved components for increased precision
Pre-drilled to accept AfterBurner light
MSRP: $69

Copper John Mark-3

CNC-machined components
3rd axis adjustable bubble level
Bright orange pin guard highlight for rapid peep alignment
Speed gap technology
IronClad fiber-optics
Extra long, ultra-protected fibers for super bright aiming points
RH/LH convertible
Dual-mount windage bracket for super wide adjustment window
Laser-engraved components for increased precision
Pre-drilled to accept AfterBurner light
MSRP: $99

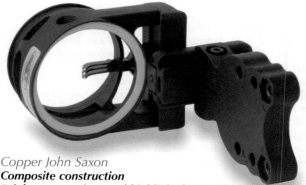

Copper John Saxon

Composite construction
Bright orange pin guard highlight for rapid peep alignment
Speed gap technology
EasyGlide technology
Ambidextrous for RH/LH shooters
Reversible windage bracket for greater windage adjustment
MSRP: $14.99

Field Logic 7 Pin IQ Bowsight

IQ Bowsight revolutionary retina lock alignment technology
Instant feedback
Forces proper form and extends effective range by 20+ yards
Available in right- or left-hand, 4 and 7 pin
MSRP: $219.99

Copper John Mark-4

Ranger-style sight
Adjustable for distance with sliding gear box
CNC-machined components
3rd axis adjustable bubble level
Bright orange pin guard highlight for rapid peep alignment
Speed gap technology zero-pin gap leaving room to spare on even the fastest bows!
IronClad fiber-optics
Extra long, ultra-protected fibers for super bright aiming points
RH/LH convertible
dual-mount windage bracket for super wide adjustment window
Laser-engraved components for increased precision
Pre-drilled to accept AfterBurner light
MSRP: $109.99

Field Logic Lethal Weapon
5-axis micro-adjustability
MicroLock Pins and pin-lock indicator
Stainless steel tubes to ensure durability
Quiver compatible
Easily adjusted for right- or left-hand use
Includes rheostat-controlled, variable intensity sight light,
and hardware/hex keys
MSRP: $299.99–399.99

Firenock Micro Adjustable and Standard AeroRests
Frictionless ball-bearing operation
Full-containment shooting flexibility
No-wear ceramic ball-bearing contact surface
Quiet design, lightweight: (1.5 oz)
Type II-aluminum anodized finish
GR2 Titanium Torx fasteners and spacers
Accommodates most arrow sizes
Available to right- or left-handed shooters
MSRP: $89.95 (camo option) (standard version)
MSRP: $174.95 (U-Frame option) (MicroAdjust version)

Firenock iBow Sight bracket
Eight-point bracket system designed
Allows up to 3 bow mounting positions
Pre-tapped holes for a bow quiver
Removable accessory mounting bar
GR2 titanium and are Torx fasteners
MSRP: $119.95

Fuse Carbon Blade

Adjustable sight rail
Carbon blade frame
3rd axis leveling
Steel encased 0.019 fiber pins in 3, 5 or 7 pin configurations
Available in micro (M-Series) or standard (G-Series) gang adjustment
RealTree Xtra, AP, Max-1 and Black Out
MSRP: $149

Fuse Pro Fire

Twelve inches of wrapped fiber-optics
Metal pins
Available in 3 or 5 pin configurations
MSRP: $39

G5 Optix XR

3 fixed pin plus 1 hybrid-floating pin
New improvements to the floating pin design allows adjustment down to the yard
Larger adjustment knob with vinyl yardage tape
3x micro-adjustments
Third-axis turning
100% Magnesium
Corrosion-resistant components
Harmonic damper
Built-in visor
Arrow bumper
6 ounces
Available in 0.019" and 0.029" smart pins
Available in right- and left-hand models
Sight shown with Rheostat Light. Rheostat Light now sold separately.
MSRP: $179

Fuse Carbon Interceptor

Small, compact, and lightweight
Interceptor sight options include standard or micro-gang adjustment with 3, 5, or 7 pin arrays
Precise 0.019 steel encased pins
3rd axis leveling
Available in RealTree Xtra, AP, Max-1 or Black Out
MSRP: $159

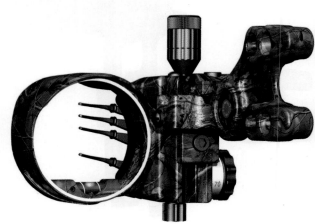

G5 Optix XR2
1 fixed pin plus 1 hybrid-floating pin design
Floating pin design allows adjustments down to the yard
Improved functionality and additional pin travel increases shootability
Larger adjustment knob with vinyl yardage tape increases visibility in the field
3X micro adjustments
Third-axis tuning
Dual riser mounting locations
Magnesium alloy construction that is 30% lighter than aluminum
Corrosion-resistant components
Harmonic damper
Built-in visor
Rubber arrow bumper
six ounces
Available in 0.019" and 0.029" smart pins
Available in right- and left-hand models
MSRP: $209

HHA DS-5019
Weight: 10 oz.
1⅝" sight housing
3 feet of fiber-optic material
Accepts lens kit b and all HHA blue burst lights
Models: DS-5000, DS-5000 LH (0.029 Fiber); DS-5019, DS-5019 LH (0.019 Fiber); DS-5010, DS-5010 LH (0.010 Fiber)
MSRP: $179

HHA DS-5519
Rapid adjustment to the yard between 20 and 60 yards using the included sight scales
CNC-machined aluminum
Yellow sight ring, lens- and light-compatible
0.019" pin with 5 feet of fiber-optic
1⅝" diameter scope
Weight: 10 oz.
Right-handed
MSRP: $199

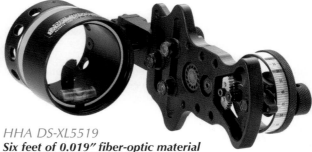

HHA DS-XL5519
Six feet of 0.019" fiber-optic material
2" sight housing with yellow sight ring
Adjustable rheostat for adjusting pin brightness in any light
Weight: 11 oz.
Right-hand only
MSRP: $279

HHA OL-5019
3 feet of wrapped 0.019" fiber-optic material
CNC-machined aluminum construction
Smooth elevation hinge with easy-access knob
Right-hand only
Manufacturer's lifetime warranty.
MSRP: $109.99

HHA OL-5519
Integral rheostat dial
5 ft. of wrapped 0.019" fiber-optic material
CNC-machined aluminum construction
Vibration-resistant cap screw and windage lock
Right-hand only
Manufacturer's lifetime warranty.
MSRP: $139

HHA XL-5519
0.019" pin
Rheostat Scope
Right-hand
Weight: 9 oz.
2" sight housing
6 feet of fiber-optic
Accepts lens kit x and all HHA blue burst lights
Exclusive mechanical rheostat feature adjusts pin brightness in seconds
MSRP: $125

HHA SD-L4
Accurate to the yard (20 to 80 yards for crossbows 260 to 410 feet per second)
Fits most crossbows
Optimizer X Scopes Manufactured by Hawke Optics LLC
Mounts any scope with 1" Weaver-style rings
Aluminum Chassis
Illuminated Hybrid L4 Single
Crosshair reticle
½-inch M.O.A. finger adjustable turrets
five-setting rheostat brightness adjustments in red and green
Waterproof, shockproof, and fog proof
MSRP: $319

Hind Sight Basic Add-on Hind Sight II
Pivot Arm
Matches best with fixed-pin front sights that employ round pin guards.
Weight: 1.8 oz.
MSRP: N/A

Hind Sight CrossFire

Fully protected sight pins with spooled fiber-optic cable
LED ultraviolet light
Glow-in-the dark shooters ring
A twilight-rear aperture
CNC-machined parts for precession fit
Circle alignment technology for positive alignment and good form
Calibrated for easy field adjustments
Weight: 7.8 oz
MSRP: N/A

Hind Sight Equalizer

Quick release of the rear aperture
Tuning knob
Sturdy mounting bracket with two locations up front
Anchor-block connection
Glow-in-the-dark reference tape
Weight: 4.0 oz.
MSRP: $65.95

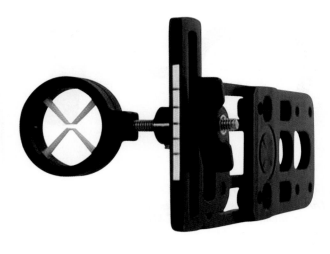

Hind Sight Ghost Rider

Dual sighting system
Compact, 60–61 aluminum, CNC-machined frame
Extra long fiber-optic sight pins in a medium 0.029" pin size
Dual pin rails
Glow-in-the-dark shooters ring
Bubble level
Ultraviolet LED lighting for less pin glare
Weight: 7.5 oz.
MSRP: $104.95

Hind Sight Dead Ringer

Dual sighting system
Compact, 60–61 aluminum, CNC-machined frame
Extra long protected fibers (0.029 inches)
Dual pin rails for pin alignment
Glow-in-the-dark shooters ring
Ultraviolet LED lighting for less pin glare
Weight: 7.5 oz.
MSRP: $99.95

Hind Sight Original Rear Aperture

Super tough nylon sight ring molded onto a stainless steel screw
Brass-thumb nut and large wing nut for easy field adjustments
1 inch inside diameter
Glow-in-the-dark crosshairs
MSRP: N/A

Hind Sight Twilight

Large magnum sight ring
Glow-in-the-dark horizontal pointers
Glow-in-the-dark tape
Available in green, hunters orange, and yellow
Weight: 1.8 oz.
MSRP: $47.95

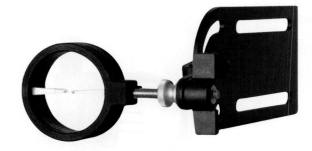

Hind Sight PathFinder

Dual roving sights that move as one
Circle alignment technology(CAT)
Magnum rear aperture and a single-pin front sight by Truglo
Extra long fiber-optic cable
Bubble level
Shooter's glow ring
Ultraviolet LED light
Quiver ready
Available in right- and left-hand models
Fully adjustable for draw lengths from 22" to 33"
MSRP: $154.95

Schaffer Performance Archery Opposition bow sight

Opposing pin technology
Pivot lock attachment
Available with 4 pins or 6 pins
Quick-detach or hard-mount versions
Mathews® Lost Camo or black anodized finish
Options include: Integrated light system, extra fiber-optic pins, and non fiber-optic stainless steel pins
MSRP: N/A

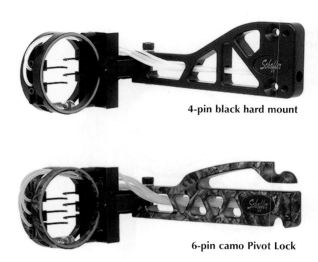

4-pin black hard mount

6-pin camo Pivot Lock

Sword Apex

100% CNC T6061 aluminum construction
2" inside diameter round aperture
5 pins available in 0.010", 0.019", or 0.029"
Laser etched elevation and windage scales
LED light
6" dovetail bar-mounting system
3rd axis adjustment
High and low sight-mounting system with built-in offset
for extended sight window
Anodized matte black finish
Available right- or left-handed models
MSRP: $125

Sword Centurion

100% CNC T6061 aluminum construction
1.5" inside diameter round aperture
Accepts 1.75" diameter lens (lens retainer ring and O-ring
included)
Solid steel machined up-pin in 0.010" or 0.019" (Multiple
pins also available)
LED light
Approx 2" in elevation travel
3rd axis adjustment
Preprinted yardage tapes
Available right- or left-handed models
MSRP: $173.99

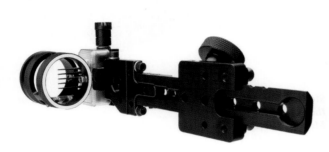

Sword Maximus

100% CNC T6061 aluminum construction
micro-adjustable elevation and windage
Tool-Less feature on windage and elevation adjustment
1.625" inside diameter round aperture
Accepts 1.75" diameter lens (lens retainer ring and O-ring
sold separately)
5 pins available in 0.010", 0.019" or 0.029"
Laser etched-elevation and windage scales
LED light
3rd axis adjustment
High and low sight-mounting system with built-in offset
for extended sight window
Anodized matte black finish
Available in left- or right-hand
MSRP: $169.99

Sword Apex Hunter

100% CNC T6061 aluminum construction
2" inside diameter round aperture
4 pins available in 0.010", 0.019", or 0.029"
Laser-etched elevation and windage scales
High and low sight-mounting bar with built-in offset for
extended sight window
Anodized matte black finish
Available right- or left-handed models
MSRP: $69.99

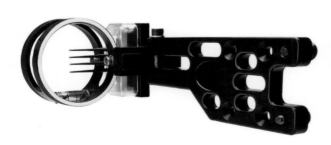

Sword Maximus Pro 2
100% CNC T6061 aluminum construction
micro-adjustable elevation and windage
Tool-Less feature on windage and elevation adjustment
1.625" Inside diameter round aperture
Accepts 1.75" diameter lens (Lens retainer ring and O-ring sold separately)
5 pins available in 0.010", 0.019" or 0.029"
Laser-etched elevation and windage scales
LED light
3rd axis adjustment
6" dovetail bar-mounting system
high- and low-sight mounting system with built-in offset for extended sight window
Anodized matte black finish
Available in left- or right-hand models
MSRP: $194.99

Sword Sabre
100% CNC T6061 aluminum construction
2" round aperture
3 pins available in 0.010", 0.019", or 0.029"
Laser-etched elevation and windage scales
high- and low-sight mounting bar with built-in offset for extended sight window
Anodized matte black finish
Available right- or left-handed models
MSRP: $59.99

Toxonics ProSlide series
Key-driven Delran slide block
Solid lock gang adjustments
Gear-driven adjustment arm
Available in single, 3-, 5-, and 7-pin models
Head is interchangeable with the ProHunter series.
MSRP: $109.99–149.99

Toxonics Solid Lock series
Steel-locking mechanism to increase the locking powers of the gang adjustments
Metal optic pins
Reversible offset bars
MSRP: $89.99–139.99

Toxonics SP319 sight
Available options include: dovetail bar, custom pin sizes, custom pin colors, custom pin quantities, and left-hand mount.
MSRP: $59.99

Toxonics ST519-CL Matthews Lost

Available options include: dovetail bar, left-hand mount, magnification, custom pin sizes, custom pin colors, and custom pin quantities.
MSRP: $99.99

Toxonics Wrangler 319

Easy access clear housing
Metal optic pins
Laser-engraved scales
Reversible extension bar.
MSRP: $42.99

Toxonics Wrangler Micro

Designed with straight pieces of 0.019 fiber-optic
Easy access clear housing
micro-adjustable
MSRP: $63.99

Trophy Ridge Alpha 1 Sight

Rugged construction combined with 14″ of 0.019
Ultrabright fiber
Rheostat sight light
100% aluminum construction
Ultrabright 0.019 fiber-optic pin
Sight level with third-axis adjustability
MSRP: N/A

Trophy Ridge Alpha V3

Exclusive Trophy Ridge vertical in-line pin technology
Three pins
Aluminum sight housing
Ultrabright 0.019 fiber-optic pins
Sight level with third-axis adjustability
MSRP: N/A

Trophy Ridge Alpha V5

Exclusive Trophy Ridge vertical in-line pins
Five pins
Aluminum sight housing
Ultrabright 0.019 fiber-optic pins
Sight level with third-axis adjustability
MSRP: N/A

Trophy Ridge Cypher 3 Pin, 5 Pin, and 7 Pin

25% lighter than aluminum
Ballistix coating delivers vibration reduction
Reversible sight mount
Tool-less windage and elevation adjustment
Rheostat sight light
Zero-pin gap spacing
Ultrabright 0.019 fiber-optic pins
Sight level
Available in 3, 5, or 7 pins.
MSRP: N/A

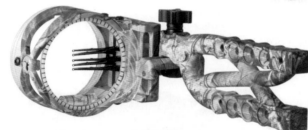

Trophy Ridge Drive Slider Sight

Adjustable indicator pin
Nylon bushings
Sight light
Low-light Glo indicator tape
Ultrabright 0.019 fiber-optic pin
Integrated sight level
MSRP: N/A

Trophy Ridge Firewire V3

Exclusive Trophy Ridge vertical in-line pins
Three pins
Composite sight housing
Ultrabright 0.019 fiber-optic pins
Sight level with third-axis adjustability
MSRP: N/A

Trophy Ridge Firewire V5

Exclusive Trophy Ridge vertical in-line pins
Five pins
Composite sight housing
Ultrabright 0.019 fiber-optic pins
Sight level with third-axis adjustability
MSRP: N/A

Trophy Ridge Hitman 3

Three-pin reversible sight mount
Rheostat sight light
100% aluminum construction
Ultrabright 0.019 fiber-optic pins
Sight level with third-axis adjustability
Zero-pin gap spacing
MSRP: N/A

Trophy Ridge Micro Alpha V3
Exclusive Trophy Ridge vertical in-line pins
Three-pin adjustable sight mount
Aluminum sight housing
Ultrabright 0.019 fiber-optic pins
Rheostat sight light
Micro-adjustment
Sight level with third-axis adjustability
MSRP: N/A

Trophy Ridge Micro Alpha V5
Exclusive Trophy Ridge vertical in-line pins
Five-pin adjustable sight mount
Aluminum sight housing
Ultrabright 0.019 fiber-optic pins
Rheostat sight light
Micro-adjustment
Sight level with third-axis adjustability
MSRP: N/A

Trophy Ridge Micro Hitman 5
five-pin reversible sight mount
Rheostat sight light
100% aluminum construction
Ultrabright 0.019 fiber-optic pins
Micro-adjustment
Sight level with third-axis adjustability
Zero-pin gap spacing
MSRP: N/A

Trophy Ridge Micro Hitman 7
Seven-pin reversible sight mount
Rheostat sight light
100% aluminum construction
Ultrabright 0.019 fiber-optic pins
Micro-adjustment
Sight level with third-axis adjustability
Zero-pin gap spacing
MSRP: N/A

Trophy Ridge Outlaw 4 Pin
Ultrabright pins
8 inches of 0.019 fiber-optics for each pin
Built-in sight light housing
Reversible sight mount
Sight light
Aluminum bracketry
Composite pin guard
Ultrabright 0.019 fiber-optic pins
Contrast Glo ring
MSRP: N/A

Trophy Ridge Punisher 3
Three pins
Field-replaceable pins
Reversible mount
Sight light
Aluminum bracketry
Composite pin guard
Ultrabright 0.029 fiber-optic pins
Contrast Glo ring
MSRP: N/A

Trophy Ridge Punisher 5
Five pins
Field-replaceable pins
Reversible mount
Sight light
Aluminum bracketry
Composite pin guard
Ultrabright 0.029 fiber-optic pins
Contrast Glo ring
MSRP: N/A

Trophy Ridge Pursuit Sight
Adjustable indicator pin
Delrin bushings
Rheostat sight light
Low-light Glo indicator tape
Ultrabright 0.019 fiber-optic pin
100% aluminum construction
Sight level with second and third-axis adjustability
MSRP: N/A

Trophy Ridge React
Smart Pin Technology
Ballistix CoPolymer System
Reversible sight mount
Right- or left-hand specific sight
Multiple mounting holes for more versatility
100% tool-less micro-adjustment
Rheostat light
0.019 Fiber-optic pins
Sight level
MSRP: N/A

Trophy Ridge Sharp Shooter ▼
Reversible sight mount
0.029 fiber-optic pins
Contrast Gloring
MSRP: N/A

Trophy Taker Top Pin 7-Pin Sight
50" of fiber-optic material
Phosphorescent details for poor lighting conditions
Glow-in-the-dark top-pin alignment ring
Large hex adjustment bolts
2nd axis leveling
All-metal construction.
Available in right- or left-handed models
Slide- or micro-adjust
MSRP: $90.99–120.99

Trophy Taker Heartbreaker Pro Archery Sight
Micro-adjustable windage
Simple and solid 2nd and 3rd axes adjustments
Multiple pin guard and configurations
Rack and spur gear thumb roller
Available in right- or left-hand
Lifetime warranty
MSRP: N/A

Trophy Taker Top Pin 10-Pin Sight
50" of fiber-optic material
Phosphorescent details for poor lighting conditions
Glow-in-the-dark top pin alignment ring
Large hex adjustment bolts
2nd axis leveling
All-metal construction
Right-hand only
MSRP: $115.99–145.99

Trophy Taker Top Pin 4-Pin Sight
50" of fiber-optic material
Phosphorescent details for poor lighting conditions
Glow-in-the-dark top pin alignment ring
Large hex adjustment bolts
2nd axis leveling
All-metal construction
Available in right- or left-handed
Slide- or micro-adjustable
MSRP: $80.99–105.99

TruGlo TG500XB Brite Site Extreme
Large circular field of view
Aperture has a 2" inner diameter
Lightweight composite pin guard
Glow-in-the-dark shooter's ring helps align peep sight
Level with two vertical bars
CNC-machined
Adjustable for left- and right-handed shooters
Markings for elevation and windage
MSRP: $39.99

TruGlo TG3515 Rite Site XS
Large circular field of view
Aperture has a 2" inner diameter
Ultrastrong, lightweight pin guard
Glow-in-the-dark shooter's ring helps align peep sight
Level with two vertical bars
CNC-machined
Adjustable for left- and right-handed shooters
Markings for elevation and windage
Includes adjustable rheostat light
MSRP: $39.99

TruGlo TG701 Range Rover One Pin
Extra long, wrapped fiber
Aperture has a 1.8" inner diameter
Glow-in-the-dark shooter's ring helps align peep sight
Glow-in-the-dark yardage tape
CNC-machined
Adjustable with one hand
Level with two vertical bars
Level is illuminated by luminescent shooter's ring
Adjustable for left- and right-handed shooters
MSRP: $99

TruGlo TG5101 Tru Site
Lightweight composite pin guard
Large circular field of view
Level with two vertical bars
Reversible bracket for greater vertical adjustability
Three sets of markings for elevation, windage, and pin adjustments
Protected fiber wraps
Glow-in-the-dark shooter ring
available in right- or left-handed
MSRP: $65

TruGlo TG5503 Micro Brite Site

Decreasing diameter pin design uses smaller pin sizes for longer yardages
Soft-feel technical coating
Ultrafine click adjustment for windage and elevation
Micro push-button light
Tool-less design
Extra long, wrapped fibers
Precision pin alignment eliminates distortion
Aperture has a 1.8" inner diameter
Glow-in-the-dark shooter's ring helps align peep sight
Adjustable level with two vertical bars
Reversible bracket for greater vertical adjustability
Adjustable for left- and right-handed shooters
MSRP: $99

Viper H250

CNC-machined from 6061 T6 aircraft aluminum
Three stainless steel pins
Available in three pin sizes: 0.010", 0.019", or 0.029"
Fixed-plate mounting bracket
MSRP: $69.99

Viper H1000

Built-in harmonic damper
CNC-machined from 6061 T6 aircraft aluminum
Oversized level
Separate windage and elevation for precise leveling
Fixed plate mounting bracket
Five Razor Edge pins
Available in three pin sizes: 0.010", 0.019" or 0.029"
7.5" of fiber-optics for superior brightness
Threaded for available ZEISS coated lenses in 2, 3, 4, and 6 power
Available in REALTREE AP®, REALTREE APG®, Mathews Lost™, Mathews Lost AT™, Pink, Black
MSRP: $100

Viper MicroTune 1750

Includes 1750P Viper Scope
Includes choice of 2, 3, 4, and 6x Viper Lens
CNC-machined from 6061 T6 aircraft aluminum
Built-in harmonic damper
Oversized level
Separate windage and elevation for precise leveling
3rd axis
6" dovetail extension and mounting block
Dovetail knob features a precise locking system
MSRP: $260

Viper Predator Microtune
CNC-machined from 6061 T6 aircraft aluminum
Built-in harmonic damper
Oversized level
Separate windage and elevation for precise leveling
3rd axis
Four stainless-steel pins
Available in three pin sizes: 0.010", 0.019" or 0.029"
7.5" of fiber-optics for superior brightness
Threaded housing and dovetail bar accepts Ultra-Violet Light
Threaded for available ZEISS Coated Lenses in 2, 3, 4, and 6 power
6" dovetail extension and mounting block
Dovetail knob features a precise locking system
MSRP: $170

Viper Predator Pro 2000Predator Pro 2000 & 2000C
Built-in harmonic damper
CNC-machined from 6061 T6 aircraft aluminum
Oversized level
Separate windage and elevation for precise leveling
3rd Axis
Four stainless-steel pins
Available in three pin sizes: 0.010", 0.019" or 0.029"
7.5" of fiber-optics for superior brightness
Threaded housing and dovetail bar accepts Viper Ultra-Violet Light
Threaded for available ZEISS Coated Lenses in 2, 3, 4, and 6 power
6" dovetail extension and mounting block
Dovetail knob features a precise locking system
MSRP: $135

Viper QuickLock 100
CNC-machined from 6061 T6 aircraft aluminum
Oversized level
Stainless steel up-pin with 2 feet of fiber optics
Fixed plate design
Available in either a single-pin or a double-pin design
Threaded for available ZEISS Coated Lenses in 2, 3, 4, and 6 power
MSRP: $55

Viper Quickset MicroTune
Oversized level
Separate windage and elevation for precise leveling
Five Razor Edge pins
Available in three pin sizes: 0.010", 0.019", or 0.029"
2" vertical adjustment with gear drive adjustability for fast accurate setup
Threaded for available ZEISS Coated Lenses in 2, 3, 4, and 6 power.
MSRP: $140

Current Arrow Rests

Bodoodle Bullet with speed fins
Lightweight
Made of rugged 6061 T-6 aluminum
Zero-play pivoting yoke assembly.
Accommodates all arrow sizes and materials.
Two stainless steel 0.015 thick speed fins come standard (with optional 0.023 thick speed fins available for heavier arrows)
Four strips of smoke quiet silencing tape
Right- or left-handed models.
MSRP: $55

Bodoodle Doodle Drop
Quick vertical and horizontal tuning
Lightweight
Made of rugged 6061 T-6 aluminum
Two stainless steel 0.015 thick Hunter Fins come standard (with optional 0.023 thick Hunter Fins available for heavier arrows)
Four strips of smoke quiet silencing tape
Right- or left-handed models
MSRP: $65

Bodoodle Game Dropper
Precision spring adjustment
Laser engraved
Lightweight
Made of rugged 6061 T-6 aluminum
Two stainless steel 0.015 thick speed fins come standard (with optional 0.023 thick speed fins available for heavier arrows as well as Hunter fins in both thicknesses)
Four strips of smoke quiet silencing tape
Right- or left-handed models.
MSRP: $70

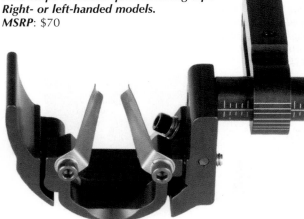

Bodoodle Pro 500
Easy to adjust with lateral, vertical, and vernier adjustments
Zero-play frictionless yoke assembly and jewel-like bearings
Lightweight
Made of rugged 6061 T-6 aluminum
Two stainless steel 0.015 thick speed fins come standard (with optional 0.023 thick speed fins available for heavier arrows as well as Hunter fins in both thicknesses)
Four strips of smoke quiet silencing tape
Available in black (right-hand only), camo, or silver (left-hand only)
MSRP: $140

Bodoodle Pro Lite

Windage and elevation adjustments for easy tuning
Zero-play frictionless yoke assembly and jewel-like bearings
Lightweight
Made of rugged 6061 T-6 aluminum
Two stainless steel 0.015 thick speed fins come standard (with optional 0.023 thick speed fins available for heavier arrows)
Four strips of smoke quiet silencing tape
Available in black, blue (right-hand only), camo, red (Right-hand only), silver, black with silver splash, and silver with black splash (right-hand only)
MSRP: $84

Bodoodle Pro Lite II

More than 1" of laser-etched windage and elevation adjustments for easy tuning
Zero-play frictionless yoke assembly and jewel-like bearings
Lightweight
Made of rugged 6061 T-6 aluminum
Two stainless steel 0.015 thick speed fins come standard (with optional 0.023 thick speed fins available for heavier arrows as well as Hunter fins in both thicknesses).
Four strips of smoke quiet silencing tape
Right- or left-handed models
MSRP: $89

Bodoodle Timber Rattler II

Adjustable launcher angle for fine tuning
Laser-etched windage and elevation adjustments for easy tuning
Lightweight
Made of rugged 6061 T-6 aluminum
Stainless steel lizard tongue available with a standard 0.010 lizard tongue with built in vibration dampener (optional 0.008 and 0.012 lizard tongues available).
Right- or left-handed models
MSRP: $82

Bodoodle Timber Rattler

Laser-etched windage and elevation adjustments for easy tuning
Lightweight
Made of rugged 6061 T-6 aluminum
Stainless steel lizard tongue available with a standard 0.010 lizard tongue with built in vibration dampener (optional 0.008 and 0.012 lizard tongues available).
Right- or left-handed models.
MSRP: $75

Bodoodle Timberdoodle

Zero-play frictionless yoke assembly and jewel-like bearings
Lightweight
Made of rugged 6061 T-6 aluminum
1 Hunter Fin (on bottom) and 1 Speed Fin (on the side)
Four strips of smoke quiet silencing tape
Right- or left-handed models
MSRP: $57

Bodoodle Timberdoodle II

More than 1″ of vertical adjustment
Zero-play frictionless yoke assembly and jewel-like bearings
Lightweight
Made of rugged 6061 T-6 aluminum
1 Hunter Fin (on bottom) and 1 Speed Fin (on the side)
Four strips of smoke quiet silencing tape
Right- or left-handed models
MSRP: $80

Bodoodle Timberdoodle High Performance

Longer arrow shelf for added protection to the bow hand
Zero-play pivoting yoke assembly
Lightweight
Made of rugged 6061 T-6 aluminum
Standard 1 Hunter Fin (on bottom) and 1 Speed Fin (on the side)
Four strips of smoke quiet silencing tape
Right- or left-handed models
MRSP: $63

Bodoodle Zapper 300 High Performance Three Blade

2 support fins and 1 bottom fin
Supports arrows weighing up to 550-grains
Lightweight
Made of rugged 6061 T-6 aluminum
Four strips of silencing tape
Right- or left-handed models
MSRP: $50

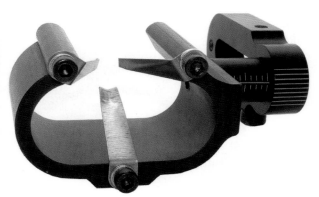

Bodoodle Zapper 300 Three Blade Launcher
3 adjustable stainless steel speed fins, 2 support and 1 bottom
Supports arrows weighing up to 550-grains
Lightweight
Made of rugged 6061 T-6 aluminum
Four strips of silencing tape
Right- or left-handed models
MSRP: $45

Bodoodle Zapper 400 Four Blade Launcher
4 adjustable stainless steel speed fins, 2 support, and 2 bottom
Lightweight
Made of rugged 6061 T-6 aluminum
Four strips of silencing tape
Right- or left-handed models
MSRP: $51

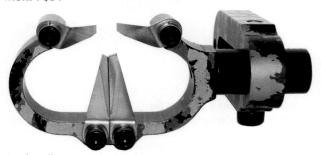

Bodoodle Zapper 400 High Performance Four Blade
4 adjustable stainless steel speed fins; 2 support and 2 bottom
Lightweight
Made of rugged 6061 T-6 aluminum
Four strips of silencing tape
Right- or left-handed models
MSRP: $54

Double Barrel Arrow Loader
Lightweight
Adjustable to fit any bow in minutes
Universally designed for left or right-handed use
MSRP: $29.99–39.99
Fuse Acculaunch Blade
Micro-adjustable technology
Laser-machined 0.010 spring steel launcher
MSRP: $124

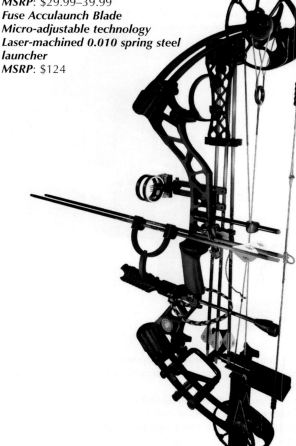

Fuse Acculaunch Fall Away
Fall away
Stainless steel launchers
Silencing material on prongs
Attaches to buss cable
MSRP: $89.99

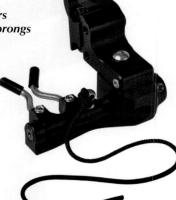

Fuse Acculaunch Prong

Micro-adjust technology
Stainless steel prongs
Silencing materials on prongs
MSRP: $124

Fuse Whisker Biscuit

Whisper-quiet operation
Shock rod technology assures consistent launch
Quick Shot design guarantees fast, snag-free arrow loading
MSRP: $119.99

Fuse Ultra Rest

Timing cord attached to the bow's and downward buss cable
Rest remains in the cocked position even on a slow let down
Only drops away if the bow is fired
Internal rubber bumpers and laser cut felt offer superior noise reduction
MSRP: $149

Mathews Ultra Rest

Velocity drop-away technology
Injection-molded rubber thumbwheel
AVT™ (Advanced Vibration Technology)
Adjustable timing cord
Built from precision CNC aluminum and stainless steel
Vertical, horizontal, and overdraw adjustments
MSRP: $149.99

NAP 360 Capture
Arrow holder secures arrows in perfect alignment
Capture brushes hold arrow without ripping fletching
Works for both carbon and aluminum arrows
MSRP: $39.99

NAP Apache
Sound dampening
Preinstalled felt silencer pad eliminates noise
Drop-away design ensures proper arrow clearance
Tool-less adjustments and laser-etched graduations
MSRP: $79.99

NAP ArmorRest
Full capture drop-away that holds your arrow no matter the angle
Fletching clearance
No bounce back
Titanium arms for less weight and added strength
Right-hand only
MSRP: $139.99

NAP Centerest Flipper
Adjustable centershot
Built-in cushion plunger action
Right- and left-handed models
MSRP: $26.99

NAP Quiktune 800
High, medium, and low tension
1 wrench adjustment
Right-hand only
MSRP: $27.99

NAP Quiktune 1000
Independent windage and elevation adjustment
Prong launcher arms with silencers
Single hex wrench adjustability
MSRP: $49.99

NAP Quiktune 2000
Drop-away rest
Spring-loaded launcher arm drops down on release
The launcher prongs act as a arrow holder
Right-hand only
MSRP: $89.99

NAP Quiktune Dropaway 4000
Drop-away rest
Cable saver
Spring-loaded launcher arm drops down on release
Launcher prongs act as a arrow holder
Micro-elevation and center shot adjustments
MSRP: $89.99

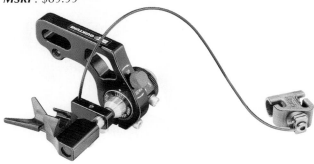

NAP Quiktune Freedom
Full capture keeps arrow in place
Cordless drop-away rest
No strings
MSRP: $49.99

NAP Quiktune Sizzor
Arrow inserts from the side
Total capture system securely holds the arrow
Total fletching clearance
Independent vertical and horizontal adjustments
Right-hand only
MSRP: $99.99

NAP QuikTune Smartrest
Fall-away style rest
Micro-adjustable drop speed
V-launcher head
Micro-adjustable centershot
MSRP: $99.99

Octane Hijack
Full-capture rest
Locks arrow at any angle
Adjustable spring plunger
Posts and plunger are felt-covered for quiet arrow flight
Right-hand only
MSRP: $49.99

Octane Hostage Pro
Right-hand only
Machined aluminum
Three-stage tuning adjustments
MSRP: $79.99

Octane Hostage XL
Simple design
No mechanical components to fail
Arrow remains enclosed and protected
MSRP: $39.99

Octane Vanish
Quick and easy setup
Loads silently at any time—even when cocked
Flared containment bar
No bounce back
Thumb cocker
Three ball bearings in a sealed housing
MSRP: $119.99

PSE Mustang Rest
Prong-style rest
Prong arrow launchers
Stainless hardware
Spring tension adjustment
MSRP: $16.99

PSE Phantom Micro
Full-capture platform
Complete arrow clearance
MSRP: $99.99

PSE Snap Shot
Bowfishing arrow rest
Designed for the beginner
High-grade aluminum and stainless steel
MSRP: $45.99

QAD Ultrarest HDX

Velocity drop-away technology
Injection-molded rubber thumbwheel
AVT™ (Advanced Vibration Technology)
Adjustable timing cord
Built from precision CNC aluminum and stainless steel
Vertical, horizontal, and overdraw adjustments
MSRP: $139.99

QAD Ultrarest Hunter

Timing cord attached to the bows downward buss cable
Rest remains in the cocked position even on a slow let down
Only drops away if the bow is fired
Internal rubber bumpers and laser-cut felt offer superior noise reduction
MSRP: $59.99

QAD Ultrarest LD

Lockdown technology with an eccentric cam and brakes
Locks down into the drop-away position
Total fletching clearance
Falls away only when the bow is fired
Black
MSRP: $114.99

Shaffer Opposition

Full containment arrow rest
Riser lock side plates
Interchangeable side plates for Mathews®, Hoyt®, and PSE® plus a universal fit model
MSRP: $159

Spot Hogg Edge
No-clamp vertical and horizontal micro-adjust
Micro-adjustable blade angle
Self-centering blade
MSRP: $129

Trophy Ridge Drop Zone Hunter
Original vertical drop-away rest
Rubber dampening
For use with right- or left-handed bows
MSRP: $99

Trophy Ridge Revolution Rest
Arm rotates 90° counterclockwise out of the fletching's way
Internal mechanisms prevent bounce back and dampens noise
Remains in the containment position even after let down
Silencer pads quiet arrow through load, draw, and release.
MSRP: $54.99

Trophy Ridge Bowfishing Biscuit
Compact, aluminum-encased Whisker Biscuit
Rock-solid, dual-bolt mount and set screw
Simply attaches to riser mounting holes
Holds arrow securely
Windage adjustments
Laser-engraved reference marks
Custom rubber boots to silence arrow reloading
For use with right- or left-hand bows.
MSRP: $39.99

Trophy Ridge Quick Shot Whisker Biscuit
Reference marks for windage adjustment
Nylon bristles completely hold the arrow in place
Available in universal right- or left-handed designs
MSRP: $39.99

Trophy Ridge Whisker Biscuit Micro
Micro-adjust windage and elevation adjustment
Nylon bushings
Aluminum-encased biscuit
Custom rubber boots silence arrow loading
Laser-engraved reference marks
MSRP: $89.99

Trophy Ridge Tack Driver Micro
Available in three thicknesses of blue steel blade launchers (0.008, 0.010, 0.012)
Pitch of the launcher arm is adjustable
Fully radiused bottom of the launcher arm
MSRP: $89.99

Trophy Taker Pronghorn
Drop-away
Rugged, all-metal construction
MSRP: $49.99

Trophy Taker SmackDown PRO
Non-containment
Prong horn launcher
Low-profile ring
Easy cord length adjustment
Built-in silencing
Lifetime warranty
MSRP: $114.99

Trophy Taker Spring Steel 2 Micro
Adjustable blade angle
Fixed flexible launcher system
Micro-adjustable windage and elevation adjustment
0.010″ launcher
Short Bar, micro-short bar
MSRP: $99.99

Trophy Taker Spring Steel
Wide-fixed arrow launcher
Machined slot to guarantee best blade alignment
Two hex bolts locate and secure best blade launcher
Windage and elevation marks
MSRP: $59.99

Trophy Taker Spring Steel PRO
Adjustable blade angle
Fixed flexible launcher system
Micro-adjustable windage and elevation adjustment
0.010″ launcher
MSRP: $89.99

Trophy Taker X-Treme FC
Arrow capture and retention of 320° of rotation
Top-loading slot
Rugged, all-metal construction
Rubberized, PVC-coated containment ring
Launcher silencer
***MSRP**: $99.99*

Vapor Trail Limb Driver
Limb driven
Full-capture
Adjustable spring tension
Free-floating launcher arm
Rubber dampener
***MSRP**: $129*

Trophy Taker X-Treme SL
Lightweight aluminum mounting bar and housing
60% glass-filled nylon ring and windage adjustment
Loads quickly and easily but holds securely
Ultra-quiet full-capture launcher
No tools or fasteners quick-install cable clamp
***MSRP**: $39.99*

Vapor Trail LimbDriver Pro
Limb driven
Full-capture
Adjustable spring tension
Free-floating launcher arm
***MSRP**: $129*

Whisker Biscuit Kill Shot

Fully adjustable
100% full arrow containment
Composite-encased biscuit design is 150% stronger than previous models
Windage/elevation adjustment with reference marks
Custom rubber boots for completely silent arrow loading
For right- or left-hand bows
MSRP: $49.99

Xtreme Hardcore Gear V Twin

Independent adjustable spring tension
Fluoropolymer launchers
Custom tuning of side and downward tension
Billet machined aluminum body and fluoropolymer launchers
MSRP: $89.99

Current Releases

Allen Caliper
Traditional straight shaft caliper release
Adjustable hook and loop strap assembly
Head rotates 360 degrees
T-style pivot reduces wrist torque
Symmetrical release jaws for a consistent string clearance
Ergonomically designed trigger
MSRP: $24.99

Allen Elite Adjustable Caliper Release
Adjustable length of pull
Micro caliper
Adjustable padded wrist strap
Symmetrical release jaws for a consistent string clearance
Ergonomically designed trigger
T-style pivot reduces wrist torque
MSRP: $30.49

Allen Exacta Buckle Caliper
Micro-caliper release head is precision machined
Buckle release on the strap designed to incorporate a keeper system
Easy one-hand installation
MSRP: $29.99

Allen Exacta XX Quick Adjust Release
Rubber frame eliminates head flop
Infinite adjustment of the perfect trigger pull length
Wrist strap can be silently attached with one hand without hook and loop
Micro-caliper release head is precision machined
MSRP: $29.99

Allen Nu Glove Caliper
Full wrap design
Suede leather lining
Adjusts to fit hands from medium to extra large
Head rotates 360 degrees
Symmetrical release jaws for a consistent string clearance
Ergonomically designed trigger
T-style pivot reduces wrist torque
MSRP: $31.99

Allen Thumb Style Release
Rugged composite construction
Easy to use thumb trigger
Automatically locks on the bow string
MSRP: $19.99

Bass Pros Shops XPS Caliper

Dual caliper release with a contoured machined release head
Lengthen or shorten using the two-piece adjustment module for a custom fit
Curved trigger
Camo-padded Velcro wrist strap
MSRP: $39.99

Bass Pro Shops XPS Deluxe Caliper

Slim caliper head with adjustable curved trigger
E-Z adjust module
Swing away feature
Padded leather buckle strap
Easy on and off
MSRP: $39.99

Cabela's Marksman

Tool-less length adjustment
Highly adjustable trigger travel and poundage
Precision-machined head assembly made of ultradurable aluminum
Teflon-coated for optimum smoothness
Spring-loaded jaws and fail-proof steel jaws
Padded camo buckle strap
MSRP: $59.99

Carter Enterprises Like Mike

Reliable, double sear interior for increased accuracy
Trigger also has minimal "over travel" and 0 to 5 lb range adjustable with a simple screw
Features popular open jaw design that loads quickly and silently on a D-loop
Scott adjustable leather buckle strap
MSRP: $191.99

Carter Enterprises Lucky

Shorter head, reduced body size, and a highly customizable trigger tension system
The new Magnetic
Attraction Tension System (MATS)
Double-sear interior design
Consistent trigger fire regardless of bow weight
Scott adjustable leather buckle strap
MSRP: $152.99

Carter Enterprises Quickie
Open, self-closing hook that quickly relocks following each shot
Silent loading and silent shooting without sacrificing accuracy
MSRP: $104.99–117.99

Carter Enterprises RX1 & RX2
Brand new magnetic self-closing, open-hook
Fast, quiet, and accurate.
Premium, fully adjustable leather buckle strap made by Scott
MSRP: $151.99

Carter Enterprises Quickie I Plus
Open, self-closing hook that quickly relocks following each shot
Silent loading and silent shooting without sacrificing accuracy
New version of the popular Interchangeable Tension System
MSRP: $124.99–134.99

Carter Enterprises Quickie II
Reverse-pivoting, self-closing hook
Silent loading on a D-loop or serving and silent shooting
MSRP: $104.99–117.99

Carter Enterprises Strapless
Smooth swept back design with a peg on the thumb to assist in pulling
The trigger on the strapless is based on Carter's design
The open jaw design adds accuracy and quicker loading to the string.
MSRP: $180.99

Carter Enterprises Quickie II Plus
Reverse-pivoting, self-closing hook
Silent loading on a D-loop or serving and silent shooting
New version of the popular interchangeable tension system
MSRP: $124.99–$134.99

Carter Enterprises Whatever

"One push" closed, jaw system with an angled loop channel

Versatile tension changing system and travel adjustment system

Dowel Interchangeable Tension System (DITS) allows trigger tension customization

Scott leather buckle strap with easy slide length adjustment

MSRP: $152.99

Cobra Dual Caliper

Precision-machined center release jaw
Padded nylon strap with adjustable extension
Gun-style curved trigger
MSRP: $29.99

Cobra EVI Bravo Pro Caliper

Dual caliper design
Machined-aluminum construction with positive-locking center release
Dual caliper jaws
360° rotating heads with chrome-moly pivot bearing
Peg-style trigger
Bravo-style padded loop lock strap
Black anodized release head
MSRP: $39.99

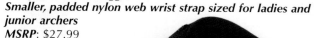

Cobra Junior Pro Caliper

Dependable, dual caliper design
Machined-aluminum construction with positive-locking center release
Dual caliper jaws
360° rotating heads with chrome-moly pivot bearing
Compact, curved trigger release
Smaller, padded nylon web wrist strap sized for ladies and junior archers
MSRP: $27.99

Cobra Lady Serpent Deluxe
Double-jaw caliper release with a compact head to maximize draw length
Buckle strap
Torque-eliminating rotating module
Adjustable trigger
MSRP: $49.99

Cobra Mamba 2 Swing Away
E-Z adjust camo strap
Dual caliper design for clean releases
Adjustable trigger
360° swing away module
E-Z Adjust camo strap for a custom fit
MSRP: $49.99

Cobra Mamba 1 Swing Away
Stainless steel single jaw
Forward mounted trigger
360° swing away module
E-Z Adjust camo strap for a custom fit
MSRP: $49.99

Cobra Pro Caliper
Accommodates the heaviest draw weights
Machined from solid aluminum
Deluxe, curved gun-style trigger
Black anodized release head
Center release caliper-style jaws
Stainless steel pins
Premium coil spring
Chrome-moly pivot bearing for a consistently smooth release
MSRP: $39.99

Cobra Serpent E-Z Adjust

Freely rotating dual caliper bow release with no-tool length adjustment
Thin tip dual caliper release jaw design
E-Z adjust module
Module also provides tool-free custom length adjustment
Padded RealTree® camo buckle strap
Forward mounted, fully adjustable trigger
MSRP: $54.99

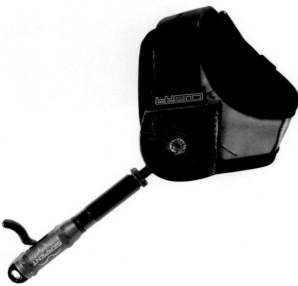

Fletcher .44 Caliber

Interlocking jaw-system
Hardened trigger and roller design
Deluxe Velcro wrist strap
Adjustable to exactly the right length
MSRP: $49.99

Fletcher F-Hook

Nock loop or D-loop hook design
Roller system for smooth performance
Trigger adjustable from heavy to hair
Includes removable knurled sleeve
MSRP: $69.99

Fletcher Flathead

Exclusive self-locking, over-center trigger design
Fully adjustable trigger pull
CNC-machined aluminum construction
Hard anodized finish for rugged use
MSRP: $69.99

Goat Tuff Equalizer Release

Wider draw shelf and repositioned trigger
Increases arrow speed and performance without increasing draw weight
Ergonomic straight-line design
Machined-aluminum body with SS internal parts
Adjustable plunger-style trigger and leather wrist strap
MSRP: $199.95

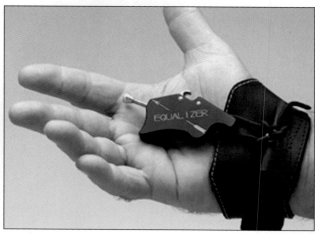

Hot-Shot Infinity II Buckle
Single jaw-style release
Alloy construction for ultrasmooth function
Lever link trigger system for less creep
Precise pull for more consistent shots
Cat's Eye™ hook design
MSRP: $54

Hot-Shot Nano
Lever-link trigger system for less creep
Precise pull for more consistent shots
Trigger and internal components are comprised of a proprietary self-lubricating alloy
Trigger tension and travel is adjustable
Nylon tether and synch-plate system promotes the ability to micro-adjust release
MSRP: $64.99

Hot-Shot Infinity II Velcro
Single jaw style release
Alloy construction for ultrasmooth function
Lever-link trigger system for less creep
Precise pull for more consistent shots
Cat's Eye™ hook design
Features fully adjustable Velcro closure system
MSRP: $54

Scott Caliper
Machined-aluminum construction featuring heat-treated steel
Pair of moving jaws
Pivoting head
Padded nylon wrist strap with Velcro closure
MSRP: $54.99

Scott Little Bitty
Single-caliper release design
Fully adjustable forward trigger maximizes draw length
Exclusive angled-jaw design with improved jaw radius
NCS connection system to minimize rotational torque
MSRP: $59.99

Scott Little Bitty2
Micro version of the Little Goose
A single caliper design
Nylon Connection System (NCS) system minimizes rotational torque Adjustable length
Adjustable trigger tension
CNC-machined aluminum construction
MSRP: $69.99

Scott Mongoose
Time-tested design
Equipped with NCS (Nylon Connection System) for a precise fit
Fully adjustable trigger
Machined-aluminum construction with hard anodized finish
MSRP: $69.99

Scott Mongoose 2
Time-tested design
Slightly slimmer design than original Mongoose
Fully adjustable trigger
Machined-aluminum construction with hard anodized finish
MSRP: $69.99

Scott Rhino XT
Single sear release with spring-loaded stainless steel hook
Interchangeable spring system for a range of sensitivity adjustment
Internal components machined from highest grade steel
Extreme forward, knurled trigger
Swept-back, curved trigger included
MSRP: $119.99

Scott Sabertooth
Dual-jaw design and pivoting head for accuracy and consistency
Streamlined for increased comfort and precision
Hand-polished stainless steel jaws for durability
Forward knurled trigger to maximize draw length
4-hole length adjustment
MSRP: $79.99

Scott Silverhorn
Roller Sear™ technology design offering a very light trigger pull
Hooks onto string loop for fast, no-look loading
Auto-cocking design
Solid swivel connector with 9-hole length adjustment
Nylon strap connector offers infinite length adjustment, reduces torque
Forward-positioned knurled-trigger maximizes draw length
MSRP: $69.99

Scott Wildcat
Dual-jaw design and pivoting head
Streamlined for increased comfort and precision
Hand-polished stainless steel jaws for durability
Forward knurled trigger to maximize draw length
4-hole length adjustment
MSRP: $79.99

Spot Hogg Wiseguy
Light, adjustable trigger with zero travel
Adjustable length with self-reloading hook
Open jaw for ultrafast D-Loop hook up
Forward trigger design for maximum draw length and speed
For use with a D-loop only
MSRP: $79.99

Spot-Hogg WiseGuy Tethered
Light, adjustable trigger with zero travel
Adjustable length with self-reloading hook
Open jaw for ultrafast D-Loop hook up
Forward trigger design for maximum draw length and speed
For use with a D-loop only
MSRP: $79.99

TruBall Assassin SST
Stainless steel version of Assassin
Dual-caliper design
6061 aircraft aluminum body with tough stainless steel trigger and jaws
Black leather strap buckle
MSRP: $69.99

TruBall Bandit
Features a rope connection covered in weather-resistant flexible tubing
Available with a black anodized head only
MSRP: $29.99

TruBall The Beast

A solid rod connection and an 11-oz trigger
Relaxed trigger with swept back design
Quick-load open-hook design allows a hunter to hook the string loop without looking
Includes drop-away solid rod swivel connection with draw length adjustment
Black Velcro strap
MSRP: $99.99

TruBall Black Hornet

Anodized metal head and rod design
Folds away into sleeve when not needed
Flat black finish on head and rod
MSRP: $69.99

TruBall Bone Collector Assassin

Stainless steel version of Assassin
Dual caliper design
6061 aircraft aluminum body with tough stainless steel trigger and jaws
Black leather strap buckle
MSRP: $79.99

TruBall Center X

Micro-adjustable wrist straps
Individual micro-adjustment screws for the sensitivity and travel
Forward trigger to provide increased arrow speed by increasing bow draw length
Swept back comfort-plus trigger
Features open-hook-style connection to the D-Loop for fast and accurate attachment
The new flip sear internal trigger mechanism allows for light trigger settings
MSRP: $99.99

TruBall Cyclone

A web strap connection with easy draw length adjustment
Aluminum head swivels or locks down
Pull trigger to open, let up to close
MSRP: $59.99

TruBall Fang

Hook-style release

Rubber insert in the trigger for improved feel

Two trigger options included in package; a straight trigger for more draw and speed and a relaxed trigger for greater comfort

Two-screw trigger sensitivity setting

Featured with a black or Mathews® Lost Camo™ anodized head with your choice of a camo Velcro strap or black leather buckle strap

MSRP: $119

TruBall Outlaw

Rope connection generates less torque

Quiet load jaws

Ball release system

MSRP: $29.99

TruBall Predator

Micro-adjustable wrist strap release

½″ sized ergonomic head and jaws attached to swivel to reduce torque

Micro-adjustable screw to wrist strap connection allows infinite length settings

MSRP: $49.99

TruBall Max 3 Hunter

Maximizes draw length

Head swivels 360° to kill torque

Adjustable sensitivity screw

Push trigger to open jaws, release to close

MSRP: $94.99

TruBall Quickdraw Outlaw

Rope connection generates less torque

Equipped with speed buckle connection

Dual-caliper design

Adjustable head length

MSRP: $49.99

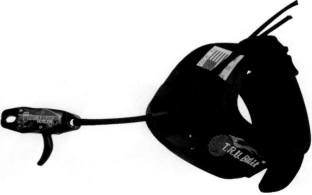

TruBall Short N Sweet

Open head design attaches quickly and easily to D-loops without looking
CNC machined components
Fully adjustable trigger tension and length
MSRP: $69.99

TruBall Sniper 2

Ribbed body with 5 draw length positions
Silent loading
Folds away into sleeve when not needed
Includes 2 triggers for hunting or tournaments
MSRP: $79.99

TruBall Sniper 2 Scout

"Jaw and a half" release design adds forgiveness to a single-jaw-caliper release
Two trigger options (spring trigger included)
Available Wrist Straps: Camo Velcro, Black Buckle
MSRP: $64.99

TruBall Stinger

Free-floating jaws with a unique ball release system
Ultra-quiet, easy-to-load jaws provide forgiveness
Smooth operation
Pull trigger to open, let up to close
MSRP: $44.99

TruBall Super Hornet

Anodized metal head and rod design
CNC-machined components
Patented trigger design for easy, silent loading
Folds away into sleeve when not needed
Fully camouflage covered
MSRP: $69.99

Tru-Fire 3D Hunter Camo

Solid CNC-machined handle
Head rotates independently from the handle
Steel, heat-treated, Teflon-coated jaws
Adjustable thumbar and trigger travel
Camo anodized
MSRP: $84.99

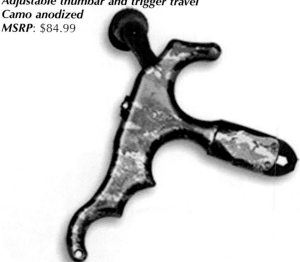

Tru-Fire 360 Buckle Foldback
Dual caliper releases
360 degree head rotation in front of the trigger
Dial located inside the body for trigger pressure sensitivity
Trigger travel and length adjustment
Camo nylon foldback Evolution buckle strap and short body design
MSRP: $59.99

Tru-Fire Edge 4 Finger
Super-sleek, solid CNC-aluminum handle
Head provides 360 degrees rotation
Fully adjustable trigger travel adjustment
Adjustable thumb knob
MSRP: $104.99

Tru-Fire Bulldog Buckle Extreme Foldback
Single-steel jaw coated in Teflon for a smooth release
Works off of string loops, serving, or aluminum loops
Trigger spring and forward trigger
Length adjustment
Camo nylon foldback Evolution buckle strap
MSRP: $69.99

Tru-Fire Edge Buckle Foldback
Utilizes a linear motion bearing to deliver a smooth trigger feel
Pull the trigger back to open the jaws, and let up on the trigger to close the jaws.
Lockdown-screw set for length adjustment
Over 1" of length adjustment
Camo leather foldback Evolution buckle strap
MSRP: $79.99

Tru-Fire Hurricane Buckle Black Foldback
Utilizes a free-floating, self-centering steel roller
Heat-treated, Teflon-coated jaws and triggers
Adjustable trigger pressure
Foldback buckle strap
32-position length adjustments
Left- or right-handed use
MSRP: $64.99

Tru-Fire Team Realtree Buckle Foldback
Utilizes a free-floating, self-centering steel roller
Heat-treated and Teflon-coated jaws and triggers
Adjustable trigger pressure
32-position length adjustments
Foldback buckle strap
Left- or right-handed use
Team Realtree camo and logo on head
MSRP: $74.99

Tru-Fire Patriot Junior
Shortened version of the Patriot
Release head utilizes the same parts as the adult model
Economical and comfortable nylon power strap with Velcro closure system
Guaranteed to fit the smallest of hands
MSRP: $19.99

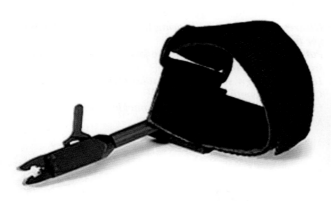

Tru-Fire X-Caliper Extreme
Non-Tru rotating calipers
Heat-treated and Teflon-coated trigger and jaws
The X-Caliper line has been redesigned for easier use on string loops
Power strap made from cotton camouflage
Fits both left- and right-hands
MSRP: $39.99

References

Books and Periodicals

Anderson, John D. Jr. *Introduction to Flight*.

"BBC News - Oldest evidence of arrows found." BBC. 08-26-2010. Retrieved 08-26-2010.

Campbell, Duncan. *Greek and Roman Artillery 399 BC-AD 363*. Oxford: Osprey Publishing, 2003.

Griffith, Samuel B. *The Illustrated Art of War*. Oxford University Press, 2005; p. 17, 141–143.

Hardy, Robert. *Longbow: A Social and Military History*. Lyons & Burford, 1992.

Jain, Mahesh C. *Textbook of Engineering Physics (Part I)*. PHI Learning Pvt. Ltd, 2009.

McGaffigan, Patricia A. "Hazards of Hypoxemia: How to Protect Your Patient from Low Oxygen Levels." *Nursing*, May 1996.

Norton, Robert L. *Design of Machinery* (3rd ed.). McGraw-Hill, 2004.

Payne-Gallwey, Ralph. *The Book of the Crossbow*. Dover, 1995.

Sears, Francis Weston and Robert W. Brehme. *Introduction to the Theory of Relativity*. Addison-Wesley 1996.

Schellenberg, Hans Michael. *Diodor von Sizilien 14,42,1 und die Erfindung der Artillerie im Mittelmeerraum*. Frankfurter Elektronische Rundschau zur Altertumskunde, 2006.

Wagner, Donald B. "Iron and Steel in Ancient China: Second Impression, With Corrections." Leiden: E.J. Brill, 1993.

Websites

"A Crossbow Mechanism with Some Unique Features from Shandong, China." Asian Traditional Archery Research Network. Retrieved on 08-20-2008.

http://www.pope-young.org/bowhunting_equipment.asp

http://www.uwlax.edu/MVAC/educators/Glossary/MP.htm

http://en.wikipedia.org/wiki/History_of_crossbows

Index

ALSO AVAILABLE

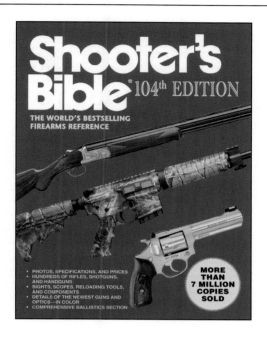

Shooter's Bible, 104th Edition
The World's Bestselling Firearms Reference
by Jay Cassell

Published annually for more than eighty years, the *Shooter's Bible* is the most comprehensive and sought-after reference guide for new firearms and their specifications, as well as for thousands of guns that have been in production and are currently on the market. Every firearms manufacturer in the world is included in this renowned compendium. The 104th edition also contains new and existing product sections on ammunition, optics, and accessories, plus up-to-date handgun and rifle ballistic tables along with extensive charts of currently available bullets and projectiles for handloading.

With timely features on such topics as the fiftieth anniversary of the Remington Model 700, and complete with color and black-and-white photographs featuring various makes and models of firearms and equipment, the *Shooter's Bible* is an essential authority for any beginner or experienced hunter, firearm collector, or gun enthusiast.

$29.95 Paperback • ISBN 978-1-61608-874-3

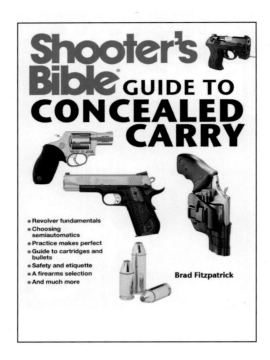

Shooter's Bible Guide to Concealed Carry

by Brad Fitzpatrick

Don't wait to be placed in a dangerous setting faced with an armed attacker. The *Shooter's Bible Guide to Concealed Carry* is an all-encompassing resource that not only offers vital gun terminology but also suggests which gun is the right fit for you and how to efficiently use the device properly, be it in public or at home. Firearm expert Brad Fitzpatrick examines how to practice, how to correct mistakes, and how to safely challenge yourself when you have achieved basic skills. Included within is a comprehensive chart describing the various calibers for concealed carry, suitable instructions for maintaining it, and, most importantly, expert step-by-step instructions for shooting.

$19.95 Paperback • ISBN 978-1-62087-580-3

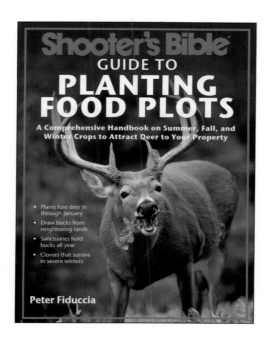

Shooter's Bible Guide to Planting Food Plots

A Comprehensive Handbook on Summer, Fall, and Winter Crops to Attract Deer to Your Property

by Peter Fiduccia

Planting a well-balanced, well-planned food plot for deer can be a great resource for any hunter: it attracts and holds deer in the area, and creates a healthier herd. This detailed, hands-on guide will teach you everything you need to know about planting food plots for deer like a pro. Author Peter Fiduccia shares the time-tested planting knowledge he has used on his farm to help anyone grow more successful food plots.

$19.95 Paperback • ISBN 978-1-62087-090-7

ALSO AVAILABLE

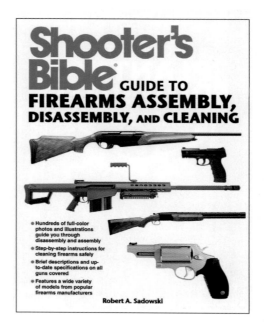

Shooter's Bible Guide to Firearms Assembly, Disassembly, and Cleaning
by Robert A. Sadowski

Shooter's Bible, the most trusted source on firearms, is here to bring you a new guide with expert knowledge and advice on gun care. Double-page spreads filled with photos and illustrations provide manufacturer specifications on each featured model and guide you through disassembly and assembly for rifles, shotguns, handguns, and muzzleloaders. Step-by-step instructions for cleaning help you to care for your firearms safely. Never have a doubt about proper gun maintenance when you own the *Shooter's Bible Guide to Firearms Assembly, Disassembly, and Cleaning*, a great companion to the original *Shooter's Bible*.

Along with assembly, disassembly, and cleaning instructions, each featured firearm is accompanied by a brief description and list of important specs, including manufacturer, model, similar models, action, calibers/gauge, capacity, overall length, and weight. With these helpful gun maintenance tips, up-to-date specifications, detailed exploded view line drawings, and multiple photographs for each firearm, the *Shooter's Bible Guide to Firearms Assembly, Disassembly, and Cleaning* is a great resource for all firearm owners.

$19.95 Paperback • ISBN 978-1-61608-875-0

ALSO AVAILABLE

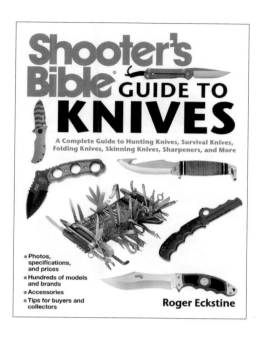

Shooter's Bible Guide to Knives

A Complete Guide to Hunting Knives, Survival Knives, Folding
Knives, Skinning Knives, Sharpeners, and More

by Roger Eckstine

The new *Shooter's Bible Guide to Knives* sets the standard for comprehensive
publications by carrying on the *Shooter's Bible* tradition of bringing together
more products and information than any other source. With photographs and
descriptions of more than four hundred knives, readers are treated to product
highlights from major manufacturers and custom knife makers. This book brings
you from the blacksmith shop to high-tech influential designers with insights into
blade steel, locking mechanisms, and handle materials. When it comes to knives,
this book is the source for the products and the passion.

$19.95 Paperback • ISBN 978-1-61608-577-3

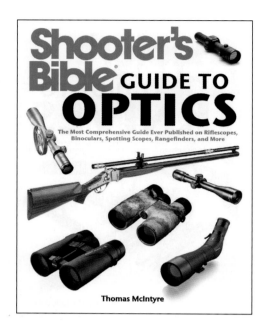

Shooter's Bible Guide to Optics
The Most Comprehensive Guide Ever Published on Riflescopes, Binoculars, Spotting Scopes, Rangefinders, and More
by Thomas McIntyre

Whether you are a target shooter, hunter, guide, tactical user, birder, or sports spectator, optics play a vital role in enhancing and facilitating your sport or profession. To help you figure out which optics best fit your needs, as well as your budget, the *Shooter's Bible Guide to Optics* lists every quality sporting optic on the market today. Loaded with color photographs, this 288-page book features a new products section, listing all new riflescopes, binoculars, rangefinders, and spotting scopes, plus in-depth features on how to use binoculars, how to mount and sight in a rifle scope, and much more.

$19.95 Paperback • ISBN 978-1-61608-632-9

ALSO AVAILABLE

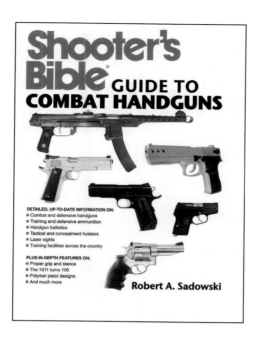

Shooter's Bible Guide to Combat Handguns
by Robert A. Sadowski

For more than one hundred years, *Shooter's Bible* has been the ultimate comprehensive resource for shooting enthusiasts across the board. Trusted by everyone from competitive shooters to hunters to those who keep firearms for protection, this leading series is always expanding. Here is the first edition of the *Shooter's Bible Guide to Combat Handguns*—your all-encompassing resource with up-to-date information on combat and defensive handguns, training and defensive ammunition, handgun ballistics, tactical and concealment holsters, accessories, training facilities, and more. No *Shooter's Bible* guidebook is complete without a detailed products section showcasing handguns from all across the market.

Author Robert Sadowski proves to be a masterful instructor on all aspects of handguns, providing useful information for every reader, from those with combat handgun experience in military and law enforcement fields to private citizens, first-timers, and beyond.

$19.95 Paperback • ISBN 978-1-61608-415-8

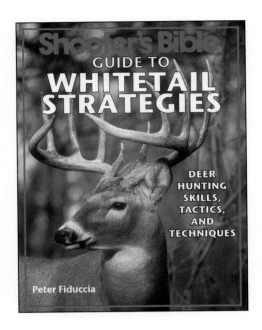

Shooter's Bible Guide to Whitetail Strategies
Deer Hunting Skills, Tactics, and Techniques
by Peter Fiduccia

Shooter's Bible Guide to Whitetail Strategies is the ultimate guide to hunting whitetail deer, from tracking strategies that include recovering wounded deer, to cooking with venison, to scoring and field-judging bucks, this book is the guide that every whitetail strategist must own. With Fiduccia's expert advice, both the novice and the seasoned hunter will have newfound confidence when heading out into the woods for a trophy buck.

$19.95 Paperback • ISBN 978-1-61608-358-8

ALSO AVAILABLE

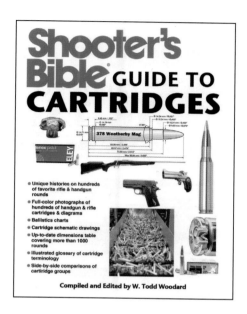

Shooter's Bible Guide to Cartridges
Compiled and Edited by Todd Woodard

A guidebook designed specifically to teach gun users everything they need to know to select the right cartridge for their shooting needs, this title is written in an accessible and engaging style that makes research fun. The *Shooter's Bible Guide to Cartridges* is packed with full-color photographs, clear and detailed diagrams, and easy-to-read charts with cartridge data.

The *Shooter's Bible* name has been known and trusted as an authority on guns and ammunition for nearly a century and has sold over seven million copies since its start. Now the *Shooter's Bible* offers readers this comprehensive and fascinating guide to cartridges. Complete with color and black-and-white photographs showcasing various makes and models of firearms and equipment, this guide to cartridges is the perfect addition to the bookshelf of any beginner or experienced hunter, firearm collector, or gun enthusiast. No matter what your shooting background is, you'll learn something new. This guide is a great introduction that will make readers want to seek out and get to know all the titles in the informative *Shooter's Bible* series.

$19.95 Paperback • ISBN 978-1-61608-222-2

ALSO AVAILABLE

Shooter's Bible Guide to AR-15s
A Comprehensive Reference to One of America's Favorite Rifles
by Doug Howlett

There's no denying the popularity and intense fascination with AR-15s among firearms enthusiasts today. Here, inside the most comprehensive source to date, is Doug Howlett's expert approach to everything from the intriguing history of the AR to breaking down the weapon piece by piece, choosing ammunition, and even building your own gun.

In this complete book of AR-style firearms, you can peruse the products of all manufacturers, learn about the evolution of the AR from its uses in the military in the 1960s to its adaptation for law enforcement and civilian uses, and gain essential knowledge on the parts and functions of the rifle. Also included are chapters on customizing and accessorizing ARs, with special focus on small gun shops and makers and their unique and successful products. Look into the future of the AR straight from top gun authorities!

$19.95 Paperback • ISBN 978-1-61608-444-8